THE NEW INTERNATIONAL COMMENTARY ON THE
NEW TESTAMENT   —F. F. BRUCE, *General Editor*

THE EPISTLES OF PAUL TO THE EPHESIANS
AND TO THE COLOSSIANS

COMMENTARY ON
THE EPISTLES TO THE EPHESIANS
AND THE COLOSSIANS

THE ENGLISH TEXT WITH
INTRODUCTION, EXPOSITION AND NOTES

by

E. K. SIMPSON, M.A.

Trinity College, Oxford,
Formerly Lecturer in New Testament
Language and Exegesis in the
Free Church College, Edinburgh

and

F. F. BRUCE, M.A., D.D.

Professor of Biblical Criticism and Exegesis
University of Manchester

WM. B. EERDMANS PUBLISHING
GRAND RAPIDS, MICHIGAN

WM. EERDMANS PUBLISHING CO.

GRAND RAPIDS, MICHIGAN

First published, December 1957
Second printing, May 1962
Third printing, January 1965
Fourth printing, February 1968
Fifth printing, August 1970
Sixth printing, June 1972
Seventh printing, December 1973

Library of Congress Catalog Card Number 57-13040
ISBN 0-8028-2193-6

CONTENTS

Abbreviations 6

THE EPISTLE TO THE EPHESIANS 9
Editor's Preface 11

INTRODUCTION 15

TEXT, EXPOSITION AND NOTES
    CHAPTER I 23
    CHAPTER II 45
    CHAPTER III 69
    CHAPTER IV 87
    CHAPTER V 114
    CHAPTER VI 135

THE EPISTLE TO THE COLOSSIANS 159
Author's Preface 161

INTRODUCTION 163
    (a) Origin and Purpose of the Epistle to the
        Colossians 163
    (b) The Colossian Heresy 165
    (c) Some Critical Questions 170
    (d) Analysis of the Epistle to the Colossians . . 174

TEXT, EXPOSITION AND NOTES
    CHAPTER I 177
    CHAPTER II 222
    CHAPTER III 257
    CHAPTER IV 296

INDEXES 314

105971

ABBREVIATIONS[1]

ARV — American Revised Version (American Standard Version, 1901)
AV — Authorized Version (King James Version, 1611)
BGU — *Griechische Urkunden* from *Berlin Aegyptische Urkunden*
BJRL — *Bulletin of the John Rylands Library* (Manchester)
CNT — *Commentaire du Nouveau Testament* (Delachaux & Niestlé)
EGT — *Expositor's Greek Testament* (ed. W. R. Nicoll)
EQ — *Evangelical Quarterly*
ERE — *Encyclopaedia of Religion and Ethics* (ed. J. Hastings)
ERV — English Revised Version (1881–85)
EVV — English Versions
Exp B — *Expositor's Bible* (ed. W. R. Nicoll)
Ex T — *Expository Times*
FS — *Festschrift*
HNT — *Handbuch zum Neuen Testament* (ed. H. Lietzmann)
IBNTG — *Idiom Book of New Testament Greek*, by C. F. D. Moule (Cambridge, 1953)
ICC — *International Critical Commentary* (T. & T. Clark)
JBL — *Journal of Biblical Literature*
JThS — *Journal of Theological Studies*
LS[9] — Liddell and Scott's *Greek-English Lexicon*, 9th edition
MK — *Meyer-Kommentar* (Göttingen)
MNTC — Moffatt New Testament Commentary
NICNT — New International Commentary on the New Testament (Eerdmans, Grand Rapids)
NTS — *New Testament Studies* (Cambridge, 1954–)
P Oxy — Oxyrhynchus Papyri
RB — *Revue Biblique*
RSV — Revised Standard Version (1952)

---

[1] For both commentaries.

6

RThR — *Reformed Theological Review* (Australia)
SJTh — *Scottish Journal of Theology*
TB — Babylonian Talmud
TR — Received Text
TWNT — *Theologisches Wörterbuch zum Neuen Testament* (ed. G. Kittel and G. Friedrich)
VGT — *Vocabulary of the Greek Testament* (Moulton and Milligan)
VT — *Vetus Testamentum* (Leiden)

COMMENTARY ON
THE EPISTLE TO THE EPHESIANS

THE ENGLISH TEXT WITH
INTRODUCTION, EXPOSITION AND NOTES

by

E. K. SIMPSON, M.A.

Trinity College, Oxford
Formerly Lecturer in New Testament
Language and Exegesis in the
Free Church College, Edinburgh

EDITOR'S PREFACE

A distinguishing feature of this volume, the seventh in order of publication in this Commentary, is that of dual authorship. Since Professor Bruce has been introduced at some length in the preface to his Commentary on *The Book of Acts,* and is so generally and favorably known from his other widely read writings, this preface may understandably concentrate on the author of the exposition of Ephesians. Some account of the origin and development of this joint enterprise may well also be given, and this will afford a suitable opportunity of acknowledgment of the distinctive contribution made by the author of the latter portion of the volume.

E. K. Simpson has long been known, especially to readers of *The Evangelical Quarterly,* as a scintillating writer on New Testament themes, whose distinctive contributions have reflected especially his masterly knowledge of Hellenistic Greek literature. These contributions include his articles on "Vettius Valens and the New Testament" (II, 1930); "The Apostle John's Diction" (XIV, 1942); and "The Vocabulary of the Epistle to the Hebrews" (XVIII, 1946). An interesting example of the same approach is found in his Tyndale Lecture for 1944, *Words Worth Weighing in the Greek New Testament* (Tyndale Press, London, 1946). This expert knowledge was also turned to splendid account in his important book, *The Pastoral Epistles* (Tyndale Press, London, 1954). His competence in the New Testament field was recognized, though he was neither an ordained minister nor a professional scholar, when he was invited to serve as Lecturer in this field in the Free Church College of Edinburgh in 1935, a post he filled for two years.

Mr. Simpson was educated at Oxford University from 1892 to 1896, where he was Ford Student of Trinity College and where he was graduated with Honors in Classics and History. He spent some time on the continent, and later was to utilize his mastery of German to good effect when in 1903 he translated into English *Modern Science and Christianity* by Professor F. Bettex. Mr. Simpson has lived the life of a private gentleman throughout most of his life, and has taken advantage of the leisure afforded him to delve deeply into a wide range of literature. Besides his

11

intense interest in Hellenistic literature, he has been known also for his delight in the writings of the Puritan divines, and for a time he was jointly responsible for a periodical entitled *The Puritan Quarterly*, which sought to stimulate a like interest in and commitment to Puritan theology among twentieth-century readers. His writings accordingly reveal a man who, besides being a humble and forthright Christian, is marked by a rare and quite unaffected love of learning. Those who have had the privilege of informal personal contact with him, as the editor did on a memorable occasion in his home in Malvern, have received an even more vivid impression of these qualities as his discourse has proved to be a veritable fountain overflowing with good things, old and new.

At Edinburgh Mr. Simpson had lectured on Ephesians *con amore*, and hence when he was approached about a decade ago in the interest of securing his participation in the Commentary, he himself suggested the possibility of expounding this Epistle. This task was indeed completed so long ago that, if it had seemed practicable to publish his manuscript as an independent volume, his contribution might have been the first or at latest the second in order of publication. The plan for the Commentary called, however, for the combination of the treatment of Ephesians and Colossians in a single volume. Unfortunately, in spite of urgent petition, he felt that he had to decline an invitation to expound Colossians also, especially because of the precarious condition of his eyesight. There was a further distressing postponement of the publication of Mr. Simpson's work when for a number of years a suitable contributor could not be found to undertake Colossians, or at least one who had the time to give to it.

At last, however, the time came when F. F. Bruce, having completed his work on Acts, agreed to undertake the exposition of Colossians. His gracious response to the invitation extended him has been a particularly happy memory in the development of the entire enterprise. Moreover, he has made a significant contribution to the integrity of the volume, not only by taking account of the earlier work as he prepared his own brilliant exposition, but also by generously supplying additional footnotes to the work on Ephesians. Thus the two parts reflect the diversity of viewpoints and qualifications of the two authors, a factor which may possibly add to the interest and value of the work for many readers, but they also disclose a significant degree of unity. Although, then, some regret may be expressed that Mr. Simpson found it impossible to undertake the work on Colossians, the turn of events has been largely felicitous since Mr. Bruce, whose background for New Testament studies was in important respects the same as those of the older scholar, and who had won wide acclaim as a learned and lucid expositor, agreed to complete the volume.

As this new volume goes forth, concerned as it is with the lofty themes of these kindred Epistles, and marked by illuminating exposition and spiritual stimulation, may the God of our Lord Jesus Christ, the Father of glory, give its readers "a spirit of wisdom and revelation in the knowledge of Him."

NED B. STONEHOUSE
General Editor

Note: Upon the death of Ned B. Stonehouse, November 18, 1962, F. F. Bruce accepted the publishers' invitation to become General Editor of this series of New Testament commentaries begun under the very able and faithful scholarship of Professor Stonehouse.

The Publishers

INTRODUCTION

The city of Ephesus and capital of proconsular Asia was the metropolis of a large and populous region.[1] A Greek colony by extraction, it had become a rendezvous of many nationalities. Its situation on the main thoroughfare from East to West, not unlike that of Venice in the Middle Ages or of Constantinople today, accounts to a large extent for its history. Jew and Gentile rubbed shoulders in its streets, and the ramifications of its mercantile trafficking gave it the motley characteristics of a cosmopolitan mart. Its busy port lay on the river Cayster, and its subsequent decay and downfall may be traced principally to the gradual silting up of its once busy harbour. In the first century A.D., however, it teemed with wealth and luxury. Its chief architectural boast consisted of the Temple of Artemis, reckoned one of the seven wonders of the world, whose treasury formed the bank of Asia Minor, an immense edifice of dazzling marble, situated outside its gates, the admiration of sightseers from every quarter. It was also proud of the largest of all Hellenic open-air theatres, capable of holding 50,000 spectators. In the vicinity of this spacious area lay a stadium for races and wild-beast fights, to which Paul makes allusion in 1 Corinthians, probably using a metaphorical figure of speech.

The apostle's first visit to this haunt of idolatry, this *arx Paganismi* (as Bengel styles it) was very brief, and might rather be termed a reconnoitre of the field than an occupation of it. Aquila and Prisca (Priscilla) were left behind on that occasion as a kind of provisional evangelists, perhaps in the character of *helpers,* mentioned in 1 Cor. 12:28, and their labour was evidently not unfruitful. When Paul returned on his third missionary journey he himself took up his abode in Ephesus for the space of two years or more. Opposition was of course encountered, mainly from the Jews in the first instance; and in view of that condition of things the apostle, as his custom was, turned to the Gentile population. In process of time the disciples drawn together by the bond of

---

[1] *Cf.* W. M. Ramsay, *Letters to the Seven Churches* (London, 1909), pp. 210 ff.

the Gospel gathered statedly in the lecture-hall of Tyrannus, where presumably a school of philosophy or rhetoric was wont to meet. The name was not uncommon, and might denote either a Hebrew or Greek proprietor; Sir William Ramsay surmised that Paul plied his trade of tent-making there during the forenoon and preached at a later hour of the day.[2] At any rate this assembly grew into a focus of illumination under his ministry which spread its radiancy far beyond the city's compass; for during this spell of tireless activity it would seem that the foundations of all the Seven Asian Churches were laid. In Ephesus itself an extensive Christian brotherhood sprang up, although full data of its stages of development are lacking. Missionary communities seldom attain full church organization whilst they are still "in the gristle."

This Hebrew of the Hebrews, we may be sure, could not but view the spectacle of rampant idolatry and its brood of lascivious orgies with kindling indignation. He was too dexterous a strategist however to denounce the cult of Artemis blatantly in the city which boasted itself her *Neokoros*[3] or sacristan, literally *shrine-sweeper*, a term that had risen to dignity in correspondence with the status of Ephesus itself. Yet he could not fail to reprobate the sin of idol-worship, and his arraignment of their cult ere long came to the ears of those who had vested interests at stake. The potent effects of Paul's preaching may be traced both in the avowed endangerment of their craft and in the holocaust of necromantic books willingly sacrificed by some of his converts; but its most conspicuous upshot meets our gaze in that tumult which Luke has so graphically portrayed, an indisputable tribute to the apostle's widespread influence, and a signal proof of the notability he had acquired. The hubbub excited, the fanaticism displayed by the vociferous mob, the solicitude of the friendly Asiarch officials, the grave *eirenicon* of the town-clerk, all bespeak the resonance of the voice uplifted so strenuously in their midst and the publicity it had achieved. "These things were not done in a corner."

It is instructive to note that the worship of Artemis, as it was practised at Ephesus, partook of an Oriental type. Like Phoenician

---

[2] *St. Paul the Traveller and Roman Citizen* (London, 1920), pp. 269 ff. Ramsay's surmise is based on the Western text, which at the end of Acts 19:9 adds ἀπὸ ὥρας πέμπτης ἕως δεκάτης ("from 11 A.M. to 4 P.M.").

[3] *Cf.* the town-clerk's words in Acts 19:35, τὴν Ἐφεσίων πόλιν νεωκόρον οὖσαν τῆς μεγάλης Ἀρτέμιδος.

16

or Syrian Astarte, with whom she appears to have been identified, the goddess was honoured as the source of fertility and patroness of propagation. It may be imagined how foul were the orgies sanctioned under such auspices, and, worst of all, sanctioned in the outraged name of religion. A vast jungle of fanaticism and superstition had grown up to luxuriant rankness around this lying wonder of an image fallen from heaven, the city's boasted palladium, a mine of wealth to all manner of speculators in the market of human credulity. And in such a congenial soil, as might have been anticipated, all manner of abominations, whether juggleries or positive works of the devil, throve as in a hothouse. It was in this deeply vitiated atmosphere, where sorcery or arts of crafty illusion tainted the very air, that the intrepid apostle, mighty through faith to the pulling down of Satanic strongholds, had planted so staunchly the banner of the cross. Whether we hold this epistle to be addressed exclusively to the Ephesians or no—and about that we shall have a word to say directly—Paul's success bears witness to his being Christ's chosen vessel for the achievement of an unparalleled task; and this *fait accompli* was only one among many of his Herculean labours.

From the Apocalypse of John we gather that the Ephesian church, when later on it was assailed by false apostles, preserved its integrity in the main, though chidden for decadence of fervour and zeal. According to a persistent tradition, John's own last years were spent in that sphere. Timothy presided over it for a season in the interim. It continued to bear a good name during the second century. One of Ignatius's Letters is addressed to it. Ultimately it became sacerdotalized, and waned with the waning fortunes of Ephesus, now a sorry heap of ruins.

The authenticity of the epistle, called in question by the Tübingen school, largely because it did not tally with their arbitrary hypotheses, now happily effete, is amply sustained by evidence, both external and internal. The critic who carps at its contents betrays his own incapacity to appreciate one of the loftiest products of inspiration, fitly termed by Dr. Pierson "the Switzerland of the New Testament." Here is in sooth a Pisgah survey of the land of promise. It may be hard to decide whether this or the kindred letter to the Colossians was the prototype;[4] but that they

---

4   See Introduction to Colossians, p. 172.

both issued from the glowing heart of the self-same apostle only violent prejudice can question. G. G. Findlay has pointed out how in its firm grasp of first principles, its attitude towards Judaism, its doctrine of the cross and of personal union with Christ, the most dominant themes of Paul's teachings find utterance here. All his favourite chords of spiritual melody are struck or recalled in this grand effusion.

The point most open to dispute concerns its title. The words "in Ephesus" (Ch. 1:1) are omitted from the Vatican and Sinaitic uncials and from the Chester Beatty papyrus, their senior in date; though in the former case supplied in the margin; but this phenomenon is virtually unique. From passages in Origen and Basil it appears that the enigmatical reading thus produced was known to them, and they spend idle pains in discovering allegorical senses in the cryptic phraseology resulting from their omission, scarcely construable apart from the missing link. Beza, however, has proffered an elucidation of the problem which obtained the endorsement of Archbishop Ussher and has been very widely adopted since. He holds the Epistle to have been of an encyclical character, designed for general circulation, a blank being, it may be, left in its foreword to be filled in, according to the community to which a particular copy was dispatched. In support of this theory it is urged that no personal greetings, such as are found in Colossians and might be expected surely in a letter addressed to a church in which Paul had laboured in person so long and with such signal effect, relieve its close. Again, we read in Colossians of an authoritative letter from Laodicea, public in its destination, circulating among the churches at this very juncture.[5] May that not be identified with ours? Moreover we note the absence in Ephesians of personal appeals to his children in the faith prominent in other cases, and remark that even the final benediction is couched in the third person. Was it not befitting that the epistle of catholicity should carry no peculiar greetings?

There is certainly a *prima facie* case for this supposition. Yet, like so many other plausible suggestions, it raises difficulties of its own. How is its universal currency under an Ephesian title to be accounted for? Is it quite true that no passages bear a particular application? Have not many discovered in the figure of a spiritual

---

[5] See exposition and notes on Col. 4:16 (pp. 310 f.).

temple an oblique reference to Diana's vaunted shrine? The only early disputant of its Ephesian designation, according to Tertullian, was the heretic Marcion, and neither Clement of Rome, our earliest patristic witness, nor the Muratorian Canon, nor Irenaeus, all of whom show acquaintance with its contents, lend any support to the circular hypothesis. Was it a custom of the ancients, to leave blank forms to be labelled *seriatim* after publication? The evidence appears to be indecisive. The omitted greetings may have been conveyed by Tychicus in person in consequence of their very multiplicity.

The date of the Epistle has been shifted by some writers to the period of Paul's detention at Caesarea or even to an Ephesian imprisonment nowhere on record;[6] but the Roman captivity holds the field. For the controversy with Judaistic Christianity seems over, that battle won. Gentile believers have gained a right to participate in all the privileges of the new covenant without embargo. And this Epistle manifestly belongs to what is known as the Christological group, marked by distinct features and topics from the rest.

The witness to it from antiquity is especially strong and clear. Ignatius and Polycarp quote the letter and so does the Shepherd of Hermas. Peter's First Epistle too is held to bear traces of acquaintance with it. Despite striking coincidences with the Colossian Epistle, its next-of-kin, the two letters are quite distinct and disclose independent tokens of their authorship as well as mutual assimilations. Deissmann infers from Gal. 6:11 that Paul's handwriting was sprawling, a rather gratuitous assumption; but at any rate it was eminently recognizable and intrinsically his own. The signature of Saul of Tarsus is not one to be counterfeited by the adroitest adept in forgery.[7]

---

6 See Introduction to Colossians, pp. 164 f.
7 See the literature cited at the end of the Introduction to Colossians (p. 172, n. 25).

ANALYSIS OF THE EPISTLE TO THE EPHESIANS

PART I (Chs. 1-3)

I. SALUTATION (Ch. 1:1-2)

II. THANKSGIVING FOR THE RICHES OF GRACE: PAST, PRESENT AND TO COME (Ch. 1:3-14)

III. PRAYER FOR THE ENHANCED ILLUMINATION OF HIS READERS (Ch. 1:15-20a)

IV. CHRIST'S EXALTATION AND ITS CONCOMITANT ISSUES FOR HIS CHURCH (Ch. 1:20b-23)

V. THE OLD AND THE NEW MANHOOD CONTRASTED (Ch. 2:1-7)

VI. SALVATION BY GRACE (Ch. 2:8-10)

VII. THE INCLUSION OF THE GENTILES (Ch. 2:11-13)

VIII. CHRIST THE PEACEMAKER (Ch. 2:14-18)

IX. THE ARCHITECTURE OF THE LIVING TEMPLE (Ch. 2:19-22)

X. THE APOSTLE'S MANDATE (Ch. 3:1-4)

XI. THE PURPOSE OF THE AGES (Ch. 3:5-13)

XII. PAUL'S ENRAPTURED SUPPLICATION (Ch. 3:14-19)

XIII. DOXOLOGY (Ch. 3:20-21)

PART II (Chs. 4-6)

I. THE TRAITS OF CHRISTIAN MANHOOD (Chs. 4:1-5:2)
   1. UNISON (Ch. 4:1-10)
   2. DIFFERENCE OF FUNCTION SUBSERVING UNITY (Ch. 4:11-13)
   3. SPIRITUAL DISCERNMENT AND GROWTH (Ch. 4:14-16)
   4. OLD TRAITS TO BE DISCARDED; NEW TO BE CHERISHED (Ch. 4:17-32)
   5. THEIR IDEAL (Ch. 5:1-2)

II. A TRUMPET-CALL TO PURITY (Ch. 5:3–7)

III. LIGHT VERSUS DARKNESS (Ch. 5:8–21)

IV. RELATIVE DUTIES (Chs. 5:22–6:9)
    1. THE NUPTIAL BOND: ITS SANCTITY AS A TYPE (Ch. 5:22–33)
    2. THE PARENTAL BOND (Ch. 6:1–4)
    3. THE DIGNITY OF SERVICE (Ch. 6:5–9)

V. THE CHRISTIAN PANOPLY (Ch. 6:10–17)

VI. THE DYNAMISM OF PRAYER (Ch. 6:18–20)

VII. FINAL GREETING (Ch. 6:21–24)

PART I

CHAPTER I

I. SALUTATION

Ch. 1:1-2

1 Paul, an apostle of Christ Jesus through the will of God, to the saints that are at Ephesus,[1] and the faithful in Christ Jesus:
2 Grace to you and peace from God our Father and the Lord Jesus Christ.

1-2 Like most of the Pauline Epistles, it commences with a paean of thanksgiving, prefaced by a brief salutation, couched in almost identical terms. The strong term for *will*[2] employed is of rare occurrence outside the LXX and N.T. His divine commission was never long absent from the apostle's thoughts. He has not run without being specifically sent. Grace may be viewed as the antecedent of peace, the corner-stone, as we shall learn from the succeeding verses, of the mighty fabric of redeeming love, in which the Father and the Son act in unison. Mark how indissolubly they are here coupled together as the transcendent sources of benediction. The Father and the Son cannot be parted asunder nor honoured in disjunction.

---

[1] The phrase ἐν Ἐφέσῳ is omitted by P⁴⁶ ℵ B 1739 and the corrector of 424 (whose corrections were based on a manuscript of great antiquity). See Introduction, p. 18. J. Mill suggested that the Ephesian destination was attached to the epistle through a combination of Eph. 6:21 f. with 2 Tim. 4:12.
[2] Gk. θέλημα.

II. THANKSGIVING FOR THE RICHES OF GRACE: PAST, PRESENT AND TO COME

Ch. 1:3-14

> 3 Blessed *be* the God and Father of our Lord Jesus
> Christ, who hath blessed us with every spiritual
> blessing in the heavenly *places* in Christ.

3 As Paul muses on the fathomless Fountain of grace, his soul is stirred to its depths, and we see him sally forth, if we may risk the simile, like some long-winded racehorse, impatient of every intervening barrier and careering onward at full speed beyond the middle of the chapter ere he can check his impetuous pace and draw bridle. Even the grammatical construction has to give way to the afflatus that has seized him, as he chants a sevenfold benediction, varied by a threefold refrain, "to the praise of the glory of God's grace." The initial doxology before us embraces the whole of the far-reaching series. We bless the Lord when we ascribe to Him the honour due to His holy Name, when we bow in adoration of His essential perfections and in thanksgiving for their manifestations in His mighty acts. But *He* blesses *us* in a sublimer sense; for we exist and subsist by His fiat, and all the material good we enjoy flows from His bountiful stores. But, to such erring creatures as we are, spiritual well-being constitutes the crowning mercy of all. We are here taught that its well-springs inhere in Christ alone and are not to be tapped apart from Him. The plenitude of life everlasting is vested in Immanuel in trust for us, His mortal brethren. That phrase *in Christ* strikes the keynote of the entire Epistle; from that prolific germ ramifies the branching oak of the forest.

The phrase "God and Father of our Lord Jesus Christ" seems to express the double filiation of the Son, His trinitarian Sonship and that of His humanity as the Sent of the Father. These divine mysteries can only be rightly viewed from "the heavenly places"[3] —another peculiar phrase of this letter—"above the smoke and

---

[3] Gk. τὰ ἐπουράνια.

stir of this dim spot which men call earth," from that supramundane plateau to which faith is privileged to soar, an altitude where the orbit of eternity circumspheres the horizons of time and space. Mountain crests have always typified communion with the Most High; but Paul's mind may be reverting to his own transit to the third heaven, that region of unutterable intercommunications. Such ecstatic raptures may not befit our frail selves, yet there are seasons of heaven upon earth which impart a foretaste of the spirit's perfected energies, a prelibation of glory, when we obtain transfiguring glimpses within the veil and breathe the air of immortality.

> 4   even as he chose[4] us in him before the foundation of the world,[5] that we should be holy and without blemish before him in love:[6]

4   From this exalted vantage-ground the apostle proceeds to cast a rapid glance over the chief landmarks in the majestic panorama of Divine grace. First in order he signalizes *election,* that sovereign ordination whereby the Father chose the recipients of His saving grace for reasons not derived *ab extra* but interwoven with His own unsearchable counsels, irrespective of merit or faith foreseen in their future demeanour. The will of God is, as Payson said, "the very perfection of reason", but He does not give us the key of His cabinet secrets. What we do descry is "a mighty maze, but not without a plan"; for a personal Deity must assuredly have a purpose enshrouded in His creative workmanship. Is men's free-will to be deemed inviolable? Much more so must the perfect will of the Most High have free scope and suffer no abridgment by reason of His creatures' lapse into revolt. Grace is not measured by desert, but bestowed at the option of the donor. If I give all my goods to feed the poor or ransom a crew of galley-slaves I have an undoubted right to select my beneficiaries as I think best.

---

4   The middle voice (Gk. $\dot{\varepsilon}\xi\varepsilon\lambda\dot{\varepsilon}\xi\alpha\tau o$) may be rendered "chose for Himself".

5   Gk. $\varkappa\alpha\tau\alpha\beta o\lambda\dot{\eta}$ $\varkappa\dot{o}\sigma\mu ov$ — a characteristic NT phrase not extant elsewhere in this form, except in an astrological reference. But Aristeas (129) and Plutarch (*Moralia* 956) employ $\varkappa\alpha\tau\alpha\beta o\lambda\dot{\eta}$ in the sense of "creation"; and the Koiné generally for the foundation of a building.

6   An alternative punctuation puts a heavy stop after "before him" and attaches "in love" to the opening words of v. 5 (which then reads, as in ARV margin, "having in love foreordained us . . .").

25

The Lord God can do nothing indeterminately, nor can His designs miscarry, nor be checkmated. An infinite will which is validated or invalidated, as the case may be, at the beck of finite humanity dwindles to the dimensions of an obsequious lay-figure, shorn of awe and dominion, a debilitated travesty of Godhead that confutes and discredits itself. Let us worship an untrammelled Potentate, *God over all.* We have Christ's own affidavit that the whole of that aggregate (John 6:37) given Him by the Father shall infallibly come to Him, and that august edict secures the content of redemption from contingency. Salvation is no precarious half-measure but a foundation laid in heaven; *Heilsart ist Schöpfungsplan.* The work of the Spirit, the Author of the new creation, is not tentative but determinate. Mark how all its subjects are elected to holiness. Sanctification is an integral part, nay, the goal, of our reinstatement. For the new nature will not contravene but cherish the regenerate aspirations implanted within it. *Noblesse oblige!* And the freer the Lord's paramount choice, the deeper the debt of the chosen to love divine.

> 5 having foreordained us unto adoption as sons through Jesus Christ unto himself, according to the good pleasure of his will,
> 6 to the praise of the glory of his grace, which he freely bestowed on us in the Beloved:

5 Foreordination is one of the unique prerogatives of Jehovah, to whom all His works are foreknown from eternity; nor can there be certain foreknowledge without certainty of futurition. A primordial purpose underlies creation and governs its labyrinthine folds, but in the case of moral agents one exempt from all trace of coercive necessitation. The Lord of all abides Monarch in the kingdom of the human will without the least violation of its innate properties. The lock is not forced but opened; we are made willing to do our Maker's will. *Acti agimus,* we act under actuation, as Augustine has put the matter in a nutshell. In effectual calling the inscrutable operation of grace emerges into the visible sphere and *adoption*[7] unfolds some of the more palpable phases of its working. It transfers the enfranchised soul from the serfdom of

---

[7] Gk. *υἱοθεσία.* The classical term for "adoption" is *εἰσποίησις,* and for "adopted" *θετός.* But the NT vocable occurs in Diodorus and Laertius, and the legal phrase *καθ' υἱοθεσίαν* ("by adoption") is frequent in the papyri.

Satan's slave-camp to the family circle of God's favour and invests the believer with its heavenly citizenship and untold privileges. The choice of Israel of old as a firstborn son (Ex. 4:22) *in statu pupillari* prefigured this "purpose of the ages", the reservation namely to Himself of an elect host of loyal hearts for ends transcending our power to conceive. The metaphor of adoption is fetched from the usages of Roman law in particular, where it was regarded as the appropriate remedy for childlessness. Though not unfamiliar to Greek legislators, it seems to have been foreign to Hebrew usage, its place being taken by the levirate law of the Jewish economy. Some theologians have discovered an analogous design in election, viewed as a divine corrective for foreseen unbelief. They argue that human depravity is so deep-seated and antipathetic to the humbling message of the cross that the Second Adam would not have "seen His seed" (Isa. 53:10), but remained a Head without members, were it not that sovereign grace has furnished a "people for His own possession," cured of their obduracy and indissolubly knit to their Elder Brother. At any rate, as a new covenant blessing, adoption displays the Father's good pleasure that a company of "sons of God" should be gathered one by one from our race, stamped with the image of His eternal Son, made co-heirs with Him, and enabled to breathe the homefelt cry, "Abba, Father" (Rom. 8:15).

6   Thus the harvest of redemption is not suspended on changeable factors nor is salvation an afterthought, the outcome of a chain of temporal circumstances; for the immutable Jehovah has no occasion for second thoughts, seeing that He beholds the end from the beginning in one simultaneous conspectus and "wills what He wills once for all" (Augustine), ordaining the entire catena of intervenient means as well as the ultimate result. The manifestation of His glory, as Jonathan Edwards has shown, is the highest conceivable final cause of creation; and in the sacrificial death of Jesus Christ, pregnant with the never-ending bliss of a countless host of immortals whom He rescues from perdition singlehanded, the praise of the glory of God's grace attains its floodmark and the cosmos its vindication from vanity.

The clause appended, "which He freely bestowed on us in the Beloved", clenches the truth the apostle has just enforced. It is generally agreed that in the older version, "accepted in the Beloved", is incorrect, though that sentiment is eminently scriptural.[8] The verb appears elsewhere only in the angel's greeting to the Virgin Mary (Luke 1:28), where it is rendered "highly favoured". We should prefer in both passages the marginal version *endued with grace*. Paul is reiterating his previous declaration (v.4) that it is "through Jesus Christ" that these distinguishing mercies reach us. The Father loves the Son so unspeakably that His love overflows upon all who are "found in Him", castled in the security of the everlasting covenant ratified at once with Him and with all whose names are written in the "oldest of scripts", the Lamb's book of life.

"My beloved Son" was the testimony thrice borne by the Father to Immanuel in the days of His flesh.[9] Moses had styled Jacob's "right-hand son", Benjamin, "the beloved of the Lord (Deut. 33:12), and the Christian Church has appropriated to her Bridegroom those endearments of the *Canticles,* and pregnant in Ps. 45, which Paul must have had in mind. Full well may all whom he has re-affiliated with the heavenly family by the travail of His soul count Him *their* well-beloved and crown Him Lord of all!

Thus far the dominant theme has been the ineffable *love of the Father*. No one has summed it up better than an American preacher, Herbert Lathe, when he wrote: "The Christian's title to heaven as joint-heir with Christ is unchallengeable. It is not because his life has been free from marked wickedness. It is not because God is indulgent or because all sinners will sometime and somehow be brought home. It is because God for unfathomable reasons chose him and raised him up from the grave wherein he lay bound and loosed him from sin and gave him a new heart and made him a son for ever. It is all of grace". And he adds

---

8 Gk. ἐχαρίτωσεν. The concisest rendering of this verb would be "graced". The Puritan Thomas Goodwin coins the word "bemercied" to translate it. The conception is Hebraistic, like the locution "to find favour". In Aristeas (225) it signifies "to be favoured."

9 We take the title ὁ ἠγαπημένος to be a more emphatic declaration of the Father's love for the only-begotten Son than is conveyed by the Evangelists' adjective ἀγαπητός, which in the singular often in classical Greek carries the sense of an *only* son. *Cf.* Plutarch, *Moralia* 94, 595; Xenophon, *Cyropaedia* ii. 6. The participle ἠγαπημένος is applied by the LXX to Israel (Isa. 5:1); and the appellation Jedidiah, bestowed by Nathan upon Solomon (2 Sam. 13:25) is its Hebrew counterpart. We might fitly render it "well-beloved." (*Cf.* Col. 1:13 for the Hebraism "the son of his love".) The Western text amplifies "the Beloved" to "his beloved Son."

a word peculiarly applicable to our day: "impatience with divine sovereignty is not the mark of a sanctified mind".

> 7   in whom we have[10] our redemption through his blood, the forgiveness of our trespasses, according to the riches of his grace,

7   Hitherto the Father's work has engrossed our view. That is indivisibly correlated with the mission of the Son; for, as Ambrose has worded it; Christ is our mouth and eye and hand whereby we have dealings with the Father, *quo nisi intercedente nec nobis nec omnibus sanctis quicquam cum Deo est.* Accordingly we are now bidden to bend our gaze on the *love of the Son,* displayed at its acme when in His Person "the offended died to set the offenders free". So cardinal is this statement that it reappears *verbatim* in the Colossian letter (1:14).[11]

Redemption primarily denotes release from a state of servitude effected by payment of a ransom-price. In a laxer acceptation it is applied to the exodus of Israel from their house of bondage, the power displayed engaging attention rather than the medium employed. Yet the stricter sense has its place in the O.T., as in Ps. 49:7f., Job 33:24, Isa. 43:3. Moreover in the institution of the Paschal lamb as a ransom for the Hebrew firstborn we recognize a prophecy of the Lamb of God's own passover. The Ritschlian school, it is true, have laboured, like their forerunner the wily Socinus, to dilute the significance of the term.[12] But in this epitome of the divine evangel it evidently carries its full sense; for, as Spurgeon pithily puts it, "the High Street of the Gospel runs crosswise". It is the Redeemer's bloodshedding that avails for the cleansing of the guilty. What else could serve as a valid detergent?

---

[10]   A few authorities (א* D* with the Coptic and Ethiopic versions and the Latin Irenaeus) read ἔσχομεν ("we have received") for ἔχομεν ("we have").

[11]   See exposition and notes *ad loc.*, pp. 190 f.

[12]   In confutation of the alleged latitude of meaning ascribed to ἀπολύτρωσις by liberalist hermeneutics, B. B. Warfield has conclusively proved that the verb ἀπολυτροῦν, ἀπολυτροῦσθαι, took the place in later Greek of the older ἀπολύειν on purpose to express more determinately the concept of *ransom*, which it implies wherever it is found, and signally so in reference to the atoning work of Christ (*The Person and Work of Christ* [Philadelphia, 1950], pp. 429 ff.). The apparent exceptions to this standing rule (which is implied by the incorporation in the verb of the definite term λυτρόν, "ransom")—namely, Dan. 4:27 (LXX) and Heb. 11:35—can be shown to involve no real departure from its uniform usage. It belongs to literary diction; consequently the papyri supply no illustrations of it. *Cf.* p. 190, n. 50 (on Col. 1:14).

For the Most High is most *glorious* in point of holiness. That attribute sheds an incomparable lustre on all the rest. And being what He is, He must "glow with fiery indignation against sin" (Dale), inasmuch as sin is not only creation's cancerous curse, menacing the moral universe with devastation, but it offers the deadliest affront to divine purity. The impunity of such an incubus would be tantamount to the abdication of the Judge of all. The sovereign Justiciar *must* exercise unswerving justice or deny Himself; for the scales of justice are never sliding-scales. It is mercy that has an optional province. How then shall a Just God be a Saviour as well, without dishonour?

In face of that tremendous deadlock all created intelligences stand nonplussed. It seems absolutely insuperable. Nothing save "love divine, all love excelling", could effect its displacement. The Trinity is involved in that stupendous elimination of obstacles and restitution of creation's equipoise, that triumphant proof that ours is not a ramshackle universe, however awry, but a cosmos presided over by a supreme moral Governor. The travail of man's redemption throbbed in the bosom of the Godhead ere time began, when the Eternal Son covenanted to become our Proxy, to fulfil all righteousness and sustain the penalty of the broken law in our nature and room. "Only the Holy One could satisfy the claims of holiness" (Forsyth). "The paradox of the pardon of sin by a holy God cannot be solved apart from an expiation of it" (Warfield). Behold the comprehensive Sin-bearer so sorely needed, "worth all that God is worth" (Goodwin), wounded for our transgressions, and you behold justice and mercy so harmoniously coadjusted that they become joint-pleaders for the prisoner at the bar. The stainless rectitude of redeeming love, the fact that it is a flawless settlement, is its peculiar glory and perfection. All is love; but all is law (Moule); and at the cross holiness gives the law to love (Forsyth). Need we add that the "riches[13] of grace" are resplendent in this wondrous counsel? Had the universe been tendered for the sinner's ransom, the indemnity would have been but finite; whereas in the unspeakable Gift high heaven comes to our aid and allocates to our bankrupt funds its own illimitable wealth, "infinite riches

---

[13] The neuter πλοῦτος for the regular masculine occurs repeatedly in Paul's epistles, possibly to avoid confusion with Plutus, the god of wealth. There is, however, a distinct tendency in Hellenistic Greek to interchange the second and third declensions, exemplified in the neuter forms of ἔλεος, ζῆλος, σκότος.

in a little room". And the Lord's forgiveness is as complete as its procurement was costly. His is no grudging, but a cordial, an *abundant*, an exhaustive pardon.

> 8 which he made to abound toward us in all wisdom and prudence,
> 9 making known unto us the mystery of his will, according to his good pleasure which he purposed in him
> 10 unto a dispensation of the fulness of the times, to sum up all things in Christ, the things in the heavens, and the things upon the earth;

8 Opinions are divided whether the "wisdom and prudence" here signalized relate to God or man. Many expositors contend that the latter term is inapplicable to the Most High. *Judgment* or *discernment* might be a more suitable rendering; the O.T. phrase corresponding (Prov. 3:19) runs, *wisdom and understanding*. But surely there is room for the display of wisdom in operation as well as principle in the unveiling of the messianic purpose and the process of restitution of a chaotic world, matured by slow degrees. In the parallel passage of Colossians (1:9)[14] unquestionably, the apostle prays that his readers may themselves be equipped with spiritual wisdom and understanding; but here his outlook is theocentric throughout. He is contemplating the "purpose of the ages", divinely decreed and incapable of frustration, a ground-plan formed in eternity by omniscience and a palatial structure, erected in time, like some vast pyramid, from base to topstone, presided over by a Master-builder who cannot err. It is that sublime spectacle that draws forth his impassioned doxology. Divine wisdom may be seen in the ordering and overruling of events, in the graduated timing of interpositions and dispensations, and in the governance of individual lives and histories to subserve its own transcendent ends.

9 *Mystery* in Scriptural usage does not denote "a secret doctrine of the initiated" and has, therefore, no lineal connection with the pagan mystery-cults, the stock-in-trade of parties dealing in occult Eastern theosophies. As H. A. A. Kennedy has shown,[15]

---

14 See exposition of Col. 1:9 on pp. 185 f.
15 *St. Paul and the Mystery Religions* (London, 1913).

they were poles asunder from the revelation from on high of which Paul was the chosen mouthpiece. We are now eyeing the disclosure of the design of sovereign grace in time,[16] concentred in Christ Jesus,[17] Himself both the sum and the solution of all unsearchabilities of the eternal will. This masterpiece of mercy, founded in reasons beyond our scrutiny, constitutes a system of its own, as co-operant as the solar, ordered in all things and sure. "God never forgets His purposes, though He executes them in His own way and at His own pace" (Chalmers), and His holy character vouches that His state secrets are "mysteries of godliness". He is the unhurried Arbiter of time and its manifold issues. At the centre of the wheeling orbs subsists unruffled calm, a serenity tranquil as that of the azure skies on a cloudless midsummer morning, "one of those heavenly days which cannot die".

10 These majestic purposes of the Most High attain their fruition "in the fulness of times"; for with Him "a thousand years are as one day". Man was left to his own inventions long enough to demonstrate the futility of his vaunted wisdom and the inadequacy of his cherished resources. The anticipations raised by the triumphs of modern science are pursuing the same track. They modify the externals of life, not always beneficently, but do not fill its aching voids nor quench its raging thirsts. God waited till the impotence of the ancient world to heal its own wounds was patent before He sent His Son to be the Physician of souls. "We can neither endure our vices nor their remedies", wrote Livy in the preamble to his Roman history. Yet with all its aberrations the Christian church has shown itself to possess a sovereign panacea for all manner of social and ethical degradation. Wherever it has had due scope and secured fair trial the Lord's antidote for the epidemic of moral evil has wrought signal marvels.

Christ is the summation of the temporal series which was created by Him and for Him (Col. 1:16, 20),[18] and its consummation is

---

[16] See exposition and notes on Col. 1:26 f. (pp. 218 f.), for comparison of the uses of μυστήριον in the two companion epistles.

[17] The words ἣν προέθετο ἐν αὐτῷ (v. 9) may bear either of two significations: (a) "which He set forth (Lat. *proposuit*) in Him", the paramount expression of the Father's tender mercy, or (b) reading αὐτῷ, "which He purposed in Himself." The former version accords best with the use of the verb in Rom. 3:25.

[18] See exposition and notes *ad loc.*, pp. 197 ff., 206 f.

bound up with His enthronement at its head. "Whatever persists
in opposing Him must be put under His feet; whatever accords
with His sway shall be conserved among His trophies" (Dale).
We can perceive the process of renovation here and there at work,
but its operation seems to us tardy and partial; for we do not see
all things as yet unified under the regency of God's anointed King.
In fact, the cycle of this spiritual palingenesis, this cosmical
revolution of a higher order, by which a perfect readjustment of
the moral system shall finally be attained, is on too vast a scale
for our mortal apprehension. The scaffolding must be removed
before we can discern the edifice. To-day we know in part; we
see through a glass obliquely. But when the perfect day dawns,
our fractional judgment will be merged in comprehensive vision
of a rounded whole. Of this much meantime we have assurance,
that, in accordance with the divine programme[19] of history, all
things in heaven and earth shall be reconstituted[20] "in Christ".
There is no expanse of empire that He cannot fill, no aspiration on
which He cannot bestow heart's content. He was the Alpha of
time's first pulsebeat, and He shall be the Omega of its parting
gasp, and gather centripetally to Himself all that survives the

---

[19] Gk. οἰκονομία. This favourite word of Polybius literally designates the
office of stewardship, on which the translation "dispensation", in the Latin
sense of that term, is founded. But the noun acquired a much wider range in the
course of time, connoting "arrangement" or "regulation", almost like our own
derivative "economy." It is often found in this broader acceptation in the
papyri, and Cicero and Quintilian thus employ it. A vocable such as "ordination" or "administration" might not unsuitably convey the marshalling notion
inherent in the term. See Ch. 3:2, 9 (pp. 70, 75).

[20] Gk ἀνακεφαλαιοῦσθαι, strictly speaking, is a technical term of rhetoric,
"to summarize"; that is to say, of literary, not popular, provenance. Quintilian
(vi. 1) construes the substantive ἀνακεφαλαίωσις by *rerum congregatio*, "recapitu-
lation." Some exegetes surmise that this usage of the word prevails in the
present passage: that as all things were made by and for Christ, and seeing that
He has assumed our nature and that man is the microcosm of the physical
creation, He has traversed the full gamut of being and, so to speak, epitomized
the cosmos in His own person. But this suggestion wears an artificial colouring
foreign to the solemn intensity of the context. It is evident from the parallel in
Col. 1:16 (*cf.* p. 197) that the conception—underlying the Prologue to St. John's
Gospel—of the Son's centrality to creation is predicated. The way is being
prepared for the affirmation in v. 22 of His supreme headship as the Keystone
of the universe, whether κεφαλή or κεφάλαιον be the proximate formative. In this
sublimer sense He becomes its focal point and redintegrating centre, the summation of its complex series, entwining the entire *catena* of existence with His
august divine humanity; the cynosure of that grand readjustment of its dislocated harmonies "to which the whole creation moves."

crash of worlds and the supersession of the seen and temporal. If we are His, He abides our central Sun and we shall find our orbit as His satellites, attendant on "the Light of Lights".

Whether "in heaven and earth" refers to the church militant and triumphant co-united under one Captain and King or comprises the angelic hosts within its purview we should hesitate to pronounce, did not the term *all* seem to imply, and the Colossian parallels[21] affirm the latter. At any rate the myriad mirrors destined to reflect His image, the race preordained to be bound to Him by a closer nexus than any beside, will consist of human beings, not superhuman princedoms and dominions, His lieges likewise but not, as we, His brethren; for the unique vinculum betwixt heaven and earth is none other than our enthroned Kinsman, the Crown-prince of the new creation, Victor Immanuel, the grand Emancipator from sin's iron yoke, whose service is perfect freedom.

> in him, *I say,*
> 11 in whom also we were made a heritage,[22] having been foreordained according to the purpose of him who worketh all things after the counsel of his will;
> 12 to the end that we should be unto the praise of his glory, we who had before hoped in Christ:
> 13 in whom ye also, having heard the word of the truth, the gospel of your salvation,—

11–13a Once more the apostle iterates his solemn affirmation that God is the Source and Christ the Medium of the soul-melting counsel of redeeming love. It "flows from the heart of the Father through the blood of the Son" (John Owen). Nor is he unmindful of the work of the Spirit, the superlative *promise* of the new covenant. In the phrase "those who beforehand hoped in Christ" the reference appears to be to the spiritual Israel, those compatriots of Paul's who waited for the true Messiah. But his survey extends to the Gentile believers, the firstfruits of the wild olive grafted into the parent stock. They had received the truth in the love of it by a reflex act of faith or "recumbency on Christ". The use of the word *heritage* or allotment recalls the installation by divine appointment of the Hebrew settlers in Canaan; and the

---

[21] *Cf.* Col. 1:16, 20 (pp. 197 ff., 206 f.).

[22] Gk. ἐκληρώθημεν (some Western authorities read ἐκλήθημεν, "we were called").

characteristic *aposiopesis* after "salvation" seems not unsuitably supplied by the verb *believed,* implied in the ensuing participle. Belief and truth are correlatives. A false representation has no title to credit; it is the conviction of its divine verity that renders the gospel worthy of all acceptation. But the writer is hurrying onward to the experimental evidence these converts from heathenism enjoyed of the transformation they had undergone.

> in whom, having also believed,[23] ye were sealed with the Holy Spirit of promise,
> 14 which[24] is an earnest of our inheritance, unto the redemption of *God's* own possession, unto the praise of his glory.

13ᵇ The image of sealing is capable of a variety of interpretations, among which *authentication* and *appropriation* are the most outstanding.[25] Christ Himself received the seal of the Father's attestation during His earthly ministry; and so the believer possesses the witness of the indwelling Spirit to his place in the new creation; for grace has given him a new palate and pabulum; his tastes and satisfactions are being purged from their carnal propensities; what he could not do in his unregenerate days he is enabled now to perform, and what he could not once upon a time resist, he now staunchly withstands. He is conscious of a new manhood and so are his associates. "Jehovah hath set apart for Himself him that is godly", says the Psalmist (Ps. 4:3); and that may be viewed as the O.T. aspect of this N.T. credential, lit up with a fresh lustre since Pentecost shot forth its quickening beams.

14 Furthermore, this Divine Indweller, independent of national distinctions, who causes men to differ from their former selves by His subduing energy, is Himself the Earnest of the glorious inheritance already foreshadowed (2 Cor. 1:22). The

---

23 Gk. πιστεύσαντες, the "coincident aorist participle" which is "doctrinally important" (J. H. Moulton, *Grammar of NT Greek* i [3rd edn., Edinburgh, 1908], p. 131 n.). *Cf.* the same form in a similar context in Acts 19:2, with remarks *ad loc.* in NICNT.

24 Gk. ὅς (masculine) although the antecedent πνεῦμα is neuter. This has been taken as proof of the personality of the Spirit (although it might be explained on grammatical grounds as the result of attraction to the gender of the masculine ἀρραβών, "earnest").

25 See G. W. H. Lampe, *The Seal of the Spirit* (London, 1951), pp. 3 ff. *et passim.*

Hebrew word *'erabhon* seems to have found its way into Greek through Phoenician traders. It conveys the meaning of a *token in kind*, viewed as the harbinger of future possession. The Spirit's agency affords a foretaste of bliss; for the life He implants in the saved soul partakes of the quality of that of heaven. In hours when the wings of faith bear him aloft, the saint enjoys a prelibation of glory. He knows he is still "in the making", but rests assured of the perfect product in prospect, when the Lord's people shall be finally redeemed from the hand of the enemy. Redemption in this broader sense comprises (Rom. 8:23) investiture with a spiritual body accoutred for heavenly service. Thus the sanctification of the Spirit completes the far-reaching design of a re-established universe of holy and happy beings, blessedly secured against defection for ever and ever.

Thus all the multitudinous strands of the vast web of creation converge in Jesus Christ, "by whom are all things and we by Him", and Milton's sonorous anthem of praise recurs to our memories:

> Sin jarred 'gainst nature's chime and with harsh din
> Broke the fair music that all creatures made
> To their great Lord, when love their motion swayed
> In perfect diapason, when they stood
> In their obedience and first state of good.
> But once again we shall renew that song
> Keeping in time with heaven, when God ere long
> To His celestial quire shall us unite
> To live with Him and sing in endless light.

And when that ultimate resolution of discords and restitution of concords takes place, its keynote will be struck in grateful celebration of Him whose name is music and whose crown of crowns is love.

We have been listening to an overture of the hallelujahs of the blest, and it closes, as it began, on the note of the praise of God's glory, the highest of all themes. We scan a veritable gulf-stream of thanksgiving, as it were, flowing out at those golden gates. False and true theology may be discriminated by a simple criterion. Do they magnify God or man? Why should the creature resent the controlling, encompassing hand of the Creator? Why in particular should any child of God exalt man's will above the Father of spirits' unerring ordinations, sovereignly wise and holy as they of necessity are?

36

III. PRAYER FOR THE ENHANCED ILLUMINATION
OF HIS READERS

Ch. 1:15–20a

15 For this cause I also, having heard of the faith in the Lord Jesus which is among you, and the love[26] which *ye show* toward all the saints,

16 cease not to give thanks for you, making mention[27] of you in my prayers;

15–16 Therefore, subjoins the apostle, in view of all this divine expenditure of grace, and of the tidings conveyed to me of your spirit of faith and love, I am moved to fervent prayer on your behalf, not unmingled with praise. He uses the selfsame expression in Colossians (1:4) to a church which he had never visited; and from the use of the term *heard* in both cases a plausible argument has been framed in support of the circular nature of this Epistle, for how should Paul thus write to his old Ephesian hearers? Yet a passage in 1 Thess. (3:5, 6) shows us that he felt a solicitude touching the constancy of his newly fledged converts which could only be relieved by news of their spiritual welfare, attested by the practice of the two foremost Christian graces. But his ardent soul can never rest content with present attainments, either for himself or others; so he breathes a glowing supplication for the increase of their heavenly-mindedness.

17 that[28] the God of our Lord Jesus Christ, the Father of glory, may give[29] unto you a spirit of wisdom and

---

26 Gk. τὴν ἀγάπην, omitted by P46 ℵ A B and a number of other authorities, yet obviously necessary to complete the sense (as against the view that the fuller reading has borrowed τὴν ἀγάπην from Col. 1:4).

27 Gk. μνείαν ποιεῖσθαι. Deissmann adduces this phrase as a notable instance of popular diction, illustrated from letters and inscriptions in the vernacular. But the expression is pure classical Greek, as old and of standard quality as Aeschines and Plato (*Protagoras* 317).

28 The conjunction ἵνα loses its telic force in relation to prayer. Precedents for this idiom reach back indeed to Homer's λίσσομαι ὅπως (*Odyssey* iii. 19).

29 The Greek verb should be read as the optative δῴη, but Blass and Moulton view it as the Ionic subjunctive δώῃ, preserving the customary sequence of moods. Cod. B reads the Attic subjunctive δῷ. Cf. p. 78, n. 24 (on Ch. 3:16).

revelation in the knowledge of him;

18 having the eyes of your heart[30] enlightened,[31] that
ye may know what is the hope of his calling,[32] what
the riches of the glory of his inheritance in the saints,

19 and what the exceeding greatness of his power to usward who believe, according to the working of the
strength of his might

20 which he wrought in Christ, when he raised him[33]
from the dead,

17 If God overrules all things for His own glory, He can
bestow on these Gentile converts an enlarged capacity of grace
and make them rise to the full dignity of their high calling.
Observe that this aspiration on their behalf is not addressed to
some esoteric circle of believers, like the favoured few selected
as pupils by the Greek philosophers, but to the rank and file of
the Christian community.[34] All alike are to covet the best gifts
of the Spirit, the full stature of manhood in Christ. The title "the
Father of glory", like the Psalmist's *God of glory* (Ps. 29:3),
represents the Father as the radiant-point of all glory, both of
efflux and influx, and the locution "the God of our Lord Jesus
Christ" (already met with in v. 3) must not be construed in detraction of the Deity of the Son, but in the light of His mediatorial
subordination to the Father. Paul seeks for his Ephesian circle the
spirit of wisdom and revelation, an open-eyed, increasing discernment of the things of God, the insight of "men in understanding".
The beautiful metaphor he employs, "the eyes of your heart being
enlightened"—the true reading—must have been quite novel when
he used it. It reminds us that the illumination he desiderates is

---

[30] Gk. τοὺς ὀφθαλμοὺς τῆς καρδίας ὑμῶν. This fine expression represents
the correct reading, found in the vast majority of manuscripts (a few read
διανοίας, "understanding," for καρδίας, "heart"). Its prototype meets us in the
Psalmist's prayer (Ps. 13:3): "lighten mine eyes" (*i.e.*, my soul's eyes).

[31] Gk. πεφωτισμένους. This accusative absolute apparently breaks the syn-
tactical construction of the sentence and is usually regarded as modified by the
subsequent infinitive (εἰδέναι, "to know") but really dependent on the preceding
ὑμῖν. The verb occurs in the LXX to signify instruction or illumination, and
repeatedly in Polybius to denote enlightenment as to the truth of a matter or
report. Thucydides indulges a good deal in accusative absolutes, irregularly
introduced. They lend additional saliency to a proposition.

[32] Gk. κλῆσις. This is a good instance of the enhanced significance imparted
by Christianity, that of a *divine call*, to a term already in general use.

[33] Gk. ἐγείρας αὐτόν, which might here be rendered: "by raising him."

[34] *Cf.* Col. 1:28, with exposition and notes *ad loc.* (p. 219).

inward, not dependent on the senses or even the mental activities, so much as on the spiritual enlightenment that assimilates divine truth as its congenial aliment, and descries objects invisible to the worldling's myopic vision; for the heart may have sounder perceptions than the head.

18–19   The apostle offers three signal petitions for these sheep of Christ ingathered from the heathen pale. The first is that they may recognize fully *the hope of the call*[35] they have obeyed, fraught with such ample benedictions in reversion. Let them realize its mighty compass and entrancing vista. Heaven lies ahead of them and they are to be made meet for it, commingling in its holy joys and bearing the image of their chosen King. Secondly, he prays that they may appreciate *the riches of the glory of His inheritance in the saints.* Christ has taken His people to be His everlasting portion, and the cost of His purchase must endear it to Him as well as to them. He has wound bonds of .love and gratitude round them that can never be snapped asunder. They are wondrous trophies of His reclaiming and upraising power, a spectacle to angels of beings brought back from exile at a tremendous outlay and reinstated after grievous rebellion in unshaken fealty to their true sovereign. Thirdly, let them reflect upon *the exceeding greatness of the Lord's power to usward who believe.* The dethronement of self and enthronement of Christ in them has already yielded proof of that. What less than an almighty arm could thus reverse the bent and bias of a sinner's character for good and all? They bear the impress of divine workmanship; but the pattern is still incomplete; they are in the making, yet not left to manufacture themselves into full-sized saints unaided; for the *working of the strength* of almightiness, put forth in bringing them from death unto life, is of the same wonder-working efficacy as that which raised Christ from the dead and has seated Him on high.

20ᵃ   Do they desire to gauge the plenitude of their resources in Him? Would they measure the dynamic force at their back? Let them not conceive of the grace he has been extolling as a slender rivulet, capable of turning the water-wheel of their souls in favoured moments, when in flood, but as a surging river of life,

---

[35]   On Christian hope *cf.* Col. 1:4, with exposition and notes *ad loc.* (p. 180).

a motive force of power to drive before its invincible energy all the obstacles it may encounter. If straitened, they are straitened in themselves; for all fulness resides in their risen Head, and, in Thomas Goodwin's phrase, "His resurrection has *the power of all resurrections* contracted in it"; His exaltation is the guarantee that His people shall be exalted in and with Him; Paul had learnt to appropriate all-sufficiency and to gird himself for his Herculean task in the panoply of his heavenly Co-worker. So he covets for his recruits reliance on their divine reserves. Their own funds might fluctuate largely with the state of the market, but they were partners in a grand alliance; for a man in Christ Jesus is more than a man by himself. He is an organ of divine puissance, an instrument "in tune with the infinite", a probationer for entire sanctification under the potentiation of the almighty Spirit.

IV. CHRIST'S EXALTATION AND ITS CONCOMITANT ISSUES FOR HIS CHURCH

Ch. 1:20b–23

> and made him to sit at his right hand[36] in the heavenly *places*,
> 21 far above[37] all rule, and authority, and power, and dominion, and every name that is named,[38] not only in this world, but also in that which is to come:
> 22 and he put all things in subjection under his feet,[39]

20ᵇ‑22ᵃ Not only has the Redeemer been released from the icy grip of death, the most tenacious of all turnkeys, but God has set Him at His own right hand, robed in mediatorial sovereignty, upraised triumphantly above all the heavenly hierarchies—their enumeration is a Pauline trait—and given Him a name loftier than every other name however preeminent of whatsoever dynasty or domination, present or to come. "The highest place that heaven affords is His, is His by right". Moreover, all things without exception are subordinated to His sway; His might matches with His majesty. And that imperial sway has for its final goal the investiture of His ransomed lieges with glory everlasting. That is the revealed programme of human history. Not the mailed fist but the pierced hand holds the rod of empire. The stone rejected by blind builders is made the chief Cornerstone of the preordained edifice projected by the Divine Architect. The best of the best is incontestably our Lord's due; and so illustrious is the self-devotion of the Lamb of God, so transcendent the glory that irradiates His dying love, that "it demands a compensation that taxes the resources of Omnipotence" (Thornwell). How suited is such a perspective to enhance the believer's estimate of his high calling and august patrimony and of the inexhaustible amplitude of his assets *in Christ,* at once his inviolable Sanctuary and Wellspring of refreshment!

---

[36] An echo of Ps. 110:1, a basic *testimonium* in the apostolic preaching.

[37] Gk. ὑπεράνω (*cf.* κατενώπιον in v. 4) is an example of the compound preposition characteristic of later Greek, reinforcing weakened verbalisms.

[38] Gk. παντὸς ὀνόματος ὀνομαζομένου. *Cf.* Phil. 2:10, where God gives to the highly exalted Christ τὸ ὄνομα τὸ ὑπὲρ πᾶν ὄνομα.

[39] An echo of Ps. 8:6 (*cf.* 1 Cor. 15:27; Heb. 2:8).

and gave him to be head over all things to the church,
23 which is his body,[40] the fulness of him that filleth
all in all.

22^b–23 The dominion here ascribed to the ascended Saviour
accords with His own testimony: "Behooved it not the Christ to
suffer these things and to enter into his glory?" (Luke 24:26). In
His quality of Mediator, the cross was the dark background to
the crown, *devestiture* the strange prelude to *investiture*. In
Philippians His passion is set forth as the pathway to theanthropic
enthronement. What inferior honour could requite an obedience
so absolutely faultless, so incomparably perfect? His singlehanded vanquishment of death and sin and hell must needs have
for its sequel a division of the spoil correspondingly sublime, a
universal lordship commensurate with the grandeur of His self-
dedication to the pangs of Gethsemane and Golgotha for our sakes.
That travail bears peculiar relation to His mystical body, the
church of which He is Head; the sheep for whose rescue the great
Shepherd shed His lifeblood and whom He tends with such loving
care. But what is the *pleroma* spoken of and what the declaration
made concerning it?[41] Here expositors part company. The
majority construe it of the church of God's elect; and unquestionably there is a sense in which Christ and the church are
complementary terms. The Bridegroom must have a bride or
renounce the title. The Head must possess a body in order to
constitute a whole. If the church be the counterpart of her Consort,
intent on glorifying Him to whom she owes her elevation, He lacks
His full aurora without her bright reflection of His beams, her
responsive greetings to His gracious caresses. Did He not say in
prayer for His disciples: "the glory which thou hast given me,

---

[40] On Christ's relation as head to the church as His body, see exposition and
notes on Col. 1:18 (pp. 201 ff.).

[41] *Cf.* Lightfoot's elaborate disquisition on πλήρωμα in his *Colossians*
(pp. 257 ff.), combated to some extent by J. A. Robinson (*Ephesians*, pp. 255 ff.),
but sounder than his own analysis of the term, which normally conveys a
passive meaning. It denotes entirety of content, and not seldom means "sum-
total." In extension of that sense we find it applied to a ship's complement or
the aggregate of a military corps. Philo uses it of the assemblage of animals
housed in Noah's ark, regarded as its freightage, and he writes elsewhere
(ii. 418) of a soul which has a full cargo of virtues *(πλήρωμα ἀρετῶν)*. The
fulness may be inherent, as in Christ, or communicated, as in the church, from
her divine treasure-chest (*cf.* Ch. 4:13). See further the exposition and notes on
Col. 1:19 (pp. 206 f.) and 2:9 f. (pp. 232 f.).

I have given them; I in them and thou in me" (John 17:22, 23)? In the terminology of the old divines, Christ figures not only as a Head of authority, but of influence. One Spirit indwells His human nature and the souls of His people. Is not the apostle magnifying the dignity of Christ *mystical*, as in 1 Cor. 12:12, viewed as the Redeemer's peculiar treasure? In His essential deity the Son of God cannot but be self-sufficing; but mediatorially He interlinks Himself with His spiritual offspring, bereft of whom He would be dismembered. To them He assumes a relative office and they are indispensable to its discharge. A physician cannot practise without patients nor a guardian exist without wards. Thus the church forms the integration or complement of Christ's saving mission, requisite to His fulfilment of the work, inasmuch as He has been pleased to identify His interest with hers and enclasp her in a spiritual wedlock supremely intimate and endearing.

The grounds for accepting this exegesis of a difficult phrase doubtless preponderate; but we cannot accede to the Old Latin and Vulgate version, sanctioned by Origen and Chrysostom, whereby the ambiguous voice of the verb *to fill* is here rendered in the passive.[42] Westcott and Armitage Robinson have endorsed that translation. The latter's version runs: "the fulness of Him who all in all *is being fulfilled*". High churchmanship may favour this not very intelligible construction of the clause for its own aggrandizing ends, and kenotic speculations may chime in with it. But "the Christ to be" of a poet's dream, in process, as it were, of evolution, has no Scriptural warrant. What is the burden of the context if not the paramount, inalienable exaltation of the Lord Jesus? In His church He deigns to dwell and purposes to raise her to His side, but she is not His co-efficient. His overflow replenishes her circumscribed streamlets; but it would ill beseem her to count herself an affluent requisite for His entirety in whom all her fresh springs take their rise, and whose plenitude as the Son of God does not permit of enhancement *ab extra*. Enough for

---

[42] Gk. πληρουμένου is rendered ambiguous by its employment both in a middle and passive sense. In the former case there is a suggestion of reciprocal action, such as "to fill for oneself" (*cf.* Ch. 4:10). On the whole, we take that to be the meaning in this passage: that, as all things are *for* Christ, He Himself being their consummation, so the decree of redemption confers on His mystical body the distinction of constituting His *mediatorial* fulness or, as the Latinists were wont to express it, His "adimpletion" or supervenient fulness. *Cf.* Col. 2:10, "in him ye are made full" (ἐστε ἐν αὐτῷ πεπληρωμένοι).

the church to reflect the radiance of her heavenly Sun, to be the recipient of His princeliest rarities *ad modum recipientis*; but it is not hers to eke out the content of her Bridegroom's full-orbed sufficiency. "The Lord makes Himself our debtor", says Augustine, "not by appropriating anything from us but by promising us all things". Is He not in Himself *semper idem, heri, hodie, in saecula*?

Bengel, and G. G. Findlay in *Exp. B.*, solve the difficulty by understanding this finale of a grand eulogium of Christ as referring not to the church, but to her Lord, arguing that "which is His body" is parenthetical.[43] Findlay points out the emphasis placed on *Him*, set in the Greek at the head of the sentence, and that the image of *filling all things* designates omnipresence in O.T. diction, so that the term *all-fulness* pertains only to One vested with divine prerogatives. The harsh construction involved seems to invalidate this line of interpretation; yet it is, surely, preferable to the cryptical passive construction noticed above.

---

[43] *Cf.* p. 207, n. 122, for the similar view of A. E. N. Hitchcock and C. F. D. Moule.

CHAPTER II

V. THE OLD AND THE NEW MANHOOD CONTRASTED

Ch. 2:1–7

In order to set forth the magnitude of the change wrought in the believers' emancipation from the power of darkness (*cf.* Col. 1:13) and the splendid possibilities consequent on their translation into the kingdom of God's Son, the apostle now proceeds to depict their former experience of the power of Satan and to contrast it with their present immunities and resources. There is no real break in the line of thought. As signal an energy as that which raised the Lord Jesus from the grave has been put forth in their regeneration.

1   And you *did he make alive,* when ye were dead through your trespasses and sins,
2   wherein ye once walked[1] according to the course of this world, according to the prince of the powers of the air,[2] of the spirit that now worketh in the sons of disobedience;

---

[1] This ethical use of περιπατεῖν (*cf.* Heb. *halakh*), a Hebraism common to Paul and John, frequently replaces the more idiomatic Hellenistic term ἀναστρέφεσθαι (*cf.* Lat. *versari*) found in the next verse. It occurs in this sense in the Palestinian writer Philodemus.

[2] Gk. κατὰ τὸν ἄρχοντα τῆς ἐξουσίας τοῦ ἀέρος. This difficult phrase admits of divers interpretations. ARV, in accordance with Grimm, alters the singular number of the text to an ideal plural "powers," but we doubt whether with adequate warrant. For NT usage distinguishes between the abstract idea of *authority* inherent in the singular and the concrete sense of *authorities* prevalent in the plural. Rationalistic critics are not slow to detect here a tinge of rabbinism and adduce Philo's speculations on intermediary powers occupying an aery citadel between heaven and earth. But these fantasies have very slender Scriptural support. Demiurgic surveillance of creation appertains to theosophic theory. It is the Most High who is "Lord of air and earth and sea" and "maketh the clouds His chariot." What is wanted is something that can be coupled with the remainder of the sentence, introduced by a genitive in apposition with the preceding genitive; something akin to a *current* of diabolical influence, to an *animus* of a sinister kind running counter to the motions of the Divine Spirit.

Some have sought to solve the riddle by attaching a rare signification to the term ἀήρ. In epic poetry, from Homer downwards, the word assumes now and then the meaning of "mist" or "vapour," with its associations of misguidance or

3 among whom we also all once lived in the lusts of our flesh, doing the desires of the flesh and of the mind, and were[3] by nature[4] children of wrath, even as the rest:—

1 We have here another of Paul's broken sentences; so that a verb *made alive* has to be supplied from v.5 for the initial pronoun *you*. He sketches the sombre background of a benighted polytheism as a foil to the sunlit slopes that these Gentiles were now scaling. The Lord of light and life has ushered them from a region of the shadow of death into an expanding morn. Once upon a time (he reminds them) they were pining away under the wasting scourge of prevalent iniquity, feelingly alive to all the lures of sin, but moribund on the Godward side.

There are three outstanding schools of moral pathology traceable throughout the centuries. Pelagianism asserts the convalescence of human nature. Man merely needs teaching. Semi-pelagianism admits his ill-health, but affirms that the symptoms will yield to proper treatment, to a course of tonic drugs and a scrupulous regimen. But Biblical Christianity probes the patient to the quick. Its searching diagnosis pronounces that mortification has set in and that nothing less than infusion of fresh lifeblood can work a cure. Nostrums and palliatives aggravate rather than allay the disease. Sin is an organic epidemical malady, a slow devitalizing poison issuing in moral necrosis; not a stage of arrested or incomplete development, but a seed-plot of impending ruin.

It seems hardly possible to differentiate the two terms *trespasses and sins*, unless we make up our minds to restrict the former to shortcomings and the latter to sins of commission. The language

---

beguilement, a sense which it shares with the epithet ἠεροειδής. In the *Argonautica* of Apollonius Rhodius that is its standing usage, and one passage of Polybius (xviii. 20) approximates thereto. It is noteworthy, moreover, that Lat. *aer* carries this sense of "mist" occasionally, as in Virgil's *aere saepsit* (*Aeneid* i. 411), *in nubem cogitur aer* (*Aeneid* v. 20). The notion therefore was "in the air." But evidence of its provenance in Hellenistic Greek is lacking, to warrant our picturing Satan here in the guise of a vapour- or film-weaver, as he is depicted in 2 Cor. 4:4.

[3] Gk. ἤμεθα. This form (in place of ἤμεν) is uniformly employed in LXX and is not uncommon in later Greek and the papyri.

[4] Gk. φύσει. Not merely "in ourselves," as J. A. Robinson contends (*ad loc.*), but as members of a fallen race. *Cf.* φύσει ἀσθενές (Xenophon, *Memorabilia* i. 6), φύσει δίκαιος (Philodemus, *Rhet.* ii. 259), φύσει σπουδαῖος (Aristotle 1237). So in Gal. 2:15, "we being Jews by *extraction*" (φύσει).

recurs in Col. 2:13.[5] Death spiritual has analogies worth pondering with death physical; but in some respects a distinction should be drawn between them. Walking, for example, is here predicated of the ethical death; for it does not connote lifelessness so much as induration. All the intellectual faculties may be in full play with a man spiritually callous. He may pursue sedulously a score of worldly aims; his human sensibilities may be wide awake. Nevertheless obtuseness may signalize the higher plane of his being. His heavenward hemisphere may remain a blank. We all know people enthusiastic for earthly gewgaws who have no taste for higher things and are lapped in soporific unconcern regarding them. Their souls have no windows "commercing with the skies"; for they are governed by the standards ascendant in their nether environment, being "alienated from the life of God because of their hardening of heart".

2 These parties are the unconscious dupes of an invisible thaumaturgist of whose deft legerdemain they have little or no suspicion. The engineer of prevalent "winds of doctrine" makes them his facile puppets. We are all under spiritual influence of some sort. Spiritualism itself constitutes one of the devil's decoys, whether we view it as a rank fraud or as actually impregnated with diabolism. For in proportion as a man draws near to Satan, Satan will draw near to him. His spirit is described as *working* energetically in the children of disobedience.[6] Such wickedness as his forms much too restless an agency to slumber. It craves insatiably a sphere of active operation. Paul had encountered many flagrant ebullitions of its malignity in Ephesus and elsewhere. So has many a modern missionary in the wilds of heathendom. What thoughtful surveyor of the scene presented by our globe to-day can stand in doubt that the lord of misrule has his myrmidons at work in every continent, imbued with his own fell passion of lawlessness? May we not say that he has had a hand in some recent scientific inventions, fraught with dire possibilities of mischief? And what other verdict can we pass on the fiendish atrocities perpetrated by Adolf Hitler and his accomplices in the late war? Were they not hatched in hell in order that these

---

5 See pp. 236 ff.
6 Gk. τοῖς υἱοῖς τῆς ἀπειθείας (a Semitism); the phrase recurs in Ch. 5:6, whence perhaps it has found its way into the text of Col. 3:6 (see pp. 266, 270 f.).

"instruments of darkness" (to borrow Shakespeare's phrase) might glut their rabid bloodthirstiness with infamous carnivals of slaughter and torture?

But not only is this evil spirit spoken of as fermenting in the hearts of mutineers against heaven; he is also styled "prince of the power of the air". The ARV, whose text we adopt, renders *powers*; but the noun is in the singular and should denote *ruling sway*, lawful or otherwise.[7] That title has given rise to rather whimsical theories. Some contend that the seat of Satan's regency is in the air that enspheres our planet. Such a notion, like many other queer fancies, undoubtedly prevailed among the Jewish rabbis, but has very slender basis in Holy Writ; else, we should urgently dissuade all Godfearing souls from setting foot in an aeroplane! Not a syllable, however, in the context suggests such an inference. We prefer to view the designation in connexion with the rest of the sentence. The air may indicate a specific locality, but it is also an appropriate emblem of the prevailing influence or surroundings amid which an individual or community breathes and moves. In that sense it answers to the German compound *Zeitgeist* and to our own *spirit of the age*. It is a leading aim of "the god of this world" to control that outlook and colour its nuances to suit his own nefarious designs. The German commentator Beck and the elder Candlish and G. G. Findlay have adopted this interpretation, and the reference to "the course (or lifetime) of this world"[8] confirms it. The main objection pleadable against that view arises from the fact that the Greek word for air is not elsewhere employed metaphorically. But surely St. Paul, under the Spirit's afflatus, had genius enough to raise the term, as Latin parlance had already done in its *popularis aura,* from a physical to an ethical plane. For in this heavenly *coup d'œil* he is not framing a cosmology after a Talmudic pattern, but engrossed with purely spiritual values. When Lowell writes of the *malarious atmosphere* in which Rousseau grew up he is using the same image, indeed illustrating the passage before us by a case in point. Is there any feature of the arch-cajoler's tactics in which he displays more adroitness than in capturing for his propaganda the shifting phases of public opinion, the claptrap of the day and the hour?

---

[7] See p. 45, n. 2.

[8] Gk. τὸν αἰῶνα τοῦ κόσμου τούτου. The idea that αἰών should be taken personally here, as in gnosticism, has little to recommend it.

Every time-serving trimmer, congenially "servile to all the skyey influences", sucks in that circumambient atmosphere like a miasma and succumbs to its infection with fatal flexibility.

3 But the apostle is far too ingenuous to exempt himself from the black list of those whom the old serpent has thus outwitted. We all carry about with us the tinder of corruption and our crafty adversary knows how to apply a match to the combustibles at hand. A powder-magazine can be commendably quiet so long as it keeps cool; but let a spark alight upon it and you may look for an explosion. The lusts of the flesh and of the mind only need provocatives to flare up in baleful conflagration. Even apostles have no ground of boasting here; for they have not made themselves to differ from what they were aforetime. Paul can never forget his quondam career as a persecutor, nor does he shrink from a place in the ranks of the natural "children of wrath", liable to seduction both by sensuous and mental appetencies. *All* alike, Jew and Gentile, are by natal proclivity[9] inchoate children of wrath. We swerve from the very outset. "An evil ground exists in my will previous to any given act" (S. T. Coleridge).

This bill of indictment cannot but grate harshly on the ears of shallow religionists of effeminate sensibilities and an extenuating temper; and manifold are the attempts they make to elude its impact by the help of evolutionary or philosophical presuppositions. Fond of patting human nature on the back and of glossing over its vicious propensities, they persuade themselves to regard it as innocent in the main, or, if somewhat of a scapegrace, "more sinned against than sinning". Its obliquities are frequently attributed to the development of the passions in advance of the judgment. But that complacent theory does not tally with the facts of the case. For, as the history of humanity abundantly proves, *all* mankind without exception turns aside to its own way. We are sinners *in grain*; every mother's son learns to be naughty without book. Nor will either impulse or example suffice to account for the anomaly of wrongdoing co-extensive with an entire species of moral agents, whilst our fellow-lodgers, the animal creation, fulfil their instinctive ends without fail. To confine sin to outward acts is merely resorting to a hollow euphemism; for whence these uniformly corrupt fruits save from a corrupt tree? Deny original

---

9 See p. 46, n. 4.

49

sin and the state of our world becomes harder to construe than if
you embrace the tenet. The evil principle lurks beneath the
surface, seated in the hidden man of the heart. Godlessness is its
most decisive trait, a latent or patent antipathy to our Creator's
will and law; and that abnormal phenomenon cannot but evoke
a louring reaction of divine holiness against it, a thunderstroke
of wrath hovering over the impenitent offender, peremptorily
claiming redress in the name of the affronted majesty of righteousness. But "he who doubts human depravity had better begin to
study *himself*" (Spurgeon).

We admit that at first sight this interlacement of the race seems
a strangely weak point in the constitution of the human family,
this liability to contamination at its primal source, resulting in
the transmission of the contagious virus *seriatim* by the law of
propagation to the collective species. Yet it must be borne in mind
that the very principle of heredity entails interdependence and
vicarious representation both for good and evil. And just because
of that ordination whereby we labour under the handicap of
"children of wrath", reproductive of the disfigured image of the
parental *radix* of mankind, redeeming love could provide for the
insition in the race of a last Adam as its restorer; so that "the
unity of the old man becomes the postulate of the new man in
Christ" (Warfield). That generic constitution which occasioned
our downfall thus paves the way for the transfer of our liabilities
to a heavenly Kinsman, and authorizes His voluntary assumption
of sponsorship on our behalf. If we are "communists in sin and
death" by virtue of an interrelated lineage, we may become communists in life and holiness by vital union with God's federal
"Head unto His church", the Firstborn among many brethren,
ingrafted as branches into the true Vine. By this masterstroke of
grace a seed of evil-doers can be transformed into trophies of an
immaculate purification and made joint-heirs of a salvation
crowned with glory everlasting.

> 4 but God, being rich in mercy, for his great love
>   wherewith he loved us,[10]
> 5 even when we were dead through our trespasses, made

---

[10] Gk. τὴν ἀγάπην ... ἣν ἠγάπησεν ἡμᾶς, as in John 17:26, constitutes a
"cognate accusative of the inner content" (Robertson).

us alive together with Christ[11] (by grace have ye been saved),[12]

6 and raised us up with him and made us to sit with him in the heavenly *places,* in Christ Jesus:

4–5ᵃ Paul has a gospel to proclaim radiant with life, a resurrection from a living death to a deathless vitality. Its recipients are upraised from "sin's dark sepulchre" to the panoramic observatory of the skies. What can reanimate the cold sterilities of such a necropolis as he has just portrayed? The enquiry dates from the days of Ezekiel and admits of only one answer. The Spirit of the Lord must breathe on these dry bones. In the act of re-vivification the Creator must take the initiative. And how plenteous in mercy must He be to brood over the skeletons in that grim charnel-house of souls beheld in the valley of vision, despite all their offensiveness, and to deign to requicken them by His own invincible energy!

5ᵇ–6 Have we never felt a thrill of copartnership in the triumphs of a comrade or kinsman and been moved by the spectacle of their hard-won distinction, counted as our own? Then let us scan with exultation a vastly sublimer theme of transport, the mystical tie, namely, that knits the saint indissolubly in the "bundle of life" with his Redeemer, who has pledged Himself, "because I live, ye shall live also."[13] The Bridegroom and the bride are no longer twain, but concorporate through the sanctifying agency of the Spirit, who renders each recipient of divine grace increasingly approximate to the image of his Lord in whom he is embosomed. Nay by anticipation Paul seats him already beside his Prince Consort on the heavenly table-land of vision.

The apostle is not merely framing an analogy between the experiences of the heirs of salvation and their Ransomer, but asserting a sublime fellowship in process of consummation. The

---

[11] P⁴⁶ B and a few other authorities read "*in* Christ" (ἐν τῷ χριστῷ) for "*with* Christ" (τῷ χριστῷ, dependent on συν- in συνεζωοποίησεν).

[12] The Western authorities read "by *whose* grace..." (οὗ χάριτι ...).

[13] It is noteworthy that here the death from which believers have been "made alive together with Christ" is their spiritual death through their "trespasses and sins"; elsewhere in the Pauline letters the pattern is *dying with Christ* followed by rising with Christ to new life in Him. *Cf.* Rom. 6:3 ff.; Col. 2:11 ff., 20 ff. (see pp. 234 ff., 253 f.); 2 Tim. 2:11. Yet in Rom. 8:10 f., where the death of the body "because of sin" is counteracted by the indwelling Spirit of life, there is an approach to the sequence of thought of the present passage.

principle of eternal life begotten within them results in such an internexus of the risen Christ and His members as raises them in His train above the storm-line of mortality. Grace is glory in the bud, and the blissful issue assured, even while they are detained, like vessels in the workshop, to obtain the final touch of the unerring Fashioner of His diamonds.

Mark the note of exclamation here interjected; *by grace ye have been saved,* inserted like a hand in the margin (Goodwin). So intense is Paul's conviction of the sovereignty or divine grace that he cannot refrain from breaking in parenthetically on the thread of his discourse to place that all-important truth in boldest relief. The dominant note of the gospel must not be kept waiting for expression; rather let it vibrate in advance with piercing resonance. J. H. Moulton in his *Prolegomena* endorses the above translation of the perfect tense, as indicative that the work of redemption stands fulfilled on its divine side; only its realization lingers.

> 7 that in the ages to come he might show the exceeding riches of his grace in kindness[14] towards us in Christ Jesus:

7 Testimony has already (Ch. 1:6) been borne that our adoption as sons betokens ultimate glorification (*cf.* Rom. 8:30). Each saved soul is a monument of matchless benignity, not only when we reflect on the record of its guilty past, so completely blotted out, but when we scan its high and holy destiny, resplendent with a lustre eclipsing all the poets' golden dreams. Ranked as princes of the blood royal, the ransomed of the Lord will everlastingly embody the *ne plus ultra* both of unstinted love and princely munificence. Severity might have fulfilled its part by visiting a sin-laden race with condign judgment, in proof that it had no "fellowship with iniquity". But in that event the sweet countenance

---

[14] Gk. χρηστότης. R. C. Trench has analysed this arresting word with much nicety in his *NT Synonyms.* The term is applied to the Emperor Titus (*amor ac deliciae humani generis,* as Suetonius calls him) by Plutarch, and to Timon in the days of his munificence by Lucian; it is employed by Josephus to characterize Isaac's placidity of temper. As used of God, it represents Him as delighting in mercy (*cf.* Rom. 11:22); in short, it signalizes His graciousness and lovingkindness. In one passage of his *Meditations* (viii. 34), Marcus Aurelius ascribes χρηστότης to the dealings of the Deity with mankind, obviously meaning "benignity," as in Tit. 3:4.

of mercy would have been veiled. As it is, the claims of rectitude have not been shelved, but triumphantly shouldered and safeguarded by the great Justiciar Himself, and mercy has free scope for manifestation in all her captivating charms.

Some understand *the ages to come* of the consecutive epochs of the Christian dispensation; but it seems better to interpret the phrase of the eternal commonwealth yet to be, and of the signal guerdons awaiting the Lord's faithful lieges at the final adjudication of honours and rewards.

VI. SALVATION BY GRACE

Ch. 2:8–10

8 for by grace[15] have ye been saved through faith; and
that not of yourselves, *it is* the gift of God;
9 not of works, that no man should glory.

8 Here we sight what may fairly be termed the central
message of this Epistle, already not obscurely foreshadowed.
Salvation is of Jehovah (Ps. 3:8), His august monopoly. We have
undone ourselves, but in Him resides our help. The Creator
mends His spoiled *chef d'œuvre* with His own hands, nor will He
"split the praise of grace". In this domain the sinner must owe
Him everything, or else figure as the pilot and coxswain of his
own frail craft. Every plea based on self is ruled out of court
when we sue for terms of rehabilitation. We must apply *in forma
pauperis* or not at all. "Grace is love passing beyond all claims
to love, conferring on a revolted race honours which no loyalty
could have earned" (Dale). All notions of qualifying for a place
at God's right hand, whether by piecemeal accumulations of merit
or signal feats of asceticism, by ritual treadmills or bodily macera-
tion, all taskworks wrought with an eye to procuring acquittal, are
misguided devices of self-righteousness, tendered as entrance-fee
or purchase-money towards a percentage at all events of the soul's
ransom. But the least admixture of faith and works proffered as
a ground of acceptance mars the whole transaction. Justification
in God's sight is cost-free and our effects nil. We must go out of
ourselves and put our trust solely and wholly in Immanuel's person
and work, to be cleared at His charges, or else abide under sentence
of condemnation.

Faith embraces Christ as our sin-proof Righteousness, satisfying
all the divine claims. In Luther's figure, it is the marriage-ring
wedding us to Him, not a trafficking but a trysting act. Even that
medium of salvation has no inherent merit of its own. Faith does
not save us as a psychological quality (Carlyle's fatuous dream),

---

[15] Gk. τῇ ... χάριτι (the article points back to the previous occurrence of
the term in v. 5). The Western codex D, the Peshitta and the Ethiopic read
"by His grace" (τῇ ...ʼαὐτοῦ χάριτι).

but by virtue of the peerless Object it enclasps and holds fast. Nor is this very faith a product of the soil, but a gift of God imparted from on high conjointly with a change of heart. Those who dispute this reading of the passage maintain that Paul is stressing the truth that *salvation* is the Lord's handiwork. That is assuredly a main plank in the Gospel platform; but he has clenched that point already and is now driving home a cognate truth, namely that salvation is altogether of grace, not of works; for even the copula interlinking the believer with his Redeemer has been welded in heaven. Faith *per se* excludes all self-congratulation; for, as the sister-epistle reminds us (Col. 2:12), it is not a self-elicited *volte-face*, springing from some *nisus* of the will resolving, "I *will* believe", but "of the operation of God". We do not box the compass for ourselves. The soul's lever is not reversed by a convulsive effort. If we breathe, it is because life has been breathed into us; if we exercise the hearing of faith it is because our ears have been unstopped. We are born *from above*. Spiritual life is not of the nature of a subsidy supplementing dogged exertion or ruthless self-flagellation, but a largess from the overflowing well-spring of divine compassion, lavished on a set of spiritual incapables.

9 The addition, "lest any man should glory", bears out this exegesis. The same phrase appears in Rom. 3:27, where boasting is shut out in the name of faith and the key turned on self-applause (Moule). Not even a gush of tears can be presented as legal tender for forgiveness. *L'orgueil ne veut pas devoir,* says Rochefoucauld, pride likes not to be beholden; but mendicants at the gate of mercy must not angle for titbits of commendation. The Gospel "cuts the very comb of pride. When thou hast thy best suit on, Christian, remember who paid for it!" (Gurnall). It is sin in fact that has bred self-sufficiency and suspicion of our Maker's trustworthiness; nor is there any effectual antidote for that fatal mischief but saving faith, "the missing link between the soul and God" (Spurgeon), the suspension-bridge flung across the yawning chasm, spanned from the heavenly, not the hither strand.

10   For we are his workmanship,[16] created in Christ Jesus

---

[16] Gk. ποίημα, "handiwork"; certainly not to be rendered, as Stalker and F. B. Meyer have understood it, "poem"—a conceit quite foreign to Paul's style

for good works, which God afore prepared that we should walk in them.

10 The new birth, introductory to a new manhood, has the Spirit for its Author. It may take place amid thunder and lightning or in the serene dawn of nascent reanimation. There may have been a time when the most obvious feature about us were the marks we bore of the devil's foundry-work, legible to every keen-eyed observer. But now we are in process of reconstruction on a new model, prepared for an habitation of God in the Spirit. There are good works likewise made ready for our performance. Lie-a-bed slackers, alas! eager to be cosily fondled, but loth to do a day's work in the Master's vineyard, half-breeds at best, are only too common. Many Christians contrive to spend their lives in canvassing the question, "Lord, what wilt Thou have me to do?" and having made extensive preparations for living to good purpose, end their days "caught napping", a prey to chronic indecision, inmates of the Castle of Indolence to the last.

When the Lord has worked *on* us, however, He works *by* us (Manton), along the line of our talents and circumstances; for the Divine Craftsman empowers and employs human effort. Most vocations are not so much chosen as committed to the parties concerned. "The situation of a man", wrote Burke, "is the main preceptor of duty"; and that situation is not the outcome of chance, but the appointment of the Disposer of all things. Good works are never to be relied on as items placed to our credit in the running account with our supreme Creditor; yet they are indispensable testifications of love and gratitude to an untold Benefactor and Saviour. "It is not against works that we contend", said Luther, after trying both plans, salvation by dint of hard labour and then by faith, "but against *trust* in works", a very different affair.

By nature we are would-be autocrats, persons of quality and standing; but new creatures in Christ Jesus ought to carry the mint-mark of humility. They should be content to serve their generation according to the will of God, to rank as trees of the Lord's planting, bearing fruit unto Him. A "self-made man" is almost inevitably badly made, a jerry-built sample of overweening

and one that would strike a falsetto note in this solemnly impressive paragraph. Greek writers discriminate carefully between the two concepts, nor do we meet with a witticism fabricated out of their confusion except among the fopperies of the late story-teller Longus, who dubs flowers "Cupid's *poems.*"

self-esteem; but when our Maker recasts us in His own image we
are assimilated to the primeval pattern of manhood,[17] no longer
intent on steering our vessel for ourselves, but willing to will and
do God's good pleasure even at the expense of our own wills.

---

[17] *Cf.* Ch. 4:23 f.

VII. THE INCLUSION OF THE GENTILES

Ch. 2:11–13

11 Wherefore remember, that once ye, the Gentiles in the flesh, who are called Uncircumcision by that which is called Circumcision, in the flesh, made by hands;[18]

12 that ye were at that time separate from Christ, alienated[19] from the commonwealth of Israel, and strangers from the covenants of the promise,[20] having no hope and without God in the world.

11 The full recognition of the glory of that grace whereof they have been made partners is now brought home to these Gentile fledglings by reverting afresh to their unregenerate days. Nothing is so apt to promote gratitude as a retrospective glance fixed on the hole of the pit from whence we have been dug out. These exiles from the pale of the promise were by birth and environment beyond the radius of those heavenly beams that cheered the inhabitants of Zion. They had hitherto dwelt in Erebus and been suffered to walk in their own devious by-paths. It is true, the gate of Judaism was left ajar for the admission of duly certified proselytes; yet it was but a postern-door, at best obscurely visible; whereas the frowning ramparts of the Holy Land reared a formidable barrier of severance not readily overleapt. Moreover, carnal pride entrenched in sanctimonious observances had warped the Jewish mind to a settled disdain of the uncovenanted peoples outside their sacred precinct and devoid of their passport of circumcision.

12 Yet it was no slight calamity to be estranged from that

---

18 Gk. περιτομή ... χειροποίητος, "*material* circumcision"; for there is a spiritual *(ἀχειροποίητος)* counterpart specified in Col. 2:11, *i.e.* the renunciation of carnal indulgences by the Christian disciple, already prescribed by the great Hebrew lawgiver (Deut. 30:6). See pp. 233 ff.

19 Gk. ἀπηλλοτριωμένοι, as in Ch. 4:18, *cf.* Col. 1:21, with exposition and notes *ad loc.* (pp. 210 f.).

20 The "covenants of the promise" (Gk. αἱ διαθῆκαι τῆς ἐπαγγελίας) are probably so called because promise is the dominant feature in the successive affirmations of God's covenant with His people: "a divine covenant is a sovereign administration of grace and of promise" (J. Murray, *The Covenant of Grace* [London, 1954], p. 31).

land of Judah where God was known, no minor evil to reside in centres of pagan idolatry, foul with obscene temple-orgies, or where altars reared to an unknown Deity bore witness to an aching void, an unsated famine of the heart. A dense cloud of withdrawal such as often wraps a mountain-peak in its enswathing folds, shrouded the Most High within an impenetrable tabernacle; and vain were all the efforts of philosophers and mystagogues to break through the nebulous pall or read the cipher of the Godhead unaided. The Hebrew theocracy, despite its decadence, abode the pharos of the world's illumination, and to be remote from its beacon-gleam was to dwell in darkness or be mocked by tantalizing wild-fires. Substance, solidity, satisfaction, the cults of heathendom had none to proffer. Their forlorn plight is delineated in three sable strokes as *Christless, Godless, hopeless.* That last-named stigma may appear an overcharged representation to a superficial spectator. But it was mournfully true of the pagan world of Paul's day, plunged in cynical pyrrhonism or squalid profligacy. The phrase *in the world* somewhat puzzles the commentators. But may there not be a reference here to the banishment of our first parents from the purlieux of Eden to the outer world and consequent debarment from the ensigns of a divine presence? For the writer goes on to speak of the outcasts as beyond the scope of illumination, till the celestial peep of day sheds its rays upon them. The settled pessimism of the bulk of heathen epitaphs attests the cheerless gloom that brooded like a nightmare over the burial-places of a pagan community. Their golden age lay not in front but behind them.

> 13 But now in Christ Jesus ye that once were far off are
> made nigh[21] in the blood of Christ.

13 Godlessness genders hopelessness; that is the nadir to which it gravitates. But Christianity wings the flight of hope blithesomely upwards to heaven's gate. Its joyous tidings sound the knell of despair. *Nil desperandum Christo duce et auspice Christo.* However far astray from their proper orbit the vagrants in the Babylon of benightment may have roved, they are capable of reclamation by the spell of Christ's love and grace. The centrifugal

---

[21] In these words we may detect an echo of Isa. 57:19, quoted more clearly below in v. 17.

bias of erring mankind may be stemmed by a centripetal current of vaster potency flowing from one Almighty to save. The blood of the Lamb has a strangely melting power over congealed hearts. "Medusa's head was fabled to turn every one who looked on it to stone; but the cross is a sight that converts the beholder from stone into flesh" (Shedd).

That atoning death forms the meridian-line of all the Lord's ordnance-surveys of the continent of Mansoul. Full well did Paul nail his colours to the cross. *We preach Christ crucified* is the device on his banner, to Jews a stumbling-block and to Gentiles foolishness; but unto them that are called (from both encampments) the power of God and the wisdom of God (1 Cor. 1:24). It seemed as if no cohesive could reunite parties so profoundly cleft asunder. But Omniscience had devised its sublime medium of reconciliation. Upon these Gentile dwellers in darkness the glory of the Lord had uprisen, bringing health as well as day-dawn, peace as well as enlightenment. There is no dissolvent of concord like sin, sundering what it cannot re-combine, a makebate loosening all the sutures of the social fabric, shattering the comity of nations, barring inter-communion except in crime, gendering fratricidal ill-will.

Who can counteract such a dismembering agency? Who can repair the riven tapestry of humanity? One alone can charm confusion into fusion, separation into sympathy, Himself the vital Ligament of re-adjustment, incorporated in whom Jew and Gentile, Greek and barbarian, bond and free, may couch together amicably like the prophet's kid and leopard, in heartfelt affinity.

VIII. CHRIST THE PEACEMAKER

Ch. 2:14–18

14 For he[22] is our peace, who made both one, and brake
down the middle wall of partition,[23]

15 having abolished[24] in his flesh[25] the enmity, *even* the
law of commandments *contained* in ordinances;[26]
that he might create in himself of the two one new
man,[27] *so* making peace;

16 and might reconcile[28] them both in one body unto

---

[22] Observe the emphatic αὐτός at the head of the sentence: "He Himself is our peace."

[23] Gk. τὸ μεσότοιχον τοῦ φραγμοῦ. The vocable μεσότοιχον, "partition-wall," is a rare one, found elsewhere only in an inscription, where it is masculine, and figuratively in a fragment of Eratosthenes, used of a *boundary-line*. Josephus, however, employs the separate words ὁ μέσος τοιχός for the inner wall of the Temple. Φραγμός is a classical term for a "fence" or "railing", found in the Evangelists (Matt. 21:33; Mark 12:1; Luke 14:23). Here the immediate allusion seems to be to the barrier placed in the Court of the Gentiles in the Temple to prevent them from penetrating further within (resembling the sacerdotal device which excludes choir and altar from the profaning tread of the laity). Two copies of the actual inscription forbidding any foreigner (ἀλλογενής), on pain of death, to "enter within the barricade which surrounds the temple and enclosure" have been found in the neighbourhood—one in 1871 and the other in 1935. See *Acts* in NICNT, p. 434, n. 44 (on Acts 21:29).

[24] Gk. καταργήσας. This is a favourite verb of St. Paul's, most difficult to render by a single translation. Jerome styles it one of Paul's "Cilicisms." Luke uses it in a solitary instance (Luke 13:7) of the "cumberground" fig-tree sterilizing the soil it occupied. But Paul's meaning is harder to hit. In one or two cases in the papyri it appears to signify "to bring to a standstill" or "put out of gear." Here it might be rendered "to invalidate" or "to nullify, annul, quash." The clumsy word "depotentiate" would nearly represent the general sense of this peculiarly Pauline verbalism. (Paul probably intended it to serve as the equivalent of the Hebrew Pi'el *bittel*, so frequently found in the rabbinical literature with the meaning "to make of no effect.")

[25] *Cf.* Col. 1:21 f.: "And you ... hath he reconciled in the body of his flesh through death"; see p. 212 with nn. 144, 145.

[26] Gk. τὸν νόμον τῶν ἐντολῶν ἐν δόγμασιν, an elliptical phrase for the Mosaic ordinances, viewed as a statutory code. Winer furnishes a comparable construction with ἐν in the phrase ἐν δραχμαῖς—as we might say: "so much in dollars." *Cf.* Col. 2:14 ("the bond written in ordinances that was against us") with the discussion in the exposition and notes *ad loc.* (pp. 237 ff.).

[27] *Cf.* the "fullgrown man" of Ch. 4:13 and the "new creation" of Gal. 6:15.

[28] The word ἀποκαταλλάσσειν is uniquely Pauline, appearing here and in Col. 1:20, 22. The prefix ἀπο- may either (as in other late Greek compounds) strengthen the verb, or mean "again." *Cf.* p. 207, n. 125 (on Col. 1:20). In Col. 1:20–22 God's reconciliation of rebels to Himself through Christ is in view; here Paul emphasizes the corollary of that prior reconciliation—the mutual

God through the cross, having slain the enmity thereby:

14 The old covenant had been in the main a dispensation of distance. It had unveiled the awful majesty of holiness and brought home to every reflecting worshipper a sense of the defiling leprosy of sin. The statutes of Judaism not only erected barricades between Israel and the rest of the nations, but they kept the Israelite himself under a rigorous yoke of discipline, sorely irksome in its pressure. Albeit a chosen people, brought nigh to the Most High, their access had its galling aspects. The terrors of Sinai formed the lurid background of their horizon; and the provisional sacrifices obligatory upon them could not appease the qualms of conscience they aroused, apart from the perfect expiation they fore-shadowed.

In this arena of strife and discord, only one Peacemaker can be found competent for the task of mediation. G. G. Findlay has epitomized the situation admirably. "The groaning frame of nature declares the world unhinged and out of course. Things have gone amiss between man and his Creator. The field of history is scarred with the thunderbolts of His displeasure. The King of the Ages is not the almighty Sentimentalist some would make Him out to be. God is love; but He is also a consuming fire.... Yet in His wrath He remembers mercy: hence the cross. No peace without that; no peace that did not satisfy God in *all* His attributes and that law, deep as the deepest in God, that binds suffering to wrong-doing and death to sin".

15 Mark how staunchly the apostle plants that unique panacea in the midst, to quench all the animosities sin foments. Goodwill betwixt man and man hinges ultimately on a will consonant with the Lord's will. It is the dying Saviour who hushes the clangours of dissonance and quells the ranklings of estrangement. The Divine *Atonemaker* (the word is a fine coinage of Tyndale) coadunates the jarring elements in the temple of His own body. There is but one authentic armistice-day, that on which the oecumenical Saviour made satisfaction for sin by the outpouring of His soul unto death and brought in a catholicity incapable of

---

reconciliation of those who, formerly estranged from one another, have now been reconciled to God. See exposition and notes on Col. 1:20 ff. (pp. 207 ff.).

rupture or dismemberment. Other foundation of peace, divine or human, none can lay. The conflict between the claims of justice and mercy ended when Jesus cried, *It is finished!* When those two great attributes of Jehovah kissed one another over our Champion's broken body, Master of the Field in the article of death, the major pacification had been achieved; and the minor, that of the transgressor with his Maker, or with his brotherman, follows wheresoever the supreme eirenicon is not spurned or ignored.

16 At Calvary as nowhere beside, a perfect chord has been struck which re-attunes the rasping discords of human jealousy and rancour. A higher unity, even in the mundane sphere of things, may absorb feuds seemingly inveterate. We might instance the coalition of the Norman and Saxon or the Scot and Englander by way of proof. But the secret of all union worth the name lies here, the heavenly talisman under whose magnetic spell "Ephraim shall no longer envy Judah nor Judah vex Ephraim".

In Christ Jesus is the point of convergence. He forms the Lodestone of concord that draws all kinds of waifs and strays to itself, the Rendezvous of seekers after a city of refuge. It is not by others resorting to us nor by our going over to them, but because both they and we come to Him that harmony is attained (Adolphe Monod).

> 17   and he came and preached peace to you that were far off, and peace to them that were nigh:[29]
> 18   for through him we both have our access[30] in one Spirit unto the Father.

---

[29] There are echoes here of Isa. 52:7 ("How beautiful upon the mountains are the feet of him that bringeth good tidings, that publisheth peace") and Isa. 57:19 ("Peace, peace to him that is far off and to him that is near, saith Jehovah").

[30] Gk. προσαγωγή. Sir John Mahaffy sought to identify the material image of a *landing-stage* with the usage of this word. But that notion is misleading in view of the various abstract significations it assumes. Such are (1) a solemn approach to a deity (Herodotus ii, 58), or (2) access to a king's presence (Xenophon, *Cyropaedia* vii, 5). Deissmann's assumption that a physical figure underlies all popular diction is erroneous, especially in advanced stages of a language. Who that says "forfeit" in English or talks of "circumstances" colloquially has their etymology consciously before his mind? Nor are the Pauline writings properly vernacular documents. The translation "footing" might be more germane, since we do employ that expression figuratively, oblivious of its latent imagery.

17 The hostility of Jew and Gentile appeared to be insurmountable. Dissevering institutions relative to ritual pollution and civil ordinances, the confinement of temple-worship to the Holy City and its concomitant enactments, repelled outsiders no less than the warning notice: "trespassers will be prosecuted". Elements so incongruous could never be amalgamated save in the alembic of a new birth, nor could the baser materials in question be melted down save in the crucible of the cross. Thus alone could the ever seething exacerbations of mutual repugnance be transmuted into a cordial *rapprochement*.

18 We have already been apprised that Christ is the Keystone of creation, its co-ordinating Clasp and Staple (*cf.* Col. 1:17). Taken up into the orbit of the heavenly Daystar, reassigned to its rightful station in His train, human nature may yet reach the goal of its creation; but not otherwise. At the day of Pentecost through the Paraclete, as well as more reticently in His personal ministry, He had preached peace to the far-off and the nigh (Acts 2:39), in accordance with Isaiah's oracle (Isa. 57:19). We meet a clear intimation in this passage of the co-working of the Trinity in the plan of redemption. By that wondrous dispensation a new type of manhood, whereby a distinct family resemblance modifies old racial distinctions, emerges from the secret laboratory of divine grace. The binding of the living epistles varies, but not their contents. "The saints are strangely akin. Voice answers to voice across the centuries; they tell in different tongues of the same wonderful discovery. Their songs are on our lips; they seem to have been written for us; their confessions of sin are a fuller expression of ours. Their life is our life; they and we are brethren" (Dale).

IX. THE ARCHITECTURE OF THE LIVING TEMPLE
Ch. 2:19–22

19 So then ye are no more strangers and sojourners,[31] but ye are fellow-citizens with the saints,[32] and of the household of God,[33]

20 being built upon the foundation of the apostles and prophets,[34] Christ Jesus himself being the chief corner stone;[35]

21 in whom each several building, fitly framed together, groweth into a holy temple in the Lord;

22 in whom ye also are builded together for a habitation of God in the Spirit.

19 In the next four verses we are presented with a development of the positive aspect of the calling of the Gentiles. Not only is their severance from the true God remedied by the mediatorial work of Christ, but they are instated in all the peculiar privileges of children, housemates no longer domiciled in the spiritual Zion, as it were, by sufferance, but far more intrinsically members of

---

31 Gk. πάροικος, which in Hellenistic tends to supplant μέτοικος, "authorized sojourner," half-way between an alien and a native. To the Jewish ear it would correspond with the proselyte from Gentilism, after the pattern of Ruth the Moabitess. Thus Babrius (*Fables*, 118) designates the swallow πάροικος ἀνθρώπου "man's *visitant*" rather than *resident*, *advena* and not *indigena* in character.

32 Gk. συμπολῖται τῶν ἁγίων, the "saints" being those of God's true Israel within the wider, national Israel.

33 Gk. οἰκεῖοι τοῦ θεοῦ, "housemates of God", or (in the Wycliffite version) "household men of God" (*cf.* Gal. 6:10 and the use of φιλοίκειος); less probably "cognate with God." It carries obviously its strongest sense, which Plato contrasts with ὀθνεῖος ("strange," "foreign"). So Philodemus (*De Ira* 56) contrasts οἱ ἔξωθεν and οἱ οἰκεῖοι, that is, "outsiders" and "insiders."

34 These are doubtless the apostles and prophets of the first Christian generation, mentioned in Ch. 4:11 as the first gifts bestowed by the ascended Lord upon His church. (*Cf.* 1 Cor. 12:28, "God hath set some in the church, first apostles, secondly prophets.") They are further referred to in Ch. 3:5.

35 Gk. ἀκρογωνιαῖος (*sc.* λίθος) recurs in the NT only in 1 Pet. 2:6, in a quotation of the one passage where it appears in LXX, Isa. 28:16. (There it represents Heb. *pinnah*; in the similar messianic passage Ps. 118:22 Heb. *rosh pinnah*, "head of the corner," is translated in LXX as κεφαλὴ γωνίας, and so quoted several times in NT. See *Acts* in NICNT, p. 99, n. 17.) Infrequent as it is, the epithet ἀκρογωνιαῖος well beseems the Messiah, for "the corner-stone fixes a standard for the bearings of the structure throughout." See J. Jeremias in TWNT i (Stuttgart, 1933), pp. 792 f. (*s.v.* γωνία); S. H. Hooke, "The Corner-Stone of Scripture," in *The Siege Perilous* (London, 1956), pp. 235 ff.

the sacred homestead than the retainers of the imperial court were part of Caesar's household. They are introduced within that home-circle under no embargo whatsoever, with no brand of inferiority attaching to them. Their adoption is as complete as that of firstborn Israel; for the partition-wall is razed and the countersign is common to both.

20 The figure of an edifice symmetrically planned by the supreme Architect aptly rounds off the picture; for it shows that the newcomers do not form a mere annex, but an integral part of the structure, which without their inclusion would fall short of its design. They are reared on the foundation of the apostles and prophets to whose witness they have paid heed. These testifiers do not seem to be the foundation referred to; for Christ Himself is the Corner-stone whereon the whole fabric rests. If so, the similitude recalls that of the rock in its application to Peter in the Gospels. Not Simon personally, but the confession he uttered, was the rock on which the church was built. He himself more than once betrayed the shelving properties of sand, but his Spirit-taught confession no gates of hell could shake. Apostles and prophets share the common salvation, and the charter of their confidence is identical with that of the obscurest follower of the Lamb. Christ alone consolidates the mystical structure; to Him belongs the title of *pierre angulaire*, Head of the Corner, the stone from which all its dimensions are measured. Apart from Him the edifice would crumble to dust; He is its essential Mainstay and Bond. His reconciling blood cements its segments in one indissoluble fabric.

Calvary has not inaptly been likened to the golden milestone in the centre of the Roman forum, whence all distances throughout the Empire were computed. All Scripture, said Denney, converges to that point. The temple here delineated owes all its augustness to the foundationstone at its base, laid in a bedrock of propitiation and identified with it (1 John 2:2), and to its vital intertexture with the whole *shrine*; for Paul so entitles it (*naos*), the sacrosanct adytum innermost of all. Is it not set apart for the residence of the Spirit? Of the ancient Zion, that hermitage where truth was cloistered awhile, the Lord had said, "Here will I dwell; for I have desired it" (Ps. 132:14). Accordingly a true, typical glory invested that hallowed spot, the only locality on the earth's surface in authentic communication with heaven.

But this tract sequestered from the world's wide wilderness for pious uses could lay claim to no charter of perpetuity. It was mundane, consequently provisional and evanescent, the harbinger and earnest of an ampler epiphany one day to supersede it. The expansiveness of Paul's world-wide gospel proclaims its nobler character; for in the new economy quondam aliens obtain reaccess to the holiest of all by the blood of Jesus. Their status is here signalized by three degrees of comparison: (1) They present themselves as fully qualified burgesses of the heavenly Jerusalem, enfranchized denizens of "no mean city". (2) Then they are pictured as inmates in the household of faith, sharers in the "priorities" of God's family circle. (3) And, best of all, they are inwrought in the Lord's unique temple not made with hands, cells in the living organism whose Builder is the Lord God Almighty, fashioned by His ever-watchful skill and care to be His dwelling-place in the Spirit.

Thus once more the Shekinah-glory of yore overarches the entire camp of the pilgrim-saints, the collective tribes of the spiritual Israel. The Redeemer's own body was the *seminal* temple (Howe), the ideal archetype after which His people should be modelled, the perfect exemplar of all their imperfect replicas.

21–22 In this imagery we descry a spiritual sanctuary of which the stateliest sublunary fane presents but a faint adumbration. It is reared on a palatial scale in multitudinous compartments of such intricacy that only the Master-builder's draft can furnish a key to their correlation.[36] To an uninitiated looker-on nothing wears an aspect of greater disorder than the area of a colossal edifice, partly commenced, partly projected, and bestrewn with materials in seemingly hopeless confusion. Once upon a time such a tower was designed by its ambitious promoters to be a rendezvous of profane self-assumption. It came speedily to grief and the fabricators of the aspiring pile were ignominiously dispersed. Not so with the Lord's own masonry of living stones. Unlike dead

---

[36] Gk. πᾶσα οἰκοδομή appears here to mean "all the building" rather than "every building" or "each several building" (ARV). The omission of the article has NT sanction in other passages (*e.g.* Matt. 28:18) and is the regular usage in the case of πᾶσα σάρξ, which according to Blass is a distinct Hebraism. There remains a possibility, however, of the correctness of the second version, if the apostle is distinguishing the several segments of the edifice from the resultant shrine (ναός). Some uncials add the article, reading πᾶσα ἡ οἰκοδομή.

matter this monumental structure possesses a capacity of growth and interaction. It is not held in position by artificial clamps or grooves, by mechanisms of pressure or resistance. The station of each individual constituent has been preordained with regard to the contour of the aggregate fabric.[37] Every believer has his own niche to fill. In the eyes of the Architect of this masterpiece of constructive skill, no dull uniformity of outline, but a diversity unmarred by discordance, finds favour. There is an ideal "union in partition". Personality and assimilation coalesce therein. The façade of God's temple is symmetrical, but it eschews a monotonous sameness. All the variegated details contribute their share to the *tout ensemble*. At the end of the vista, seen in the interim through the perspective glass of prophecy, a majestic edifice, absolutely flawless, looms in view; and when the copestone shall be laid atop with anthems of jubilation this house not made with hands, founded on God's own Cornerstone and indwelt by His Holy Spirit, shall be right glorious to behold.[38]

What a fellowship rivets our gaze in the communion of saints! Where shall we find its like? Gathered from east and west, from patriarchs of the prior and laggards of the last times, from the courts of kings and the cabins of beggars, from babes-in-arms and centenarians, right honourables and ragamuffins, from the ranks of the learned and the ignorant, the pharisee and the publican, the sharp-witted and the feeble-minded, the respectable and the criminal classes—what a divine power must be put forth to mould all these incongruous elements into one consentient whole, stamped with one regenerate likeness for evermore, the radiant image of the "Alpha and Omega," God's Yokefellow and theirs, coequally David's Son and David's Lord!

---

[37] Gk. συναρμολογουμένη. This verb is again peculiar to Paul; but ἁρμολογεῖν occurs rarely in the sense of *compacting* masonry *together* and once metaphorically in Sextus Empiricus. To the architectural metaphor here there is a close correspondence in the physiological terminology of Ch. 4:16, where we have the only other known occurrence of συναρμολογεῖν.

[38] *Cf.* A. Cole, *The New Temple* (London, 1950).

CHAPTER III

X. THE APOSTLE'S MANDATE

Ch. 3:1-4

Hitherto, since the apostle launched forth on this world-surveying epistle, we see him borne along as on the bosom of some broad sheet of water, sailing before the wind with every stitch of canvas fully set. There now ensues a pause, a lull in the strength of the breeze that has wafted him onward; and in the broken sentences which we now encounter we feel as if we were watching the shifting of the sails and the tentative expedients for making headway available of yore, when almost becalmed, to a wind-wafted mariner. The beckoning current of the Spirit has by no means ceased, but the next tack he is to make is not so immediately evident. Such we judge to be the explanation of the grammatical hiatus prominent in the former half of the third chapter, a hiatus only closed up in v. 14, where the *for this cause* of v. 1 is reiterated after a batch of parentheses.

1 For this cause I Paul, the prisoner of Christ Jesus in behalf of you Gentiles,[1]—

2 if so be that ye have heard of the dispensation[2] of that grace of God which was given me to you-ward;

3 how that by revelation was made known unto me the mystery,[3] as I wrote before in few words,[4]

---

[1] Gk. ὑπὲρ ὑμῶν τῶν ἐθνῶν. The Western text represented by Cod. D and Ambrosiaster's reading tries to mend the anacoluthon here by adding πρεσβεύω ("serve as an ambassador") after ἐθνῶν (cf. Ch. 6:20). Paul might well style himself Christ's prisoner in behalf of the Gentiles, since his arrest in Jerusalem and consequent remission in custody to Rome were the direct result of his Gentile evangelization, and in particular of his journey to Jerusalem as leader of the delegation carrying gifts from the Gentile churches to the impoverished believers of Jerusalem (cf. Rom. 15:15–32).

[2] Gk. οἰκονομία (cf. p. 33, n. 19, on Ch. 1:10, and p. 217, n. 166, on Col. 1:25).

[3] On the aspects of the "mystery" entrusted to Paul as presented in Colossians and Ephesians respectively, see pp. 218 f., nn. 168, 173 (on Col. 1:26).

[4] Gk ἐν ὀλίγῳ, "in brief," for which both Shakespeare and Milton now and then substitute the locution "in few." The reference is not to a former letter, but to the compendium (a *multum in parvo*) of Christian doctrine outlined in the foregoing chapters. The expression occurs elsewhere in NT only in Acts 26:28 f.,

4   whereby, when ye read, ye can perceive my understanding in the mystery of Christ;[5]

1-4 In this intermediate paragraph Paul lingers wonderingly
around the theme, so engrossing to minds nursed in the lap of
Judaism, of the calling of the Gentiles and his own official mandate
in connexion therewith. It was as their chosen apostle that he was
toiling and suffering on their behalf; and that ordination fully
warranted his intense zeal for their welfare and passionate concern
that their spiritual insight and devotion might be raised to the
highest pitch.

He had himself been obliged to defend his apostolical standing
strenuously against gainsayers, and he therefore lays stress once
more on its unexceptionable validity. The "mystery of Christ",
the distinctive peculiarities of His gospel, had been supernaturally
imparted to him at first hand. He was "a chosen vessel" selected
for this very enterprise; in no wise an interloper, but the accredited
mouthpiece of divine grace to the major portion of the human
family. He points his readers to that compendium of heavenly
lore summarized in the two preceding chapters by way of proof
that he was entitled to rank as a privy-councillor of the Most High.
Was the claim to be a special channel of revelation fallacious or
presumptuous? Far from it. His message was one of truth and
soberness, so worthy of all acceptation indeed that it was slighted
at the peril of its contemner. The cringing homage so dearly prized
by hierarchical grandees Saul of Tarsus disdained to court; but
for his inspired message he claimed a deferential reception.
Minimizing himself he magnified his office.

He styles himself the *prisoner of Jesus Christ*. See what the
grace of God can accomplish! Scan not without wonder the bearing
of this caged eagle penned within Nero's prison-bars. Here is a
veteran soldier of the cross, seamed with many a battle-scar, shut
out from the high places of the field where he had so gallantly
trodden down strength, cramped within painfully narrow precincts,
his untamed spirit shackled by manacles of inaction and suspense;
the churches whose names were graven on his heart left meanwhile

---

where Chrysostom's rendering "almost" in currently rejected as lacking confirmation, though none of the versions replacing it is convincing. We should
take it there in the same sense as here, but tender a fresh explanation of its
cryptic significance. (*Cf. Acts* in NICNT, p. 494, n. 30.)
[5]   *Cf.* Col. 2:2 (pp. 222 ff.).

untended, and he himself to all seeming laid aside as a "vessel wherein is no pleasure". Does he faint or repine? Nay, he glories in tribulations. Nero's prisoner? Nothing of the sort! He is the prisoner *of Jesus Christ* and that makes a world of difference; renders him far freer than his jailors in fact. What is best for the Lord's cause the Lord knows best. It was for an Ephesian convert's sake (Acts 21:29) that Paul had been mobbed at Jerusalem; and in their cause he is right willing to spend and be spent, to be chained or at large, as the Supreme Will decrees.

The query here put—*if*[6] *ye have heard*—at first sight bears out the theory that the Letter is a general one, implying, as it would seem, that he was personally unknown to the bulk of his readers. It is, however, uncertain whether the Greek necessitates a conditional interpretation of the clause.

---

[6] Gk εἴγε. At first sight this parenthesis appears to lend support to the hypothesis of a circular letter. But Meyer, in accordance with the judgment of Hermann, maintains that εἴγε may mean "seeing that." At any rate the stress does not fall on the conjunction, but extends to the whole proposition. *Cf.* Lucian (*Jupiter Tragoedus*, 36), εἴγε ἀκούουσιν, "if they *do* hear." Moreover, the Ephesian hearers must be included in the description. There is plausibility in Bishop Moule's suggestion that the form of the sentence is ironical, challenging in fact an affirmative as the only possible answer. Other examples of this rhetorical meiosis are found in St. Paul's writings. The Socratic irony figures largely in classical literature, especially by way of preface to an air of self-assertion or claim of distinction. Thus Aeneas employs this very figure (Virgil, *Aeneid* i. 375 f.) by way of preface to the wide-wafted story of Troy and his share in its catastrophe: *si vestras forte per aures / Troiae nomen iit.*

XI. THE PURPOSE OF THE AGES

Ch. 3:5–13

5 which in other generations was not made known unto
the sons of men,[7] as it hath now been revealed unto
his holy apostles[8] and prophets in the Spirit;

6 *to wit,* that the Gentiles are[9] fellow-heirs, and fellow-
members of the body,[10] and fellow-partakers of the
promise in Christ Jesus through the gospel,

7 whereof I was made a minister, according to the gift
of that grace of God which was given me according
to the working of his power.

8 Unto me, who am less than the least of all saints, was
this grace given, to preach unto the Gentiles the
unsearchable riches of Christ;

5–8 Hebrew prophecy had not been silent respecting this
divine secret (*cf.* Isa. 56:5); but it had remained an unwelcome
topic to the Jewish mind, absorbed in the contemplation of its
own peculiar privileges and construing any ultimate extension
of their compass only as foreshadowing accessions of Gentile
proselytes to the ranks of the theocracy. To us indeed, as we
look back over nineteen centuries of the out-workings of Christianity, God's wider purposes may sound almost a commonplace.
To Paul, however, they stood out in relief above every other
phenomenon in the annals of mankind, as the veriest clue of the
ages, the disclosure of the divine program touching mankind. And

---

[7] *Cf.* Rom. 16:25 ("the revelation of the mystery which hath been kept in
silence through times eternal"); also Col. 1:26 ("the mystery which hath been
hid for ages and generations") with exposition and notes *ad loc.* (pp. 218 f.).

[8] Gk. τοῖς ἁγίοις ἀποστόλοις αὐτοῦ. Cod. B and Ambrosiaster (a most
remarkable conjunction!) omit ἀποστόλοις, thus assimilating the text to Col. 1:26,
where the mystery is revealed τοῖς ἁγίοις αὐτοῦ ("to his saints"). Lachmann
and Tregelles put a comma after ἁγίοις, as though the meaning were "to the
saints—His apostles and prophets"; but this is an unnatural way to construe
the text.

[9] Gk. εἶναι τὰ ἔθνη κ.τ.λ. The infinitive is epexegetic, opening up the nature
of the secret previously specified.

[10] Gk. σύσσωμα, "concorporate": a Pauline coinage to match the other
epithets *(συνκληρονόμα ... συμμέτοχα)*. The obtuse suggestion of certain
German critics and their understudies that it means "fellow-slaves" confutes
itself. Not only does it stultify the sentence, but there is only one NT passage
where that secondary acceptation of σῶμα prevails (Rev. 18:13). It could never
be used like δοῦλος of an honourable style of service.

that *he* should be deputed for its setting on foot sent a thrill through his inmost being, at once elating and blended with awe and wonder.

The phrase *holy apostles and prophets* is a little puzzling. De Wette argued that Paul would not have classed himself as *holy*; but the term signifies "set apart", and it is of that very fact he is treating. Most exegetes view the prophets here referred to as NT prophets, and as they are named after the apostles and are presented as organs of a fresh revelation, that judgment would appear to be correct.[11] The truth set in the light of noonday is, as the epithets used demonstrate, the closing up in Christ of the old cleavage, so that Jew and Gentile form one body in Him, with no rift between them and no inequality in their respective standing. Where is there a fraternity so close and real as that of sterling Christian brotherhood?

Yet lest the apostle should seem to think of himself "above measure", he hastens to designate himself by a double diminutive[12] "less than the least of all saints". The magnitude of the function entrusted to him abases Paul to the dust when he contrasts it with his own unworthiness and insignificance; and only the counterweight in the other scale, "I can do all things through my Enabler Christ" (Phil. 4:13) can redress the tilting balance.

Hereupon he breaks forth into one of those ecstatic acclamations of the peerless pre-eminence of his Conqueror and Counsellor and Captain in the holy war from which he cannot be withheld for any length of time. What a glow enspheres the compound he here employs, "the *untraceable* riches of Christ", those illimitable resources and assets of His! How redolent it is of Paul's *immanuelized* soul! How he delights to lose himself in the halo that encircles his glorified Lord! Nothing in his eyes is good enough

---

[11] *Cf.* Chs. 2:20 (p. 65, n. 34) and 4:11.

[12] Gk. ἐλαχιστότερος, an expressive double comparative, like our *lesser* and German *mehrer*, comparable to anomalous superlatives found in the papyri such as ἐλαχιστότατος, μεγιστότατος, πρώτιστος, but also paralleled in literary quarters; for ἀμεινότερος is quoted from Mimnermus and τοῦ ἐσχάτου ἐσχατώτερος from Aristotle. We imagine that Paul is making playful allusion to his own name and rather diminutive stature. (Let us recall Shakespeare's "most unkindest cut of all," or such redundancies as "nethermost," "the very slightest.") Why E. J. Goodspeed should think that this self-description "gives scholars who maintain that Paul wrote it great embarrassment" (*Introduction to NT* [Chicago, 1937], p. 231) is difficult to understand. To many it strikes the same authentic note as ὧν πρῶτός εἰμι ἐγώ of 1 Tim. 1:15.

to be predicated of Him. "Imagination's utmost stretch in wonder dies away" as it strives to compress within finite dimensions the infinitude of the Lamb of God and the amplitude of His royal magazines.

For all spiritual wealth is vested in Jesus Christ. Two golden spheres He fills to overflowing, the sphere of glory and the sphere of grace. As the only-begotten Son, His uncreated beams flooded a past eternity and furnished an adequate object of complacency to the Eternal Father, a perfect reflex of an ineffable effulgence. What plummet can sound the ocean? But the preacher of the gospel is concerned not so much with a fathomless pre-existence as with the Saviour's riches funded in the covenant of grace. It is Christ manifest in the flesh, tempering His heavenly resplendence with a terrestrial veil, that the apostle is contemplating. Glory holds high festival above, but grace commiserates and stoops below in the guise and trappings of a servant. Jesus espouses utter poverty that we might become unutterably rich. Love is best gauged by sacrifice. Here then is One who for our sakes gave up more than any other being ever possessed, nay yielded Himself up body and soul to inexpressible pangs as our Hostage. Will He grudge us aught that is His? Far from it. The Prince of givers shares even His crown-jewels with His redeemed. No calculus can compute the purchasing-power of an infinite propitiation focussed in a Divine Sponsor, staking His all in ransom for the sheep of His pasture. How exhaustible are all sublunary mines, how evanescent all worldly hoards or estates! But the King of Glory is His own *El Dorado*; and His exchequer of pardoning mercy, His gems of lifelong loving kindness, His bullion of immortal joy, are as exhaustless as the everlasting surplusage of Deity lying at their base.

> 9 and to make all men see what is the dispensation[13] of the mystery which for ages[14] hath been hid in God who created all things;[15]

---

[13] Gk. *οἰκονομία*. The reading *κοινωνία*, underlying AV "the fellowship of the mystery", has exceedingly poor attestation.

[14] Gk. *ἀπὸ τῶν αἰώνων*, "from eternity"; it may be classed as a Hebraism. *Cf.* Col. 1:26 (p. 218, n. 169).

[15] It must be allowed that the added words in AV, "by Jesus Christ" (Gk. *διὰ Ἰησοῦ Χριστοῦ*) lack the support of the best uncials.

10   to the intent that now unto the principalities and the
powers in the heavenly *places* might be made known
through the church the manifold[16] wisdom of God,

9 The reading *fellowship* of the AV has been replaced on good
authority by *dispensation,* the topic in hand. But we hesitate to
expunge, even in deference to the best uncials, the concluding
clause *through Jesus Christ*; for it has better support, and its
deletion deranges the contexture of the passage, which corresponds
with the declaration of Col. 1:16. By its removal the statement
who created all things forfeits all relevance or indeed meaning.
Ellicott and others discover in it a reference to God's omnipotence,
but surely that thought is out of place; whereas when the share of
Christ in creation obtains recognition, the "purpose of the ages"
centering in Him forms the pertinent sequel.

10 At any rate that purpose sets the sovereign choice of the
Lamb's bride in a wondrous aspect and irradiates her with an
extramundane lustre and distinction all her own. She is not only
emblazoned as a signal trophy of divine counsel, but is discerned
to be such by a galaxy of higher intelligences who mark the
unfolding of her destiny.[17] The church is a spectacle to angels as
well as men. From her chequered story and long-drawn conflict
the celestial hosts learn secrets of the Creator's wisdom not elsewhere divulged. The strange vicissitudes in her status, the yet
stranger throes of tribulation through which she is called to pass,
and, strangest sight of all to the heavenly onlookers, the submission
of her illustrious Head to the reproaches and agonies of the cross,
are fraught with priceless instruction to these sons of the morning,
themselves not wholly unscathed by the internecine feud between
light and darkness. We are their graduating school. It is a
captivating glimpse we here gain of the repercussions of the
battle-fields of earth, audible in "the heavenlies" by spirits attent
to listen and perceptive by intuition of *arcana* which we must spell
out letter by letter. Here we descry unsuspected witnesses of our

---

[16] Gk. πολυποίκιλος, "variegated" like Joseph's coat, "diversified," "multi-
form," is a rare poetical adjective, indicative of the complexity of the divine
counsels, their versicoloured intertexture and reticulation.

[17] On "the principalities and powers" see the exposition of Col. 1:16 (p. 198).
Here (as in Ch. 1:21) both good and evil beings of this order are probably in
view; in Colossians generally (owing, no doubt, to the content of the Colossian
heresy), as in Eph. 6:12, they are evil.

prowess or pusillanimity, whose keen vision pierces through "the dim inane" and scans from afar the bearing of the victors and the vanquished, the unquailing heroes of faith or the inglorious herd who fall a prey to the shafts of unbelief.

Oftentimes must they have puzzled over the story of man's fall and the permission of moral evil. For they themselves form units in the order of the universe. Their hermit spirits dwell apart without point of intersection. Sweet communings may be theirs, but no ties of consanguinity. How diverse from the mortal constitution of things, in which, as Whittier's haunting lines remind us,

Like warp and woof all destinies are woven fast,
Locked in sympathy like the keys of an organ vast:
Pluck one thread and the web ye mar;
Break but one of a thousand strings and the painful jar
Through all will run.

To these watchers of the skies the first human pair could not but present an amazing phenomenon, the mysterious hyphen between matter and spirit, in Scaliger's apt phrase, *utriusque mundi nexus.* In contrast with their own insulation they at length scan an interlinked procession of beings, and by that very sequence susceptible of a common lapse and a common salvation implicit therein. Is not the wisdom of God, impeached in the catastrophe of the fall, vindicated by that inconceivably wondrous dénouement? Assuredly the final key to the first creation is the second (Forsyth).

One thing at any rate is clear. We are parts of a larger whole, designed to read an impressive lesson to the universe, an absorbing object of scrutiny to the observant hosts of light, our present coadjutors and class-mates, our future colleagues and comrades.

11 according to the eternal purpose which he purposed[18] in Christ Jesus our Lord:
12 in whom we have boldness and access in confidence[19] through our faith in him.

---

[18] Gk. ἣν ἐποίησεν, "which He *formed*" rather than "*executed.*" To refer the relative ἥν, with many of the Fathers, to σοφία ("wisdom") of v. 10 seems forced.

[19] Gk. πεποίθησις, a word of late formation, derived from πέποιθα reckoned as a present tense ("I trust"), is used in NT by Paul only. It was current in Jewish circles, as Philo and Josephus evince; but has no place in the papyri and is found elsewhere solely in Babrius (43. 19) and thrice in Sextus Empiricus. The first hand in Cod. D adds to "confidence" the gloss "by having been freed" (τῷ ἐλευθερωθῆναι).

13 Wherefore I ask that ye may not faint[20] at my tribulations[21] for you, which are your glory.

11-13 All the Father's counsels find their consummation in the Son of His love. For His sake the cosmos was framed and furnished to be the theatre of a battle royal between the rupturer of its harmony and our mightier Kinsman-Redeemer. All the believer's confidence of a welcome in approaching the eternal throne hinges upon his filial standing in Christ and unchallengeable access to the mercy-seat. Planted on that ground, let not one of his readers be cast down by tidings of his imprisonment. No brand of infamy is it, but a badge of honour. Is he not their hostage, nay their tribune, in subordination to the supreme Advocate on high?

---

[20] Gk. ἐνκακεῖν and ἐκκακεῖν, which appear as variants here in the MSS, appear to be variations of a single verb, signifying "to be dispirited", "to be downcast," "to wax remiss"; used once by Luke (Luke 18:1) and five times by Paul (the other occurrences being 2 Cor. 4:1, 16; Gal. 6:9; 2 Thess. 3:13), but scarcely met with elsewhere, save in one passage of Polybius (iv. 19). The related verb ἀποκακεῖν (Jer. 15:9, LXX), "to swoon," "to faint away," has a more emphatic connotation than disheartenment.

[21] Gk. θλίψεις, literally "squeezings" or "pressings"; in English the word *straits* comes nearest to it (*cf.* Lat. *angustiae*). Its conjunction in Lucian and Epictetus with στενοχωρία corresponds with the same phraseology in Isa. 8:22; 30:6 (LXX) and three passages in Paul (Rom. 2:9; 8:35; 2 Cor. 6:4); *cf.* Trench, *NT Synonyms*. The metaphorical sense is predominantly Biblical. With the reference to Paul's tribulations on behalf of his fellow-Christians *cf.* the fuller statement in Col. 1:24, with exposition and notes *ad loc.* (pp. 214 ff.).

XII. PAUL'S ENRAPTURED SUPPLICATION

Ch. 3:14–19

14 For this cause I bow my knees unto the Father,[22]
15 from whom every family[23] in heaven and on earth
     is named,
16 that he would grant[24] you, according to the riches of
     his glory, that ye may be strengthened[25] with power
     through his Spirit in the inward man;[26]
17 that Christ may dwell in your hearts through faith;
     to the end that ye, being rooted and grounded[27] in
     love,
18 may be strong[28] to apprehend with all the saints
     what is the breadth and length and height and depth,
19 and to know the love of Christ which passeth know-
     ledge, that ye may be filled unto all the fulness of
     God.

14–15 Of such a transcendent intercession as this, offered on
bended knee by such a suppliant, it seems wellnigh impertinent
to indite an annotation. Comparable to some heavenly breeze, set
in motion by the Spirit of the Lord, it sweeps across the aeolian

---

22 Some Western authorities and the bulk of the Byzantine witnesses add
"of our Lord Jesus Christ" (*cf.* AV).
23 Gk πατριά, a term of rare occurrence, except in Herodotus, where it
means "lineage" or "clanship." The abstract idea of *paternity* seems uppermost
here (*cf.* Athanasius, *Against Arius*, i. 23).
24 Gk δῷ. Modal sequence requires the optative mood; but many scholars
hold that this *prima facie* subjunctive form represents an Ionic optative, conforming to rule. *Cf.* p. 37, n. 29 (on Ch. 1:17).
25 Gk κραταιωθῆναι, a Septuagintalism, found four times in NT, the three
other occurrences being Luke 1:80; 2:40, and 1 Cor. 16:13 (where it is paired with
ἀνδρίζεσθαι): "to be fortified, braced, invigorated."
26 Gk. εἰς τὸν ἔσω ἄνθρωπον. The "inner man" (ὁ ἔσω ἄνθρωπος) is a
Pauline coinage (Rom. 7:22; 2 Cor. 4:16) meaning "the man within the man."
27 Gk ἐρριζωμένοι καὶ τεθεμελιωμένοι. The duplicate metaphor is facilitated
by the figurative use of ῥιζοῦν, dating from Plato and exemplified in Plutarch,
Appian and Vettius Valens. *Cf.* Col. 2:7 ("rooted and builded up"). For
τεθεμελιωμένοι *cf.* Col. 1:23 ("grounded"), and for the whole sentence *cf.* Col.
2:2, with exposition and notes *ad loc.* (pp. 223 f.; especially p. 223, n. 9).
28 Gk ἐξισχύσητε. The version "be strong" is questioned by Moulton and
Milligan; but the word clearly means "to acquire power" in Plutarch, *Moralia*
801. The fervency of the prayer requires a strenuous diction to bear it out.
The word signifies "to prevail" in Vettius Valens (288, 353).

harp-strings of the apostle's soul, waking chords of celestial music of unearthly beauty and superlative grandeur, to which it beseems us to give audience in "expressive silence" rather than mar the strain by the incongruity of a fumbling accompaniment. It is in such passages as these that inspiration rises to its full stature and, like the colossus of Rhodes, dwarfs its puny inspectors. Enough to eye with due reverence its main dimensions. First of all Paul invokes the *Father of all fatherhoods,* from whom every family in heaven and earth derives its appellation. This rendering is entitled to strong support, although the felicity of the original paronomasia cannot be preserved in our English version. God Himself is the archetype of parentage, faintly adumbrated by human fatherhood. From His creative hand have proceeded all rational beings in all their multiplicity of aspects and manners and usages, divergent or interrelated. To the "Father of Spirits" they owe their existence and the conditions that have stamped it with both an individual and collective impress, an actual or potential scope and orbit.

Doubtless the oecumenical fatherhood of beneficence (Acts 17:28) is uppermost in the writer's mind; yet the appended clause *in heaven and on earth* warrants a secondary reference to the household of faith, conjointly perhaps with their angelic fellow-tribesmen, as Calvin terms them, who are specifically alluded to in the context. For the time being it is located in two worlds, yet constitutes in the aggregate a blessed entirety. Mundane families severed in time and place are incomplete; but here is a fraternity scattered through all ages and climes which is clasped indissolubly in one family register and cast in one identical mould. The saints are of one type, though not of one pattern, alike burgesses of Jerusalem which is above, the mother of them all.

16–17 It is for the church militant however, battling in the thick of the fray, that Paul's soul is fired to an incandescent glow in this sublime petition. *Enablement* is the primary prerequisite to that science of measuring the immeasurable to which he bids them aspire. "Unless above himself he can erect himself, how weak a thing is man" wrote Seneca, and Samuel Daniel and Wordsworth have echoed the sentiment. But the Christian does not rely on his own endeavours to scale heights hitherto untrodden, apart from the Spirit's potent aid. By His indwelling our natural impotence may be sublimated into supernatural energy. Firmly

79

rooted in the rich soil of love, our revitalized natures, instinct with the reflex influences of prevenient love divine, may effloresce in spiritual discernment of objects surpassing computation or admeasurement. By virtue of their new birth believers possess an enlargement of vision of which worldlings are destitute. Let them improve the God-given faculty, meant to be exercised wherever it is bestowed, to the full.

All the outfit for their sacred warfare must come from head-quarters, inasmuch as we need empowerment not only for the field of action, but for spiritual insight itself. Faith is the visive organ, as here set forth; yet its blossom love has illuminating virtue likewise. It sheds a light of its own on the object seen, a glow of soul-sympathy. Love elicits insight. Thus equipped the believer may make glorious advances in the quest of divine mysteries. Yonder Alpine peak seems to mock its would-be climber; but Paul is pointing out the secret track whereby that inaccessible summit may be scaled. Himself no mean proficient in the art of mountaineering, he prays that his neophytes may buckle to the arduous task in God's name and strength. *Excelsior* should be their motto and loving gratitude their mainspring.

18-19 What a noble estimate the apostle makes of his disciples! The ancient mystagogues restricted their choicest teachings to an esoteric circle, industriously sifted from the vulgar herd of auditors, admission to which was counted in itself no small privilege. But Paul reckons every convert a candidate for honours, or he would not have offered such an exalted prayer on their behalf.[29] Under the tutelage of the Spirit there is nothing to preclude the rank and file[30] from apprehending, as well as aspiring to, a vastly enhanced realization of the love of Christ towards His own. True, it passes knowledge and may well be termed unsearchable; but the Spirit "searcheth all things, even the depths of God". Through His illumination the scholars may transcend themselves and launch out into an expanse of divine fullness scorning circumnavigation. Cudworth in his discussion of the mystery of the

---

[29] What is a statement in Ch. 1:23 is voiced as a prayer here. *Cf.* Ch. 4:13, where the fulness $(\pi\lambda\dot{\eta}\varrho\omega\mu\alpha)$ to which they are to attain is Christ's; but He is the embodiment of the fulness of God (Col. 1:19; 2:9 f.). See E. Best, *One Body in Christ* (London, 1955), p. 144.

[30] *Cf.* exposition of Col. 1:28 (pp. 219 f.).

Trinity observes that we may scan a range of hills confronting us without being able to perambulate them. The object cognized may outreach our grasp, yet be accessible to our ken. Such is our notion of infinity; we seize its purport, but explore it we cannot.

As shoreless an ocean stretches before us in the love of the Saviour. Its dimensions can only be gauged by the implications it suggests. Not but what love both divine and human has balances of her own, a far more delicate instrument than the scales of the goldsmith, capable of weighing emotions otherwise imponderable, and worthier to be prized than any metewand beside. Has love then a length and breadth and depth and height? In predicating such properties are we not materializing spiritual values? We grant that analogical language of this kind is liable to misconstruction; yet what imaginative mind does not resort to it when profoundly moved? In cold blood men exact logical precision from a speaker; but when the whole being is stirred figures of speech crowd on the electrified faculties and commend themselves to his sympathetic hearer. If genius at such a moment has, in Milton's phrase, its "nimble servitors", much more has inspiration.

For surely we cannot maim this magnificent effusion by adopting the tasteless view of many expositors that the mensuration here visualized is that of the church regarded templewise. That would be a relapse into bathos. Have we mounted a breathless ascent to an ethereal table-land only to descend as steeply? What is more disappointing than to scale the crest of some abrupt acclivity in expectation of a commanding prospect, only to find a slope trending downwards ahead of us, leading into some valley-basin that affords no view at all? That is not the case here. We are still mounting aloft and breathing a rarefied air impregnated with spiritual ozone.

It is urged, to be sure, that the image of Ezekiel's mystic temple is reintroduced here as a sort of pendent to Ch. 2, and that we are invited to become adepts in the art of surveying its dimensions. We are not surprised that those who make the church their idol, until she virtually usurps the place of her Lord, should be beguiled by such a fancy; but we wonder that Bengel and a number of evangelical interpreters since his day have followed in their wake. The city of God, "builded compact together" after its great Architect's model, could not with any propriety be portrayed as measureless; but the love of Christ which passes knowledge does

expand to an infinitude baffling creaturely cognizance. In the act
of mensuration we discover its immeasurability.

> The first-born sons of light
> Desire in vain its depths to see,
> They cannot reach the mystery,
> The length, the breadth, and height.

For what other love can enter the lists with this competitor?
Human love has its choice gallery of masterpieces of devotion,
full comely to behold. Parents have spent themselves for their
bairns and bairns tended their parents affectionately. Husbands
and wives have almost merged personalities. It is this capacity
for absorbing attachment that qualifies us for appreciating the love
of the heavenly Bridegroom for His bride. Shakespeare reminds
us that "love lends a precious seeing to the eye"; and that is why
our rooting and grounding in love forms a preparative for
discerning the love unspeakable. What of its *longitude*? It began
ere the stream of time issued from its fountain and will endure
when that stream loses itself in the ocean of eternity. What of its
latitude? It has room for all diversities of race and culture. In its
circumference, east and west find their meeting-point and co-insec-
tion. What of its *altitude* and *profundity*? Here thought and
speech are stranded. How far is it from the regalia of universal
empire to the dereliction of the accursed tree? Or conversely, what
is the interval between the miry clay of our lost estate and the
perspective of joint-heirship with a glorified Redeemer? When we
can span the illimitable and sound the inexplorable, then may we
hope to fathom the deep that coucheth beneath and to scale the
height that overarches us in the transcendental hemisphere of love
divine. It is its own hyperbole and nonpareil. Stretch our faculties
as we may, they are but finite and their most extended vistas
partake of our circumscription.

Nevertheless He "who only doeth wondrous things" can effect
more than we can conceive. The anticipation of being filled with
His fullness evidently glances forward to an ultimate goal. Paul's
unblenching spirit, rapt into the society of saints made perfect,
espies vessels of mercy charged with all they can hold of Deity,
"plunged in the Godhead's deepest sea", their boundless sphere of
expatiation.

Has he not trespassed out of bounds? Is not this utterance

tinctured with extravagance? Can it be reconciled with his
habitual sobriety of mind? Nay! he has ample warrant for his
temerity; for prayers of ours can never outstrip the Lord's munifi-
cent bounty.

> Thou art coming to a King;
> Large petitions with thee bring;
> For His grace and power are such,
> None can ever ask too much.

XIII. DOXOLOGY

Ch. 3:20–21

20 Now unto him that is able to do exceeding abundantly
above all that we ask or think, according to the power
that worketh[31] in us,

21 unto him *be* the glory in the church and in Christ
Jesus[32] unto all generations for ever and ever.[33]
Amen.

20–21 Consequently he closes his impassioned prayer with an
equally impassioned doxology, as one accustomed to expect from
the Lord loftier benedictions than can be put into words. He
expresses the transcendent conception by an adverb of his own
coinage, *vastly more than more*.[34] To us the reading "in the church
and in Christ Jesus", adopted in the text (not without variants)
out of deference to the most valued uncials, sounds somewhat like
an ecclesiastical gloss. We question whether it can be alleged to
be after the apostle's manner to partition off the church from her
Head in this fashion, or to place her in the foremost rank. We may
well be thankful that the measure of God's power to enrich us is
not our measure of that power. There are ineffable potentialities,
plenitudes more than superlative, in an infinite Deity. On such a
theme *vox faucibus haeret*. We recall the signal experience that
befel the Puritan John Flavel on one of his ministerial journeys on
horseback in the neighbourhood of Dartmouth, when the sense of
Christ's inexpressible love so overcame him that he no longer knew

---

31 Gk. ἐνεργουμένην, taken as middle voice. If it be taken as a passive, the
sense will be: "according to the power that is wrought (*or*: made to work) in
us." *Cf.* p. 221, n. 183 (on Col. 1:29).

32 The Western texts reverse the order, so as to read: "in Christ Jesus and
in the church"; some later uncials (K L P etc.) omit "and", whence AV "in the
church by Christ Jesus."

33 εἰς πάσας τὰς γενεὰς τοῦ αἰῶνος τῶν αἰώνων, an intensive Hebraism for
"eternity." *Cf.* our idioms of a corresponding nature: "for evermore"; "for ever
and ever"; "world without end."

34 Gk. ὑπερεκπερισσοῦ, "superabundantly"; "transcendently more"; "far in
excess." This is one of Paul's characteristic outbursts with ὑπέρ. The form ἐκ
περισσοῦ is a Platonic combination, meaning "surpassingly" or "beyond comparison"; it is perfectly classical. Clement of Rome borrows the apostle's
hyperbole in his Letter to the Corinthian church of the next generation.

his whereabouts; and when he recovered himself found his steed standing stock-still by a brookside and his nose bleeding copiously. He washed his face in the rill and rode on; but that night he passed in such a spiritual trance that he left supper untasted and lay awake till day-break, bathed in a flood of serene exaltation and beatitude.

Such a rapture of adoration seems to master the apostle at this point and language fails him to express his unutterable transports. Our loftiest supplications in this life—what are they but the babblings of spiritual infancy, rudiments of an intercourse as yet imperfectly attained? And what our choicest yearnings but conscious emptiness in quest of replenishment at the wellspring of all-sufficiency which "pours forth its undiminished superabundance from the throne of God and of the Lamb" (Spurgeon)? R. W. Dale waxes eloquent on the prospect opened up to faith's far-seeing eye by this passage. His rythmical English is worth quoting for its stately march and rapt jubilation. "The love of Christ", he writes, "has not only been unquenched; it has never even sunk. In His resurrection and ascension He has illustrated the immense expansion possible to human nature. Through ages without end, inspired with His life and sustained by the Divine power which wrought in Him when raised from the dead, we shall ascend from height to height of righteousness, of wisdom and of joy: with unblenched vision we shall gaze on new manifestations of the light in which God dwells: with powers exalted and enlarged we shall discharge ever nobler forms of divine service and be filled with ever diviner bliss; and through eternity the infinite love of Christ will raise us from triumph to triumph, from blessedness to blessedness, from glory to glory". Does it not defy definition and baffle appraisement, this idealized counterpart of that "fourth dimension" of which mathematical theory has occasional inklings and premonitions?

PART II

CHAPTER IV

I. THE TRAITS OF CHRISTIAN MANHOOD

Ch. 4:1–5:2

1. UNISON

Ch. 4:1–10

Hitherto, under Paul's trusty guidance, his crusaders have
been threading the loftiest passes of revelation, absorbed in the
panorama of a massive mountain-chain of Christian doctrine,
outspread around their line of march. Now it is time for them to
descend from these craggy altitudes, intersected by many a cross-
track opening into regions yet unexplored and cloud-capped, to
the lower levels of everyday duty and demeanour; from the
credenda, in short, to the *agenda*; for all doctrine truly held
prompts to corresponding practice. If faith be the candle, works
are the light; take one away and you cannot keep the other
(Selden).[1] Our belief fixes the trend of our footsteps. We *are,*
in fact, what we believe (Hodge). And such a faith as they have
imbibed lays them under stringent obligation to "walk as becometh
saints." Trophies of grace raised from the dead to form an integral
part of God's living temple, let them aspire to applied Christianity,
the fulness of life in Christ; else they will belie their profession
and dwindle to "evangelical hypocrites", as Payson styles those
whose conduct disaccords altogether with their calling. The foliage
and fruit tell a tale of the root at their base. Some people's lives
confute their professions. If they are to maintain that "truce of
God" whereof they have been made partakers and to demonstrate
its reality, the first desideratum is humility and self-repression,
that serenity of temper unvexed by pique or peevishness which
makes charitable allowance for the infirmities of fellow-members
and is not oblivious of its own foibles and indiscretions. Later on

---

[1] *Table-talk.*

(Ch. 4:32)—and in Col. 3:12[2]—the prompting consideration, Forgive as ye have been forgiven, is explicitly enounced. Knowledge or privilege must not engender freaks of pride or petty resentment. One Spirit indwells the collective church; and His dominating presence should ensure a consensus of good feeling, the imprint of a homogeneous mould stamped upon their moral physiognomy. His baptism makes the whole communion blessedly akin. Is not the mind of Christ their lustrous fair copy?

1 I therefore, the prisoner in the Lord,[3] beseech you to walk worthily[4] of the calling wherewith ye were called,
2 with all lowliness[5] and meekness, with longsuffering,[6] forbearing one another in love;
3 giving diligence to keep the unity of the Spirit in the bond[7] of peace.
4 *There is* one body, and one Spirit, even as also ye were called in one hope of your calling;
5 one Lord, one faith, one baptism,
6 one God and Father of all, who is over all, and through all, and in all.

1-3 In point of fact a prisoner on their behalf, Paul has a peculiar title to plead with them to exercise that mutual forbearance which averts rifts and heart-burnings among those who are essentially brethren, but cannot always see eye to eye. Not a few

---

[2] See exposition and notes *ad loc.* (p. 280).
[3] *Cf.* Ch. 3:1 (pp. 69 ff.).
[4] *Cf.* Col. 1:10 (p. 186).
[5] Gk. ταπεινοφροσύνη, "humble-mindedness," is a NT compound expressive of the Christian virtue of humility, requisite because ταπεινότης meant the crouching submissiveness of a slave, regarded as a despicable trait. It had been employed without disdain in LXX; but even the longer term retains its contemptuous connotation in Josephus (*War*, iv. 9), Epictetus (iii. 24), Plutarch (*Moralia*, 336). *Cf.* Col. 2:18, 23; 3:12.
[6] Gk. μακροθυμία, "forbearance"; what in older English was sometimes called *longanimity*. In the Greek *Anthology* the epithet is applied to the patient-spirited ass. *Cf.* Trench, *NT Synonyms*, § 50.
[7] Gk. σύνδεσμος, the grammatical term for that part of speech which we call a conjunction, metaphorically denotes a copula or vinculum uniting its components as in a wreathed chaplet. Thus Plato (*Republic* 616) poetically styles light the σύνδεσμος τοῦ οὐρανοῦ, Plutarch (*Numa*, 6) writes of the σύνδεσμος εὐνοίας, and Philodemus (*Rhetoric*, iii *init.*) refers to τῶν τεχνῶν σύνδεσμος, the bond of the arts. In Col. 2:19 Paul uses it of the ligaments of the body (see p. 251), and in Col. 3:14 figuratively, with an objective genitive, of love as the consolidating cement of Christian fellowship (see p. 281).

genuine, but crotchety, believers have no sense of proportion or perspective. To their distorted vision molehills and mountains are much alike; either of them presents a fatal barrier in their cantankerous judgments to co-operation. But asperity and fidelity are no more synonyms than unity and uniformity, the wide interval between which Bacon has so sagely noted.[8] Personal tastes and predilections and likes and dislikes have no business to intercept feelings of brotherly kindness. The uniting bond of love precludes all ranklings of petulance or ill-will. Religious embitterments are too often works of the flesh, products of the proverbial *odium theologicum*. Joseph's counsel, "See that ye fall not out by the way", has its pertinent application to the church of God. Let them set themselves to deal not only discreetly but magnanimously and genially with their fellow-pilgrims in the heavenly pathway.

4–6 In contradiction to a cross-grained, disputatious temper the apostle inculcates the unruffled unity of the Spirit's inbreathing, grounded in the very nature of their common faith. Its sevenfold enumeration follows, and that resolves itself into an ultimate triunity; one Spirit, body, hope; one Lord, faith, baptism;[9] and one Father of all.[10] The rhythmical cadence suggests a metrical source for this classification. The Trinity itself, reckoned upwards from the Third Person to the First, lies at the base of the whole survey.[11] Without the Holy Spirit's operation as its Organizer there would be no true *ecclesia*: for its fellowship does not hinge on official succession or corporate visibility, but on the interpenetration of a common life identified with His own, wrought by its Divine Author. Why then is hope subjoined? Because saving faith, the nursery of Christian hope, forms the proper antidote to disintegrating forces. Manzoni has happily styled the Christian

---

[8] *Essays: On Unity in Religion.*

[9] Gk εἷς κύριος, μία πίστις, ἕν βάπτισμα. This collocation of three genders (masculine, feminine and neuter) with their relevant nouns strongly confirms the supposition of a metrical source of this quadrisyllabic triad. It reads like a mnemonic cadence in currency among the Gentile believers or catechumens.

[10] The repeated "one" in this confessional summary is characteristic of Eastern as distinct from Western creeds. Contract the Nicene Creed ("I believe in *one* God the Father Almighty...") with the old Roman or "Apostles'" Creed ("I believe in God the Father Almighty..."). See R. R. Williams, "Logic *versus* Experience in the Order of Credal Formulae," NTS i (1954–5), pp. 42 ff.

[11] Compare the coordination of "the same Spirit," "the same Lord," and "the same God" in 1 Cor. 12:4–6.

church "the camp of those that hope".[12] Other expectations of a moral Utopia disperse like a fleeting mirage and the fond somnambulists wake disenchanted from their cherished illusion. Only one anticipation of human perfectibility "maketh not ashamed", because it is no chimera or fool's paradise, but based on the adamantine platform of the Lord's own sovereign fiat and backed by His own paramount decree. And how sublime the vista of a divinely ordered commonwealth that hope unfolds! Findlay boldly designates the church a "Society for the Abolition of Sin and Death", the gloomiest spectres that haunt mankind. A fresh heaven and a fresh earth clad in stainless array under the sway of the King of Righteousness and Peace casts all other programs of betterment into the shade.

The midmost group in this sacred heptad comprises one Lord, one faith, one baptism. Note that the true church is not a creedless community, not a "congeries of religious miscellanea." The church rests on the *given* (Forsyth), not on conjectural or subjective data. Christ occupies the central place, and with Him are linked the inward and outward *vincula* that bind His people to the Saviour. *Faith* may signify the instrument of justification or carry the more objective sense of Christian doctrine. The initiatory rite of baptism seems selected to represent all external ordinances of worship, such as prayer, praise, preaching, the Lord's Supper and His Day, in the practice of which, broadly speaking, all branches of the church, despite its fissures, may be said to coincide. Finally, the vision of one God and Father of all believers, over all by His transcendence, through all by His immanence, in all by His Executive, the Holy Ghost, that majesty on high which eclipses all false gods and local divinities of paganism, invests the spiritual edifice with an unearthly halo of matchless sanctity and beauty. In the Divine Fatherhood thus interpreted all lines of unity converge, an intrinsic unity surpassing uniformity as life outvies mechanism. The pristine Fount of Life, in whom we live and move and have our requickened being, constitutes its vital element and sphere of expatiation. The visible church may be described as the casket of the invisible, whose precious stones are encased within that integument; yet they may ever and anon be found detached from their encasement, members linked with the Head of the church, albeit outside the visible fold.

[12] *Chiesa di quei che sperano, campo di Dio vivente.*

7   But unto each one of us was the grace given according
     to the measure of the gift of Christ.
8   Wherefore he saith,[13] When he ascended on high,
     he led captivity captive, And gave gifts unto men.[14]
9   (Now this,[15] He ascended, what is it but that he also
     descended[16] into the lower parts of the earth?[17]
10 He that descended is the same also that ascended far
     above all the heavens, that he might fill all things.[18])

7–10   All ascriptions of honour to Christ fall short of the
Lord's intrinsic glory. In proof of His exhaustless treasury of

---

[13] Gk. διὸ λέγει. It is disputed whether this form of quotation (cf. Ch. 5:14,
p. 121) is, as Lightfoot holds, impersonal, or whether "He saith" is to be understood of God speaking in His Word. Meyer, Winer and Blass uphold the latter
assumption, and Meyer regards it as a proof of the NT writers' conviction of the
theopneustia of the OT. Dr. Warfield has supported this contention at length,
instancing in particular Philo's usage when quoting the living oracles, "the
crystallized voice of God." See his *Inspiration and Authority of the Bible*
(Philadelphia, 1948), pp. 299 ff.

[14] Gk ἔδωκε δόματα τοῖς ἀνθρώποις. The last clause of the citation varies
both from the LXX and the Hebrew text, which read: "*received* gifts for (or
among) men"— by which some understand in *human nature (ἐν ἀνθρώποις)*. But
what Christ receives mediatorially He receives to bestow on His people, as
Peter reminded his hearers on the day of Pentecost (Acts 2:33). They are
blessed with all spiritual endowments in and through Him. NT quotations of
OT passages are also authoritative interpretations of the significance of these
passages. The Spirit of God knows His own letter-press better than the most
lynx-eyed modern critic, so often "all eyes and no sight." (It is noteworthy that
the Aramaic Targum on the Psalter and the Syriac Peshitta both read "thou hast
given gifts to men" in Ps. 68:18, in accordance with what was probably a long-
standing oral interpretation. The Targum understands the words as referring to
Moses, who *received* the Law on Sinai that he might *give* it to the people of
Israel.)

[15] Gk. τὸ δέ, introducing a comment on the word ἀνέβη ("He ascended").
So τὸ δὲ Ἅγαρ (Gal 4:25); τὸ δὲ Ἔτι ἅπαξ (Heb. 12:27).

[16] Cod. B and most of the later manuscripts and versions add "first" (πρῶτον)
after "he descended" (κατέβη).

[17] Gk. τὰ κατώτερα μέρη τῆς γῆς. Even "the lowest pit" in Ps. 87:6 is not
Sheol, but a state of complete destitution. The noun μέρη is omitted in some
uncial texts (including P[46]), in which case it might be rendered "the netherlands
of the earth." The alleged descent of Christ into Hades, in support of which
the Fathers are fond of citing this verse, was no original part of what is called
the "Apostles' Creed." *Descendit ad inferna* is a late intercalation (Schaff,
History of the Church: Ante-Nicene, II. 540), grounded mainly on Petrine
passages literally construed in conformity with familiar legends of Greek
mythology. The descent and ascent here correspond to the humiliation and
exaltation of Phil. 2:6–11. See also S. S. Smalley, "The Eschatology of Ephesians," EQ xxviii (1956), pp. 152 ff., especially p. 155.

[18] He in whom all the fulness (πλήρωμα) dwells is the One who fills
(πληροῦν) the universe.

91

fulness, the apostle now adverts to a prophetic Psalm (Ps. 68:18). The primary application of the passage relates doubtless to David's capture of the Jebusite acropolis and the triumphant ascent of the ark to Mount Zion ensuing thereupon (*cf.* Ps. 24). But that *epinicion* attains its germinant fulfilment in David's greater Son, the antitypical Ark of an auguster tabernacle than any made with hands. Living Christianity is an efflux from the heart of the Lord Jesus, by whose self-existent life all its streamlets are fed. The investiture of mediatorial sovereignty, however, thus foreshadowed presumes His previous *devestiture,* His descent into this sublunary arena of conflict to wage battle with the usurping archenemy. For this end the Captain of our salvation must abase Himself to our low estate (Ps. 136:23), this "undervault of the creation," in Rutherford's phrase, not, as the Fathers maintain, to some subterranean limbo vaguely denominated hell, but either to (1) the ignominious status of a homeless Nazarene or the netherlandish level of an itinerant Galilaean rabbi (Isa. 44:23), or (2) to the virgin's womb (*cf.* Luke 1:48), that secluded birth-chamber designated in these very terms in Ps. 139:15, or possibly (3) in reference to the occupancy of the garden-tomb (*cf.* Ps. 71:20). For "the increase of His government" was to be sown in a lowly furrow here below, and to be fertilized with a dread baptism of agony and vilification and hidden in a rock-hewn sepulchre; so that in Ps. 22 He accepts the menial title of a worm, the undermost of creeping things. Only in the subsoil of Calvary can God's imperishable grain of wheat be sown or His church planted with Him; nor could she burgeon until the kindly springtide of Pentecost, when the eternal doors had lifted up their golden heads for the re-entrance of the travail-worn Immanuel to receive the sceptre of universal dominion. David's cavernous bivouacs, his tugs-of-war, his spoils so hardly won, preceded his enthronement and enfolded within their issues Solomon's jubilant temple-dedication and its attendant Shekinah-glory. In analogy wherewith we behold the Lord's spiritual house of habitation, unlike Caesar's *domus aurea* reared by forced labour, waxing to its consummation without sound of hammer or chisel by the successive labours of a divinely apportioned guild of masons whose several functions Paul proceeds to enumerate. For it is no soulless mausoleum, but an expansive and regal abode of the Eternal, instinct with the power of an endless life of His own infusing.

2. DIFFERENCE OF FUNCTION SUBSERVING UNITY

Ch. 4:11–13

11 And he gave some[19] *to be* apostles; and some, prophets; and some, evangelists; and some, pastors and teachers;

12 for the perfecting[20] of the saints, unto the work of ministering, unto the building up of the body of Christ:[21]

13 till we all attain unto the unity of the faith, and of the knowledge of the Son of God, unto a fullgrown man,[22] unto the measure of the stature[23] of the fulness of Christ:[24]

11 The imagery of an edifice must not be suffered to obscure the fact that the church is no less a body than a temple, a sympathetic organism than a stable structure. Her divine Head

---

19 Compare the list of ministrations which "God hath set ... in the church" in 1 Cor. 12:28; there too apostles and prophets take first and second places respectively. *Cf.* Chs. 2:20; 3:5.

20 Gk καταρτισμός. This term indicates "equipment" or "coadjustment." The verb καταρτίζειν is used in Heb. 10:5 of the body prepared for Christ's incarnation; but it can also be employed of the setting of a fractured limb, the repairing of a dislocation or rent, as in Matt. 4:21. Perhaps "coordination" would best represent its scope here.

21 Here, where the church is viewed as the body of Christ, the thought of building (οἰκοδομή) is introduced (*cf.* v. 16); conversely, where the church is presented as an edifice in Ch. 2:20 ff., the biological concept of "growing" is imported. The apostle's mind passes readily from the one figure to the other.

22 *Cf.* the "new man" of Ch. 2:15.

23 Gk. ἡλικία. Souter and others prefer the rendering "age," in deference, no doubt, to the current sense of the word in the papyri and later Greek. But what intelligible meaning can be attached to "the age of Christ" in this passage? The idea of adolescence has been already emphasized in the figure of the ἀνὴρ τέλειος, which so naturally merges in the picture of a corresponding stature, developed to a Christlike maturity of conformation with the ideal Prototype. Moreover, the signification "stature" cannot be eliminated from the NT while the story of Zacchaeus remains on Luke's page (Luke 19:3), nor is it by any means unknown to literary Hellenistic. *Cf.* Lucian, *True History* i. 40; *In Defence of Portraiture* 13; *On the Syrian Goddess* 28; and F. Field, *Notes on the Translation of the NT* (Cambridge, 1899), pp. 6 f. (on Matt. 6:27). Epictetus (iii. 2) speaks of a soul's growth from a fingerbreadth to a two-cubit compass, a much more recondite sample of mensuration.

24 The church is already the πλήρωμα of Christ by the call of God (Ch. 1:23); she is now summoned to attain that πλήρωμα in the life and experience of her members.

replenishes her energies out of His own essential vitality. Apostles and prophets do not spring up at random; they are largesses from His royal exchequer of grace, shafts of His polishing, arrows hid in His mighty quiver. The church has not been left an orphan by her Founder to make headway as best she can by manipulating auspicious circumstances, courting diplomatic alliances or adopting inflated titles. A spiritual house must grow, not by astuteness of tactics, but by spiritual agencies and methods.

Those agencies are manifold. The seeing eye and the hearing ear and the skilful hand all contribute their quota to the church's true weal. She has a visible orbit of expatiation, which called for extraordinary pioneers to stabilize its incipient motions, when as yet the canon of Scripture lacked completion as her authentic chart or standard of measurement. The apostolate was an inner circle of privy councillors or plenipotentiaries entrusted with the task of foundation-laying, and the New Testament prophets and evangelists might be entitled their *aides-de-camp*, auxiliaries inferior in status or catholicity of embassage and amenable to their endorsement and location. Nor is the pastoral office which they transmitted to later generations to be dispensed with or reconstituted on grounds of expediency or self-conceit; for it carries the Lord's own *imprimatur*. He selects His chosen heralds as He sees fit. Now a Boanerges and anon a Barnabas is requisite; a vehement Elijah at one epoch, a plaintive Jeremiah at another. The sagacious vigilance of the church's Head dispenses "the residue of the Spirit" to its chosen envoys, empowered to serve their generation according to His sovereign will. For Christ Himself is in the vessel He has chartered, piloting her course, ruling her destiny, and manning her decks, with the perfect intuition of omniscience.

The Lord's Anointed has taken captivity captive that He may confer gifts on men. The language pictures a recapture of prisoners of war analogous to the rescue of Lot when reclaimed by Abraham from the clutches of the predatory kings. The powers of hell were triumphantly routed at Calvary, as Col. 2:15 testifies,[25] and their prey disenthralled by the divine Bondlooser of souls held in thraldom. Having regained His lieges from their enslaver's grasp, He assigns them their befitting posts of ministration. Lordly

---

[25]   See exposition and notes *ad loc.* (pp. 239 ff.).

functionaries ambitious of secular pomp, in Milton's caustic phrase, "the poppies among the corn", have wrought grievous mischief in the church of God, but the permanent ministry of the Word bears His signature and its institution carries His warrant. The New Testament affords no hint of a priestly caste, "commanding all the approaches of the soul to Him", usurpers of the title they clutch at; but the universal priesthood of believers, each occupying his proper place in the body of Christ, has its clear authorization. In the theocracy of grace there is in fact no laity.

12–13 Paul seems to address his admonition primarily to particular churches, such as were in process of formation under his apostolate, to instruct them how their divinely instituted overseers should contribute to the attainment of an enlightened and robust standard of Christian manhood, reflecting in miniature the lineaments of its great Exemplar. Multiplicity of agencies empowered from on high is to promote unity of type. We are not "violating the unities" in likening them to a gallant flotilla bound for a common haven rather than a solitary ark breasting the waterfloods. Syncretism effects juxtaposition, a mere caricature of unison; in fact, a smothered discord; but a variegated unity embellishes the world of nature and of grace. Neither oddity for oddity's sake nor quadrangular monotony is its ruling principle, but circumstantial diversity subserving a harmonious whole. Bald identity is much less attractive than multiplex coadaptation. The perfecting of the saints in like manner does not blot out their personalities nor pool them. We are to be ourselves throughout eternity, veritable integers, not atomic particles of the universe.

How exalted are Paul's ideals of holy living! To his purged vision the weakliest saplings of the Lord's planting, when acclimatized to their new seed-plot, fostered by the heavenly sunbeams and watered with the celestial dews, may in process of time tower into cedars of Lebanon whose leaf shall not wither. They are destined to grow upward to a stature kindred with that of Christ Himself, so unified with Him as to reflect the image of the Firstborn in a full-orbed adolescence; for glorification is the complement of justification, the coming of age of His fraternal seed royal.

The chief aim of the provision of shepherds, here only so designated in the New Testament, is to supply plentiful and wholesome pasturage for the flocks. Some follow Calvin and Owen in differentiating *pastors* from *teachers*; but the omission of the Greek article between the two substantives militates against this duplication of functions. The ministry has not only the duty of promoting an intelligent insight into the Christian verities, but also the task of winning over outsiders. It serves as a means to an end and appertains to a provisory and intermediate stage of the church's history. When the believer's preparatory schooling is over and the loftier employments of the heavenly world engross his full-grown energies, these exterior adjuncts will be superseded. There are plants that call for the nurseryman's tendance at a certain period of development that become independent of his care when they have reached maturity.

The apostle's keen solicitude for his nurslings is ever apparent. Will they weather the bleak spells they must encounter or will they quail? Will these recruits of his show their mettle by grappling sturdily with the tussles that face them and emerge unscathed from the ordeal? That will depend largely on the tenacity of their hold of the truth and of Him who is its final Amen. Are they being changed by communion with Him into His likeness, weaned from the frailties of childhood and acquiring stamina by virtue of the very wear and tear they meet? Then they will win their spurs in the testing battle-field of life. All is well if they are being moulded into the image of the Second Adam, the Archetype of regenerate humanity. A certain statue chiselled by Polyclitus was awarded the palm by cultured Greece as a faultless work of art, and reckoned the canon of manly physique. So Jesus Christ forms the standard of Christian appraisement, and approximation to His holy walk and gracious demeanour constitutes the gauge of His people's sanctification. "When their garments are white the world will count them His".[26] They should be putting on the new man day by day; but not, as some allege, by a process of discarding that personal identity which raises them high above the marionettes of pantheism. Stephen's transfiguration betokened no "reabsorption in the oversoul", no jugglery of dehumanization, but the attainment of a full-sized Christian stature, commensurate with the inheritance of the saints in light.

Paul cannot, however, ignore the painful alternative to this heavenward impulsion, pursuing lovingly through cloud and sunshine the track of Christ's unerring steps.

---

[26] Bunyan, *Holy War*.

3. SPIRITUAL DISCERNMENT AND GROWTH

Ch. 4:14-16

14 that we may be no longer children, tossed to and fro and carried about[27] with every wind of doctrine, by the sleight[28] of men, in craftiness, after the wiles of error;[29]

14 The apostle is well aware how readily his converts may cool from their first love; how they may be fluttered, or drift with the encircling tide instead of breasting its perilous suction. That very undertow beguiled the Ephesian craft later on (Rev. 2:4). Neophytes have ever been prone to be ensnared by glib-tongued dissemblers masquerading in the guise of angels of light. Paul had himself warned them (Acts 20:30) that false brethren would infest their ranks. Such a propaganda is denounced yet more explicitly in the Colossian Letter. Without firm anchor-ground in Christ, unstable adherents of the new faith resembled a rudderless, wave-tossed skiff, caught in the swirl of a transverse current in the vicinity. They might become the catspaws of prowling waylayers; or, like the parasites of ancient comedy or the trencher-chaplains of English satire, take their cue from the tone and sentiments of their novel patrons, sage oracles in pretension, oily charlatans in practice.

---

27 Gk. περιφερόμενοι. This picturesque verb forms the proper military phrase for *wheeling*. In Plato's *Republic* (436) it is employed of the whirligig of tops, and in Xenophon (*Cyropaedia* 3) of dogs dancing round their master's person. It also expresses physical dizziness or mental distraction (Plutarch, *Caesar* 32, 60; *Moralia* 77). So the adjective περιφερής is used of revolving eyes (Lucian, *Jupiter Tragoedus* 30). The compound συμπεριφέρεσθαι indicates specially obsequious concurrence (Polybius iv. 35; Plutarch, *Moralia* 468), or a molluscous frame of mind swayed by the prevalent trend of which it is the index (Philodemus, *On Piety* 27)—in Shakespeare's phrase, "wind-changing."

28 Gk. κυβεία, a term borrowed from dicing and gambling. In Arrian's Epictetus (ii. 19; iii. 21) κυβεύειν means "playing the cheat."

29 Gk. μεθοδία τῆς πλάνης, "sleights of deception." The word μεθοδία acquired a depreciatory sense, like the English nouns *device, manipulation, manœuvre.* Cf. the recurrence of the word in Ch. 6:11, of "the *wiles* of the devil." The form μέθοδος bears the meaning of "ruse," "stratagem," in Vettius Valens (238, 242) and 2 Macc. 13:8; of "artfulness" in Plutarch *(Moralia* 168), and of wrestling tricks *(Moralia* 638). Instances also occur of the use of the verb μεθοδεύειν to mean "bamboozle" (2 Sam. 19:27, LXX; Dionysius of Halicarnassus ii. 27).

Believers are to be children, yet not absolutely such. Certain qualities of the child they are to emulate; for, if destitute of its simplicity and guilelessness, they cannot possess true infancy of heart. But *childish* traits should be shunned as resolutely as *childlike* graces should be fostered. What is here censured is the fickleness of children's volatile moods, shifting like a kaleidoscope, dazzled by the first glittering bauble or flimsy distraction that catches their eye, and liable to be beguiled by every siren ditty of allurement within earshot. How incongruous with Christian "hearts of oak" is this humorsome and ductile temper! How unstable those whirligigs whose brains are turned by the boluses of any quack skilled to make aconite taste like ambrosia! What an old writer terms a *clinical* church, "sicklied o'er with a pale cast of" unwholesome teaching, belies its avowed profession. It is sunk to the level of a religious infirmary for neurasthenic patients.

The underhand tactics of the intriguers in question must not be overlooked. "By the sleight of men and their chicanery in shifts of deception." These adepts in duplicity do not show their hand to their dupes; their dice are perfidiously loaded. Sinon's wooden horse glides into Troy in disguise; *hostis ut hospes init.*[30] Ruse and subterfuge are the favourite policy of seducers from the faith, falsetto their native dialect. Their spells are woven in silence and secrecy till they have trapped their prey in the fine-spun meshes of their net. In like manner it is the settled policy of Romanism in Protestant lands to patronize toleration till she can secure her own dominance. Then that patentee of jesuitical reservations drops her mask and refurbishes her quondam engines of coercion. We learn what she would fain do from what she has done when she held undisputed sway—

> From east to west while priesthood's banners flew,
> And harnessed kings her iron chariot drew.[31]

It was the Lord Protector of the meek and unsuspecting who uttered the significant warning, "Beware of men" (Matt. 10:17)! No superfluous caution assuredly in our fairspoken, double-dealing day.

Having diagnosed the malady Paul prescribes the medicine for it.

---

[30] Ovid, *Fasti* ii. 787 (of Sextus Tarquinius entering the house of Lucretia).
[31] James Montgomery.

15 but speaking truth[32] in love, may grow up in all
things into him, who is the head, *even* Christ;
16 from whom all the body fitly framed[33] and knit
together[34] through that which every joint supplieth,[35]
according to the working[36] in *due* measure of each
several part, maketh the increase of the body unto
the building up of itself in love.

15 The victim of these guileful seducers cannot escape blame
for his weak-kneed pliancy to persuasion. He should have stood
his ground without budging, in fixed conviction that his Lord is
Truth personified, resolute where there was no ground for vacilla-
tion. So the apostle ranges the Christian stalwart of his portrayal
alongside of truth, a model of sincerity uninveigled by the
chicaneries of smooth-tongued religious quacks. The closer we
keep to Christ, the more we shall enjoy of certainty and be the less
liable to be wheedled by newfanglers and their catchpenny wares.
Whether the verb used means to *speak* or *act truly* is hard to
decide. Our version adopts the former alternative, in accordance
with Gal. 4:16. Yet Robinson justly contends that the proper
antithesis to compliance with error consists in maintenance of
truth both in lip and life. "Truthing it in love"—better *truthify*
(Trapp)—is a clumsy rendering. It may well denote *keeping truth*
or even *troth* or cleaving to it. This notion of sterling integrity
covers a wider area than veracity of speech and more aptly

---

32 Gk. ἀληθεύοντες. In confirmation of the wider sense of this verb compare
the compound ἐπαληθεύειν, which means "to verify, corroborate," by acts rather
than words (Josephus, *War* vii. 8. 1).
33 Gk. συναρμολογούμενον, as in Ch. 2:21 (*cf.* p. 68, n. 37).
34 Gk. συνβιβαζόμενον, expressing the sequel of the divine conjunction, a
juxtaposition resulting in harmonious coalescence, a correlation as of a functioning organism. It is used in a similar context in Col. 2:19; *cf.* also p. 223, n. 7
(on Col. 2:2).
35 Gk. διὰ πάσης ἁφῆς τῆς ἐπιχορηγίας. For ἁφή ("ligament") see J. B.
Lightfoot's note on its occurrence in Col. 2:19; *cf.* also p. 251, n. 101. The noun
ἐπιχορηγία, "furnishment," is found in NT only here and in Phil. 1:19, which
accentuates the fulness of the provision. It occurs, however, in one *Ephesian*
papyrus, and the cognate verb appears elsewhere in NT (notably in Col. 2:19,
where it is rendered "supplied" in a similar context to this) and in later Greek.
Strabo uses ὑποχορηγία with the same meaning.
36 Gk. κατ᾿ ἐνέργειαν. P46 reads καὶ ἐνεργείας, which would have to be taken
with the preceding phrase, as though the meaning were "adjusted and fitted
together through the supply *and functioning* of every ligament, in the due
measure of each several part"—but the accepted text should stand. Several
Western authorities omit κατ᾿ ἐνέργειαν altogether.

introduces the resplendent ideal which irradiates the rest of the sentence. Truth of utterance finds place later on (v. 25). "Be thou the true man thou dost seek" is Whittier's counsel, both loyal and frankhearted. "Truth without love", says McCheyne, "lacks its proper environment and loses its persuasive power; love without truth forfeits its identity, degenerating into maudlin sentiment without solidity, feeling without principle."

16 An elaborate physiological metaphor, already familiar to students of 1 Corinthians, sums up the apostle's injunction to walk worthy of the high vocation of saintship. It is once more echoed in Col. 2:19.[37] Two conceptions of the relation to Christ implicit therein have been competing for utterance. He is the all-in-all of His people, at once their impregnable Rampart and the Cornucopia of their spiritual enrichment. Their life subsists by intercommunion with His perennial fulness. But He is also the sovereign Head of His new creation, the Shekinah-sheen of its mantling day and Polestar of its receding night. His risen life diffuses itself by means of an invisible fellowship scattered throughout space and time, to which the physical organism offers a close analogy. We have seen architectural terminology pressed into service; we now have imagery borrowed from medical science presented to our view. Did Luke suggest the technical terms? At any rate the Spirit was their ultimate prompter. It is a diagram of the complete system of nerves and muscles that lock the limbs in co-ordination and coadjustment with the controlling mind. Unity of structure in the whole and variety of function in the parts are the conditions of growth on which he is insisting (Robinson).

Beginning with the Father's eternal purpose we have traversed the mystery of redemption embodied in the Son and reached the ligatures interwoven by the Spirit between the segments making up the aggregate whole, fixing the status of the component elements of the body of Christ and attempering it into symmetrical cohesion. The similitude of a living organism intricately coadjusted presents difficulties when unduly elaborated, but the broad outline is clear-cut. In the body, the head fills a function corresponding to that of the root in the vegetable creation. Unobstructed conduits must subsist between the reservoir of supply and its ramifying

---

[37] See p. 251 and especially n. 100.

channels of distribution; and the circulation of life needs to be equably apportioned in order that the organism may exhibit a consonant whole. Harmonious setting or articulation is requisite for the conveyance of vital energy from the "power-house" to its preordained outlets of distribution. Each member of this mystical body has a certain province assigned him to fill. All the other members with whom he is providentially consorted should (such is the ideal) act in concert to discharge their several parts, not merely without friction and grating, but with the nicest inter-adaptation; even as the joints and muscles of an athlete collaborate in his feats of agility with such litheness that the service they render seems not constrained but instinctively tributary to the exploit. Thus should each tenon and sinew, ministrant in its own sphere, however tiny, fulfil the task entrusted to it, each saint diffuse a savour of Christ in his environment to the well-being of his brethren whose good he seeks and also with a view to the incorpora-tion of "those without" in the living temple of redeemed souls. For a day will speedily dawn when the mystery of God shall be finished and the celestial bride emerge immaculately adorned for her Husband. And the liker the church militant to the church triumphant, the church in her budding promise to the church in her bridal glory, the better will she fulfil the end of her vocation and the nearer will the consummation of her training be brought. She cannot stoop to affect "the image of the earthly" without relaxing all her spiritual fibres and sullying the chastity of her heavenly betrothal.

4. OLD TRAITS TO BE DISCARDED; NEW TO BE CHERISHED

Ch. 4:17–32

17 This I say therefore, and testify in the Lord, that ye
no longer walk as the[38] Gentiles also walk, in the
vanity of their mind,[39]
18 being darkened[40] in their understanding, alienated[41]
from the life of God, because of the ignorance that
is in them, because of the hardening[42] of their heart;
19 who being past feeling[43] gave themselves up to
lasciviousness, to work all uncleanness with greedi-
ness.
20 But ye did not so learn Christ;
21 if so be that ye heard him, and were taught in him,[44]
even as truth is in Jesus:[45]

17–19 From the portrayal of this sublime climax of attainment the apostle turns forthwith to practical admonitions. Paul's

---

38 The intrusive λοιπά (whence AV "other Gentiles") is supplied by later
hands in Codd. ℵ and D, in the bulk of the later manuscripts, and in some
versions, but is absent from the most reliable witnesses for the text.

39 Gk. νοῦς. See p. 250, n. 99 (on Col. 2:18).

40 Gk. ἐσκοτωμένοι. The verb σκοτοῦσθαι from Plato downwards suggests
the effects of stupefaction or vertigo. It thus prepares the way for the subsequent figure of insensibility (πώρωσις). With ἐσκοτωμένοι τῇ διανοίᾳ here cf.
ἐσκοτίσμεθα τὴν διάνοιαν in the Ancient Homily falsely ascribed to Clement of
Rome (19:2).

41 Gk. ἀπηλλοτριωμένοι. See p. 58, n. 19 (on Ch. 2:12).

42 Gk. πώρωσις. See n. 40 above.

43 Gk. ἀπηλγηκότες. This verb may signify in Hellenistic "to be despondent
or despairing" (de-sperare) (cf. the variant ἀπηλπικότες in the Western text);
but the conetxt here supports the other rendering "desperate," "infatuated" or
"past feeling"—the sense borne out by the term in Polybius (i. 35; xvi. 12) and
Philo (ii. 430). For ἐν πλεονεξίᾳ at the end of v. 19 see p. 118, n. 10.

44 Cf. Col. 2:6 f., with exposition and notes ad loc. (pp. 226 f.).

45 Gk. καθὼς ἔστιν ἀλήθεια ἐν τῷ Ἰησοῦ. Not a few expositors boggle at
this clause as it stands, and some would read ἀληθείᾳ, "in truth," to the detriment
of the sense. We should accent ἔστιν as the emphatic word (cf Plato, Cratylus
386), and interpret "according as truth is embodied in Jesus," comparing
Rom. 9:1, "I speak the truth in Christ," its Impersonation. The historical Jesus
claims to be the Truth and to be its final Witness (John 14:6; 18:37). Those
who have "learned Christ" aright as the pharos of all real illumination have
reached the fountain-head of certainty, found the pole-star of their life-voyage
throughout its whole passage.

loftiest flights are never merely speculative excursions; they are incentives to unflagging perseverance. *Therefore* walk no more in the halting gait of the old man, but step out with the sturdy pace and in the stalwart trim of the new.

Another of the apostle's contrasted pictures now meets our gaze. What these Gentiles had been is retraced by way of warning, what they might be is held up as their *beau idéal*. In the background stretches a pagan civilization rank with pollution and slowly succumbing to a complication of moral disorders terrible to contemplate, its very mentality a simmering Tophet, darkling amid fancied enlightenment. Professing wisdom, ancient culture had branded itself with the stigma of downright futility. Its fatal hollowness could no longer be hid. Its sapient insipidities of diet supplied nothing to sate the gnawing hunger of the human heart. In Plato's day ethical theory had ranked as a captivating intellectual pastime, a palaestra of dialectical gymnastics. Now its hair-splitting logomachies had sunk to the level of an oppressive nightmare. The verdict, "all is vanity", was forcing itself on a generation sick of a surfeit of pretentious but paralytic philosophies wrangling for pride of place without intelligible distinction or issue. Is it not so to-day? A septic civilization harbours within itself the germs of dissolution or universal overturn. Godlessness always lies under sentence of death (Carlyle). Deserved devastation is its doom. Sin's firstborn is invariably the grisly sergeant-at-arms Death, the grim-visaged janitor of judgment. For much more pestilent agencies than a decrepit scholasticism were undermining the bases of society with inveterate omens of disintegration. The deadliest symptom of all was that necrosis of soul which supervenes upon the putrefaction of a moral charnel-house. Darkened perceptions bred mischief enough, but brazen-faced ossification wrought worse havoc by far. Unblushing obscenity and infamous orgies of lasciviousness were become a stupefying opiate, under whose narcotic fumes the sense of shame was vanishing from a bestialized community. An American traveller in Italy has noted how fully the demoralizing frescoes of Pompeii account for the downfall of Rome. It was not lava but lewdness that buried Herculaneum. To be "past feeling" is to wear the mark of the beast and be sealed as the devil's own, among those in whom a seared conscience has completed its perfect work, already ensured for perdition and shrouded in the grave-clothes of the second death, prematurely defunct ere the passing-bell has tolled over an expiring lease of life vilely misspent. The doom of such moral lepers is the sentence: "let them be filthy still!"

20–21 But Paul augurs better things of his children in the faith. To them falsehood has lost its glamour and vice its fulsome lure. Sitting at the feet of Jesus is the touchstone of sound-mindedness, a grander tutelage than the curriculum of any other training-school could furnish. "Initiated in the secrets of the skies", invested with such a patent of nobility, be it theirs to imbibe their Master's lessons and reproduce them in miniature, catching His likeness and conforming to His summons to holy living. Let them echo the rapt prayer of Alexander Vinet: "Disrobe us of ourselves and clothe us with Thyself, O Lord!" We are pledged to doff the old man and don the new. Truth "from falsehood cleansed and sifted," than which naught can be truer, has Jesus for its perennial wellspring, and it permeates as an effluent principle the life yielded to its crystal outflow. Notice the cogent incentive: "Ye have not *so* learned Christ." Usually we learn subjects, not persons; but the Christian's choicest lesson-book is his loveworthy Lord. Instruction about Him falls short of the mark; personal intimacy is requisite to rivet the bond of union with the Saviour. Our partial conceptions must be rectified by His indisputable *Ipse dixit's*, whom, rather than in whom, we believe (2 Tim. 1:11).[46] The Teacher is the theme, His own Body of Divinity and Text-book. Is He not the Focus (Col. 2:3) of all wisdom and knowledge?[47] Are not truth and His "Verily, verily" convertible terms? Where is its embodiment if not in Him? The human intellect spells out the paradoxes of mortality piecemeal, with faltering, tentative, ever fallible scrutiny. He probes human nature to its core and brings its most recondite secrets to light. There needs no proof for the truth of anything Christ has said but that He has said it.[48] "Truth came once into the world with her divine Master," says John Milton, "and was a perfect shape most glorious to look upon."[49] Thus He becomes the complete Spectrum of our colour scheme, our Quintessence of reality, the Oracle of our inner

---

46 See E. K. Simpson, *The Pastoral Epistles* (London, 1954), pp. 126 f.
47 *Cf.* p. 224.
48 John Locke.
49 *Areopagitica.*

104

world; and apart from His irradiation man's vaunted sagacity stumbles in the dark. By this rectifying medium we correct the distortions of our dim-sighted vision; and it is the heavenly Daystar that reveals to us the sad soilure of our plight. The length and strength of the chain let down to draw us up discloses the slough wherein we weltered, but withal the mighty leverage set in motion for our upraising from the pit of corruption, the dynamic commensurate with our disability and ignorance, stranded, as we are, in an islet of existence belted with unvoyageable tracts of space and baffled by myriads of inscrutabilities. The "background of the unresolved" invariably keeps pace with our vaunted discoveries, those complex webs of knowledge and nescience interwound.

> 22 that ye put away,[50] as concerning your former manner of life, the old man,[51] that waxeth corrupt after the lusts of deceit;
> 23 and that ye be renewed in the spirit of your mind,[52]
> 24 and put on the new man,[53] that after God hath been created in righteousness and holiness of truth.[54]

22-24 Renunciation and appropriation are to be concurrent processes. To the old self, at once misguided and defiled, no clemency is to be shown. Summary crucifixion is its desert. And if the full-grown brood of mischiefs is to be extirpated, even the freakish little foxes that spoil the grapes must not be spared for all their whining. Else like the too sleek and self-applauding Quaker audience which Stephen Grellet arraigned for being "starched before they were washed", the believer will incur the charge of scamped work. Vivification should be coextensive with mortification. Who is content with half a pair of scissors? "The renewal of the spirit of the mind" enjoined is thorough-going, and it exhales a perfume replete with the fragrance of the ambrosial odours of Eden. That transition implies a whole-hearted transfer

---

[50] Gk ἀποθέσθαι. For the catechetical import of this word see p. 271, n. 59 (on Col. 3:5 ff.).
[51] Cf. Col. 3:9, with exposition and notes ad loc. (pp. 272 f.).
[52] Cf. Rom. 12:2.
[53] Cf. Col. 3:10, with exposition and notes ad loc. (pp. 272 ff.). But there the word translated "new" is νέος, whereas here it is καινός, "fresh." The believer is a new creature; his outlook and aims, his tastes and inclinations, are novel. See Trench, NT Synonyms, § 60.
[54] Cf. Col. 3:10, where the new (νέος) man "is being renewed (ἀνακαινοῦσθαι, from καινός) unto knowledge after the image of him that created him" (see p. 272, nn. 64, 66).

from a shelving gravitation downwards to a capacity of mounting aloft. For "the new moral self Christ gives us", as Forsyth aptly styles it, is created *God-wise* in the image of sanctified reason, moulded of a superhuman make. Henceforward it behooves us to grow upward into the similitude of our august Prototype, the "Perfection of Beauty" and Nonpareil of His own curriculum. For so close is His interfusion with His teaching that in imbibing the one we absorb the other. Gospel theology merges in Christology (Isa. 53:11). Beginning to teach in His earthly ministry, He completes His course of instruction from His chair on high, and we may without irreverence designate the Holy Spirit His Broadcaster.

This passage gives us to understand that Christian profession cannot consist of negative traits, of fair-seeming leafage devoid of fruit. Even in the coarse scales of worldly valuation a conventional propriety of deportment, frostbitten and prudential to a fault, coupled with keen-eyed regard for the main chance, will not win hearty esteem. The *bona fide* follower of the Lamb cannot rest satisfied with a shabby-genteel religion, an orthodox head ill-matched with heterodox feet. Has he not been recast after a new pattern and qualified for likeness to his divine Head, his radiant Paragon? It was Paul's intense Christ-mindedness which lent such overpowering weight to his biddings and beseechings. And so true eaglets of the celestial eyrie must needs acclimatize themselves to "the heavenlies" by taking flight into the empyrean possible only to "children of the day." What was to be the pledge of their new birth, their spiritual disenthralment? Not austerity of mien pulling a long face, but transparence of aim and motive authenticates the device on their banner, "holiness unto the Lord". In the choice wording of Lavater's hymn, not quite reproduced in the current English version of the German original:

> O Jesus Christ, grow Thou in me
> And *vanish* all beside!
> Farther from sin each day may I,
> Closer to Thee, abide.

25 Wherefore,[55] putting away falsehood, speak ye truth

---

[55] The logic of Christian ethics appears in this "Wherefore" *(διό)* with which the injunction to put away the old vices is repeatedly introduced in NT (*cf.* Jas. 1:21; 1 Pet. 2:1).

each one with his neighbor: for we are members one of another.[56]

26 Be ye angry, and sin not: let not the sun go down upon your wrath:[57]

27 neither give place to the devil.

28 Let him that stole steal no more: but rather let him labor, working with his hands the thing that is good, that he may have whereof to give to him that hath need.

The apostle's wings are now definitely furled and his feet pace the beaten causeway of life. Having laid an impregnable basis of Christian doctrine for his striplings in the faith, he proceeds to erect thereupon an analogous superstructure of Christian ethics. Total abstinence from iniquity and unalloyed zeal for rectitude are to distinguish their carriage from the unregenerate world around them; for saving faith acts both as a solvent and a cement.

25 First we hear him insist on sterling *veracity* (*cf.* Col. 3:9); for "lying lips are an abomination unto the Lord, but they that deal truly are His delight" (Prov. 12:22). The practice of deception and fraud has invariably signalized idolatrous communities and been reckoned by the votaries of false gods an exceedingly venial offence. Debased moral standards sanction, and in effect beget, a prolific brood of mendacities, until the dishonour of double-dealing is almost effaced by its prevalence. That rampant evil could only be counteracted by godly principle, actuated in all its doings by a sense of the all-seeing eye. Mark that Paul's lofty standard of conduct is not educed from the maxims of moral philosophy, but from his readers' relationship through Christ to one another and its appropriate outworkings. His people share a common life and a common fraternity. On these grounds what can be more culpable than insincerity of dealing among kindred spirits? As Chrysostom remarks, it is monstrous for the foot or the arm to play false to the eye or the ear.

If we look for truthfulness in others we must needs be transparently truthful ourselves. Speech has not been bestowed on us that we may prevaricate or "give truth a sprain", as the French have it, but fulfil the offices of social beings, mutually supple-

---

[56] *Cf.* 1 Cor. 12:12 ff.

[57] Both parts of this verse are quoted in Polycarp's *Epistle to the Philippians* (12:1).

THE EPISTLE TO THE EPHESIANS

mentary the one to the other. Jesuitical equivocation injects a dismembering virus into the body politic, subversive of all good faith and public credit. The apostle is here citing verbatim from the prophet Zechariah (8:16) as his "senior counsel", so to speak.

26-27 *Be angry and sin not.*[58] A chastened temper must accompany avoidance of random or deceptive language. It becomes us to be zealous in God's cause, cool in our own. The term used in the second clause suggests the idea of embitterment or exasperation. Trench is no doubt correct in saying that the injunction not to let the sun set on your wrath signifies your *irascibility* rather than *ire*. Suffer no indulgence in sinful resentment to engender a splenetic frame of mind. That explains the addendum "neither give place to the devil".[59] Practice the noble art of selfrestraint. Give no handle to the adversary.

These precepts cover a wide area of social conduct. It is not righteous indignation, the reaction of purity against corruption, one of the purest emotions we can feel, that is inhibited; for cases not seldom occur where charity is irrational and lenience tantamount to treachery; but the grudge which springs from haughty self-assumption or a spirit of revenge fomented by wounded pride. Lawful and unlawful anger both find their exemplification in the leading case of Moses. When he broke the tables of the Law he was justly incensed against a sottish multitude; his inmost soul was stirred by zeal for the Lord's honour. But not so when he lost his temper and struck the rock in a fit of choler. A man totally destitute of indignation is a maimed sample of humanity. In such a world as this the truest peacemaker may have to assume the role of a peacebreaker as a sacred obligation. Not then strong passions,

---

[58] Gk. ὀργίζεσθε καὶ μὴ ἁμαρτάνετε, a quotation from Ps. 4:5 (LXX); the Hebrew text has "Stand in awe, and sin not" (ARV, v. 4). Let godly fear curb ungodly exacerbation. The Pythagorean parallel alleged (Plutarch, *Moralia* 488), "Let vituperation *(λοιδορία)* cease at nightfall and shake hands," is a very different maxim in principle. Imperturbability may be the mask assumed by moral obtuseness. The compound παροργίζειν ("to provoke") occurs in Aristotle; the noun is confined to Biblical Greek.

[59] Gk. μηδὲ δίδοτε τόπον τῷ διαβόλῳ. The phrase διδόναι τόπον (*cf.* Lat. *dare locum*) is Hellenistic, meaning "to give scope or range to" (Plutarch, *Moralia* 462) or "to make room for" (Luke 14:9; Plutarch, *Gaius Gracchus* 13). Some would render διάβολος here by "slanderer," but this is contrary to NT usage. Ephesians (*cf.* also Ch. 6:11) and the Pastorals are the only Pauline epistles to use διάβολος. (In the others Σατανᾶς is preferred.) *Cf.* Acts 13:10 for another Pauline use of διάβολος.

but their legitimate scope or vicious misdirection, merit respectively praise or blame. Brave censure may be eminently salutary either to an individual or a nation. An honest love is not afraid to frown (Young).[60] Cantankerous ebullitions of passion on the other hand are criminal lapses from self-control. Thereby we lay ourselves open to the encroaching tactics of Satan, and permit him to gain an entrenchment within our lines of defence. God has given us those passions "under lock and key". We must never allow the infernal housebreaker to pick the lock and gain entrance unawares. Give him a loophole of admission and he will soon dilate the aperture till he secures a firm foothold of occupation that will cost the capitulator dear. *De puerta cerrada el diablo se torna,* from a fast-bolted door the devil turns away, says a Spanish proverb. Wherefore bolt the old serpent out, head and tail!

28 Another rampant sin of heathendom now falls under stricture. *Theft* is selected as the foil to sterling honesty and wise generosity. Where the fear of God is lacking, petty larcenies are sure to abound, even if depredations on a more extensive scale do not prevail. Respect for other people's property, whether personal or public, distinguishes a law-abiding community from a social congeries of unstable equilibrium, deficient in cohesion and void of principle, held together mainly by considerations of self-interest. Pilferings cannot always be detected or exposed, because many situations necessitate the exercise of trust. Unscrupulous characters may avail themselves of "the false balances of deceit" in such cases and their defalcations escape discovery. The petty larcenies of slaves in particular formed a kind of retaliation for their iniquitous thraldom and became such a foregone conclusion that no master but had his eye on them, and his precautions for circumventing their malpractices. But Christians, like Caesar's wife, have a prestige all their own to maintain, and ought to be above suspicion of filching what is not theirs. Let them be hard workers and blameless members of society, not clutching all they can get, but finding satisfaction in giving, out of the earnings of honest industry, needful succour to impoverished children of want. The helping hand is the best index of the feeling heart.

We hear much to-day of "unearned increment" as a problem in economics; but by far the worst purloiner is the gambler who picks

---

[60] *Night Thoughts.*

another man's pocket (or else his own) under cover of a game of chance. Let him that has stolen in this genteel fashion steal no more a march on his neighbour.

> 29 Let no corrupt[61] speech proceed out of your mouth, but such as is good for edifying as the need may be,[62] that it may give[63] grace to them that hear.

29 This bolt is launched against the offence of *impure utterances,* baneful in their influence as a malarial gas. Many of these Gentile converts had been living in an impure environment, where soul-polluting ribaldries formed the staple of conversation among boon companions at convivial gatherings. Let them beware lest old tendencies of that sort should reassert themselves in an unguarded hour. They have been sealed as the Lord's by His Holy Spirit, and must not affront Him by unchaste word or thought. No graceless indulgences can be sanctioned in a royal priesthood like theirs, an election of grace "in holy orders", set apart to sacred uses, and imbued with sanctified motives, on pain of sullying, or at least beslurring, their Christian manhood. Flippancy or impropriety of speech falls under the head of the evil rebuked. In Colossians a kindred exhortation reappears (4:6),[64] and is clenched by the positive behest that their talk should be seasoned with salt, the antidote to corruption, of gracious savour, well-timed and suffused with a vein of piety, talk guided into profitable channels.

> 30 And grieve not the Holy Spirit of God, in whom ye were sealed unto the day of redemption.[65]

30 "God's honour," says Bengel, "is an awfully tender thing

---

61 Gk. σαπρός, "rank," "foul," "putrid," both in a literal and figurative sense. Some would emasculate the epithet by rendering it "evil"; but it carries the connotation of *pernicious* and *offensive.* Epictetus employs the term (ii. 18) to stigmatize coarse-minded boxers and swashbucklers in general. In popular usage it was closely akin to our colloquial use of the adjective "rotten." Chrysostom says that it answers to "worthless." In an illiterate papyrus letter σαπρὸς περιπατῶ means "I am walking about in rags." *Cf.* the occurrences of the word in the Gospels: Matt. 7:17 f.; 12:33; 13:48; Luke 6:43.
62 Gk. πρὸς οἰκοδομὴν τῆς χρείας, "with a view to timely instruction." *Edification* is a Christian coinage, imaging *upbuilding,* the idea that underlies the Latin *instruere;* here the befitting theme, needful to be uttered in the given circumstances.
63 Gk. ἵνα δῷ (*cf.* Chs. 1:17; 3:16).
64 See exposition and notes *ad loc.* (p. 299); *cf.* also Col. 3:8 (p. 271).
65 *Cf.* Ch. 1:13 (p. 35).

and may be injured before we are aware." The Holy Spirit's scrutiny is omniscient, and our blessed Refiner cannot but be instantly conscious of every germ of contamination latent in the souls He has sealed for the Lord's possession. Every taint of ingratitude or self-will or unbelief or positive turpitude harboured by the believer contravenes the new creation to which he belongs, entails depletion of its fibre and causes the Christian runner to swerve from his heavenward track. To tamper with sordid objects offends the dove-like Paraclete. All sinful compliances, all slighting of His monitions, wound Him to the quick; for they blur, and tend to blot out, the "spirit born of the Spirit", the stamp of sanctity and separation He imprints on His charges. It is not an influence that these sacrileges stifle, but a sacred Person they repel, one who deigns in loving-kindness to dwell in our sin-deflowered souls, to become our Teacher, our Consoler, our Warden, the earnest and ensurer of our final purification. A careless walk implies irrecognition of all we owe to His untiring patience and quickening energy. The Thessalonian church had been warned not to quench the Spirit. That outrage were suicidal: but He may be hurt by less heinous obliquities, by a spirit of laxity and half-hearted docility. Alas for the unhallowed compromises of the professing church! How prone is its gold to wax dim and discoloured, till it incurs the disrepute of sheer tinsel and dross!

31 Let all bitterness, and wrath, and anger, and clamor, and railing, be put away from you, with all malice:[66]

32 and be ye kind one to another, tenderhearted,[67] forgiving each other, even as God also in Christ forgave you.[68]

31–32 Finally, the apostle sums up his inspired exhortation in a general counsel of benignity and serenity of demeanour, illustrated after his manner by a list of the chief delinquencies against which they are to stand on guard. It behooves them to abjure

---

[66] Gk. κακία, *animi pravitas* (Calvin); more specifically, "ill-will." See Trench, *NT Synonyms*, § 11.

[67] Gk. εὔσπλαγχνος, "kind-hearted"; like σπλαγχνίζομαι a good example of Hebraistic Greek. In *Attic* poetry ἄσπλαγχνος means "cowardly" (*Sophocles, Ajax* 472). *Cf.* σπλάγχνα οἰκτιρμοῦ in Col. 3:12 (p. 279).

[68] *Cf.* Col. 3:13. On the verb χαρίζομαι, used twice here and in the parallel passage in Colossians, see p. 238, n. 62. At the end of the verse our textual authorities are divided between ὑμῖν, "you" (P46 ℵ A G etc.) and ἡμῖν, "us" (B D etc.).

111

all tartness of speech, all touchiness of temper, all propensity to brawling or detraction, much more *malice prepense*; for these are appurtenances of the old Adam, patches of the serpent's skin which is to be entirely sloughed.

The type of human nature he had to deal with was manifestly of a proletarian cast drawn from the common ranks, not much embellished with superfine manners, composed not of porcelain ware but earthen vessels, fragile at best. The most serious cleavages they might undergo were those caused by angularity or malice. In contrast with possible factious dissidences of this kind, the apostle sets in the foreground a warm-hearted, forgiving spirit. However an envious, obstreperous temper may pass muster in the world's bear-garden, it matches ill with the peaceful sheepfold of Christ. The sacred patience and gentleness of the Good Shepherd ought to distinguish His chosen flock. What business has a scowling mien or brusque manner to intrude into His hallowed precinct? Those who have themselves been cleared of a crushing debt must not exact from their brethren the petty sums they may have loaned them nor stickle for inordinate deference. Let them comport themselves forbearingly even to the erring and headstrong and sympathetically to the afflicted. Love suffereth long and puts the best construction on the most irksome behaviour. Pardoned culprits have no title to pose as fault-finding martinets, enforcing the letter of the law in violation of its spirit. Wrathful Christians are a scandal to the Prince of Peace (Watts).

Observe that the cross of Christ is the sole medium of Gospel forgiveness. All pardons pass through Immanuel's hands. God's evangel exhibits a miracle of mercy that should ensure large-heartedness in its recipients; but that mercy is essentially *cruciform*. "No Gospel was known to the primitive church which had not this foundation, that God forgives our sins because Christ died for them" (Denney). Apart from the Saviour's exhaustive satisfaction for sin, defrayed in a costlier currency than ours, we should have no plea to offer in arrest of judgment. "Remission of sins without satisfaction for them implies that *might in the Godhead is more fundamental than right*" (Shedd). We are justified without impeachment of holiness, because the Holy Redeemer is become our Proxy and our Propitiation, has cast in His lot with us and for us, and buried the confluent transgressions of His people in an ocean of reconciliation "deeper than ever plummet sounded." At

the cross alone is the Lord well-pleased *for His righteousness'*
sake; and full well may we share the rejoicings of heaven and earth
over that transcendent vindication of outraged rectitude, since
there we too "may look on *all* God's attributes and be at peace"
(Joseph Cook). Heaven's act of oblivion is no half measure. "Go
with your limited, conditional pardons to the children of men;
it may become them, it is like themselves. That of God is absolute
and perfect, before which our sins are as a cloud before the rising
sun" (John Owen).[69] The dimensions of sovereign grace overlap
our aggregate iniquities.

---

[69]   On Ps. 80 (*Works*, ed. Gould, VI, 502).

CHAPTER V

5. THEIR IDEAL

Ch. 5:1-2

1 Be ye therefore imitators of God, as beloved children;
2 and walk in love, even as Christ also loved you,[1] and
gave himself up for[2] us, an offering and a sacrifice to
God for an odor of a sweet smell.[3]

1 Paul clenches his admonitions in the bold counsel with which
the fifth chapter opens. There is no real break here. He hesitates
not to exhort them to become copyists of God, reflectors of His
measureless love, as beloved children of their heavenly Father.
Low models furnish no high incentive to those who copy them;
but to aspire to a resemblance to our Maker sets the loftiest ideal
conceivable before his readers. In an inferior sphere of things
imitation is dubbed the sincerest form of flattery; and the aphorism
suggests that what we deeply admire we shall be prone to mimic.
Some of the divine attributes lie far beyond our scope even to
measure, much more to copy; but there are communicable perfections which present to us a glorious field of emulation; and
forgiving love is conspicuous among these approximately imitable
traits of Deity. Has not Christ set us the supreme standard of

---

[1] The second person "you" (Gk. $\dot{v}\mu\tilde{a}\varsigma$) followed so closely by the first person
"us" (Gk. $\dot{\eta}\mu\tilde{\omega}\nu$) is striking; as usual, the manuscripts and versions vary con-
siderably in their support of the one or the other; but the authority of P^{46}
supports the reading of the first person in both clauses.
[2] Gk. $\dot{v}\pi\acute{e}\varrho$, in this connexion, as below in v. 25, stands for more than "in
behalf of," the sense to which many limit it. To die for another involves
substitution; for he who lays down his life for his friend ($\dot{v}\pi\acute{e}\varrho$, John 15:13)
sacrifices his own life by so doing. The *Alcestis* of Euripides hinges on such a
procedure, and in that tragedy $\dot{v}\pi\acute{e}\varrho$ alternates with the more explicit preposition
$\dot{a}v\tau\acute{\iota}$. Cf. John 10:11 and 2 Cor. 5:14. Plato and Aristotle employ the verb
$\dot{v}\pi\varepsilon\varrho\alpha\pi o\theta v\acute{\eta}\sigma\varkappa\varepsilon\iota v$ to express such an act, and the concurrent phrases $\varepsilon\dot{\iota}\varsigma$ $\dot{v}\pi\grave{e}\varrho$
$\pi\acute{a}v\tau\omega v$ (Plutarch, *Moralia* 986) and $\mu\acute{o}vo\varsigma$ $\dot{v}\pi\grave{e}\varrho$ $\pi\acute{a}v\tau\omega v$ (Plutarch, *Aratus* 19)
ratify the usage. So $\dot{v}\pi\grave{e}\varrho$ $\ddot{\omega}v$ $\ddot{\eta}\lambda\theta o\mu\varepsilon v$ $\dot{a}\pi o\theta\alpha vo\acute{v}\mu\varepsilon vo\iota$ (Plutarch, *Moralia* 236),
testified the Spartan band at Thermopylae. The preposition is used of vicarious
military service (Plutarch, *Gaius Gracchus* 6) and of hostages (Plutarch, *Demetrius* 51), and in the papyri (*cf.* Philem. 13) of signatures instead of illiterate
parties. The precise image, as Tischendorf rightly affirmed, is that of
representation.
[3] Gk. $\varepsilon\dot{\iota}\varsigma$ $\dot{o}\sigma\mu\grave{\eta}v$ $\varepsilon\dot{v}\omega\delta\acute{\iota}\alpha\varsigma$, found some forty times in the LXX Pentateuch.

attainment as our fair copy? "Ye therefore shall be perfect, as your heavenly Father is perfect" (Matt. 5:48). We know what superhuman efforts a craze for "breaking records" will elicit from the fervid soul of youth. Elihu Burritt's graphic sketch, *One Niche the Highest,* focusses in a breathless narrative this passion for reaching the summit-level of a crag. There may be a vein of selfishness in such soaring ambitions; but the sterling Christian's aim is not self-gratification. His master-motive is altruistic, love to his Redeemer and to his fellow-men. There are cross-currents; yet the bent to enthrone the usurper self is curbed in his case and the dynasty within restored to its rightful owner.

2 Let their forgiveness of wrongs be as ungrudging as their heavenly Father's of them; let it be moulded on the type of God's dealings with themselves. Thus will they prove that they are no bastards but true sons of His. For the loving-kindness the Lord has shown to us utterly eclipses any goodwill we can manifest toward our fellow-creatures. All other acts of self-abnegation pale before the dying love of the crucified Lamb of God. When He offered Himself up, the Just for the unjust, love attained its climax, its maximum. In that cross we descry a revelation of the heart of the Eternal without parallel, we behold a laying bare of the foundation of His throne sublimer than the panorama of the stellar universe, fairer than heaven's spangled causeway in all the splendour of its glistening galaxies. The duplication of the terms *offering* and *sacrifice*[4] cannot be meaningless. In the former we discover the Everliving Priest presenting His unique oblation, in the latter the oblation itself; for as John Wessel, one of the precursors of the Reformation, reminds us, Christ is Priest and Victim in one. And what a peerless Passover this snow-white Lamb, this Ransom of value measureless, unveils to our gaze! A God who stultified His own Law by connivance with lawbreakers would not be morally in earnest; but at Calvary the worst is faced and the Law not betrayed but majestically honoured. Christ does not "bring us off by some adroit management or plausible appeal to pity, but by meeting every just demand and outstanding claim *perfectly* without subterfuge" (Candlish); for "God loves sinners, but He loves the law of His own nature better still" (Forsyth). The

---

4 Gk. προσφορὰν καὶ θυσίαν. *Cf.* Ps. 40:6 (where LXX has θυσίαν καὶ προσφοράν).

co-operant grace of the Father and the Son finds expression, the One in giving His Well-beloved, the Other in charging Himself with our mountainous liabilities and defraying the sum-total. His work is perfect. Over the Lamb slain the covenant of our peace is for ever ratified. Thus amazingly forgiven talents of debt we could never discharge, how clemently it behoves us to treat our fellow-debtors who owe us a few paltry pence! Debtors to mercy must not be unmerciful to their insolvent brethren, even though their conduct gives us legitimate ground of offence.

That glorious expiation was unutterably well-pleasing to the Father of Mercies. May we not allege that this sweet-smelling holocaust, this divine antiseptic, fumigates our ill-savoured world, rising up to heaven like an aroma balmier than all the frankincense of Arabia Felix, purging the very air? But if shorn of its vicarious import, it forfeits all its infinite significance. How unworthy of divine sanction the dramatic martyrdom of modernistic thought! Viewed as a comprehensive propitiation for guilt, it towers in solitary grandeur; otherwise regarded, its sanction flouts all ethical distinctions by rewarding spotless innocence with direst obloquy and anguish for no intelligible or adequate purpose, to the glaring dishonour of moral government, outraged by the gibbeting of heaven's Darling as a malefactor, made a gazingstock and target to hellish malignity, to warn us forsooth how vilely immaculate goodness is doomed to fare! Nay, verily: the end in view must justify the tremendous avalanche of wrath and woe, or the divine administration be fatally tarnished by its permission. Eyes purged with heavenly eyesalve "see at the cross the awfulness of the lovely and the loveliness of the awful conjoined"[5] in the illustrious master-secret of the Most High. "Here the whole Deity is known."

---

[5] Wardlaw, *On the Atonement.*

II. A TRUMPET-CALL TO PURITY

Ch. 5:3-7

3 But fornication, and all uncleanness, or covetousness, let it not even be named among you, as becometh saints;

4 nor filthiness, nor foolish talking,[6] or jesting,[7] which are not befitting: but rather giving of thanks.

5 For this ye know of a surety,[8] that no fornicator, nor unclean person, nor covetous man, who is an idolator, hath any inheritance in the kingdom of Christ and God.

6 Let no man deceive you with empty words: for because of these things cometh the wrath of God upon the sons of disobedience.

7 Be not ye therefore partakers with them;

3-7 The Biblical partition of mankind is uniformly twofold. No neutral region is recognized, intermediate between day and night, in this dual analysis. The line of demarcation drawn between Christ's lieges and the unbelieving world is clear-cut and salient throughout, and their carriage must comport with their status. The *Betweenite* of formalism, that tin-soldier, Mr. Facing-both-Ways, has no place in this muster-roll of the King's troops in active service, whose discipline should challenge closest inspection. Let there be no coquetting on their part with infractions of rule, no dalliance with (1) sins of the flesh, (2) mammonism, (3) fooleries of babblement, especially drolleries verging on obscenity. These

---

6 Gk. μωρολογία, "twaddle" or "buffoonery" (Latin *stultiloquium*), the *morologi sermones* of Plautus (*Pseudolus* 5. 1).

7 Gk. εὐτραπελία, "flippant banter" (Latin *facetiae, lasciviae*), defined by Aristotle (*Rhetoric* ii. 12) as ὕβρις πεπαιδευμένη, polished wit with an element of *cheek*, the kind of chaff inspired by large potations, regardless of decorum. In Plutarch's *Moralia* (274) εὐτράπελοι are society men, good fellows. The artistic but nauseous ingredients of Plato's *Symposium* or of Xenophon's homelier companion-picture illustrate the sallies of festal licence in vogue, and the squalid indecency of Petronius's *Trimalchio* exhibits its grossest phase.

8 Gk. ἴστε γινώσκοντες. This periphrastic present (Robertson) lends emphasis to the statement: "ye are well aware." For the Attic ἴστε (whether it be indicative or imperative) Hellenistic usually substitutes οἴδατε. Cf. the Attic third person ἴσασιν in Acts 26:4; see F. Blass, *The Philology of the Gospels* (London, 1898), p. 9.

crying evils would flaunt as established conventions of society in such libertine environments as Ephesus.[9] From such vicious practices the grace of God has set them free; and it is their veriest wisdom to shun even passing fraternity with topics and scenes steeped in pernicious associations. The covetousness branded as idolatry[10] may be the cupidity indicted by the Tenth Commandment, or a spirit of envy fraught with class-hatred, or, not improbably, overreaching and exploitation in general. Madcap joviality and wassailing, the wildfire of farcicalities, or saucy sallies of persiflage, appear to be reprehended next; for a religious style of intercourse, "speech filled from heavenly urns" (Lowell), is recommended in contrast. Some profanities are kindlers of speedy judgment. Flippant *facetiae* or ribald pleasantries, garnished with blasphemous expletives, draw down vengeance sooner or later on the offender who knows better all the while. The crimson flag must never be trailed in the mire thuswise by its sworn legionaries. We have already met with the expression *sons of disobedience* (Ch. 2:3)[11] as a designation of Satan's myrmidons.

---

9   Compare the list of vices in Col. 3:5 ff. (pp. 266 ff.).

10   Gk. πλεονέκτης, ὅ ἐστιν εἰδωλολάτρης(v. 5). The noun πλεονέκτης means "money-grubber," "mammonist" (some erroneously interpret it "debauchee," because of its conjunction with lusts of the flesh); πλεονεξία represents the grabbing spirit of rapacity characteristic of the αἰσχροκερδής, while the verb πλεονεκτεῖν may comprise an element of fraud as well, like Bunyan's "Sir Having Greedy"—illicit gains due to sharp practice (*cf.* Aristotle, *Politics* 1297; Plutarch, *Moralia* 224; Lucian, *Symposium* 43; Vettius Valens 344). In Ch. 4:19 ἐν πλεονεξίᾳ seems to mean "ravenously." Lechery becomes the coveted gratification of the rakeshames there stigmatize.d See also Col. 3:5, τὴν πλεονεξίαν, ἥτις ἐστὶν εἰδωλολατρεία (p. 270, nn. 50–54).

11   *Cf.* p. 47, n. 6.

III. LIGHT VERSUS DARKNESS

Ch. 5:8–21

> 8 for ye were once darkness, but are now light in the
>   Lord: walk as children of light
> 9 (for the fruit of the light[12] is in all goodness and
>   righteousness and truth),
> 10 proving[13] what is well-pleasing unto the Lord;
> 11 and have no fellowship with the unfruitful works of
>   darkness, but rather even reprove them;

8 The practices of which he had bidden them beware were outward signs of inward benightment and wide as the poles asunder from sterling children of light.[14] Roused from their former stupor it behooves them not to drowse again within range of the enemy's forays and ambuscades. Let them reflect that once upon a time they too had been *darkness*; not merely unenlightened or ill-informed, but wrapt in a dense fog-bank of moral hallucinations, Satanically blinded therewithal and glorying in their shame. The employment of the abstract for the concrete greatly enhances the force of the contrast between their past and present; for it identifies them with their respective environments. To be ensphered in darkness is a hapless plight and that plight had been theirs. Now, however, they had quitted the realm of nightshade for an auspicious morning-land. They were basking in the orient beams of Christ's marvellous light, reflecting the rays of the uprisen Sun, the long-promised Illuminant of the Gentiles. Heretofore they had lain immured in a crypt of labyrinthine errors, till that

---

[12] The AV reading "the fruit of the Spirit" is to be rejected, although it has the signal support of P^{46}. It is probably due to the influence of Gal. 5:22 on the mind of an early scribe. "The fruit of the light" (א A B D* G P etc.) suits the context better; it forms an appropriate contrast with "the unfruitful works of darkness" in v. 11.

[13] Gk. δοκιμάζοντες, which may signify *making proof* of what is well pleasing to God (*i.e.*, by reducing it to practice), or, more probably, *approving as befitting*, the technical sense of the verb, as in Appian's phrase ἡ δοκιμασία τοῦ νόμου, "the endorsement of the law" (*Civil War* i. 10). In Lucian οὐ δοκιμάζω means "I disagree" (*Toxaris* 57; *True History* 44, 46), expressing dissent. Here *consent* is the implication upon trial.

[14] For the Pauline opposition of darkness and light, see Col. 1:12 f., with exposition and notes *ad loc.* (pp. 188 f.).

auspicious hour when the glory of the Lord arose in all effulgence upon them.[15]

9-10 Darkness, like a minus quantity, symbolizes a yawning deficiency, a destitution of the most essential element of life, the light of day. Their quondam darkness, notwithstanding all the palliatives invented to gloss over the real situation, lay under a curse and blight of sterility; but the Spirit of life by whom they have been visited vivifies all He touches and fosters in His seedlings the self-evidencing fruitage of the spiritual orchard. "What fruit had ye then", the apostle enquires in *Romans* (6:21), "in those things of which ye are now ashamed?" They concealed only black kernels of death. But "in the Lord" they are alive and astir and manifest the authentic tokens of spiritual enlightenment. Formerly night had reigned not only around but within them: and not a few could be named who had emitted streaks of pitchy darkness, miscalling the efflux illumination. Now, however, they pertained to the kingdom of light and held forth a heavenlit torch, shedding radiance both by life and lip. Solomon had employed the figure of his righteous man (Prov. 4:16), whose roseate daybreak culminates in the full blaze of noon. For God's law written in the heart will be written out in the everyday living as well. "In the Lord" they are reflectors of a flood of gospel luminosity, itself germinant with growths of righteousness, its authentication and outcome. The "fruit of the light" is the correct reading here. *Goodness* expresses unalloyed benignity, kindly disposed to all men, especially drawn to the household of faith. Without the accompaniment of *righteousness,* however, that goodness would lack character and degenerate into flabbiness. The Spirit of rectitude or sanctification of the conscience (Findlay) upholds principles and appeals to ethical standards and exalts the claims of duty and fair-dealing. We take *truth* to be opposed to hypocrisy, which constitutes mendacity towards God and duplicity towards men. The new creature will ring true and breathe an atmosphere of sincerity.

11 But light has no fellowship with darkness, and walkers in darkness have no fellowship with the Father (1 John 1:6). Its very ingress ousts that interloper. Every morning the resistless inroad

---

[15] With the injunction "walk as children of light" *cf.* John 8:12; 12:35; 1 John 1:6 f.

of the dawn arouses a dormant world and summons the labourer
to his task. During the watches of the night slumber has held
the population captive, but it wanes with the resurgence of day.
So the "sons of the morning" are wakened by the advent of the
Light of the world. Their envelope of darkness is put to flight
and decamps forthwith. Light requires no testification of its
potency; it diffuses reality without respect of persons and exposes
the works of darkness in their true nigritude. Not only must
believers not lend them countenance or partake of other men's sins
by a conspiracy of silence, but, when occasion serves, it is theirs
to drag them to light. Does a book or play enlarge one's theory
of evil? Have naught to do with it for your own sake and denounce
the pest for the sake of others; for in our plague-stricken planet
inspectors of nuisances are indispensable. Only do not thrust
yourself into the post without due warrant!

12 for the things which are done by them in secret it is
a shame even to speak of.

13 But all things when they are reproved are made
manifest by the light: for everything that is made
manifest[16] is light.

14 Wherefore he saith,[17] Awake, thou that sleepest, and
arise from the dead, and Christ shall shine[18] upon
thee.

12–14 A distinction seems to be drawn between two discrepant
classes of transgressions. Some are too foul to be mentioned by
sanctified lips. These ranker abominations, like rotting carcases,
ought to be buried out of sight. But iniquities of a less heinous
cast, compatible with a conscience not utterly seared, should be
rebuked by shedding the light of heaven on their obliquity. Light
lays bare its counterpole deformity in the very process of diffusion,

---

16 Gk. φανερούμενον, following φανεροῦται in the foregoing clause. We seem
to be constrained to understand the repetition of the verb in the same verse as
proof that it carries a single sense in both instances. But it seems possible that
that sense should be middle, not passive, and that the rendering in both places
should be "manifests itself"—this being the very nature of light, conformably
to modern theories of undulations of a luminiferous ether.

17 Gk. διὸ λέγει (cf. Ch. 4:8. with n. 13 on p. 91).

18 Gk. ἐπιφαύσει, future of ἐπιφαύσκειν, a verb otherwise found only in
LXX. Another compound, διαφαύσκειν, occurs rarely elsewhere. It was no
doubt the unfamiliarity of the verb that gave rise to the variant readings
ἐπιφαύσει σου ὁ χριστός ("Christ shall touch thee") and ἐπιφαύσεις τοῦ χριστοῦ
("thou shalt touch Christ").

robed in a beauty all its own. Its property is to act as a revelation, like the word of life its gleam symbolizes and mirrors. There are rakeshames whose hearts are set in them to do evil best shunned with abhorrence as incurable moral lepers; but others by no means so besotted may be met with, not insusceptible of enlightenment, sinners who may yet prove the raw material of saints. They are not impervious to admonition nor reprobates hardened against the entrance of the light, nor unaware of their myopic condition. To them its shimmer comes revealingly as an illuminant unmasking their malady in its true colours. They rank among those who shake off their lethargy, who "come to the light" (John 3:20) without ranklings of repugnance. Their case is hopeful: for "to know ourselves diseased (and own it) is half our cure" (Young).[19] What is thus "made manifest is light", not because darkness in their case changes its nature, but because, convinced of their moral night, wistful yearnings are stirred within them for better things. To them we judge the summons to be addressed: "Awake, thou that sleepest and Christ shall beam forth on thee!" an inspired version apparently of the tenor of more than one direction of the Old Testament.[20] They are in the track of day, emerging from the catacomb of "sin's dark sepulchre", and pursuing that path with faces turned towards the light, the Sun of Righteousness will rise upon them with healing in His wings; for that Light of Light is already up and the darkness recoiling and vanishing away (1 John 2:8). But it may be viewed as a clarion call to spiritual somnambulists in general, challenging them to resuscitation from the bed of sloth. *Cf.* the parable of the Virgins, *all* of whom slumbered and slept (Matt. 25:5), lapped as in a leaden trance. We accept accordingly the modern rendering of this somewhat abstruse passage. The older hermeneutic labours under the objection that it shifts the voice of the reiterated verb from a passive to an active meaning in the selfsame sentence, a most unlikely procedure. Whatever is exposed to the brilliance of the lamp of day is rendered visible in terms of light, which, like the chromatic scale, has an unmasking quality, constituting a touchstone of reality or decep-

---

[19] *Night Thoughts.*
[20] The wording may well be that of a primitive Christian baptismal hymn (cf. the early description of baptism as φωτισμός, "enlightenment"); the very rhythm of the three *stichoi* is of a type associated in the Greek memory with religious initiation.

tion. The presence of the Light of the World stripped the blind leaders of the blind in Judaea of their cloaks of darkness; but it did not of necessity recast their moral horizon. The detection of his guilt does not ensure a criminal's reformation. Plato's sanguine theory that the root of evil is ignorance and education its panacea has been tried scores of times and found grievously inefficient. Darkness may be innate as well as circumambient, and haters of the light like the Pharisees bitterly resent its exposure of their rogueries. Benightment may be chased from its lairs successfully by the daydawn; but a work of grace alone can make opaque bodies translucent or irresponsive ones impressibly sensitive. Visibility and vision differ as much as audibility and a musical ear.

15 Look therefore carefully how ye walk, not as unwise, but as wise;
16 redeeming the time, because the days are evil.
17 Wherefore be ye not foolish, but understand what the will of the Lord is.

15–17 The seriousness of the times in which they were living laid on these disciples a peculiar obligation to watch their steps. To-day God's people stand in similar case; for levity and trifling, at all times unbecoming, acquire an especial degree of impropriety in seasons of upheaval and insecurity. It is recorded of that noted Puritan, Col. Hutchinson, that as he foresaw the approach of the Civil War, he deliberately gave up most of the sports and diversions in which he has previously indulged, as mistimed and no longer in place. In somewhat of the same frame of mind Paul bids his readers walk warily[21] not only in view of the brevity of life here below, but of the precarious conditions environing them. A traveller crossing a tract of boggy or broken ground or traversing a corduroy road must be on the *qui vive*. He cannot afford to neglect the path of his feet as one pacing an even surface may do; he must pick his way. The train of thought recalls the language of 1 Cor. 7:30, 31, prefaced by the warning, "the time is short." If a veneer of gaiety and *insouciance* characterizes the bubble-chasers of fashionable life, stigmatized by Samuel Johnson as "an assembly

---

21 Gk. πῶς ἀκριβῶς περιπατεῖτε. We prefer this order, which has uncial support (ℵ A D G), to the transposition ἀκριβῶς πῶς (P46 ℵ * B 33 etc.), which makes ἀκριβῶς less forcibly qualify βλέπετε, itself fully expressive of meaning. It is the walk that demands exactitude.

of beings counterfeiting a happiness they do not feel," the Christian who possesses its authentic secret needs not any such artificial stimulus to give a fillip to his jaded spirits. To Christ's lieges pertains the high vocation of bearing witness to His holy name in this misguided world. They are to *market* the time allotted them,[22] to turn it to good account like the faithful servants in the parable of the Talents. Opportunities are ever on the wing: they must be seized and husbanded or else spurned and missed, for as a rule they do not recur. Paul counsels them to buy them up with sanctified ingenuity, even as shrewd hands purchase properties at a favorable juncture, or as the intelligent husbandman improves the fleeting hour. Time may be gained as well as lost. Too many dawdlers "let the years slip through their fingers like water" to no worthy purpose. He himself was an exemplary steward of his crowded span of activity. Good works are not the price of God's favour, but they are its mint-mark, and spiritual indolence a sign of light weight. The sundial mottos: *Now or when?* and *Begone about your business* are well fitted to rouse thumb-twiddlers from their torpidity. One trader prospers by wide-awake sagacity, another loses by want of enterprise or observation of the trend of the market. They are to take pains to apprehend their Lord's will and act accordingly. "A man's situation", says Burke, "is the preceptor of his duty"; and in a higher sphere the signals of providence are to be read with enlightened judgment. But duty itself is not optional, nor has the imperative mood properly any future tense. Calamity was manifestly in the air; but by prompt and watchful compliance with their heavenly Instructor they might face the day of visitation valiantly.

> "To-morrow I will live," the slothful cry;
> In what far country doth this morrow lie?[23]

18 And be not drunken with wine, wherein is riot, but be filled with the Spirit,

19 speaking one to another in psalms and hymns and

---

[22] Gk. ἐξαγοραζόμενοι τὸν καιρόν. We deem the rendering now in vogue, "buying back," less commendable than "buying up" or, in Burke's phrase, "making a market of"—that is, taking advantage of opportunities. The metaphor of buying back present time is utterly nebulous; but the redemption of it in a wider sense is most suitable and a familiar figure. Plutarch repeatedly employs the phrase ὠνεῖσθαι τὸν καιρόν (*Sertorius* 6), and κερδαντέον τὸ παρόν is an adage of Marcus Aurelius (iv. 26). *Cf.* Col. 4:5 (p. 299, with nn. 12 and 13).

[23] Cowley's translation of an epigram of Martial (v. 58).

spiritual songs, singing and making melody with your heart to the Lord;

18 The sunny clime of Asiatic Greece, prolific in the fruit of the vine, fostered the mercurial temper of its denizens, susceptible to instincts of sociability and more addicted to carousal and jollification, often interlinked with heathen festivals, than regions less luxuriant and inured to scantier fare. Excessive indulgence in wine had hastened the death of Alexander the Great himself. The term rendered riot[24] primarily denotes *wastefulness*: but as used elsewhere (*e.g.* in the parable of the Prodigal Son) connotes profligacy in general with all its vicious concomitants. In contrast to these miscarriages, to which their environment tended to render them liable, the apostle paints the picture of a Pentecostal infilling of the Holy Spirit, not less mirthful than any carnal indulgence, but infinitely purer and as salutary as the other was noxious.

19 At first sight this juxtaposition seems a trifle incongruous; but on maturer reflection we remember how the disciples on the day of Pentecost were charged with drunkenness, albeit groundlessly. Signal manifestations of the Spirit in seasons of revival have not seldom been accompanied by phenomena easily confounded with physical intoxication; and scenes of this description Paul had doubtless witnessed. The "gift of tongues" itself had features that might be stigmatized as delirium (1 Cor. 14:23). Are they in quest of sober enlivenment? Let them seek a baptism from on high, an ecstasy charged with divine exhilaration, a heaven-born rapture to which the lookers-on might be utter strangers. Let their fervour find vent, not in bacchanalian ditties, but in the songs of Zion fraught with far loftier sentiments; let their exultation of soul give birth to thanksgivings and the voice of melody couched in the language of the Hebrew Psalter, or in canticles and lyrics resonant with spiritual joy.[25] At the Reformation sacred songs

---

[24] Gk. ἀσωτία, properly "prodigality," but in a moral sense "profligacy" or "recklessness" spurning restraint; in our version "riot" in the Miltonic sense of the term for the tipsy revelry of wastrels.

[25] Gk. ψαλμοῖς καὶ ὕμνοις καὶ ᾠδαῖς πνευματικαῖς. These designations of sacred song differ but little from one another. The first title suggests the Davidic Psalter, the second effusions of praise, the third lyrics of a general description, confined only by the epithet πνευματικαῖς (omitted by P[46] and B) to a devotional sphere. Trench (*NT Synonyms*) has elaborated the lines of distinction perhaps beyond warrant, in view of Pauline usage in such amplifications. *Cf.* Col. 3:16, with exposition and notes *ad loc.* (pp. 283 ff.).

supplanted godless ballads on every hand.[26]

> 20 giving thanks always for all things in the name of
> our Lord Jesus Christ to God, even the Father;[27]
> 21 subjecting yourselves[28] one to another in the fear of
> Christ.

20 Two precepts, cognate respectively with the first and second tables of the moral law, are here stressed. The obligation of thankfulness to God for "mercies countless as the sands" holds the premier place. That we exist depends on the Creator's fiat, and that our days are passed in comparative tranquillity or within the verge of divine illumination we owe to His lovingkindness. All our positive blessings are of His bestowal. Our very deprivations and trials, frowning providences, as we deem them, if we are His by grace as well as nature, come to us as benedictions in disguise. Were we in full accord with His will we should receive them as such, like Job at the high-water mark of his faith. The Lord's sovereign dispensations are matter for gratitude, not for murmuring.

> Trials must and will befall;
> But with humble faith to see
> Love inscribed upon them all,
> *That* is happiness to me.

The mixed yarn of life, woven in the loom of heaven by the Father of mercies, traces a perfect design for those "in Christ," and their thanksgivings should reascend to Him through their mediatorial All-in-all.

21 Such a frame of heart, penetrated with a sense of indebted-

---

[26] Like *The Gude and Godlie Ballatis* which accompanied the Scottish Reformation.

[27] *Cf.* Col. 3:17 (pp. 285 f.).

[28] Gk. ὑποτασσόμενοι. It remains uncertain whether we are to regard this as a participle in agreement with πληροῦσθε or a "hanging participle", of which examples occur in Greek literature, or, as Moulton argues, with appeal to the papyri, a participle substituted for an imperative, not unexampled in NT (*cf.* p. 280, n. 99). The reader may be referred to Moulton's *Prolegomena*, p. 222, for a discussion on participial usage and to A. T. Robertson, *Grammar of the Greek New Testament*, p. 945, with reference to this passsage. It is clear that the verb must be understood in some form or other in v. 22. Regularity of grammatical construction is in rare instances transgressed by literary as well as popular writers from Thucydides downwards through a "lost construction" or one intentionally suspended in an obvious context.

ness, will not repudiate the claims of others on its service; for its self-seeking has been displaced by a nobler affection. The keynote is changed from insistence on *our* rights to a recognition of those of others. That principle implies subordination to all lawful authority, religious or secular, "in the fear of Christ," with a conscious regard to His authoritative behests. Even secular acts are to be performed from sacred motives, and the Lord to be served in one and all. The old reading, *in the fear of God,* has very weak support.

IV. RELATIVE DUTIES

Chs. 5:22–6:9

1. THE NUPTIAL BOND: ITS SANCTITY AS A TYPE

Ch. 5:22–33

22 Wives, *be in subjection*[29] unto your own husbands, as unto the Lord.
23 For the husband is the head of the wife, as Christ also is the head of the church, *being* himself the saviour of the body.
24 But as the church is subject to Christ, so *let* the wives also *be* to their husbands in everything.

22–23 The injunction of a spirit studious to serve others leads Paul to deal (as in Colossians more succinctly)[30] with the topic of relative duties pertaining to the family and household, the basal unit of society and its essential nucleus. Without a doubt, if order be "heaven's first law," Satan's pet policy is the promotion of all manner of license, with "confusion worse confounded" as its woeful epilogue. But Christianity abominates the firebrand of creation for his world-wide incitation of disorder, ruin and ravage. It enjoins on the other hand the dutiful observance of the ties of kinship or subservience recognized by the law of nature itself as of cogent validity. Among the most sacred of these bonds of human society is the tie of marriage. The family is the primordial cell of the body politic, closely interlinked with the welfare of the species; and to tamper with it brings disaster to the state dissolute enough to sanction its desecration. Those who are busy undermining the chastity of wedlock to-day are the worst enemies of the commonweal. Its inviolability is not a question to be settled on grounds of expediency. The corner-stone of society is at stake in the matter. Zolaism in fiction or on the stage ought to be hooted out of the community as an anti-social pest.

---

[29] The verb has to be supplied from v. 21. The bulk of later manuscripts actually supply it, either in the second person ὑποτάσσεσθε or in the third person ὑοπτασσέσθωσαν. See p. 287, with n. 128.

[30] Col. 3:18 ff. (see pp. 287 ff.). In both epistles the code of household duties is subsumed under the catechetical heading "Be subject."

24 The apostle enhances the dignity of this relic of Eden by likening it to the believer's relationship with his Lord. It is no fanciful comparison that he institutes; for the type was ordained to adumbrate the antitype. Christ has chosen a mystical bride, to whom He performs the part of Bridegroom; and the loftiest aspect in which an earthly nuptial can be viewed consists in the analogy it bears to the heavenly affinity. The loyal wife's subordination to her husband founds itself in part on her physical constitution; but the Christian spouse discerns therein a similitude of her union with the Kinsman-Redeemer of His people. For conscience' sake she will comply with all lawful requisitions of her human head, pledged to minister to her preservation and well-being. As they keep tryst with one another, so will the Founder of marriage with them. Let her exhibit in the home circle those queenly virtues so much more potent and precious in many respects than the kinglier prerogatives of the legislature or office or bench. The ambitiously masculine woman has the reward, such as it is, of her *tour de force,* but it often proves an apple of Sodom to her sated palate in the long run.

The husband's love towards his bride is measured by a superlative standard of self-sacrifice when it is likened to that of Christ for His church. The voluntary election of the lover and its implications chiefly point the comparison; for in expanding his similitude, as we shall see, the apostle shows how far this love of Jesus transcends conjugal affection at its summit-level.[31]

25　Husbands, love your wives, even as Christ also loved the church, and gave himself up for it;

26　that he might sanctify it, having cleansed it by the washing of water with the word,

27　that he might present the church to himself a glorious *church,*[32] not having spot or wrinkle or any such thing; but that it should be holy and without blemish.

28　Even so ought husbands also to love their own wives

---

[31]　The hierarchical order of creation, in which "the head of the woman is the man" (1 Cor. 11:3), is carried farther here, for the husband's headship in relation to the wife is viewed as a reflection of Christ's archetypal headship in relation to the church—a theme developed in the earlier part of this epistle. *Cf.* exposition and notes on Col. 3:18 (pp. 289 f.).

[32]　Gk. ἵνα παραστήσῃ . . . ἔνδοξον τὴν ἐκκλησίαν. Note the predicative adjective exterior to the article, precisely similar to Plutarch's τὴν ʽΡώμην ἐνδοξοτέραν ἀπέλιπε (*Pyrrhus* 19). We might render "present the church in her glory."

as their own bodies. He that loveth his own wife loveth himself;

29 for no man ever hated his own flesh; but nourisheth and cherisheth it, even as Christ also the church;

30 because we are members of his body.

31 For this cause shall a man leave his father and mother, and shall cleave to his wife; and the two shall became one flesh.[33]

32 This mystery is great: but I speak in regard of Christ and of the church.

33 Nevertheless do ye also severally love each one his own wife even as himself; and *let* the wife *see* that she fear her husband.[34]

25-33 This marvellous analogy, like the paean which closes the third chapter, defies exhaustive analysis. It is impossible to partition its intricate fabric into segments. The earthly and heavenly bridal are inextricably blended. All we can do is to gather up its pregnant instruction under four outstanding heads.

1. *Dominion.* We must banish all thoughts of an overbearing sway or cringing subservience; for a passion of mutual love glows in the bosoms of the ideal Bridegroom and His ideal bride. There is in fact a measure of equality between the human contracting parties, attempered by a measure of precedence. The true wife's compliance with the will of her spouse rests partly, as we said, on her physical build and consent to be his helpmeet; but the Christian wife perceives in it a verisimilitude of the grander union with her Divine Lord who has chosen her for His own. She will therefore submit, not merely by reason of terms of stipulation, but lovingly, to the behests of her human head, himself bound up with her well-being by the most intimate of earthly bonds, cemented by their joint approval. They are pledged to reciprocal conservation and cherishment, even as the Saviour to the weal of His people. Keeping tryst with one another and fulfilling the law of their conjunction, they will blend in happy unison. The husband bears rule, but his is no capricious or exacting priority. His lordship is

---

[33] Quoted from Gen. 2:24 (*cf.* Mark 10:7 f., for our Lord's application of the passage). In some patristic citations the clause "and shall cleave to his wife" is omitted—an omission probably due in the first instance to Marcion.

[34] Gk. ἡ δὲ γυνὴ ἵνα φοβῆται τὸν ἄνδρα. This construction may be viewed as a syncopated imperative, akin to Mark 5:23, but (judging by 1 Cor. 16:10) βλεπέτω is to be understood, governing ἵνα in its qualified sense.

not arbitrary but constitutional, and her deference not constrained, but spontaneously yielded.

2. *Devotion.* Another characteristic of marital love here brought to our notice is the devotion it inspires to its chosen object. Wondrous have been the exhibitions of self-sacrifice, even in the human sphere, that the spirit of deep affection has elicited; its transactions of disbursement and receipt make us marvel. Love speedily outstrips law in the race of achievement. Constancy and self-abandonment ennoble her feats of arms. Who would wish to tarnish her escutcheon by disparaging these trophies of love's power? Paul is careful to differentiate wedded love from that of kindred; for a man will forsake father and mother that he may cleave to a wife, and forfeit life unquailingly for her dear sake. Philip Bliss lost his, we remember, in a heroic effort to save his beloved partner from peril of drowning consequent upon a railroad catastrophe at Ashtabula.

But the apostle exalts the love of Christ, as well he may, far above the human image of its dominance. That pales in presence of the more illustrious passion of Christ crucified, lit up with a radiance all its own. Such unspeakable self-devotion has no parallel elsewhere. Every renewed heart can exclaim ecstatically, not without a thrill of holy awe, "He hath set His love upon me, I cannot tell why"; "I was the flax and He the flame of fire; so I am my Beloved's: He is mine" (Quarles). The ransomed of the Lord owe their very salvation to their Bridegroom. He has cleansed them by the washing of regeneration with the word (v. 26). The reference is obviously to the Spirit's own cleansing[35] by virtue of

---

[35] Gk. τῷ λουτρῷ τοῦ ὕδατος ἐν ῥήματι. As advocates of baptismal regeneration persistently translate λουτρόν here and in Tit. 3:5 as "laver," it is needful to remark that ὁ λουτήρ, not τὸ λουτρόν, is the LXX vocable for the laver of Judaism, and that λουτρόν, both in Attic and Hellenistic Greek, as often signifies the act of washing as the vessel or locality of ablution. The terms ἄλειμμα and λουτρόν are conjoined, e.g., in Plutarch (*Alexander* 40) and in inscriptions. Elsewhere we have elaborated this point at length (*cf.* E. K. Simpson, *The Pastoral Epistles*, pp. 114 f.) and furnished plentiful examples, ranging from Sophocles (*Oedipus at Colonus* 1599, 1602) to Lucian (*On Mourning* 11; *The Ass* 20). Purifications were prerequisite for an Eastern bridal (Esth. 2:12), and "water and the Spirit" are the standing emblems of purgation (Ezek. 36:25-27; John 3:5). The phrase "in (or by) the word" is difficult; but Chrysostom's identification of the terms with the baptismal formula savours of the sacerdotalism of his age. In Ch. 6:17 ῥῆμα θεοῦ means "God's word"; and John 17:17 ("sanctify them in the truth: thy word is truth") conveys the same

the pellucid stream of divine purification. The word read or spoken or preached constitutes the instrument of purgation. "Ye are clean because of the word which I have spoken unto you" (John 15:3). Many curious meanings have been foisted upon this sentence. Upholders of baptismal regeneration, for instance, discover the Trinitarian formula in the term *word* and the baptismal font in the *washing*, with equally slight warrant.[36] Baptism proclaims need of purgation, but cannot furnish what it requires. Outward water cannot convey inward life.[37]

The Lord's chosen are His both by purchase and possession. When Margaret Wilson suffered martyrdom for befriending a hunted Covenanter her last utterance was: "I am one of Christ's children: let me go." The call of her Beloved drew her out of time into eternity. Here then is a ligature that swallows up death itself in victory, binding faster than the closest human ties can conjoin.

For Christ's love to His elect passes knowledge; its depths are beyond the plumblines of created intelligences, its flame self-fed, self-kindled, aglow with an incandescence that many waters could not quench; a purpose to redeem which nothing could divert from its resolve, nor any obstacle, however tremendous, deter from achieving it once for all. The king of terrors, armed with his fellest sting, had no power to withhold this unblenching Lover from standing proxy for the bride of His choice. What an amazing spectacle this, of Life essential plunging into a dread abyss of dereliction that His bride might partake with Him of everlasting bliss and joy! Is He not the mirror of chivalry no less than of devotion? No human suitor has ever loved, or ever will, on such a scale as that.

3. *Design.* We cannot enlarge on the *Design* of this matchless self-abasement; how the Lord Jesus has formed His people for Himself, the fruit of His travail rendered an object of eternal complacency in His eyes by sanctifying grace, a baseborn folk made gloriously pure and spotless by His sleepless watchfulness, to be presented to Himself, when their fashioning season is over-passed, clad in a strangely radiant investiture of immortal loveli-

---

line of thought. *Cf.* also John 15:3; Ps. 119:8; Zech. 13:1. *In Christi morte habemus et λύτρον et λουτρόν,* says Turrettine, mindful of the variation of reading in Rev. 1:5.

[36] *Cf.* J. A. Robinson, *Commentary, ad loc.* (pp. 205 ff.).
[37] S. Charnock, *Works* II, 75 (*Nature of Regeneration*).

ness. When their corruption has put on incorruption, they shall
shine forth in His likeness; for the clothing of the bride imparadised
is to be of wrought gold and she is made one spirit with her Lord,
even as the ideal wife fuses her nature with her husband's and
finds in him her rounded whole and complement.

4. *Derivation.* Here we come face to face with the marvel of
the *mystical union.* "Because the children are sharers in flesh and
blood, He also Himself partook of the same" (Heb. 2:14). It is
not, as many would have it, a sequel attendant on the incarnation;
for then it would extend to all mankind; much less is it mediated
through the hocus-pocus of the mass. Believers are members of
His body by participation in the same quickening Spirit that
indwelt Christ's human nature. The inmost secret of redeeming
love discloses itself in this conjunction. Thus the confluence of
two lives in holy matrimony typifies a sublimer relation than its
own, the union of the Song of Songs, a betrothal inward, reciprocal,
everlasting.

By way of illustration of this heavenly espousal Paul adverts to
the moulding of Eve at the first, educed from her sleeping spouse's
side, and in that respect more intimately incorporated with him
than any other consort on record, and elicits from it an emblem
of the church, taken in a spiritual acceptation out of the Redeemer's
wounded side. The additional clause of the quotation, omitted in
modern recensions of the text out of deference to certain somewhat
overprized uncials, has strong MSS. support and seems to us
unlikely to have been inserted by copyists without warrant.[38] It
delineates with a realism no other phraseology could equal the
inwardness of the union of the Lord and His people, and accords
with the previous declaration that he who loves his wife loves
himself and that none hate their own flesh. Of course abnormal
cases, such as that of the Gadarene demoniac or self-torturing
fakir, do not count in a broad survey of normal human nature.[39]
Moreover the corollary drawn that the nuptial pair are no longer

---

[38] The words ἐκ τῆς σαρκὸς αὐτοῦ καὶ ἐκ τῶν ὀστέων αὐτοῦ are absent
from P^{46}ℵ* A B and other early authorities; they are present in ℵ^c D G and
the bulk of later authorities. They echo the words of Adam in Gen. 2:23 ("This
is now bone of my bones, and flesh of my flesh"); *cf.* the immediately following
quotation from Gen. 2:24 in v. 31.
[39] Compare the Latin phrase *curare carnem.* The sentiment of care for the
body is a favourite classical image (*cf.* Xenophon, *Memorabilia* i. 2; Seneca,
Epistles i. 14).

twain, but virtually unified, husband and wife but one humanity, appears to match with the enlarged reading. A solidarity of accord and coalescence out-weighing even the filial tie renders them not plural but *dual,* interknit without absorption in one another. So Christ having loved His affianced partner with undying affection, loves her to the end, till her assimilation to her illustrious Paragon grows into a speaking likeness.

Note how pointedly this organ of inspiration ratifies the historicity, so widely discounted, of the Biblical narrative concerning the origination of mankind, regarding it not only as authoritative but decisive of the type of conjugal society ordained thence-forward. The progenitors of "all living" ensphere all their posterity as the circumambient globe their physical habitat. Consanguinity determines to a large extent the shape of their moral government. What is a *species?* The American scientist Dana defined it as "an enlargement of the individual, the repetition of the type-idea." If so, we need not wonder that pristine divine ordinations control the ensuing stages of development as the preordained first term of a concatenated series.

CHAPTER VI

2. THE PARENTAL BOND

Ch. 6:1–4

1 Children, obey your parents in the Lord:[1] for this is right.

2 Honor thy father and mother (which is the first commandment with promise),

3 that it may be well with thee, and that thou mayest live long on the earth.

4 And, ye fathers, provoke not your children to wrath; but nurture them in the chastening and admonition[2] of the Lord.

1–3 Our apostle is now setting the most salient earthly relationships in a heavenly framework. He has just exalted marriage to the celestial domain; now he uplifts filial obedience to the same altitude by the adjuration "in the Lord."[3] Chrysostom understands his language to signify the earliest announced injunction; but Paul is evidently rehearsing the Fifth Commandment of the decalogue. Filial piety has won high eulogy from the bulk of pagan moralists and oftentimes proved a stepping-stone to nobility of character. If a rebellious temper ferments where nature itself dictates gratitude and attachment it augurs ill for the life thus sullenly overclouded at the outset. Offspring are sadly deficient in natural affection who act impatiently or callously towards those that gave them birth. Any child of right feeling would be concerned to hide rather than disclose a parent's infirmities, hesitate to cross even their prejudices, and indignantly resent any unjust aspersion cast upon their name. How many a sacrifice fathers and mothers

---

[1] Gk. ἐν κυρίῳ, omitted by B D G and some patristic citations.

[2] Gk. ἐν παιδείᾳ καὶ νουθεσίᾳ. Trench deals with these words (*NT Synonyms*, § 32). He regards νουθεσία as expressive of verbal admonishment; but it may include castigation as a practical mode of reproof. The process is disciplinary. Plato compares τὸ νουθετητικὸν τῆς παιδείας (*Sophist* 230) to the physician's prescription of deobstruants before he permits liberty of diet. *Cf.* νουθετεῖν in Josephus (*War* ii. 21), and the use of ἀνουθέτητος (Menander, *Gnomai* 49; Plutarch, *Moralia* 283) in reference to one who will not take warning in any shape.

[3] *Cf.* p. 290, n. 139 (on Col. 3:18).

have made on their behalf! Surely a sense of indebtedness of itself enjoins that we should requite the loving care of our parents by every means in our power. The voice of nature in this connexion coincides with the revealed will of God; it is invested therefore with the highest of all sanctions, and coupled with a promise of longevity fulfilled in many Scriptural and profane biographies, perhaps even nationally, as Dr. Pierson argues, in the perpetuation of the Chinese people through two changeful millenniums. Observe that the new dispensation does not abrogate the moral law, but enhances its dignity, and that the mother's authority obtains a place side by side with the father's in this realm of her special supervision. Both the parental relationship and the filial can only be safeguarded by recognizing them as divine appointments. The Christian child in particular is born into the household of faith and in a special relationship to the covenant promises. In any case their responsibility for the little one's welfare gives to the commands and prohibitions of fathers and mothers a weight attaching to no other human authority.

4 The father as the paterfamilias is singled out by the apostle for admonition.[4] His sway must comprise a positive and negative element, a blend of firmness with gentle treatment. The child must be taught the lesson of obedience betimes, if it is ever to become fit to bear rule itself. Susannah Wesley makes the subjugation of a child's will the first element in its training. But that delicate operation must not be performed in such a fashion as to exasperate the building consciousness of free agency and engender a rebellious temper. "Whipping the offending Adam out" of the juvenile scapegrace may conceivably be requisite, but only as a last resort. Even then it may cow but not cure the delinquent's malapert spirit. But too many parents nowadays foster the latent mischief by a policy of *laissez faire*, pampering their pert urchins like pet monkeys whose escapades furnish a fund of amusement as irresponsible freaks of no serious import. Such unbridled young scamps, for lack of correction, develop too often into headstrong, peevish, self-seeking characters, menaces to the community where they dwell, and the blame rests with their supine and duty-shirking seniors. The revolutionary Thelwall told Coleridge that he thought

---

[4] See, however, p. 291, n. 147 (on Col. 3:21), for πατέρες in the more general sense of "parents."

it very unfair to give a child's mind a certain bent before it could choose for itself. "I showed him my garden," says Coleridge, "covered with weeds, describing it as a *botanical* garden." How so? he asked. I replied that it "had not yet come to years of discretion. True, the weeds had taken the mean advantage of growing *ad libitum*; but I could not be so unfair as to prejudice the soil in favour of roses and strawberries." There must be either discipline and control or invertebracy and chaos, either Abraham's seeds or Eli's weeds in embryo, vegetant for good or ill.

Christ set His broad seal on parental claims when he censured the Pharisees' hypocritical cant in evasion of them; and yet more impressively by His own example in submitting without a jot or tittle of impatience to the yoke of Joseph and Mary at Nazareth. Studied disrespect and pretence of superior enlightenment on the part of young people in the home are at once offences against the divine law and prognostics of evil omen to the body politic. Religious households constitute the nurseries of freedom and social tractability.[5]

---

[5] *Cf.* pp. 290 ff. (on Col. 3:20 ff.).

137

3. THE DIGNITY OF SERVICE

5 Servants, be obedient unto them that according to the flesh are your masters, with fear and trembling, in singleness of your heart, as unto Christ;

6 not in the way of eyeservice, as men-pleasers;[6] but as servants of Christ, doing the will of God from the heart;

7 with good will doing service, as unto the Lord, and not unto men:

8 knowing that whatsoever good thing each one doeth, the same shall he receive again from the Lord, whether *he be* bond or free.

9 And, ye masters, do the same things unto them, and forbear threatening: knowing that he who is both their Master and yours is in heaven, and there is no respect of persons[7] with him.

5-8 As in the Colossian epistle,[8] Paul's searching glance rests not only on the children of the church, but on the slave, of whom so few took account. True, there were sundry grades of servitude in the ancient world, not all alike in degradation. The Greek slave for the most part was more humanely treated than the Roman and mainly regarded as a source of revenue to his master. The New Comedy moreover assigns noteworthy licence of speech to household slaves. Brutality of handling embittered the lot of the Roman serf more keenly, abjectly at his master's mercy or worn to death in forced labour on the public lands. In some cases, however, the yoke of bondage was distinctly lighter than in others,

---

[6] Gk. μὴ κατ' ὀφθαλμοδουλείαν ὡς ἀνθρωπάρεσκοι. These compounds are unique, except that they occur in the parallel passage Col. 3:22 (*cf.* p. 294 with n. 156), while the latter is found also in LXX (Ps. 52:6). Ignatius (*Epistle to the Romans* 2:1) coins the verbal form ἀνθρωπαρεσκῆσαι.

[7] Gk. προσωπολημψία. None can deny that this vocable presents a typical sample of Hebraistic Greek, the lifting up of the face upon a person unwarrantably, in a perverse manner. It stands to reason that this obliquity pertains to the sphere of judicial awards, not to the free bestowal of favours which the recipient has not strictly merited. *Cf.* Col 3:25 (p. 295 with n. 164).

[8] *Cf.* pp. 293 ff.

pressing least of all on the privileged class of "hired servants," with bread enough and to spare (Luke 15:17). A dawning sense of cosmopolitanism was in a measure modifying Aristotle's famous definition of the slave as a "living tool" or chattel[9] (*Nicomachean Ethics* 8.11) and leading philosophical minds, with Seneca, to talk grandiloquently of equality of souls. But practice by no means corresponded with that purely theoretical assumption. It was left for Christianity to soften the fate of these downtrodden beings, possessed of no substantial rights as against the free citizens for whom they toiled so incessantly. To bondservants of this description the apostle's exhortation is addressed; but it embodies principles applicable to all posts of subordination. Three constituent elements of Christian service, humility, honesty and heartiness, are set in strong relief. The aspirant to the gold-medal of service should dismiss every vestige of self-assertion and obey his earthly master with scrupulous submissiveness as one serving Christ. The "fear and trembling" specified[10] cannot mean fawning servility, for Paul uses the same phraseology elsewhere (1 Cor. 2:3) of his own ministry and of the welcome given by the Corinthian church to Titus (2 Cor. 7:15). It suggests meekness and diffidence no doubt, in contrast with the self-assurance that clamours for all it can possibly get. Drudgery becomes "divine" when rendered ungrudgingly and with honest goodwill; for conscientious service disarms even severity of its frown. The treadmill of menial employment ceases to be bitterly irksome, moreover, when trodden in obedience to the will of the sovereign Employer whose rewards are priceless and inviolably guaranteed. Let them imbibe the mind of Christ Himself. Jesus has served in the ranks of duteous obedience without a trace of impatience or repining. Singleness of aim, the polar opposite of duplicity, should betoken His disciples. They will not stint themselves to the minimum of performance that will pass muster; their motto must be *thorough*. Evasion of displacent jobs will be at times their temptation; but they will scorn eye-service to man, when they feel conscious that they are

---

9   See p. 276.
10   Gk. μετὰ φόβου καὶ τρόμου. From Paul's use of this phrase elsewhere concerning his own ministry we infer that it had acquired a softened meaning by usage, like many phrases in English. "All in a tremble," "with a vengeance," "head foremost"—these are vigorous tropes not to be literally construed. So we talk of "rising to speak *with trepidation*," when *diffidence* only is signified.

working under their heavenly Master's eye and striving to please Him, solicitous most of all that their labours should bear inspection from the viewpoint both of earth and heaven.

9 But life's poor distinctions vanish when they are scanned from "the heavenly places" of spiritual insight. Let the master in turn ponder his accountability to his and his servant's Overlord, who cannot be biassed to award a partial sentence, like so many of this world's tribunals.[11] Instead of truculence or resort to threats, the common expedient of arbitrary power, let him exercise lenity and kindly consideration towards those amenable to his control, and abstain from scolding severity.

The majestic horizon of eternity reduces the temporal status of the believer to a minor consideration. He who is the Lord's freeman, though outwardly debased, has a far grander heritage and destiny than his pagan employer. It is his to discover in every mundane relationship scope for manifesting a heavenly frame of mind and thus recommending his religious faith to favourable notice. Even Menander could write: "Serve freely and thou shalt be no slave".[12]

Of course many a superficial thinker has blamed Christianity for lending any sanction whatsoever to the rank injustice of slavery. But its mission was spiritual in essence and only collaterally social. Had it assailed the established system of serfdom point-blank, it would have ruined that primary object by inflaming political antagonisms to an incandescent furnace-heat. Servile wars had already shaken Roman society to its base and helped to precipitate imperial dictatorship as the sole effectual preservative against social insecurity. The institution of slavery was in fact bound up inextricably with the legislation of the ancient world and could only be dissolved with its dissolution. By attacking that deep-rooted curse directly the new faith would have come into deadly conflict with "the powers that be", and merged itself in a

---

[11] With Eph. 6:8, where every man is to receive the good that he has done, compare Col. 3:25, where the converse is stated, that every man will correspondingly receive the evil that he has done. Note also that here the impartiality of the Divine Judge is affirmed in the injunction to masters, whereas in Col. 3:25 its context is the injunction to slaves (see pp. 294 f.).
[12] *Fragment* 857. *Cf.* Seneca (*Epistles*, 47): *Servi sunt? immo humiles amici. servi sunt? immo conservi.*

gigantic extrinsic upheaval fatal to its intrinsic purpose. Divine wisdom is not so shortsighted as to be thus side-tracked.

In the unsullied cosmos of God's creation slavery could have found no place. That inhuman abuse sprang from the infraction of the moral order. It was one of the outgrowths and evidences of a polity unhinged by sin. Fraternity with our Maker alone can secure fraternity with our brother-man; for even communism can enforce bondage of dissidents with ruthlessness. And if that shattered fellowship were to be restored, as the Epistle to Philemon intimates, it could only be conclusively re-erected through the restoration of a befitting relationship with the Most High. The truths of the gospel laid the axe at the roots of the evil; for they proclaimed spiritual liberty, equality and fraternity *in excelsis,* they revealed one Potentate and Governor, the universal House-holder and Judge, under whose audit all alike are to be mustered for appraisement. The decisive judgment of human rights and claims is reserved for the supreme court of appeal. "Christianity," says one writer, "is eminently economic; it never does too much. Slavery was like a tree notched, that it might be felled in due season." The unhurried Christ's triumph tarries during the hand-breadth of time because His empire is coeval with eternity.

V. THE CHRISTIAN PANOPLY

Ch. 6:10–17

10 Finally,[13] be strong[14] in the Lord, and in the strength
of his might.

10 During the last two chapters the apostle has laid weight
on the gracious and pacific traits of the new manhood incorporated
as members of Christ's body; but she sails with her High Admiral
not in a pleasure-yacht but a man-of-war. As we recall the
transcendent perspective and passionate fervour of the earlier half
of the Epistle we feel the aptness of a finale set to a martial strain,
of a rousing charge to be sounded forth to the church *militant*.
Nor are we disappointed. There is a holy war afoot with the
powers of darkness; and who so qualified to animate the sacra-
mental host of God's elect as this scarred veteran of the cross,
himself no carpet-knight, but versed in all the strategy of the
campaign and cognizant of all the tactics of the enemy?

Paul was in the imperial city, the arsenal of that incomparable
engine of conquest, the Roman army, and peradventure chained
to one of her ironsides, accoutred with the gear of a soldier on duty.
He finds his text in the Old Testament battle-cry, "Quit you like
men, be strong" (1 Sam. 4:9), which he had already enforced on
the Corinthians (1 Cor. 16:13); but the striking illustrations that
succeed are unmistakably borrowed from the Roman style of
equipment within survey of the prisoner. Paul gleans his imagery
from objects close at hand. One preliminary caution needs to be
insisted on. The Christian soldier must not dream of entering on
this spiritual warfare at his own charges or with his own equipment.
Let him cry with David, "It is God that girdeth me with strength;

---

13 Gk. τοῦ λοιποῦ. This reading of Westcott and Hort (attested by P46
ℵ * A B 33 etc.) has strong support. It should signify "henceforward" (χρόνου
being understood). But τὸ λοιπόν of the Received Text, meaning "in conclusion"
or "in consequence" (*cf.* Lucian, *Parasite* 13) is far more pertinent, for the
military emblems that follow mark a practical application most appropriate at
this point (*cf.* Lat. *ceterum* and French *enfin*). We frequently find λοιπόν joined
with an imperative in Marcus Aurelius, meaning "wherefore" (*cf.* 1 Cor. 7:29).
14 Gk. ἐνδυναμοῦσθε. A LXX verb used of Gideon (Judg. 6:34), a favourite
with Paul. Outside Biblical Greek it appears only in Christian writers like
Clement of Rome (*Ep.* 55:3).

Hy teacheth my hands to war." His resources must be procured from headquarters, not self-devised. We that can do nothing in ourselves, we are such weaklings, can do all things in Christ as giants (John Owen).[15] In Him we have righteousness and strength, justification by faith and sanctification by the Spirit, the whole armour of God, defensive and offensive combined.

11 Put on the whole armor of God, that ye may be able to stand against the wiles of the devil.[16]
12 For our wrestling is not against flesh and blood, but against the principalities, against the powers,[17] against the world-rulers[18] of this darkness,[19] against the spiritual *hosts* of wickedness in the heavenly *places.*[20]

11 For this internecine conflict moreover no partial equipment will suffice. The spiritual warrior must be armed cap-a-pie, or his accoutrement rests incomplete. It comprizes in all a sevenfold panoply, the first draft of which had already been sketched in 1 Thess. 5:8 and Rom. 13:12. For he will have to dispute every inch of the ground with an adversary unrivalled in crafty ruses as well as open assaults. No constituent part of this divine armour-of-proof for all conceivable exigences can be safely omitted. We cannot forge our own weapons, nor rely on the fencing-foils of human intuition or reason or the pinchbeck shield of ethical science as our palladium in the day of battle. The subtle strategy of Satan's

---

15 *Works* II, 110 (ed. Gould).
16 See Ch. 4:27 (p. 108, n. 59) for διάβολος.
17 See Col. 1:16; 2:10, 15, with exposition and notes (pp. 198, 233, 239 ff.).
18 Gk. κοσμοκράτορες. This was one of the Greek terms adopted by the Talmudists (*cf.* M. Jastrow, *Dictionary of the Talmud*, p. 1325, col. 2) to signify a world-ruler like Nebuchadnezzar—Tertullian's *munditenentes*. Here it extends to unseen spiritual potentates who make human despots and false systems of thought their tools of dominion. It is one of the adulatory titles of the Roman Emperors found in inscriptions. In Vettius Valens it is used astrologically of the sun and moon (360).
19 After "darkness" the bulk of later authorities for the text add "of this age" (Gk. τοῦ αἰῶνος); cf. AV.
20 τὰ πνευματικὰ . . . ἐν τοῖς ἐπουρανίοις, "spiritual forces in the upper realm." These forces of wickedness are contrasted with flesh and blood as viewless, impalpable; nor does it seem in keeping with that statement to fix their location specifically in the firmament. We take "the heavenlies" here to be the region of spiritual intercourse. These evil beings claim human surrender to their dominating influence; and war must be waged against that demand of allegiance. Byron makes Satan boast: "He who bows not to God has bowed to me."

masked batteries or flaming vollies, as the case may be, demands all the weaponry of heaven for its discomfiture.

12 We may descry no hostile forces confronting us save those of flesh and blood; but Paul knew by pungent experience that antagonists take the field against Christ's soldiery far too formidable for carnal arms to parry. Wherefore he utters this solemn injunction to all and sundry, apprizing them that it is a world-war they are called on to wage, that they are picked out to wrestle against principalities and powers supernaturally marshalled and not to be coped with except by virtue of supernatural aid. Christian Science (so-called) instructs its votaries to view disagreeables and portents of evil as non-existent, to shut their eyes to all perturbing phenomena; but the word of truth does not lull us asleep by rosy-tinted pictures of our state or environment. Christ by no flowery pathway came to our succour, nor did He veil unwelcome tidings from his weak-kneed disciples. We are not to compliment with Apollyon but resist him tooth and nail, sustained by the conviction that if his depredations are licensed, they are likewise limited. The Captain of our Salvation cut His way through the serried hosts of hell, massed for His destruction, unaided; and His crucial victory assures that of His redeemed, clad in His own everlasting strength;

> And when the strife is fierce, the warfare long,
> Steals on the ear the distant triumph-song,
> And hearts are brave again, and arms are strong.

The title of *world-ruler*, as inscriptions testify, was one of the fulsome adulations laid at the feet of the emperor Caracalla. At the instigation doubtless of his infernal principal, this brutal and murderous potentate depicted himself on his coinage with the radiate crown as lord of the stars, occupant of the "heavenly places."[21]

Alas! how many wicked tyrants since his day have been the willing tools of the arch-usurper and manslayer! What fell embodiments of force and fraud, leagued against the Lord's Anointed, the noble army of Christian martyrs and confessors have been fortified to face! Note how fully Paul here identifies himself with the rank and file of the church militant, staff-officer though he were by divine warrant. "*We* wrestle, you and I alike."

As in Bunyan's *Holy War*, a twofold infernal policy meets our

---

[21] *Cf.* Moulton and Milligan, *Vocabulary of the Greek Testament* (London,

scrutiny in this passage. The tactics of intimidation and insinuation alternate in Satan's plan of campaign. He plays both the bully and the beguiler. Force and fraud form his chief offensive against the camp of the saints, practised by turns. His subalterns, ecclesiastic and secular, have shed torrents of innocent blood in bygone days to efface vital Christianity from the annals of the globe. But faith at bay, invincible as her Author, has risen to her full stature in the dread hour of persecution and martyrdom and bidden brave defiance to the gates of hell. Far sorer damage has resulted from the clandestine wiles of the wicked one than from his "big battalions," from covert tare-sowing than from overt trampling down of the Lord's cornfields. Those viewless miasmas, the poison-gases of spiritual wickedness, do most execution by their ravages. "I love a rumbling, raging rather than a subtle, sleepy devil," wrote Rutherford.[22] The father of lies works his deadliest havoc by "shamming dead" and writing his own obituary in unctuous terms; the wolf preys fellest when he masks himself in sheep's clothing. It is his success in eliminating the frontier-lines of truth and falsehood under colour of broadmindedness, and in securing the ascendancy of "scientific thought" or rather its counterfeit, that has paved the way for his most signal inroads of unbelief on the pale of true religion in modern times. The capture of heavenly outposts like the Christian pulpit for the propaganda of infidelity is a *coup d'état* peculiarly congenial to the old serpent, one of whose favourite methods of warfare consists of an occupation of sacred ground by the enemy's troops, surreptitiously plotted amid ostensible professions of peace.

> 13 Wherefore take up the whole armor of God, that ye may be able to withstand in the evil day, and, having done[23] all, to stand.

13 So urgent is his mandate that the apostle reiterates it with a reason for his insistence. Divine equipment alone can enable the believer to foil the foe's guileful machinations or overwhelming irruptions. Two postures of defence are requisite to ensure his

---

1930), *s.v.* κοσμοκράτωρ, and E. Stauffer, *Christ and the Caesars* (Eng. tr., London, 1955), pp. 228 ff.

[22] *Letters* (ed. Bonar), 90.

[23] Gk. κατεργασάμενοι. This verb is classical for *achievement* either in war or in the Grecian games.

safety, an active and a passive style of resistance, of attack and
defence respectively. Paul had already (5:16) described the days
as evil, and he now specifies the armour and ammunition procur-
able for successful encounter with the spiritual adversary. He is
to be confronted valiantly in close combat, not evaded by withdrawal or adroit manoeuvring. The Lord's lieges are to fight the
good fight of faith, quitting themselves like men-at-arms, and
replenished from their arsenal at headquarters to hold the field[24]
unrepulsed. It is not theirs to shirk the battle-royal with Apollyon
but to "fight to a finish."

14 Stand therefore, having girded your loins with truth,
    and having put on the breastplate of righteousness,
15 and having shod your feet with the preparation of
    the gospel of peace;

14 Full well had the veteran apostle of the Gentiles tried
every piece of gospel armour which he proceeds to enumerate.
Experto crede, he might have averred to the Roman soldier to
whom he was chained, whose outfit doubtless suggested the imagery
here borrowed. The engirdling *Belt* (*cingulum*) at first glance
identifies the soldier on duty, styled by Tacitus, *miles accinctus*.[25]
It is hard to decide whether it represents truth of doctrine or
sincerity of character. It may of course embrace both; for the true
gospel begets truth in the inward parts. It tells the truth about
human nature and prescribes the sole effectual remedy for its ills,
so many of which are falsely diagnosed by physicians of no value.
It substitutes an infallible for an erratic criterion, reality for
speculation, appealing to Him whose name is Truth as its ultimate
authority. Resolution of soul springs from settled conviction, from
a full persuasion that the cause championed is not merely legitimate
but supremely loveable, a trust of untold value and validity,
compared with which terrestrial prizes are but baubles. Faithfulness will be the girdle of such a warrior's reins. The heart made
upright by divine grace will be nerved for any fray, outnumbered
though it may be by the satellites of error; whereas the lurking
consciousness of an unsound foundation, either without or within,
palsies the combatant's arm forthwith. He who contends for the
truth with no hypocrisy, because he prizes it above rubies, will deal

---

24 *Cf.* Luther's version, *das Feld behalten.*
25 *Annals* xi. 18.

such decisive strokes that he will daunt the militia of craft and
subtlety assailing him before they can task his mettle or offer a
counterbuff to his heavenly battle-axe. Sincerity may be attacked
by passing qualms; but it will not flinch from its colours in earnest,
and those colours themselves are colours in grain, ineffaceable and
deluge-proof.

The next piece of armour signalized is the *Breastplate* (*lorica*)
of righteousness. Here again, is the appellation objective or subjective? Are we to understand imputed or inwrought righteousness
thereby? Most expositors give their vote in favour of the latter;
but surely the former cannot be excluded from the picture. The
cuirass here depicted covers the vital organs and serves as the
soldier's staple protection in a conflict wherein heart-issues lie at
stake. Now the Epistle to the Romans settles the question what
it is that inspires the Christian trooper with inextinguishable
confidence and unblenching fortitude. His impenetrable mail
consists of a righteousness enthroned at God's right hand in the
person of His well-beloved Son, absolutely flawless, the very
"righteousness which God's righteousness requires Him to require"
(Cunningham), reckoned to the combatant's account; his authentic
regimentals, so to speak. His own godliness and integrity, the
radical change wrought within him which implanted a sanctified
principle inseparably linked with justification, inwoven with the
moral texture of his being, unquestionably yields its serenity to
his spirit; but his capital confidence lies in his Captain's victory, the
basis and pledge of his own. Self-reliance in any shape would
constitute no bulwark for his soul and but ill withstand hostile
missiles; it would crinkle or warp in the hour of peril. The Lord
our Righteousness must be our trusty munition, our sevenfold
Shield and Buckler which no sword-thrust can pierce, our
impregnable Rampart and Buttress which no volleys of the pit can
batter or raze (Isa. 59:17).

We conclude therefore with Charles Hodge that this staunch
metal breastplate needs to be of more impermeable texture than
personal godliness. Sanctification is the befitting bearing of the
militia of the cross, their proper posture of soul, and in a subordinate sense, their "armour of righteousness," yet scarcely its
defensive frontispiece. It was the ark of God itself, not the
gallantry of its henchmen, that was Israel's safeguard in times of
calamity and stress. The saint's derivative holiness should animate

him with unflagging zeal and courage and give him the staying-power he needs, but we cannot well ascribe to it the potency of a spiritual palladium.

15 Paul proceeds to provide his soldier with *Footgear*. He is to be "shod with the preparedness[26] of the gospel of peace;" for peace with God implies war with Satan. The Christian serves under the standard of the Prince of Peace and assumes the celestial panoply supplied for his defence at his Commander's cost in firm resistance to that worst of all incendiaries. The chief requisite in regard to an army's shoe-leather consists in facility of motion. Long marches formed one of Julius Caesar's most successful tactics; again and again his picked troops vanquished their enemies by surprising them unawares. Alexander had practised the same device long before. Readiness for the field, qualification for expeditious mobility, such as the *caliga* or military shoe of the Roman legionaries was designed to facilitate, presents an appropriate emblem of the adaptation of the gospel watchword to give alacrity to the evangelical soldier. There should be nothing slipshod about his locomotion. A light foot should be the visible evidence of a guilt-eased heart. No obstacle and no stress of weather could check for any length of time the advance of the great republic's legions. Disheartenment they deemed a failing to blush for, to be beaten a contingency out of the question. Victory seemed the presiding genius of their resistless propulsion. Did onward march entail hardship and heavy sacrifice of life? Then let it be incurred. There was nothing their steeled sinews would not undergo in order to overcome. The genuine missionary of the cross re-exhibits in a nobler cause the fervour shown by the battalions of Rome for the proud commonwealth for which they fought and bled so intrepidly. But his marching orders embrace a vastly wider circumference than the flight of the imperial eagles ever ranged. This "reasonable service" differs entirely from the irreflection of fanaticism or the precipitance of fool-hardiness. It is a disciplined zeal which counts the cost and pronounces it worth while, which brooks the roughness of the road with sturdy surefootedness, confiding in its Guide, and triumphs in the prospect of a goal aglow with rapturous satisfaction and everlasting joy.

---

[26] Gk. ἑτοιμασία, used of ship's tackling, seems best rendered "equipment," but may carry the abstract sense of "readiness."

16 Withal[27] taking up the shield of faith, wherewith ye shall be able to quench all the fiery[28] darts of the evil *one*.

16 But the combatant's equipment is still incomplete. His left hand must grasp the doughty *Shield* (*scutum*) of faith. No pasteboard targe this, but the full-sized buckler of the Greek hoplite or the Roman infantry, sometimes expanded into the complex *testudo* of shields tensely packed together to screen a band of soldiers from the enemy's projectiles. Here the reference is to the single shield, personally wielded as a protection against a rain of arrows or stones. Its fire-proof metal lining sufficed to intercept or extinguish the ignited missiles of ancient belligerents. Supplied with this inviolable *aegis* the host of the redeemed possess the secret which overcomes the world (1 John 5:4). Persecution flings its fiery bolts in vain against so invulnerable a defence. Scan the *arc de triomphe* reared in Heb. 11 or look within the veil at the apocalyptic martyrs, and mark how they vanquish all the power of the enemy by unshaken trust in the testimony of Jesus, their crucified and risen Head, and in the God-given promises of the new covenant. This heavenly-tempered shield, stouter by far than that of Achilles, defies all the infuriated malice or sinuous finesse of Satan. The accuser of the brethren is ever seeking to wound the saints' peace and inject lying or impious suggestions into their souls, or temptations to doubt their gospel standing. But "faith unfeigned" repels these onsets, strengthened with might in the inner man by the indwelling Spirit of Christ (3:17); and the believer's shelter behind the bosses of this celestial breastwork secures him from mortal injury, as he turns his buckler this way and that against the shafts of hell. Unbelief exposes its defenceless prey to the assaults of the victimizer of souls and lets his gimcrack shield drop from his nerveless arm. But Mr. Valiant-in-Fight recovers his faltering poise and grasp of the safeguard well-nigh wrested from him and holds it up, like hard-pressed Job, in the face of the implacable foe as his sovereign talisman.

---

[27] Gk. ἐν πᾶσιν. The easier reading is ἐπὶ πᾶσιν, "furthermore," or (as Bengel understands it figuratively) "over all the rest"; but if Westcott and Hort's text be adopted, the reading is approximately the same.

[28] Gk. πεπυρωμένα, "flaming," "ignited (with combustibles)." *Cf.* Lucian's ἄνθρακες πεπυρωμένοι (*True History* ii. 30). The darts may be railing accusations; for the phrase πεπυρωμένα ῥήματα occurs in the *Anthology* vii. 408 (Loeb). In the *Anacreontics* the verb is used of the pangs of love.

17 And take the helmet[29] of salvation, and the sword of the Spirit, which is the word of God:[30]

17 One more defensive item of armour finishes off the list. It supplies the head with protection in the thick of battle. The *Helmet* (*galea*) of Salvation[31] may be interpreted as emblematic of hope, which carries this title in 1 Thess. 5:8. We are inclined, however, to judge that it includes a more extended reference, in fact what the writer to the Hebrews styles (Heb. 6:11) the "full assurance of hope," persistently cherished. Paul has stressed the deadliness of the fray in prospect and the potency of the adverse powers. What will enable the Christian soldier to hold up his head unquailingly, vexed by no downcast forebodings? A buoyant hope brightens his crest and recruits his prowess, the hope of salvation in all the compass of that majestic term. Granting that the gist of the analogy lies in a forward-looking spirit, it should not be overlooked that Biblical salvation rings the changes on all tenses of the verb. In one sense it is past, achieved when the believer is "saved by grace." Then it has a present application. He is in course of deliverance from the power of sin; his new nature is showing tokens of consolation; he is being framed into "an habitation of God in the Spirit." The helmet is screening his head from the impact of evil suggestions and impulses that would put him to shame, and futurity holds out the crown of assured victory and entire riddance from susceptibility to sin. What are earthly baubles when weighed against the prizes of glorification and Christ-likeness proffered as the guerdons of this holy warfare?

We have seen the Christian crusader buckle on his harness in preparation for the toughest of conflicts; for his Zion is not merely a fane but a fortress; but what of his offensive artillery? That lies ready to his hand in the *Sword* (*gladius, ensis*) of the Spirit, backed, as we shall find, by the invisible but prevailing weapon of prayer. God's word shelters as well as slays; but its peculiar distinction consists in the havoc it works in the ranks of the foe. Recent improvements, the work of guilty science, in the arts of slaughter may have diminished the importance of the sword to-day in

---

29 Gk. περικεφαλαία, a late word, replacing the Homeric κόρυς, and extant in the papyri, Polybius, and Josephus.

30 Gk. ῥῆμα θεοῦ, not "a word of God," but succinctly "God's word," His unique revelation. *Cf.* Ch. 5:26; Rom. 10:17; Heb. 6:5.

31 *Cf.* Isa. 59:17.

martial campaigns: yet it remains the typical instrument of the military profession and, historically viewed, its supreme equipment. The Epistle to the Hebrews employs the same figure (4:12) to set forth the trenchant power of Scripture, its scimitar edge, capable of sundering the joints and marrow and dissecting the intents of the heart. This soul-searching quality makes it the chief medium of conviction, far more availing than the subtlety or eloquence of the preacher. A Bible text smites the conscience point-blank or floors self-righteousness as no weapon of mortal fabrication would do. The omniscient Spirit of the Lord breathes through its pages, that Spirit whose fathomless line can sound the depths of Deity itself, much more the shallows of human nature. By dint of that incisive probe the proudest insurgent's secrecies may be ransacked. As Dagon reeled before the ark, so have the legions of hell been palsied by the sword of the Lord in the hand of His chosen Gideons. Full often it has bent souls to its mastery, as it bent Augustine or Vanderkemp, irrespective altogether of man's agency. The plainspokenness of absolute honesty, the purity of crystal rectitude, the penetration of superhuman wisdom, vindicate its credentials, attesting its title to rank above all other scripts. It is no conglomerate of piecemeal religious miscellanea, but a living organism instinct with divine vitality. The clairvoyants of modern criticism, no doubt, treat the word of God as a half-erased or overwritten palimpsest, the original purport of which is only to be detected by a lavish use of their patent chemicals; or they read the contents asquint or upside down in their process of hypothetical re-concoction, proudly misstyled scientific. They slit the seamless robe into a thousand shreds and patches in order to mend its texture. But a mutilated Bible is what Moody dubbed it, "a broken sword." To all not deafened or scared by the clamour of pretentious pedantry the dislocated or vivisected members of Holy Writ cry aloud for replacement in their proper setting.

What a consternation the sword-play of this celestial brand has made in the ranks of the rebels against light! How many has it disarmed and shaped anew! Its rare exploits claim a scanty tribute of verse in their honour.

> Damascus steel of old was famed in fight,
> And many a chevalier of prowess bore
> Toledo's finely tempered blades of yore
> Wherewith they turned the Paynim hordes to flight;

Nor less renowned Goliath's sword of might,
That nonpareil the son of Jesse wore,
Reft from the tabernacle's treasure-store
By him whose arm to wield it had best right.
But never yet was earthly falchion seen
Of virtue both to scathe and to make whole
Like thee, sword of the Spirit flashing keen,
Excalibur whose stroke doth cleave the soul!
Thine edge hews the old man in twain, I ween,
The new thy clasp doth gird, sustain, control.

VI. THE DYNAMISM OF PRAYER

Ch. 6:18-20

18 with all prayer and supplication[32] praying at all
seasons in the Spirit, and watching[33] thereunto in all
perseverance[34] and supplication for all the saints,

18 The accoutrement cap-à-pie appropriate to the Christian
warrior has been reconnoitred; but though no piece of armour can
be said to have been overlooked, a dynamic all-important for a
campaign waged against the standing army of darkness craves
mention. What Luther says of the Reformation may be affirmed
of every stage of the conflict in the heavenlies; "prayer must do
the deed". If not strictly one of the weapons of our warfare,
it is their potent concomitant and indispensable auxiliary. By
persevering, unceasing, heart-felt prayer alone can the soldier
of Christ acquire or retain that high-souled fortitude, that
indomitable resolution, that spiritual presence-of-mind amid the
hurly-burly and din of battle, that calmness in the wearing hours
of suspense, for lack of which he may blot his escutcheon deplorably
either through temerity or treachery.

Prayer is an engine wieldable by every believer, mightier than
all the embattled artillery of hell. Never out of season, nor to be
deemed a drudgery, it is to be plied indefatigably, with a compass
coextensive with the church universal. Its circuit should be as
catholic and its importunity as fervent as the needs of the host of
the Lord in every quarter of the globe. To differentiate between
prayer and *supplication* seems hypercritical. Some would construe
in the Spirit of the human agent principally; and that appears to
be the meaning of the phrase in such contexts as Rom. 1:9, 1 Cor.
14:15; but Jude writes of "praying in the Holy Spirit" (20), and

---

32 While προσευχή means "prayer" in general, δέησις means "request."
33 Gk. ἀγρυπνοῦντες, "keeping vigilant," not drowsing; *cf.* Col. 4:2 (p. 297
with nn. 4 and 5). So ἐπαγρυπνεῖν in Plutarch and Epictetus; used of a cock
(Lucian, *Gallus* 31).
34 Gk. προσκαρτέρησις. Deissmann can discover this very rare noun only in
two Jewish manumissions of contemporary date (*Light from the Ancient East*,
p. 102). But it occurs also twice in Philodemus of Gadara (*Rhetoric* i. 11; iii. 8),
who uses a derivative adverb as well.

true prayer is both the suitor's own and the Spirit's work. The sincerity and intension of soul pertain to the human petitioner; the potency, inspiration and freedom of utterance and access (2:18) spring from "the secret touch of the Spirit" (Gurnall), generating a glow of holy emotion in the suppliant's soul.

The primary condition of true communion with the Most High is a consciousness that we are holding converse with a Divine Person, not addressing vacancy like the pantheistic word-spinner. For all prayer worth the name is "a living voice speaking in a living ear." It may be tranquil or agonistic, ejaculatory or protracted. And we may add that a routine of prayer prescribed and appointed by rote, is ill suited to an intercourse so sacredly familiar and intimate as the approach of children to a Father in heaven. Entreaty for the welfare of others is amongst the noblest privileges of the Lord's people; and observation bears record that public disasters and private distresses multiply in proportion to the decay of that importunate intercession which prevails to "move the hand that moves the world to bring salvation down." Proficients in the holy art of intercession are sorely needed by the church of God to-day, skilled to turn the battle in the gate by dint of this impalpable reagent. And may not ten praying souls avert the vials of judgment from some wrath-provoking Sodom or Capernaum?

> 19 and on my behalf, that utterance may be given unto me in opening my mouth, to make known with boldness the mystery of the gospel,[35]
> 20 for which I am an ambassador in chains;[36] that in it I may speak boldly, as I ought[37] to speak.

19-20 The ambassador depends principally on the countenance of the government he represents. But in the case of the apostle's

---

[35] The words "of the gospel" (Gk. τοῦ εὐαγγελίου) are omitted by B G and a few Western citations.

[36] Gk. ἐν ἁλύσει. Whether the singular is to be pressed remains doubtful, or whether the term is collective, as it seems to be in Polybius iv. 76, Josephus, *Antiquities* xviii. 6, and perhaps Lucian, *Toxaris* 32. But we notice that Paul invariably (Acts 28:20; 2 Tim. 1:16) uses the singular, as if descriptive of his enchainment to a soldier (*cf. Acts* in NICNT, p. 447, n. 39; p. 529 with n. 34). The paradox lay in an envoy *bound*, an ambassador placed under arrest, in violation of the law of nations.

[37] Gk. ὡς δεῖ is not merely "as I ought" but "*in the fashion I ought*"—a distinction drawn by Aristotle (*Rhetoric* iii. 1) and Plutarch (*Moralia* 804). *Cf.* p. 298, n. 9.

embassy the prayers of loyal fellow-subjects are instituted as a medium of blessing and furtherance of his mission. Their allegiance and his coincide, and their supplications on his behoof shall of a surety bear fruit in a ministry recruited and emboldened thereby; for "no faithful prayers are lost at sea" (Gurnall). Shackled in body, he yearns for enfranchisement of spirit, the outspokenness and liberty from constraint which heartens every genuine preacher of the word. Too many pulpiteers append so many qualifying clauses to their statements of divine truth as go far to nullify the main proposition. But diffidence misbecomes the fearless gospel herald. It is not the carnal self-reliance eulogized by Emerson that stiffens his backbone. That would savour of sheer presumption. His sufficiency is of God. Yet a haunting sense of infirmity may so weaken his testimony as to render it invertebrate in seasons of depression or amid outbreaks of scornful repugnance. How often has the Christian missionary to face such discouragements! Under such circumstances nothing rekindles his zeal like the consideration that he is being upheld by believing prayer, that other members of Christ's body are part and parcel of his ministrations, whilst pleading on his behalf. That thought acts as a cordial to his swooning spirit. Not for his bondloosing, be it noted, does the lorn prisoner bid the saints especially pray, but for the unfettered exercise of his world-wide commission, chained though he were meanwhile to a single spot. The Colossian parallel (Col. 4:3)[38] favours this interpretation; some, however, discover a reference to the Lord's promise of extemporaneous facility of speech in cases of judicial trial (Matt. 10:20). We think the proposition embraces a wider scope. Was not Paul rendered cosmopolitanly vocal in his prison-Epistles, whereof this one is not the least resonant? In these pages he speaks in reverberant tones across the centuries to every subsequent generation a message of certainty and energy divinely sealed and verified.

---

[38] *Cf.* exposition and notes *ad loc.*, p. 298.

VII. FINAL GREETING

Ch. 6:21-24

21 But that ye also may know my affairs,[39] how I do,[40] Tychicus, the beloved brother and faithful minister in the Lord, shall make known to you all things:

22 whom I have sent unto you for this very purpose, that ye may know our state, and that he may comfort your hearts.

23 Peace be to the brethren, and love with faith, from God the Father and the Lord Jesus Christ.

24 Grace be with all them that love our Lord Jesus Christ with *a love* incorruptible.

21-22 How entirely exempt from the odious spirit of sacerdotal domination does the chosen evangelist of the Gentile world evince himself to be! Assuredly he had not "run in vain"; the scale of his work and its fructification proclaimed his pre-eminent station and unblenching fidelity and devotion. Yet this "prince of the church" sets himself on no elevated pedestal above his brethren; for he craves the prayers of these humble folk on his behalf as no less a royal priesthood than himself, and commends his fellow-labourer Tychicus to them as an emissary qualified to inflame their zeal and to convey a just impression of his own estate and prospects. Paul's confidence in his envoy attests his messenger's sterling integrity; and all we know of Tychicus corroborates that lofty estimate. This Asian disciple had, in all likelihood, been Paul's companion in his last visit to Jerusalem, and must have served him in some capacity at this period in the midst of the imperial city. He was entrusted with this priceless Epistle and the Colossian counterpart, and reappears finally, serviceable and trusty as ever, in the Pastoral Letters (2 Tim. 4:12). The gospel-imbued self-forgetful spirit of these elect delegates of the churches discloses itself in the very obscurity of their histories. So absorbed

---

[39] *Cf.* Col. 4:7 f., with exposition and notes (pp. 301 f.).

[40] Gk. τί πράσσω, usually translated "what I am doing"; but can it not mean "how I fare"? *Cf.* εὖ πράσσειν ("to prosper") and φαύλως πράσσειν ("to fare ill," as in Babrius 119. 3). In Lucian's *Dialogues of Harlots* (9) τί ἐπράξατε, greeting a returning soldier, surely signifies: "How have you sped?" *Cf.* Lucian, *Nigrinus* 3, ἠρώτα ὅ τι πράττοιμι, and Lat. *quid agis?*

were they in their subsidiary task that they compiled no memorabilia of their redoubtable champion, or details of their own adventures as his dutiful armour-bearers and confidential scouts and message-carriers.

23–24 The syncopated benediction, accompanying the apostle's autograph at the close, signalizes the later in contrast with the earlier Epistles. Some regard the use of the third person as decisive in favour of the circular theory of the Epistle. But it accords with the specification of a class to whose circle it is restricted, those who love Christ imperishably or indefectibly.[41] The old version *in sincerity* seems no more than a paraphrase of that distinguishing feature, here couched in a negative form and so rendered in our version *with an incorruptible love*. One of two things may be signified; either love *imperishably* cherished and in perpetuity, or else *unfadingly*—if we might coin a word, *serelessly*—without waning or declension. Perhaps the keyword of Ps. 119, "Blessed are the undefiled in the way," was in the thought of the writer. The true-born heir of the kingdom is discriminated from the bastard by his inviolable affiance to his Lord. His is not a fitful, evanescent sentiment of attachment, a merely impulsive adhesion, but a *cohesion* of amaranthine stability, an intertexture of spirit, proof against all disintegrating factors. There is a love as well as faith of God's elect which from its exalted vantage-ground, seated in "the heavenly places," can chant Wade Robinson's triumphant canticle:

> Heaven and earth may fade and flee,
> First-born light in gloom decline;
> But while He and I shall be,
> I am His and He is mine.

May that ecstatic symphony be our hymeneal too in Christ Jesus, our transcendent Next-of-Kin!

---

41 Gk. ἐν ἀφθαρσίᾳ. The version "in sincerity" lacks confirmation. We must either construe the phrase to mean, without alteration, "imperishably," appealing to the counter-term εὔφθαρτος which signifies "destructible" (Marcus Aurelius, ii. 12), or "undwindlingly," "uncorrodedly"—a love the vitality of which is unsapped by the malarial influences specified in Chs. 4 and 5.

COMMENTARY ON
THE EPISTLE TO THE COLOSSIANS

THE ENGLISH TEXT WITH
INTRODUCTION, EXPOSITION AND NOTES

by

F. F. BRUCE, M.A., D.D.

Professor of Biblical Criticism and Exegesis
University of Manchester

AUTHOR'S PREFACE

The invitation to follow up my volume on Acts in this series with a commentary on Colossians is something for which I feel very grateful to my friend the General Editor, not least because it has given me the opportunity to deepen my acquaintance with Paul and appreciate more fully the mind of one who in so signal a degree possessed the mind of Christ. And it is with a real sense of honour done to me that I find myself sharing a volume with that veteran scholar and saint, Mr. E. K. Simpson, from whose writings I have derived much intellectual and spiritual profit these thirty years.

Acknowledgment is made in the course of the exposition and notes to those works which I have found most useful in this study. Unfortunately, Professor C. F. D. Moule's fine volume on Colossians and Philemon in the new "Cambridge Greek Testament Commentary" series appeared too late for me to refer to it. The same applies to W. F. Arndt and F. W. Gingrich's excellent English edition of Bauer's Lexicon to the Greek New Testament.

In writing to the Colossians, says Calvin, Paul "teaches that all parts of our salvation are to be found in Christ alone, that they may not seek anything elsewhere; and he puts them in mind that it was in Christ that they had obtained every blessing that they possessed, in order that they might the more carefully make it their aim to hold Him fast to the end. And indeed even this one article would be perfectly sufficient of itself to make us reckon this epistle, short as it is, to be an inestimable treasure. For what is of greater importance in the whole system of heavenly doctrine than to have Christ drawn to the life, so that we may clearly contemplate His excellence, His office, and all the fruits that accrue to us therefrom?" The truth of this testimony has been amply confirmed in the writing of this commentary; may it be further confirmed in the reading of it.

F. F. B.

INTRODUCTION

(a) Origin and Purpose of the Epistle to the Colossians

Colossae was a city of Phrygia, situated on the south bank of the River Lycus, a tributary of the Maeander.[1] The main road from Ephesus to the Euphrates ran through it, and it is mentioned accordingly in the itineraries of the armies of Xerxes and the younger Cyrus, which marched along this road. Herodotus, in the fifth century B.C., calls it "a great city of Phrygia";[2] at the beginning of the following century Xenophon describes it as "a populous city, wealthy and large."[3] But towards the end of the pre-Christian era it diminished in importance with the growth of Laodicea and Hierapolis, two neighbouring cities in the Lycus valley, and Strabo the geographer, writing at the beginning of the Christian era, calls it a small town.[4] The site is now deserted, but the town of Honas (formerly a Byzantine fortress and seat of an archbishopric) lies three miles to the south-east. In the apostolic age its population consisted of indigenous Phrygians and Greek settlers, together with a fair proportion of the Jewish colonists who resided in Phrygia from the time of Antiochus the Great (223–187 B.C.) onwards.

The region of Phrygia in which Colossae and its sister cities lay (sometimes called Phrygia Pacatiana) formed part of the kingdom of Pergamum, which was bequeathed to the Roman senate and people in 133 B.C. by the last ruler of the Attalid dynasty, and was reconstituted as the Roman province of Asia.

Christianity was introduced to Colossae and the other cities of the Lycus valley during the years of Paul's Ephesian ministry, recorded in Acts 19.[5] So vigorously was the work of evangelization prosecuted during those years (A.D. 52–55) that not only the people of Ephesus but "all they which dwelt in Asia heard the word of the Lord, both Jews and Greeks" (Acts 19:10). While the work was directed by Paul, he was assisted by several colleagues, and through

---

[1] *Cf.* W. M. Ramsay, *Cities and Bishoprics of Phrygia* i (Oxford, 1895), pp. 208 ff.
[2] *Histories* vii. 30.
[3] *Anabasis* i. 2. 6.
[4] Gk. πόλισμα (*Geography* xii. 8. 13).
[5] See *Acts* in NICNT (Grand Rapids, 1954), pp. 384 ff.

their ministry in various parts of the province churches were planted, some of which the apostle himself was unable to visit personally. None the less he maintained a warm pastoral interest in them.

Among these last were the churches planted in Colossae, Laodicea and Hierapolis, which appear to have been the fruit of the missionary activity of Epaphras. This is plainly to be inferred from the references to Epaphras in Paul's Epistle to the Colossians (Chs. 1:7 f.; 4:12 f.).

Within five years of Paul's departure from Ephesus, he found himself a prisoner in Rome, waiting to have his case heard by the emperor, to whose jurisdiction he had appealed from that of the procuratorial court in Judaea. He spent this time in Rome under military guard, in a relatively free and honourable custody, and was able to receive visitors without let or hindrance.

Among the visitors who came to him in Rome from all parts of his far-flung mission field was Epaphras, the evangelist of the Lycus valley. He brought the apostle news of the progress of the churches in that area. Much of his news was encouraging, but there was one disquieting feature: at Colossae in particular there was a strong inclination on the part of the Christians to entertain a form of teaching which (although they did not suspect it) would inevitably subvert the pure gospel which they had accepted a few years before, and force them to give up their Christian liberty for spiritual bondage. It was mainly to safeguard them against this threat that Paul sent them the Epistle to the Colossians.

We have said that Paul was in Rome when he wrote this letter. The question is not of the first importance, as it makes little difference to the exegesis whether it was sent from Rome or Caesarea or Ephesus. In recent years the thesis that all four of the "Captivity Epistles" were written during one or more of the apostle's periods of imprisonment at Ephesus has found able defenders.[6] In the case of one of the four—the Epistle to the Philippians—the arguments for an Ephesian origin are specially

---

[6] To the bibliography given in *Acts* in NICNT, p. 393, n. 29, add G. S. Duncan, "The Epistles of the Imprisonment in Recent Discussion," ExT xlvi (1934–5), pp. 293 ff.; "Were Paul's Imprisonment Epistles written from Ephesus?", ExT lxvii (1955–6), pp. 163 ff. For the Caesarean provenience see most recently L. Johnson, "The Pauline Letters from Caesarea," ExT lxviii (1956–7), pp. 24 ff.

strong.[7] But in the case of Colossians and Ephesians (with which Philemon necessarily goes) the arguments for a Roman origin are stronger.[8] Arguments on the supposed development of Paul's thought must be used with caution;[9] but a comparison of the presentation of the Church as the body of Christ in Colossians and Ephesians with the presentation of that doctrine in 1 Corinthians (A.D. 54) and Romans (early in A.D. 57) points very definitely to the conclusion that Colossians and Ephesians represent a later and more advanced stage of the doctrine in the apostle's mind than do 1 Corinthians and Romans. It is only in Colossians and Ephesians that the thought of Christ as the head of the body emerges. In 1 Cor. 12:12 ff., where the common life of Christians is first compared to the interdependence of the various parts of the body, the head is one "member" among others; a member of the church may be thought of as the head or as part of the head—an ear or an eye. This becomes impossible when once the apostle reaches the more advanced conception found in Colossians and Ephesians.

Whether this more advanced conception represents a spontaneous progress in the apostle's thinking about the relation between Christ and His people or arose in part from some special stimulus cannot be known for certain; but it is very probable that the form which it takes in Colossians reflects Paul's vigorous reaction to the news of the strange teaching which was being inculcated at Colossae.

(b) The Colossian Heresy

We have no formal exposition of the Colossian heresy; its features have to be inferred from Paul's references to it in the

---

[7] See Acts in NICNT, p. 395, n. 35. But see also P. N. Harrison, "The Pastoral Epistles and Duncan's Ephesian Theory," NTS ii (1955–6), pp. 250 ff., in which it is argued from Duncan's own premises that "Paul cannot have written Philippians at Ephesus, and must have done so at Rome."

[8] The value cf the statement in the Marcionite prologue to Colossians ("The apostle in bonds writes to them from Ephesus") is greatly weakened by the fact that the companion prologue to Philemon represents that epistle as written from Rome (as was also the Epistle to the "Laodiceans", according to its Marcionite prologue). The Ephesian provenience of Colossians and Ephesians is rejected by E. Percy, Die Probleme der Kolosser- und Epheserbriefe (Lund, 1946), pp. 467 ff.

[9] Cf. C. H. Dodd's two essays on "The Mind of Paul," reprinted in his New Testament Studies (Manchester, 1953), pp. 67 ff. The second of these essays contains a vigorous defence of the Roman provenience of all the Captivity Epistles.

course of the epistle and from the particular aspects of Christian truth which he emphasizes in order to provide his readers with an antidote against it.

Basically the heresy was Jewish. This seems obvious from the part played in it by legal ordinances, circumcision, food regulations, the sabbath, new moon and other prescriptions of the Jewish calendar—things which once had their place as "a shadow of the things to come" but had lost their validity now that Christ, the reality which they foreshadowed, had come and fulfilled their significance (Ch. 2:16 f.).

But it was not the straightforward Judaism against which the churches of Galatia had to be put on their guard at an earlier date. That Judaism was probably introduced to the Galatian churches by emissaries from Judaea; this Judaism was a native Phrygian variety, which had undergone a remarkable fusion with a philosophy of non-Jewish origin—an early and simple form of gnosticism.[10]

The orthodoxy of the Phrygian Jews was suspect in the eyes of their Palestinian and Mesopotamian brethren. A Talmudic saying is frequently quoted in this regard, to the effect that Phrygian wine and baths had separated the ten tribes from their fellow-Israelites;[11] but there were more subtle influences than these. The barriers between Judaism and paganism were not very effective in a region where a Jewish lady could be both honorary ruler of the synagogue and priestess of the imperial cult.[12] That might be an exceptional occurrence, but the synagogues of Phrygia were peculiarly exposed to the influences of Hellenistic speculation and consequent tendencies to religious syncretism. When the gospel was introduced to the area, a Jewish-Hellenistic syncretism would find no great difficulty in expanding and modifying itself sufficiently

---

[10] The essential feature from which gnosticism derives its name is its emphasis on right knowledge (Gk. γνῶσις) as the way of salvation, but the description "gnostic" is usually restricted to those systems which posit a clear-cut dualism between the spiritual and material realms, and envisage salvation as the liberation of those particles of the spiritual realm (especially human souls) which are imprisoned in the material realm (e.g. in bodies of flesh); asceticism was commonly regarded as an important element in the process of this liberation. See H. Jonas, *Gnosis und spätantiker Geist* i (Göttingen, 1934), ii. 1 (1954), with review of Part i by A. D. Nock in *Gnomon* xii (1936), pp. 605 ff.
[11] TB *Shabbath* 147b. The geographical reference is not certain.
[12] *Cf.* W. M. Ramsay, *Cities and Bishoprics of Phrygia* ii (Oxford, 1897), pp. 637 ff., 649 ff., 673 ff. (notes on inscriptions 530 and 559).

to take some Christian elements into its system, and the result would be something like the Colossian heresy as we may reconstruct it from Paul's treatment of it.

In this teaching a decisive place was accorded to the angelic beings through whom the law was given. They were not only elemental spirits but dominant ones as well—principalities and powers, lords of the planetary spheres, sharers in the plenitude of the divine essence. Since they controlled the lines of communication between God and man, all revelation from God to man and all prayer and worship from man to God could reach its goal only through their mediation and by their permission. It was therefore thought wise to cultivate their good will and pay them such homage as they desired.

Moreover, since they were the agents through whom the divine law was given, the keeping of the law was regarded as a tribute of obedience to them, and the breaking of the law incurred their displeasure and brought the law-breaker into debt and bondage to them. Hence they must be placated, not only by the regular legal observances of traditional Judaism—circumcision, the sabbath and the various sacred seasons of the levitical year, food restrictions and so forth—but by a rigorous asceticism.[13]

All this made an undoubted appeal to a certain religious temperament, the more so as it was presented as a form of advanced teaching for the spiritual élite. Christians were urged to go in for this progressive "wisdom" (*sophia*) and "knowledge" (*gnosis*), to explore the hidden mysteries by a series of successive initiations until they attained perfection (*teleiosis*). Christian baptism was only a preliminary initiation; if they would proceed farther along the path of truth, they must put off all material elements by pursuing an ascetic regimen until at last they found themselves transported from the material to the spiritual world, from the

---

[13] We are invited to compare Philo's description of the Therapeutae (*Contemplative Life*, 37), what Hippolytus says about the Encratites (*Refutation*, viii. 20. 1) and what Epiphanius says about the Ebionites (*Heresies*, xxx. 15. 3; 16. 1), but these people's asceticism did not have the same motivation as that inculcated at Colossae. J. B. Lightfoot (*St. Paul's Epistles to the Colossians and to Philemon* [London, 1879], pp. 73 ff.) finds Essene influence in the Colossian heresy. This can hardly be sustained, unless we stretch the meaning of "Essene" to an abnormal extent; but it should be added that the value of Lightfoot's dissertation on the Essenes, appended to his commentary (pp. 347 ff.), has been vindicated by all that has been discovered on this subject since its publication, not least in the light of the discovery of the Qumrân texts.

domain of darkness to the realm of light. This was the true redemption at which they ought to aim.

All this angel-worship is condemned by Paul as specious make-believe. Far from representing a more advanced grade of religious truth than that which was presented in the apostolic preaching, it was at every point inconsistent with that preaching and tended to undermine the whole gospel. This was something worse than the simple Jewish legalism against which the Galatian churches had to be warned some years earlier. A system in which the planetary lords played so prominent a part must inevitably enthrone fate in place of the will of God. If we may judge by the analogy of parallel systems, Christ was probably held to have relinquished successive portions of His power to these lords as He passed through their spheres, one after the other, on His way to earth. But certainly His death was believed to prove His inferiority to them, since it was they who made Him suffer. And by the same token His servant Paul, who had to endure so many afflictions in his apostolic ministry, clearly had not attained to that degree of insight into the powers of the world and of control over them which would have enabled him to avoid these sufferings.

Paul's answer to this "tradition of men" is to set against it the one trustworthy tradition, the true doctrine of Christ. Christ, he says, is the very image of God, the One who embodies the plenitude of the divine essence, in which these elemental spirits have no share at all. And those who are members of Christ realize their fulness in Him; they need not seek, and they cannot find, perfection anywhere else. It is in Christ that all wisdom and knowledge are concentrated and are made available to His people—not just to an élite, but to all. Christ is the one Mediator between God and man, not in the sense of one who occupies the lines of communication between them and can transmit messages passing from one side to the other, but in the sense that He combines Godhead and manhood in His single person and so brings God and man together. Christ is the One through whom and for whom all things were created, including the principalities and powers to which the Colossians were being tempted to pay tribute. But why should those who are united with the Creator of these principalities and powers think it necessary to appease them? Above all, Christ by His death is revealed as the Conqueror of these principalities and powers. On the cross He fought and won the decisive battle against them. Not only did He repel their attack upon Himself and turn the cross into His triumphal car before which they were driven as His vanquished foes, but by that victory He liberated His people also from their power. Why then should those who through faith-union had died and risen with Christ go on serving those beings whom He had so completely conquered? Far from being a form of advanced wisdom, this false system which they were being urged to accept, with its tabus, bore all the marks of immaturity. Why should those who had come of age in Christ go back to the apron-strings of infancy? Why should those whom Christ had set free submit to this yoke of bondage again?

Thus, in his reply to the Colossian heresy, Paul develops the doctrine of the cosmic Christ more fully than he had done in his earlier extant epistles. The doctrine was not new, indeed. To Paul there was "one Lord, Jesus Christ, through whom are all things, and we through him" (1 Cor. 8:6); to him and to his fellow-Christians this Christ was "the power of God, and the wisdom of God" (1 Cor. 1:24); and God through the Spirit had revealed to His people that hidden wisdom, "foreordained before the worlds unto our glory," through ignorance of which the supernatural world-rulers had crucified the Lord of glory and thus accomplished their own overthrow (1 Cor. 2:6–10). And the liberation which Christ procured by His death was not restricted to His people alone, but would ultimately be displayed in its cosmic outreaching (Rom. 8:19–22). But what was hinted at here and there in those earlier epistles is expounded more fully in Colossians.

Justification by faith, fundamental as it is to Paul's outlook, does not exhaust his message. It was inevitable—and most desirable—that in the age of the Reformation special attention should be concentrated on the way by which the individual soul is accepted as righteous in God's sight. But it is regrettable that in many Protestant quarters Paulinism has been equated so absolutely with the emphasis of Galatians and Romans that the corporate and cosmic insights of Colossians and Ephesians have been felt to be non-Pauline. There is room in true Paulinism for both, and contemporary evangelicalism must similarly make room for both if it is not to become lop-sided and defective.[14]

---

[14] *Cf.* O. A. Dilschneider, *Das christliche Weltbild* (Gütersloh, 1951), reviewed by W. M. Horton in *Erasmus* vii (1954), p. 131.

(c) Some Critical Questions

It has sometimes been urged against the Pauline authorship of the Epistle to the Colossians that such a gnostic heresy as is rebutted in the epistle cannot have arisen before the second century A.D. There would be substance in this argument if the Colossian heresy exhibited the features of fully developed Valentinianism or another of the gnostic systems attacked by Irenaeus and Hippolytus.[15] But, as compared with these second-century systems, the Colossian heresy must be regarded as only an incipient form of gnosticism, and in fact evidence is forthcoming in increasing measure that such incipient forms of gnosticism were current in the first century, especially in areas where Judaism of the Dispersion found itself involved in the dominant trends of Hellenistic and Oriental thought.

Another argument that has been brought against the authenticity of the epistle boils down to the feeling that the author of the Galatian, Corinthian and Roman letters could not have adapted himself as the writer of Colossians does to the situation with which this epistle deals. But this is to impose a completely unwarranted limitation on Paul's intelligence, versatility and originality. He whose settled policy was to be "all things to all men" for the gospel's sake (1 Cor. 9:22 f.)[16] was surely not incapable of confronting the false *gnosis* and worldly *askesis*[17] taught at Colossae with the true *gnosis* and spiritual *askesis* of Christ. While he opposes an uncompromising negative to the heresy which he attacks, he takes up its characteristic terms and shows how the truth which they attempt to convey is embodied in Christ, the true mystery of God.

It has been pointed out that Paul in this epistle is doing two things at once: he is acting as the apologist for Christianity to the intellectual world of paganism at the same time as he is defending

---

[15] New light on these is afforded by the lately discovered Coptic gnostic texts from Nag Hammadi. *Cf.* F. L. Cross (ed.), *The Jung Codex: A Newly Discovered Gnostic Papyrus* (London, 1955); M. Malinine, etc. (ed. and tr.), *Evangelium Veritatis* (Zürich, 1956).

[16] See the important study by H. Chadwick, "All Things to All Men", NTS i (1954–5), pp. 261 ff.

[17] Gk. ἄσκησις means primarily "training" or "exercise", such as an athlete must undertake; in a secondary sense (whence our word "asceticism") it was used of the discipline necessary for spiritual contests. *Cf.* Acts 24:18, "I also exercise myself" (Gk. καὶ αὐτὸς ἀσκῶ, the only NT occurrence of the word).

gospel truth within the Church.[18] As apologist to the Gentiles, he was probably the first to meet his pagan opponents on their own ground and use their language in a Christian sense, in order to show them that the problems to which they vainly sought an answer elsewhere found their satisfying solution in the gospel.

This employment of the technical terms of the erroneous teaching in what has been called a "disinfected" sense[19] helps to explain the difference in vocabulary which many have felt between this epistle (and Ephesians) on the one hand and the Galatian, Corinthian and Roman epistles on the other. It may have been also in reaction to the Colossian heresy that Paul developed his earlier picture of Christian fellowship in terms of the relation between the various parts of one body to the point reached in Colossians and Ephesians, where the Church is viewed as the body of which Christ is the head. In this way not only the living fellowship between the members but the dependence of all the members upon Christ for life and power is vividly brought out, and the supremacy of Christ is vindicated against a system which contrived to cast Him down from His excellency. That, in consequence, "body" is used in these two epistles in correlation with "head," rather than (as in the earlier epistles) in correlation with "spirit", may be granted; but this provides no compelling reason for denying that the writer of the earlier epistles could have written these too.[20]

Again, some of the stylistic distinctiveness of this epistle is bound up with the sustained note of thanksgiving; this consideration applies to Ch. 1, and particularly to verses 9–23, some parts of which have been singled out as specially un-Pauline in character. (The influence of the sustained note of thanksgiving on style and diction is even more relevant to the study of Ephesians.) There is the further point that the credal affirmations of Ch. 1:12–17 probably echo the language of primitive Christian confessions of faith.

There seems, in short, to be no sound argument against the genuineness of this epistle. Some scholars, represented principally

---

18 H. Chadwick, *loc. cit.*, p. 275.
19 H. Chadwick, *loc. cit.*, p. 272.
20 But *cf.* Eph. 4:4. See now P. Benoit, "Corps, tête et plérôme dans les Epîtres de la Captivité," RB lxiii (1956), pp. 5 ff.

by H. J. Holtzmann[21] last century and Charles Masson[22] in our own day, recognizing indubitably Pauline elements in Colossians, have tried to account for the presence of elements felt to be un-Pauline by supposing that Paul wrote a shorter Epistle to the Colossians. This was drawn upon subsequently by the Paulinist who is supposed to have composed the Epistle to the Ephesians. Then this Paulinist, not content with composing such a masterpiece as Ephesians, interpolated passages from Ephesians into the genuine Colossians, together with warnings against gnosticism, and thus produced our present Epistle to the Colossians. Holtzmann attempted by this hypothesis to account for the curious phenomenon that, in passages common to Colossians and Ephesians, sometimes the one epistle and sometimes the other seems to be the earlier. But "the complexity of the hypothesis tells fatally against it."[23] The literary relationship of Ephesians to Colossians (and to other Pauline epistles) presents a real problem, but the solution does not lie in this direction.[24] To the present writer it still appears most probable that Paul, having completed his letter to Colossae, allowed his thoughts to run on along the same line until he was gripped by the vision which finds expression in the companion letter, and began to dictate its contents in an exalted mood of inspired meditation, thanksgiving and prayer. The resultant document was then sent as a letter to the Asian churches by the hand of the messengers who were entrusted with the Epistle to the Colossians.[25]

---

[21] *Kritik der Epheser- und Kolosserbriefe* (Leipzig, 1872). The genuine nucleus which Holtzmann discerned in Colossians consisted of Chs. 1:1–5, 6a, 7, 8, 9a, 10 (in part), 13, 19–20 (in part), 21–23 (in part), 25, 29; 2:1, 2a, 4, 5, 6, 7b, 8, 9 (in part), 11 (in part), 12–14, 16, 18b, 20, 21, 22a, 23b; 3:3, 12, 13, 17; 4:2–5 (for the most part),6–8, 10–11, 12 (in considerable part), 13, 14, 15.

[22] *L'Épître de Saint Paul aux Colossiens*, in CNT x (Neuchatel & Paris, 1950), pp. 83 ff. Masson's argument is independent of Holtzmann's, although his conclusions are generally similar.

[23] A. S. Peake, *Critical Introduction to the NT* (London, 1909), p. 52.

[24] "The relation between Colossians and Ephesians—the principal objection urged against their authenticity—is of such a kind that the hypothesis of the authenticity of the two letters is still the best solution" (W. Michaelis, *Einleitung in das Neue Testament* [Bern, 1946], p. 200).

[25] The principal recent works which deny the authenticity of Ephesians are E. J. Goodspeed, *The Meaning of Ephesians* (Chicago, 1933), *The Key to Ephesians* (Chicago, 1956), and C. L. Mitton, *The Epistle to the Ephesians* (Oxford, 1951); the principal recent work to maintain its authenticity is E. Percy, *Probleme der Kolosser- und Epheserbriefe* (Lund, 1946). Percy concludes: "The result of our analysis of the relation between the two letters is this

Both letters (with the companion epistle to Philemon, which was despatched at the same time) are present in the Pauline *corpus* as far back as we can trace the existence of this collection, and were acknowledged as canonical from the earliest beginnings of the New Testament Canon.

—that certain circumstances do indeed appear to speak loudly in favour of the literary dependence of Ephesians on Colossians, but that even stronger arguments on the other side speak in favour of their common origin" (p. 433). The recent symposium, *Studies in Ephesians* (ed. F. L. Cross, London, 1956), opens with an essay on "The Case for the Pauline Authorship" by J. N. Sanders, followed by one on "The Case against the Pauline Authorship" by D. E. Nineham. In Sanders's judgment, Ephesians is not really an epistle (not even a circular one), though its form is epistolary; he prefers to regard it as Paul's spiritual testament to the Church.

THE EPISTLE TO THE COLOSSIANS

INTRODUCTION

ANALYSIS OF THE EPISTLE TO THE COLOSSIANS

I. SALUTATION (Ch. 1:1–2)

II. THE PERSON AND WORK OF CHRIST (Chs. 1:3–2:7)

1. PAUL'S THANKSGIVING FOR THE COLOSSIANS' FAITH (Ch. 1:3–8)

2. PAUL'S PRAYER THAT THE COLOSSIANS MAY INCREASE IN THE KNOWLEDGE AND LOVE OF GOD REVEALED IN CHRIST (Ch. 1:9–23)
   (a) His prayer for their Christian progress (Ch. 1:9–14)
   (b) Christ as Lord of Creation (Ch. 1:15–17)
   (c) Christ as Head of the Church (Ch. 1:18)
   (d) Christ as Reconciler of all things (Ch. 1:19–20)
   (e) Christ as Reconciler of His People to God (Ch. 1:21–23)

3. PAUL'S STEWARDSHIP OF THE REVELATION OF GOD (Ch. 1:24–29)

4. PAUL'S CONCERN FOR THE CHRISTIANS OF THE LYCUS VALLEY (Ch. 2:1–5)
   (a) Reassurance of his prayers for them (Ch. 2:1–3)
   (b) His anxiety lest they be misled (Ch. 2:4–5)

5. GO ON AS YOU HAVE BEGUN (Ch. 2:6–7)

III. FALSE TEACHING AND ITS ANTIDOTE (Chs. 2:8–3:4)

1. CHRIST IS ALL—AND ALL YOU NEED (Ch. 2:8–15)
   (a) The Fulness of Christ (Ch. 2:8–10)
   (b) The New Circumcision (Ch. 2:11–12)
   (c) The Triumph of Christ (Ch. 2:13–15)

2. GUARD YOUR FREEDOM! (Ch. 2:16–19)
   (a) Freedom in respect of Food and Festivals (Ch. 2:16–17)
   (b) Freedom in respect of Asceticism and Angel-Worship (Ch. 2:18–19)

3. You Died with Christ; Therefore . . . (Ch. 2:20–23)
4. You Rose with Christ; Therefore . . . (Ch. 3:1–4)

IV. THE CHRISTIAN LIFE (Chs. 3:5–4:6)

1. "Put Off" (Ch. 3:5–11)
2. "Put On" (Ch. 3:12–17)
3. "Be Subject" (Chs. 3:18–4:1)
   (a) Wives and Husbands (Ch. 3:18–19)
   (b) Children and Parents (Ch. 3:20–21)
   (c) Servants and Masters (Ch. 3:22–4:1)
4. "Watch and Pray" (Ch. 4:2–6)

V. PERSONAL NOTES (Ch. 4:7–17)

1. Paul's Messengers (Ch. 4:7–9)
2. Greetings from Paul's Companions (Ch. 4:10–14)
3. Greetings to Various Friends (Ch. 4:15–17)

VI. FINAL GREETING AND BLESSING (Ch. 4:18)

CHAPTER I

I. SALUTATION

Ch. 1:1–2

1 Paul, an apostle of Christ Jesus through the will of
   God, and Timothy our brother,
2 to the saints and faithful brethren in Christ *that are*
   at Colossae: Grace to you and peace from God our
   Father.[1]

1 As in the companion epistle to Philemon (by contrast with
that to the Ephesians), Paul associates Timothy with himself in
the salutation to the Christians of Colossae. But Timothy was
with Paul in too many places and on too many occasions for this
fact to be used as a clue to the place from which this epistle was
written. We know indeed that Timothy was in Paul's company
for much of his Ephesian ministry (*cf.* Acts 19:22; 2 Cor. 1:1, etc.),
but this does not exclude the possibility—or even the probability—
that he was in Paul's company at Rome also.

Paul, as in 2 Cor. 1:1, reserves the designation "apostle" for
himself; he does not accord it to Timothy. Nor does he accord
it to Epaphras in v. 7, although it was Epaphras who first brought
the gospel to Colossae. Paul alone was the Colossians' apostle,
even if he had never visited them in person. For, whereas he had
been independently and directly commissioned by the risen Lord,
Timothy and Epaphras and others, however much he loved and
honoured them as "fellow-servants", were his lieutenants, commissioned by him to aid him in the task of proclaiming the gospel
and planting churches. Where, as in 1 Thess. 2:6, he links Timothy
and Silvanus with himself as "apostles of Christ", he is using the
term in a wider sense, in which apostleship, instead of being based
on an immediate commissioning by Christ, is "grounded in the
preaching of the genuine gospel, under the guidance of the Holy

---

[1] The words "and the Lord Jesus Christ" (*cf.* AV) appear in the Byzantine
text, the codices ℵ A C G, and the Clementine Vulgate; they are omitted by
B D and most of our early manuscript authorities, by the oldest Vulgate codices,
the Syriac version, and Origen. See n. 6 below.

Spirit, whether in association with Paul or independently of Paul's mission."[2]

2 Paul describes those to whom he sends this letter as "saints and believing brothers in Christ" who live at Colossae. When he calls them "saints", he marks them out as the holy people of God, chosen and set apart for Him. The whole description is similar to the corresponding phrase at the beginning of Ephesians, although not identical with it: "to the saints who are [in Ephesus] and believers in Christ Jesus" (Eph. 1:1). He sends them his characteristic greeting—"Grace to you and peace from God our Father"—in which the collocation "grace and peace"[3] unites a Christianized variant of the regular Greek salutation ("Hail!")[4] with the common Jewish salutation ("Peace!").[5] The form of the greeting here is unique for Paul in that the words "and from Christ Jesus our Lord" are not added after "from God our Father."[6]

---

[2] D. W. B. Robinson, "Apostleship and Apostolic Succession", RThR xiii (1954), p. 38. On the twofold use of the term ἀπόστολος cf. also T. W. Manson, *The Church's Ministry* (London, 1948), pp. 31 ff.; K. H. Rengstorf, *Apostleship* (Eng. tr., London, 1952); J. N. Geldenhuys, *Supreme Authority* (London, 1953), pp. 45 ff.; P. Bonnard, *L'Épître de Saint Paul aux Galates* = CNT ix (Neuchâtel-Paris, 1953), pp. 58 f.; C. Masson, *L'Épître de Saint Paul aux Éphésiens* = CNT ix, p. 191; B. Citron, "The Reformed Ministry in the Contemporary Church", SJTh viii (1955), pp. 392 ff.

[3] *Cf.* Rom. 1:7; 1 Cor. 1:3; 2 Cor. 1:2; Gal. 1:3; Eph. 1:2; Phil. 1:2; 1 Thess. 1:2; 2 Thess. 1:2; Tit. 1:4.

[4] Gk. χαῖρε, which probably suggested to the apostle the similarly-sounding but richer greeting χάρις ("Grace!").

[5] Gk. εἰρήνη, echoing Heb. *shalom* (*cf.* Arab. *salaam*).

[6] See n. 1 above. The very uniqueness of this reading speaks in its favour; there would be a strong tendency to assimilate the wording here to Paul's usual practice.

II. THE PERSON AND WORK OF CHRIST

Chs. 1:3–2:7

1. PAUL'S THANKSGIVING FOR THE COLOSSIANS' FAITH

Ch. 1:3–8

3 We give thanks to God the Father of our Lord Jesus Christ, praying always for you,

4 having heard of your faith in Christ Jesus, and of the love which ye have toward all the saints,

5 because of the hope which is laid up for you in the heavens, whereof ye heard before in the word of the truth of the gospel,

6 which is come unto you; even as it is also in all the world bearing fruit and increasing, as *it doth* in you also, since the day ye heard and knew the grace of God in truth;

7 even as ye learned of Epaphras our beloved fellow-servant, who is a faithful minister of Christ on our[7] behalf,

8 who also declared unto us your love in the Spirit.

3 After the salutation, as regularly in Paul's letters to churches, comes his thanksgiving to God for the good news that he hears of his readers, and the assurance of his continual prayers on their behalf.[8] Deissmann quotes from pagan letters examples of thanksgiving to a deity immediately after the opening salutation.[9] It was,

---

7 The reading "our" (ARV, ERV, RSV) has in its favour the formidable combination of P^{46} and the Alexandrian and Western authorities; the Byzantine reading "your" is attested by Cod. C and the Latin, Syriac and other versions. In a context where either reading gives good sense, the weight of the textual evidence must be decisive. But there is constant confusion in Greek manuscripts between the various forms of ἡμεῖς ("we") and the corresponding forms of ὑμεῖς ("you"), partly because of the identity of pronunciation of the two pronouns in later Hellenistic Greek, and partly because of the rhetorical fashion of saying "we" in preference to you. Here Paul may be referring to himself in the first person plural, or associating his readers with himself. We cannot, however, in such cases wholly discount the possibility of a confusion between the two pronouns going back beyond our earliest textual evidence.

8 *Cf.* Rom. 1:8 f.; 1 Cor. 1:4; Eph. 1:16; Phil. 1:3 f.; 1 Thess. 1:2; 2 Thess. 1:3; Philem. 4.

9 A. Deissmann, *Light from the Ancient East* (Eng. tr., London, 1927), pp. 179 ff., quoting BGU ii, 423.

no doubt, a natural and common custom in letter-writing, but one which (like so many others) Paul Christianized.

4-5 As Paul enumerates his reasons for thanksgiving and prayer, we recognize the familiar triad of graces—faith, love and hope—elsewhere combined by Paul, as in 1 Thess. 1:3; 5:8, and (best known passage of all) 1 Cor. 13:13.[10] Here, however, the three are not completely coordinated; the Colossians' faith in Christ and love to their fellow-Christians are here based upon the hope which is laid up for them in heaven.[11] But this hope laid up in heaven, as we discover in the course of the epistle, cannot well be anything less than Christ Himself (cf. Ch. 1:27). "Christ Jesus" appears here to be viewed not so much as the object of their faith as the living environment within which their faith is exercised; that is to say, the faith of which the apostle speaks is the faith which they have as men and women who are "in Christ Jesus."[12]

The emphasis on hope in v. 5 reminds us that the salvation which believers already enjoy in Christ includes a future aspect. We are encouraged to expect its consummation on the day of Christ's *parousia*; in this sense Paul can speak elsewhere of salvation as being "nearer to us than when we first believed" (Rom. 13:11). We should not allow a proper appreciation of "realized eschatology" to banish from our minds the prospect of that "revealing of the sons of God" for which "the earnest expectation of the creation" waits (Rom. 8:19). This Christian hope formed part of the subject-matter of the gospel message as it was first proclaimed at Colossae.[13] We may compare the reference in Eph. 1:12 to "us who at the first placed our hope in Christ." The description of the

---

[10] Cf. also Rom. 5:1-5; Gal. 5:5 f.; Eph. 4:2-5; Heb. 6:10-12; 10:22-24; 1 Peter 1:3-8, 21 f.; Ep. Barn. 1:4; 11:8; Ep. Polyc. 3:2 f. It may well be that the triad of graces belongs to the common stock of the earliest Christianity and is not the creation of Paul; in that case a passage like this will represent Paul's own exegesis of the triad (so A. M. Hunter, "Faith, Hope, Love—A Primitive Christian Triad", ExT xlix [1937-8], pp. 428 f.).

[11] For the part played by hope in this epistle cf. vv. 23 and 27; see also Eph. 1:18; 4:4.

[12] The preposition here is ἐν, not εἰς (as it is in Ch. 2:5). For such a use of ἐν after πίστις cf. Gal. 3:26; 5:6; Eph. 1:15 (closely parallel to the present passage); 1 Tim. 1:14; 3:13; 2 Tim. 1:13; 3:15. In most, perhaps all, of these passages the sphere of faith rather than the object of faith may be in view (cf. C. F. D. Moule, IBNTG, p. 81).

[13] Cf. C. F. D. Moule, *The Meaning of Hope* (London, 1954), and J. E. Fison, *The Christian Hope* (London, 1954).

Christian proclamation as "the word of the truth of the gospel" is echoed and amplified in Eph. 1:13 ("the word of truth, the gospel of your salvation").[14]

6 This true message of the gospel, which in due course reached Colossae, and produced the vigorous and increasing fruit of Christian life and testimony there, was doing the same throughout the world. It has been thought that the expression "bearing fruit and increasing" may echo the language of a gnosticizing interpretation of our Lord's parable of the sower (Mark 4:8) which had been pressed upon the Colossian church.[15] Whether this is so or not, an echo of that parable may certainly be detected, and Paul's choice of words does not support those modern interpretations which exclude the thought of development from this and kindred parables.

Paul was writing (as we think) from Rome, but he knew that in addition to his own propagation of the gospel from Jerusalem to Illyricum, and now in the imperial city itself, the same gospel was being blazed abroad by other heralds too. "The whole gospel for the whole world" might well have been his motto, and if sometimes the language which he uses to express this idea seems to outstrip what had actually been accomplished at the time, it was with the eye of a true prophet that he descried the all-pervading course of the message of life rivalling that of the heavenly bodies of which the psalmist spoke: "their sound went out into all the earth, and their words unto the ends of the world" (Rom. 10:18, quoting Ps. 19:4).[16]

7–8 What was true of the progress of the gospel elsewhere was true at Colossae as well; the Christians of that city had continued to grow in spiritual character and in actual numbers since the day when they first heard and believed the gospel. The gospel told them of the grace of God, brought near to men in Christ, and when they yielded their allegiance to Christ as Lord and Saviour they came to know in personal and united experience the reality of that grace. The preacher from whom they first heard

---

[14] *Cf.* 2 Cor. 6:7 ("in the word of truth").

[15] *Cf.* W. L. Knox, *St. Paul and the Church of the Gentiles* (Cambridge, 1939), p. 149 n.

[16] *Cf.* v. 23; Rom. 1:8; 1 Thess. 1:8. J. Munck interprets the universal terminology of such passages (especially Rom. 10:18) in accordance with his view of Paul's eschatological significance (*Paulus und die Heilsgeschichte* [Copenhagen, 1954], pp. 45 f. *et passim*).

this message of God's grace bore the name of Epaphras. Paul refers to him in terms of affection and praise, as a dear colleague[17] in the service of God, who had gone to Colossae (and evidently to other cities in the Lycus valley) as his own representative and as a faithful servant of Christ.

Who this Epaphras was we cannot say with certainty. He is mentioned again in Ch. 4:12 and in Philem. 23. The name is a short form of Epaphroditus, and we meet with an Epaphroditus elsewhere in the Pauline corpus (cf. Phil. 2:25; 4:18), but there is no sufficient evidence for identifying the two.[18] In Philem. 23 Epaphras is described as Paul's fellow-captive,[19] but we do not know what the circumstances were under which he earned this description. Probably he shared one of the apostle's more abundant imprisonments, possibly in Ephesus. At any rate he had discharged his responsibility well as the evangelist of the Lycus valley, for there were flourishing churches in that area—in Hierapolis and Laodicea as well as in Colossae—to testify to the enduring character of his work. More recently he had paid a visit to Paul in Rome and told him how these churches were faring. Much of his news was good and encouraging, but some aspects of church life at Colossae were disquieting, and it was this that stimulated Paul to write particularly to the Christians of that city. First of all, however, he dwells on the good report which Epaphras had brought him: he "declared unto us your love in the Spirit"—that is to say, the mutual love implanted and fostered in their hearts by the Holy Spirit who dwelt within them and united them in a living bond. This, by the way, is the only explicit reference to the Spirit of God in this epistle.[20] The absence of reference to Him elsewhere is

---

17 He uses the term σύνδουλος ("fellow-slave"), used also of Tychicus in Ch. 4:7. T. R. Glover regards Paul's fondness for compounds with σύν as a mannerism which reveals somethings of his character: "The dearest of all ties for Paul is to find men sharing things with him. The work, the 'athletic' life, the yoke, the slavery, the imitation,—these are all expressions of his relation with Jesus Christ, the very essence of life; how much more it is to him when he finds his friends standing with him in that great loyalty!" (Paul of Tarsus [London, 1925], p. 180).

18 As Glover does (op. cit., p. 179), adding the two σύν compounds with which Paul describes Epaphroditus (συνεργός, συνστρατιώτης, both in Phil. 2:25) to the two with which he describes Epaphras (σύνδουλος and συναιχμάλωτος, Philem. 23), to give him four in all.

19 Like Aristarchus in Col. 4:10.

20 There is an implied reference in the adjective πνευματικός ("spiritual") in v. 9.

the more striking as there are several places where His work might have been naturally introduced, especially His rôle in baptizing believers into the unity of the body of Christ.[21] Yet His presence and activity are implied here and there (for example, in opposition to the "flesh"[22] as the source of divine knowledge).

---

[21] *Cf.* 1 Cor. 12:13; Eph. 4:3 ff.
[22] As in Ch. 2:18.

2. PAUL'S PRAYER THAT THE COLOSSIANS MAY INCREASE IN THE KNOWLEDGE AND LOVE OF GOD REVEALED IN CHRIST

Ch. 1:9–23

Paul repeats his assurance to the Colossian believers of his constant prayers on their behalf—prayers which have been redoubled since Epaphras came with news of their progress. The content of Paul's prayer for their spiritual welfare then passes into one of the great Christological passages of the NT, the signal for the transition being given in vv. 13 and 14 by Paul's reminder to them of their redemption, forgiveness and transference into the kingdom of God's beloved Son. This mention of the Son of God leads Paul on to contemplate the Son's rôle in creation and reconciliation. The language of this section is marked by a liturgico-hymnic style such as appears in certain other NT passages (*cf.* John 1:1 ff.; Heb. 1:1–4; 1 Peter 2:22–24; 3:22). This suggests that Paul is here echoing the phraseology of a primitive Christian confession of faith in Christ. This confessional style, with its piling up of participial clauses, resembles similarly constructed affirmations concerning God in the liturgy of the synagogue.[23]

(a) His prayer for their Christian progress

Ch. 1:9–14

9   For this cause we also, since the day we heard *it,* do not cease to pray and make request for you, that ye may be filled with the knowledge of his will in all spiritual wisdom and understanding,

10   to walk worthily of the Lord unto all pleasing, bearing fruit in every good work, and increasing in the knowledge of God;

11   strengthened with all power, according to the might

---

[23]   *Cf.* E. Norden, *Agnostos Theos* (Leipzig, 1912), pp. 250 ff.; A. Deissmann, *Paul* (Eng. tr., London, 1926), p. 107; E. Lohmeyer, *Der Brief an die Kolosser* (MK, Göttingen, 1953), p. 13; E. Percy, *Probleme der Kolosser- und Epheserbriefe* (Lund, 1946), pp. 38 f.

of his glory, unto all patience and longsuffering with joy;[24]

12 giving thanks unto the Father, who made us meet[25] to be partakers of the inheritance of the saints in light;

13 who delivered us out of the power of darkness, and translated us into the kingdom of the Son of his love;

14 in whom we have our redemption,[26] the forgiveness of our sins:

9 His prayer for them, then, is that they may attain to the full knowledge of God's will[27] through the insight that His Spirit imparts, and thus be able to please Him in everything and live in a way that befits His children. We have already noticed the almost complete absence of explicit reference to the Spirit of God in this epistle (there is an allusion to Him here in the phrase "*spiritual* wisdom and understanding"); on the other hand, this epistle (like that to the Ephesians) has much to say about "knowledge" as a means of promoting Christian life.[28] But the "knowledge" of which the apostle speaks is no merely intellectual exercise, no theosophical *gnosis* such as was affected by the teachers who were leading the Colossians astray.[29] He wishes to impress

---

24 Nestle punctuates after "longsuffering", taking "with joy" along with the following words "giving thanks unto the Father"; the punctuation in the text is preferable.

25 Gk. ἱκανώσαντι, for which a few authorities (mainly Western, but including the Sahidic Coptic, Armenian and Ethiopic versions) have καλέσαντι ("called"). Cod. B conflates the two readings, καλέσαντι καὶ ἱκανώσαντι ("called and made meet"). Codd. ℵ and B and a few other authorities make the object ὑμᾶς ("you") instead of ἡμᾶς ("us"); cf. n. 7 above.

26 Many minuscules add διὰ τοῦ αἵματος αὐτοῦ ("through his blood"), which has found its way into TR and AV— a patent borrowing from Eph. 1:7.

27 For the knowledge of God's will cf. Acts 22:14; Rom. 12:2. From Rom. 2:28 one might infer that "to know the will" (*sc.* of God) was a current expression in Hellenistic-Jewish religious terminology.

28 Cf. Chs. 1:28; 2:1 ff.; 3:10.

29 Perhaps one reason for his preference of ἐπίγνωσις here is his desire to point a contrast with the much canvassed γνῶσις. This seems more likely than that Paul takes over what was a catchword of his opponents, by which they emphasized the more advanced knowledge they taught as against the ordinary γνῶσις (so W. L. Knox, *op. cit.*, p. 150; cf. Moulton and Milligan, VGT, p. 237). Whether the force of the prefix ἐπί here is intensive (J. B. Lightfoot) or directive (J. A. Robinson), or whether in fact it has any special force, is uncertain; no rule can be laid down covering all instances. In many, but not all, NT instances ἐπίγνωσις, like the verb ἐπιγινώσκω, "is almost a technical term for the decisive knowledge of God which is involved in conversion to the Christian faith" (R. Bultmann, *Gnosis* [Eng. tr., London, 1952], p. 37). See J. B. Lightfoot,

his readers with the character and importance of true knowledge before drawing their attention to the dangers of that "knowledge falsely so called" which was being pressed upon them. True knowledge is founded in practical religion; it is that knowledge which, according to the OT, starts with a proper attitude towards God: "the fear of the LORD is the beginning of knowledge" (Prov. 1:7; cf. Ps. 111:10; Prov. 9:10). Right knowledge, according to Paul, leads to right behaviour;[30] and here right knowledge is contrasted with wrong teaching.

10 If the Colossian Christians are filled with this right knowledge, they will live and act in a manner worthy of the holiness of Him whom they confess as their Lord. The formula "worthily of the Lord" (cf. 1 Thess. 2:12; 3 John 6; also Matt. 10:37; Wisdom 3:5) belongs to a type which appears on inscriptions in the province of Asia; according to Deissmann, it seems to have been popular at Pergamum.[31] If even pagans had some notion of rendering worthy worship to the deities whose votaries they were, how much more should Christians render the spiritual service of obedient lives to the living and true God, and to His Son Jesus Christ![32] Thus the fair fruit of good works would spring in greater abundance from the divine seed which had been sown in their hearts,[33] and at the same time they would make ever increasing progress in the knowledge of God. For obedience to the knowledge of God which one has already received is a necessary and certain condition for the reception of further knowledge.

11 Paul prays that they may be endowed not only with

St Paul's Epistles to the Colossians and to Philemon (London, 1879), pp. 137 f.; St. Paul's Epistle to the Philippians (London, 1881), p. 86; J. A. Robinson, St. Paul's Epistle to the Ephesians (London, 1904), pp. 248 ff.; E. K. Simpson, The Pastoral Epistles (London, 1954), p. 66; J. Dupont, Gnosis: La connaissance religieuse dans les épîtres de saint Paul (Louvain, 1949).

[30] Cf. Phil. 1:9 f.; also Rom. 12:2; 15:14; 1 Cor. 1:6; 2:6 ff.; 3:2; 2 Cor. 8:7; 11:6; Phil. 3:10; Philem. 6. For the ethical use of περιπατέω ("walk") in v. 10 (cf. Chs. 2:6; 3:7; 4:5) see p. 45, n. 1 (on Eph. 2:2).

[31] A. Deissmann, Bible Studies (Eng. tr., Edinburgh, 1909), p. 248.

[32] In the phrase εἰς πᾶσαν ἀρεσκείαν ("unto all pleasing") ἀρεσκεία has a higher sense than that of "obsequiousness", which it frequently possesses; parallels to this higher sense are found in Philo. Deissmann (Bible Studies, p. 224) quotes an example from an inscription, and Moulton and Milligan (VGT. p. 75) give one from an Oxyrhynchus papyrus of the 2nd cent. A.D. We might render freely: "so as to satisfy Him in all things."

[33] Cf. v. 6 (p. 181).

knowledge, but with power, "being empowered with all power in accordance with God's glorious might." The power which he longs to see manifested in their lives is the power of God Himself— nothing less. In Ephesians this idea is made even more explicit: there he describes the "exceeding greatness" of God's power in relation to those who believe in terms of the power which God exerted when He raised Christ from the dead and exalted Him to the place of universal supremacy at His own right hand. This, we are told, is the power which God places at the disposal of His people.[34] No wonder that the apostle speaks of it as God's "glorious might" (ARV "the might of his glory" is a literal rendering of the Greek phrase, which here preserves a Hebraic idiom). We remember how in another place he says that Christ "was raised from the dead through the glory of the Father" (Rom. 6:4).[35]

Such an endowment with divine power will enable them to stand firm in the face of trial and opposition and everything else that will test their faith in Christ. Patient endurance belongs to the fruit of the Spirit (Gal. 5:22). It was, of course, a quality highly esteemed by the Stoics, but Paul adds another quality which was not so characteristic of Stoicism—joyfulness.[36] Had not Paul himself learned to combine joyfulness with patience and long-suffering on more than one occasion? A Stoic in the stocks would have borne the discomfort calmly and uncomplainingly, but would he at the same time have sung praises to God, as Paul and his friend Silas did in the prison at Philippi?[37] Early Christianity and Stoicism show a resemblance with respect to several ethical features, but the power which Christians received from God gave them something over and above what Stoicism could impart. The Stoic virtue of self-sufficiency[38] falls short of that habit of mind to which Paul referred when he said he had learned to be content

---

[34] Eph. 1:20 (see E. K. Simpson's exposition *ad loc.*, pp. 39 f.).

[35] The power of God is a prominent theme in Colossians and Ephesians; *cf.* also Col. 1:29; 2:12; Eph. 1:19; 3:7, 16, 20; 6:10.

[36] Even if we adopt Nestle's punctuation (*cf.* n. 24 above), the virtues of patience (ὑπομονή) and longsuffering (μακροθυμία) still have the graces of joy and gratitude closely associated with them

[37] Acts 16:25. Epictetus, indeed, commends the example of Socrates, who composed a paean in prison (*Enchiridion* ii. 6. 26); but such an example was more admired than followed.

[38] Gk. αὐτάρκεια (see commentary on Acts in this series, pp. 349 f.)

in all the circumstances of life, for Paul's contentment was attended by a joyful exuberance which overflowed to others.[39]

12 Patience, longsuffering and joy should continually be accompanied by a thankful spirit. In Christianity, someone has said, theology is grace, and ethics is gratitude. If God's attitude and action towards us have been characterized by grace, our response to Him, in life and behaviour as well as in thought and word, should be characterized by gratitude. Nothing less is fitting, when we consider how, in the apostle's language here, He has "fitted us to share the inheritance of His holy people."[40]

For His holy people—the people of His choice—God in earlier days provided an earthly inheritance, a land which they might enter and possess. But the inheritance of which Paul speaks here belongs to a higher plane and a more enduring order than any terrestrial Canaan.[41] Like the recipients of the Epistle to the Ephesians, these Colossian Christians are no longer "strangers and sojourners", although they were Gentiles by birth, but have been made "fellow-citizens of the holy people of God and fellow-members of His household" (Eph. 2:19), thanks to their all-powerful and all-enabling Father.

13 This inheritance is a realm of light; it is irradiated by the rays of the Sun of righteousness, shining in the hearts of His people.[42] Thus it forms a complete contrast to the realm in which they formerly lived, the realm which is here described as the jurisdiction of darkness. There is no need to see here, as some do, a reflection of Zoroastrian dualism.[43] The statement of an ethical antithesis in terms of light and darkness (light being the correlate of goodness and truth, and darkness of evil and falsehood) is too

---

[39] Phil. 4:11–13; cf. also 2 Cor. 2:14.

[40] Gk. τῷ ἱκανώσαντι ἡμᾶς εἰς τὴν μερίδα τῶν ἁγίων. With these words C. H. Dodd associates Job 31:2 (LXX), ἐμέρισεν ὁ θεὸς ἄνωθεν καὶ κληρονομία ἱκανοῦ ἐξ ὑψίστου ("and God has made distribution from above, and the inheritance of the Sufficient One is from the highest place"). There, as in some other LXX passages, ἱκανός is a divine name, representing Heb. *Shaddai* (usually translated "Almighty" in EVV). Dodd suggests that Paul's use of the verb ἱκανόω here and in 2 Cor. 3:5 f. reflects this Septuagintalism (*The Bible and the Greeks* [London, 1935], pp. 15 f.).

[41] For this heavenly inheritance cf. Acts 20:32; 26:18 (both passages in Pauline speeches); also Heb. 11:8–16; 1 Peter 1:4.

[42] Cf. 2 Cor. 4:6; 1 John 1:5–7.

[43] E.g., C. A. A. Scott, "The Dualistic Element in the Thinking of St. Paul", ExT xxiii (1911–12), pp. 488 ff.

widespread for us to assume in such a reference as this the influence of any one system of thought in which these terms played a prominent part. It may be, indeed, that the incipient gnosticism which was being propagated at Colossae made play with "light" and "darkness" as it did with "wisdom" and "knowledge"; but there is good Biblical precedent for their use, going back to the separation of light and darkness in the creation story in Gen. 1:4.

The phrase "the jurisdiction of darkness,"[44] which Paul uses here, appears in Luke's account of our Lord's arrest in Gethsemane, where He says to the men who have come to apprehend Him: "Have you come out with swords and clubs as though you had a bandit to deal with? When I was with you day after day in the temple, you never laid a finger on me. But this is your hour and the jurisdiction of darkness" (Luke 22:52 f.). These last words of His refer to the supernatural forces marshalled against Him by Satan for a decisive combat. The dark power did indeed have its brief hour of opportunity against the Son of man, but it was only a brief hour, and it ended in the utter defeat of the dark power. By virtue of His conquest then, Christ now has the authority to raid the domain of darkness and rescue those who had hitherto been fast bound under the control of its guardians. Here, no doubt, Paul has the Colossian heresy in view, for those very guardians, "the world-rulers of this darkness" as they are called in Eph. 6:10, are the principalities and powers to which the Christians of Colossae were being urged to pay some meed of homage. But why should they do any such thing? They had already been rescued from the sphere dominated by those principalities, and translated into the realm of the victorious Son of God. No longer was there any need for them to live in fear of those astral powers which were believed to control the destinies of men; their transference to the dominion of light had been accomplished once for all.

When he affirms that believers have already been brought into the kingdom of God's beloved Son, Paul gives us an example of truly realized eschatology. That which in its fulness lies ahead of them has already become true in them. "Whom he justified, them He also glorified" (Rom. 8:30). The fact that God has begun a good work in them is the guarantee that it will be brought to fruition in the day of Jesus Christ (cf. Phil. 1:6). By an anticipation

---

44 Gk. ἡ ἐξουσία τοῦ σκότους.

which is a real experience and not a legal fiction they have received here and now the glory that is yet to be revealed. The "inheritance of the saints in light" has not yet been manifested in its infinite wealth, but the divine act by which believers have been rendered meet for it has already taken place. The divine kingdom has this twofold aspect throughout the NT.[45] It has already broken into this world in the work of Christ (cf. Matt. 12:28; Luke 11:20); it will break in one day in the plenitude of glory which invests Christ's *parousia*. Those who look forward to an abundant entrance in resurrection into that heavenly realm which "flesh and blood" (the present mortal body) cannot inherit[46] are assured at the same time that this realm is already theirs.

It appears that Paul tends to distinguish these two aspects of the heavenly kingdom by reserving the commoner expression "the kingdom of God" for its future consummation,[47] while designating its present phase by some such term as "the kingdom of Christ." We may compare his language in 1 Cor. 15:24, where Christ, after reigning until all things are put under His feet, delivers up the kingdom "to God, even the Father"; Christ's mediatorial sovereignty then gives place to the eternal dominion of God.[48]

14 Because we have been introduced into this new realm, we enjoy here and now the benefits won for us by its ruler. In Him we have our redemption, the remission of our sins—in Him, because it is only as those who share the risen life of Christ that we have made effective *in* us what He has done *for* us.[49] The redemption which is ours in Him is something that He has procured for us; it implies that our former existence was one of bondage from which we required to be ransomed.[50] The ransom-price is

---

45 Cf. Acts in NICNT (Grand Rapids, 1954), pp. 34 ff.

46 1 Cor. 15:50.

47 So, at any rate, 1 Cor. 6:9 f.; 15:50; Gal. 5:21; 2 Tim. 4:1, 18. Other Pauline instances of βασιλεία τοῦ θεοῦ are Rom. 14:17; 1 Cor. 4:20; Col. 4:11 (see p. 306 below); 1 Thess. 2:12; 2 Thess. 1:5; these are more general in their reference. In Eph. 5:5 we read "the kingdom of Christ and God" (τῇ βασιλείᾳ τοῦ χριστοῦ καὶ θεοῦ), or "the kingdom which is Christ's and God's"; here the two aspects appear to be conjoined.

48 Cf. G. Vos, The Pauline Eschatology (Grand Rapids, 1952), pp. 236 ff., 258 ff.; cf. also W. D. Davies, Paul and Rabbinic Judaism (London, 1948), p. 296.

49 Cf. J. A. T. Robinson, The Body (London, 1952), pp. 45 f.

50 On "redemption"(ἀπολύτρωσις) cf. B. B. Warfield, The Person and Work of Christ (Philadelphia, 1950), pp. 429 ff.; O. Procksch and F. Büchsel, TWNT iv (Stuttgart, 1942), pp. 329 ff. (s.v. λύω, etc.); E. K. Simpson, Words Worth

not explicitly stated in the best authenticated text here; what it was is evident not only from the parallel passage in Eph. 1:7 ("in whom we have our redemption through his blood")[51] but from other Pauline passages where the same thought is expressed, notably in Rom. 3:24 f., where believers are said to be justified freely by the grace of God "through the redemption that is in Christ Jesus: whom God set forth to be a propitiation, through faith, in his blood."[52] It becomes quite plain that the emancipation which we enjoy in Christ was purchased for us at the price of His life, freely offered up on the cross as a sacrifice to God.

Deissmann asks whether this "manumission" is "merely a single summary act performed once for all in the past" or also (as he thinks probable) "an act of liberation experienced anew, in each single case of conversion, by every person newly incorporated in Christ."[53] The answer surely is that it is both: the redemption was procured by Christ for His people once for all, but it is received by them individually as they become united with Him by faith.

The companion expression, "the remission of sins," though frequent in the NT, is less characteristic of Paul; it appears in the Pauline corpus only here and in the parallel passage Eph. 1:7.[54] Normally Paul prefers to speak in terms of justification, which embraces all that is meant by "remission of sins" but includes much besides. The appearance of the expression here, however, is no argument against the authenticity of Colossians; it is very likely that here (and in Eph. 1:7) Paul is echoing what had already become standard Christian language for acknowledging the blessings bestowed in Christ; he may even be quoting from a primitive Christian confession of faith.[55]

Weighing in the Greek NT (London, 1944), pp. 8 f.; L. Morris, *The Apostolic Preaching of the Cross* (London, 1955), pp. 9 ff.

[51] See E. K. Simpson *ad loc.*, p. 29, with n. 12.

[52] *Cf.* L. Morris, *op. cit.*, p. 108 ff.; J. Behm, TWNT i (Stuttgart, 1933), pp. 171 ff. (*s.v. αἷμα*); A. M. Stibbs, *The Meaning of the Word "Blood" in Scripture* (London, 1947); W. D. Davies, *op. cit.*, pp. 232 ff.

[53] *Light from the Ancient East*, p. 330.

[54] Gk. ἄφεσις ἁμαρτιῶν (in Eph. 1:7, ἄφεσις παραπτωμάτων). *Cf.* Matt. 26:28; Mark 1:4; Luke 1:77; 3:3; 24:27; Acts 2:38; 5:31; 10:43; 13:38; 26:18. Even the corresponding verb ἀφίημι is used by Paul in this sense only in the quotation from Ps. 32:1 in Rom. 4:7. With ἄφεσις we may compare his use of πάρεσις in Rom. 3:25, in the more limited sense of "passing over" sins committed in the past.

[55] E. Percy points out that none of the distinctively Pauline terms, such as justification or the non-reckoning of trespasses, would suit the solemn liturgical

(b) Christ as Lord of Creation

Ch. 1:15–17

> 15 who is the image of the invisible God, the firstborn of all creation;
> 16 for in him were all things created, in the heavens and upon the earth, things visible and things invisible, whether thrones or dominions or principalities or powers; all things have been created through him, and unto him;
> 17 and he is before all things, and in him all things consist.

Paul follows up his reminder of the benefits which his readers have received in Christ with a statement of the primacy of Christ over the created universe. This is one of the great Christological passages of the NT, declaring as it does our Lord's divine essence, pre-existence, and creative agency. Yet, high as the Christology is, it does not appear to be original to Paul himself, but rather part of what he "received" as primitive Christian teaching.[56] Certainly the doctrine here set forth is practically identical with that set forth in two non-Pauline passages of the NT—John 1:1–4 and Heb. 1:2–4. All three passages have an OT background, which is seen especially in Prov. 8:22 ff., where Divine Wisdom, personified, claims to have been with the Almighty at the beginning of His ways and to have been His assessor, if not His agent, in the work of creation. If we ask how the early Church came so unanimously to speak of her Lord in terms of the Divine

---

diction of this passage so well as ἄφεσις τῶν ἁμαρτιῶν (*op. cit.*, pp. 85 f.). Besides, Paul may have had a special reason for bringing "redemption" and "remission of sins" together as he does here if the Colossian theorists anticipated others to whom Irenaeus refers (*Heresies* i. 21. 2), who distinguished "remission of sins" as a preliminary stage and "redemption" as the perfect stage, the former being received in the baptism instituted by the "human" Jesus, the latter coming from the "divine" Christ which descended upon Him. If such a distinction was being taught at Colossae, we can understand why Paul should emphasize that "redemption" and "remission of sins" were received together in one and the same Christ.

[56] *Cf.* J. G. Machen, *The Origin of Paul's Religion* (New York, 1921); A. M. Hunter, *Paul and his Predecessors* (London, 1940). We remain unconvinced by the arguments of E. Norden (*op. cit.*, pp. 252 ff.) and M. Dibelius (HNT xii [Tübingen, 1953], pp. 10 ff.) that the wording of this passage comes from Hellenistic-Jewish formulas, as also by the attempt of E. Käsemann ("Eine urchristliche Taufliturgie", *Festschrift Rudolf Bultmann* [Stuttgart, 1949], pp. 133 ff.) to derive it from a gnostic hymn in honour of the *kosmokrator*.

Wisdom, the answer must be sought in His own teaching.[57]

Here, however, Christ is presented as the agent of God in the whole range of His gracious purpose towards men, from the primaeval work of creation through the redemption accomplished at history's mid-point on to the new creation in which God's purpose will be consummated.

15 Christ, then, is described as the image of the unseen God. What is this but to say that the very nature and being of God have been perfectly revealed in Him—that in Him the invisible has become visible? "No one has ever seen God," says the Fourth Evangelist; "the only begotten Son, who has his being in the Father's bosom, he it is who has made him known" (John 1:18). Later, the same evangelist reports Christ Himself as saying: "He who has seen me has seen the Father" (John 14:9). In another epistle Paul affirms that since the creation of the world the everlasting power and divinity of the invisible Creator may be "perceived through the things that are made" (Rom. 1:20). But now an all-surpassing manifestation of that everlasting power and divinity has been granted: "the light of the gospel of the glory of Christ, who is the image[58] of God," has dawned upon us; He whose creative word in the beginning called light to shine forth from the darkness has now shone in our hearts, "to give the light of the knowledge of the glory of God in the face of Jesus Christ" (2 Cor. 4:4, 6). And the writer to the Hebrews expresses the same truth in another form: to him Christ is the "effulgence[59] of God's glory and the very impress of his being" (Heb. 1:3).

No reader conversant with the OT scriptures, on reading these words of Paul, could fail to be reminded of the statement in Gen. 1:26 f., that man was created by God "in his own image." Defaced as the divine image in man may be by reason of sin, yet in the order of creation it remains true, as Paul reminds us elsewhere, that man is "the image and glory of God" (1 Cor. 11:7).[60]

---

[57]   *Cf.* J. R. Harris, *The Origin of the Prologue to St. John's Gospel* (Cambridge, 1917); *The Origin of the Doctrine of the Trinity* (Manchester, 1919).

[58]   Gk. εἰκών (2 Cor. 4:4, as here in Col. 1:15).

[59]   Gk. ἀπαύγασμα, used of wisdom in Wisdom 7:26, where she is described as "an *effulgence* from everlasting light, and an unspotted mirror of the working of God, and an image (εἰκών) of his goodness."

[60]   Gk. ἀνήρ ... εἰκὼν καὶ δόξα θεοῦ ὑπάρχων. In 1 Cor. 11:7 it is man (ἀνήρ) as distinct from woman that Paul has in mind, yet he obviously bases his statement on Gen. 1:26 f., where it is mankind, male and female, that is intended.

This image of God in man, moreover, is a copy or reflection of the archetypal image—that is to say, of God's beloved Son. And so, as we are told later in this epistle, when the havoc of sin is removed and the new man appears, the latter is renewed after the image of his Creator (Ch. 3:10).[61]

It may be observed in passing that there is a close association between the doctrine of man's creation in the divine image and the doctrine of our Lord's incarnation; it is because man in the creative order bears the image of his Creator that it was possible for the Son of God to become incarnate as man and in His humanity to display the glory of the invisible God.

Christ, in addition to being the image of God, is "the firstborn of all creation." The context makes it clear that this title is not given to Him as though He Himself were the first of all created beings; it is emphasized immediately that, far from being part of creation, He is the One by whom the whole creation came into being.[62] What the title does mean is that Christ, existing as He did before all creation,[63] exercises the privilege of primogeniture as Lord of all creation, the divinely appointed "heir of all things" (Heb. 1:2). He was there when creation began, and it was for Him as well as through Him that the whole work was done.

The title "firstborn", used of Christ here and in v. 18, echoes the wording of Ps. 89:27, where God says of the Davidic king: "I also will make him my firstborn, the highest of the kings of the earth."[64] But it belongs to Christ not only as the Messiah of

---

[61] J. B. Lightfoot (*Colossians, ad loc.*) points out Philo's repeated use of εἰκών as a description of the λόγος (see further on Ch. 3:10, p. 272). "Beyond the very obvious notion of *likeness*," Lightfoot adds, "the word εἰκών involves two other ideas: (1) *Representation* ... (2) *Manifestation* ..." (*op. cit.*, p. 145).

[62] Strack–Billerbeck (*Kommentar zum NT aus Talmud und Midrasch* iii [Munich, 1926], p. 626) compare with this phrase (Gk. πρωτότοκος πάσης κτίσεως) the description of God as *qadmono shel 'olam* ("the beginning of the world") in *Bereshith Rabba* 38 (23b), where certainly there is no thought of portraying God as part—even the first part—of the world.

[63] A frequently cited parallel in English literature to this "exclusive" use of a superlative is the couplet from Milton's *Paradise Lost* iv. 323 f.:
Adam, the goodliest man of men since born
His sons; the fairest of her daughters Eve.
A. W. Argyle, remarking that most commentators are content to quote as a Biblical Greek parallel πρῶτός μου ἦν (John 1:15), adduces a closer one from the LXX: πρωτότοκος ἐγὼ ἢ σύ (2 Kingdoms 19:43), "I was born before you" (ExT lxvi [1954–5], pp. 61 f.). *Cf.* also the dissertation by E. Cerny, *Firstborn of Every Creature* (Baltimore, 1938).

[64] This OT passage is echoed also in Rev. 1:5, "Jesus Christ, who is the faith-

David's line, but also as the Wisdom of God.[65] Whereas, in the Wisdom literature of the OT, Wisdom is at best the personification of a divine attribute or of the holy law,[66] the NT writers know that, whether they speak of this Wisdom expressly or only by allusion, they are speaking of a living person, one whom some of them had met face to face. To them all, as to Paul, Jesus Christ was the incarnate Wisdom of God.[67]

As with all the other direct or indirect OT adumbrations of our Lord (including the messianic concept itself), this one is interpreted by the NT writers in terms of the historic and personal fact of Christ, and not *vice versa*. Thus, the famous passage in Prov. 8:22 ff., however its phraseology may be drawn upon by NT writers who present Christ as the Wisdom of God, is not regarded by them as a prophecy whose details may be pressed to yield Christological conclusions. Later Christian writers involved themselves in considerable embarrassment by trying to extract a Christological exegesis from the passage.[68] What Paul implies is not so much that the Wisdom of the OT books is really Christ, as that Christ—the Christ who came to earth as man, who died and rose again, "who was made unto us wisdom from God"[69]—is the One who was before all creation. He is the pre-existent, cosmic Christ.[70]

---

ful witness, the firstborn of the dead, and the ruler of the kings of the earth" (where "ruler" is the translation of Gk. ἄρχων, representing Heb. 'elyon).

65 C. F. Burney (JThS xxvii [1925–6], pp. 160 ff.) finds in πρωτότοκος πάσης κτίσεως an allusion to the words with which Wisdom introduces herself in Prov. 8:22, *Yahweh qanani reshith darko* ("The LORD begat me as the beginning of His way"). Then, in view of the rabbinic use of *reshith* ("beginning") in this verse to explain the "beginning" of Gen. 1:1, Burney goes on to treat Col. 1:15 ff. as an elaborate exposition of Gen. 1:1, in which Paul aims to show that Christ exhausts every meaning that could be extracted from *reshith*—"that in all things He might have the preeminence." See also W. D. Davies, *op. cit.*, pp. 147 ff.

66 This is true even of Philo's λόγος, even if it receives the epithet πρωτόγονος (*Confusion of Tongues*, 146); Philo's λόγος, unlike John's, could never have become flesh and tabernacled among men.

67 As in 1 Cor. 1:24. *Cf.* C. A. A. Scott, *Christianity according to St. Paul* (Cambridge, 1927), pp. 264 f.

68 They were particularly embarrassed by the LXX wording, Κύριος ἔκτισέ με ("The LORD *created me*"), which seemed to play right into the hands of the Arians and other heretics.

69 1 Cor. 1:31.

70 See F. V. Filson, *The NT Against its Environment* (London, 1950), pp. 61 f., on the primitive-Christian character of this affirmation.

The idea of pre-existence is not unknown to Jewish thought; we meet it, for example, in later discussions about the Messiah[71] and in the pre-existent Son of man of the Enoch literature.[72] But such pre-existent beings were, to the minds of those who discussed them, largely ideal; here pre-existence is predicated of a man who had lived and died in Palestine within the preceding half-century.[73] This is not the only place where Paul asserts or implies that Christ existed before His incarnation. Nor is Paul the only NT writer to teach such a thing. The same teaching is found in Hebrews (Heb. 1:2; 10:5 ff.), and the Fourth Evangelist not only makes similar assertions (e.g., John 1:1 f.) but ascribes them to Jesus Himself (e.g., John 8:58). So too in the Apocalypse Jesus is the Alpha and Omega, the First and the Last (Rev. 1:17; 2:8; 22:13); David's root as well as David's offspring (Rev. 22:16). The presence of such teaching in this passage of Colossians affords no ground for denying it to be an authentic part of the epistle.[74]

But Paul speaks not only of a pre-existent Christ, but of a cosmic Christ; that is to say, he finds in Christ "the key to creation, declaring that it is all there with Christ in view."[75] Whatever figures in Jewish literature, canonical or otherwise, may have pre-existence predicated of them, to none of them is such cosmic activity and significance ascribed as Paul here ascribes to the pre-existent Christ.[76] Yet this is not the only place where Paul makes this ascription; he has already stated in 1 Cor. 8:6 that Christians have "one Lord, Jesus Christ, through whom are all things, and we through him", while in Rom. 8:19 ff. he shows how the redemption procured by Christ works not only to the advantage of its immediate beneficiaries, "the sons of God", but through them to the whole creation.

---

[71] One example will suffice; Messiah's pre-existence was inferred from Ps. 72:17, "His name shall be continued as long as the sun" (margin: "before the sun"), where the verb *yinnon* ("shall be continued") was treated as a proper name and the clause taken to mean: "Before the sun his [Messiah's] name was Yinnon" (TB *Sanhedrin* 98b).

[72] *Cf.* 1 Enoch 48:2 f.

[73] "The heavenly Messiah of the apocalypses is a lifeless figure, clothed in unapproachable light. The risen Christ of Paul, on the other hand, is a person whom a man can love; indeed He is a person whom as a matter of fact Paul did love" (J. G. Machen, *op. cit.*, pp. 194 f.).

[74] Or for denying the authenticity of the whole epistle.

[75] A. M. Hunter, *Interpreting Paul's Gospel* (London, 1954), p. 60.

[76] *Cf.* J. G. Machen, *op. cit.*, p. 194.

196

16 Christ, then, is prior to all creation and, as the firstborn of God, is heir to it all. But more: it was "in Him" that all things were created. The preposition "in" seems to denote Christ as the "sphere" within which the work of creation takes place;[77] more commonly the preposition "through" is used,[78] denoting Him as the agent by whom God created the universe. Here again the teaching of Paul is corroborated by the writer to the Hebrews, who assures us that it was through His Son that God made the worlds (Heb. 1:2), and by the Fourth Evangelist, who affirms in his own uncompromising way: "All things came into being through Him, and apart from Him none of the things that exist came into being" (John 1:3).

This is not the same thing as Philo's doctrine of the function of the Logos in creation. Philo's Logos is practically identified with the "intelligible world" conceived in the mind of God as the blue-print for the material world;[79] its designation as God's first-begotten son is purely metaphorical. And while it is easy to see affinities between Paul's language here and Stoic terminology, Paul's thought is derived not from Stoicism but from Genesis 1[80] and the OT Wisdom literature, where Wisdom is the Creator's "master-workman"[81] (although, for Paul, the "master-workman" is no longer a figure of speech, but the personal, pre-existent Christ).

So then, the One through whom (as Paul has said already) the divine work of redemption was accomplished is the One by whom the divine act of creation also took place. Our Lord's mediatorial relation to the created universe provides a setting to the gospel of our salvation which adds greatly to our appreciation of that gospel.[82] For a man redeemed by Christ, the universe has no

---

77 E. Haupt, *Der Brief an die Kolosser* (Göttingen, 1897), pp. 30 f., points out that ἐν αὐτῷ here has the same force as in Eph. 1:4; God's creation, like His election, takes place "in Christ" and not apart from Him.

78 Gk. διά, as in 1 Cor. 8:6; Heb. 1:2; John 1:3, cited in the exposition above.

79 Philo, *On the Making of the World*, 20–23.

80 Where God speaks and creation springs into existence; *cf.* Ps. 33:6, "By the word of the LORD were the heavens made..."

81 Heb. *'amon* (Prov. 8:30), perhaps echoed in the ἀμήν of Rev. 3:14 ("the Amen, ... the beginning of the creation of God"). In normative Judaism wisdom was identified with the *torah*, "the desirable instrument through which the world was created" (R. Aqiba in *Pirqe Aboth* iii. 18).

82 I. Henderson (*Myth in the NT* [London, 1952], pp. 31 ff.) points out that the doctrine of creation cannot be "demythologized" into existential terms; any

ultimate terrors; he knows that his Redeemer is also Creator, ruler and goal of all.

With special regard to the Colossian heresy, Paul now goes on to emphasize that, if all things were created by Christ, then those spiritual powers which received such prominence in that heresy must have been created by Him. The denizens of the upper realms as well as the inhabitants of earth owed their being to His creative power—the invisible forces of the spirit world as well as the visible and material order. "Whether thrones or dominions or principalities or powers," they all had Christ as their original creator and also as their final disposer.

The early Christians had the authority of their Lord for believing in angels good and bad. What Paul here points out is that, whether good or bad, all are alike subject to Christ as their Creator. No doubt, in view of the situation at Colossae, it was hostile rather than friendly powers that he had in mind; but the first argument by which he tries to reduce those hostile powers to their proper dimensions in the eyes of Christians is the fact that they owe their very existence to the Christians' Saviour. (A second argument, developed in Ch. 2, is that they were vanquished by that same Saviour.)[83]

In all, five classes of angel-princes seem to be distinguished in the NT—thrones, principalities, authorities, powers and dominions.[84] They probably represent the highest orders of the angelic realm, but the variety of ways in which the titles are combined in the NT warns us against the attempt to reconstruct a fixed hierarchy from them. In Ch. 2:10, 15 (as in Eph. 3:10; 6:12), they are summed up more concisely as "principalities and powers." Here the point is that the highest angel-princes, like the

---

attempt to do so simply removes it altogether. The consequence would be that Christianity would have nothing at all to say about God's relation to the material world—"which includes, it must be remembered, God's relation to man in so far as the latter, having a body, is himself in some sense part of the material world."

83 See pp. 239 ff. (on Ch. 2:15). Good angels, of course, manifest their subjection to Christ by their obedience (cf. Heb. 1:14). See G. B. Caird, *Principalities and Powers* (Oxford, 1956).

84 Gk. θρόνοι, ἀρχαί, ἐξουσίαι, δυνάμεις, κυριότητες. (Cf. Milton, *Paradise Lost* v, 601: "Thrones, dominations, princedoms, virtues, powers.") The four listed here are θρόνοι, κυριότητες, ἀρχαί and ἐξουσίαι. The "thrones" may bear some relation to the twenty-four enthroned elders of Rev. 4:4. Many other grades of angelic power are distinguished in the pseudepigrapha.

rest of creation, are subject to Christ as the One in whom, through whom and for whom they were created.[85] They were created *in* Him, because all the Father's counsels and activities (including those of creation) are centred in the Son; they were created *through* Him, because He is the divine agent in creation; they were created *for* Him, because He is the goal to which they all tend.[86]

The conception of Christ as the goal of creation plays an essential part in Paul's soteriology. And this is the more impressive when we bear in mind that the person thus presented as creation's goal was Jesus of Nazareth, but lately crucified in Jerusalem, whose appearance as the risen Lord to Paul on the Damascus road had called forth that overmastering faith and love which completely reorientated his thought and action and remained thereafter the all-dominating motive of his life. Any attempt to understand the Christology of this epistle without taking into consideration this personal commitment of Paul to Christ would be the sort of understanding that Paul himself condemns as being "according to the elemental powers of the world and not according to Christ" (Ch. 2:8).[87]

This distinguishes Paul's teaching about Christ as the goal of creation from all the Jewish parallels which have been adduced for it.[88] Whatever was previously revealed about God now received fresh illumination from the fact of Christ and from faith in Christ—not only with regard to God's saving activity but also with regard to His rôle as Creator of the universe and Lord of history. That the course of history is overruled by God for the accomplishment of His purpose is a major truth of the OT, but here we learn how vitally the accomplishment of His purpose is

---

85   The tense of "were created" *(ἐκτίσθη)* at the beginning of v. 16 is aorist, referring to the historic act of creation; the tense of "have been created" *(ἔκτισται)* at the end of the verse is perfect, referring to the enduring result of the creative act.

86   For the bringing together of various prepositional phrases to express the relationship of God or Christ to the universe, *cf.* Rom. 11:36; 1 Cor. 8:6; Eph. 4:6. To relate such constructions to Stoic formulations—comparing them, *e.g.*, with Marcus Aurelius's ἐκ σοῦ πάντα, ἐν σοὶ πάντα, εἰς σὲ πάντα (*Meditations* iv. 23)—is to pay more attention to the form of words than to their substance. Paul's intention is as different from that of the Stoic philosophers as the God of whom Paul speaks is different from the pantheistically conceived world-soul of Stoicism.

87   *Cf.* E .Percy, *op. cit.*, p. 72.

88   *E.g.*, TB *Sanhedrin* 98b records the opinion of R. Yochanan (d. A.D. 279) that the world was created with a view to Messiah.

bound up with the person and work of Christ.[89] So, too, in Eph. 1:10 we are told that God's purpose, conceived in eternity by Him in Christ, that it might be put into effect when the appointed time had fully come, is that all things, in heaven and on earth, should be summed up in Christ. Or, as has been remarked already, it is by means of the mediatorial world-rule of Christ that God's eternal kingdom is finally to be established (1 Cor. 15:24 ff.).

17 The teaching of vv. 15 and 16 is now summed up in a twofold reaffirmation of the pre-existence and cosmic significance of Christ: "He is before all things, and in him all things hold together" (RSV). "In the beginning God created the heaven and the earth", says Genesis, but in that beginning, says John, which was the beginning of all created beings, the Divine Logos already existed (John 1:1). No matter how far back we may press in our imagination, we can never reach a point of which we may say, with Arius: "There was once when He was not."[90] For He is "before all things"[91]—and the words not only declare His temporal priority to the universe, but also suggest His primacy over it (as indeed the title "firstborn" has already implied).

As for the statement that all things hold together or cohere in Him, this adds something to what has been said before about His agency in creation. He maintains in being what He has brought into being. Similarly, in Heb. 1:2 f. the Son of God is not only the One through whom the worlds were made but also the One who maintains them in being by His almighty and enabling word. The Greek word translated "consist" (ARV) or "hold together" (RSV)[92] is found as a Stoic term, but the force of its use here is that for Paul it is the living Christ, who died to redeem men, that is the sustainer of the universe and the unifying principle of its life.

(c) Christ as Head of the Church

Ch. 1:18

> 18 And he is the head of the body, the church: who is the beginning, the firstborn from the dead; that in all things he might have the preëminence.

---

[89] *Cf.* v. 20 (pp. 207 ff.).

[90] Gk. ἦν ποτε ὅτε οὐκ ἦν, a proposition explicitly condemned in the Creed of Nicaea.

[91] Gk. πρὸ πάντων. The phrase denotes priority in importance in Jas. 5:12; 1 Pet. 4:8 (*cf.* C. F. D. Moule, IBNTG, p. 74).

[92] Gk. συνέστηκεν.

18 Thus far Paul has set forth the doctrine of Christ in terms which he shares with other NT writers—terms which, in fact, may have belonged to a widespread Christian confession, even if he does stamp them with the unmistakable imprint of his own experience and mind. But now he goes on to make a contribution to NT Christology which is distinctively his own. This Christ, he affirms, "is the head of the body, the church." Christ and His people, that is to say, are viewed together as a living unit; Christ is the head, exercising control and direction; believers are His body, individually His limbs and organs, under His control, obeying His direction, performing His work. And the life which animates the whole is Christ's risen life, which He shares with His people.

The use of the body as a figure to illustrate the common life and mutual interdependence of a political or social group was not unknown in antiquity. It finds classical expression in the fable of Menenius Agrippa, who persuaded the seceding plebeians of Rome to return and live among the patricians on the ground that, if the other parts of the body conspired to starve the belly because it did no work, they would soon find themselves suffering in consequence.[93] Again, Stoicism viewed the divine power as constituting the world-soul, informing the material universe as the individual soul informs the body[94]—a point of view succinctly summed up in Alexander Pope's couplet:

> All are but parts of one stupendous whole,
> Whose body Nature is, and God the soul.

But it is no mere figure of speech or philosophical concept that Paul brings to expression here, and we have to look elsewhere for the source of this way of conveying the relation that subsists between Christ and the church.

---

[93] Livy, *History* ii. 32, 9–12.

[94] The analogy of the body was also applied by the Stoics to the state, in which each citizen had his part to play as has each member of a body. According to W. L. Knox (*op. cit.*, p. 161), the political developments of the Hellenistic age modified the form of this analogy so that the emphasis was removed from the mutual duties of the members to the superior importance of the head; "it is likely enough that the transition was accomplished in Alexandria in favour of the Ptolemies before it became a convenient method of flattering the Roman Emperors." He derives Paul's conception of the church as the body of Christ from this Stoic commonplace.

The first place (taking his letters in chronological order) where Paul speaks of the church as the body of Christ is 1 Cor. 12:12–27. This passage opens with the words: "For as the body is one and has many parts, and yet all the parts of the body, many as they are, make up one body, so it is with Christ. For in one Spirit we were all baptized into one body, whether Jews or Greeks, whether slaves or freemen." And it is summed up in v. 27 by the statement: "And you are Christ's body, and severally parts thereof." Here Paul is concerned to impress upon the Corinthian Christians the fact that, as fellow-members of the body of Christ, they have mutual duties and common interests which must not be neglected.

Again, in Rom. 12:4 f. he declares that "as in one body we have many parts, and all the parts have not the same function, so we, many as we are, are one body in Christ, and as individuals we are parts of one another." Here he is thinking of the variety of service rendered by the diverse members of the church, in accordance with their respective gifts, all together helping to build up the one body to which they all belong.

In those earlier epistles Paul uses the terminology of the body and its constituent parts to express the mutual relations and obligations of church members.[95] But in Colossians and Ephesians[96] he thinks rather of the relation which the church, as the body of Christ, bears to Christ as head of the body. This is a development of the line of thought which appears in 1 Corinthians and Romans, where Christ is not described as the head in this sense.[97] Yet the differing aspects and emphases seen in the places where this terminology is used in the various epistles correspond closely to the differences in the apostle's theme and purpose while writing them.

It is unlikely that Paul derived this conception of the church as the body from Stoic thought,[98] and even more unlikely that he

---

[95] *Cf.* also 1 Cor. 6:15; 10:16 f.; 11:29 (and, in more general terms, 1 Cor. 8:12; 2 Cor. 5:14; Gal. 3:27 f.; 4:14).

[96] *Cf.* Eph. 1:23; 2:16; 4:4, 12, 16; 5:23, 30.

[97] *E.g.,* in 1 Cor. 12:21 the head is mentioned simply as one among other members of the body; there is no thought there of the head being Christ. In 1 Cor. 11:3, however, we have the statement that "the head of every man *(ἀνήρ)* is Christ."

[98] *Cf.,* in addition to W. L. Knox (see n. 94 above), T. Schmidt, *Der Leib Christi* (Leipzig, 1919); G. Johnston, *The Doctrine of the Church in the NT* (Cambridge, 1943), p. 87. Even if Paul's language is influenced by Stoic terminology, the conception expressed by his language is not the Stoic one.

was influenced by gnostic ideas.[99] He would have been acquainted with the rabbinical speculation which pictured all mankind as members of Adam,[100] and we know how he points the antithesis between being "in Adam" and "in Christ." But we need not think that his conception of all believers as members of the body of Christ was formed on the analogy of this kind of speculation. Rather, both ideas are rooted in the OT conception of "corporate personality."[101] All mankind, by natural birth, share the life of Adam and thus may be described as "in Adam"; heirs of the new creation, by spiritual rebirth, share the life of Christ and so are "in Christ." And this being "in Christ" is given vivid expression by Paul in his presentation of the church as the body of Christ.[102]

The source of this presentation, however, is not the most important question; much more important is Paul's intention in using it. He uses it when he wishes to bring out certain aspects of the relation between Christ and the church; when he wishes to bring out certain other aspects, he uses other terminology. Thus, from other points of view, the church is presented as the bride of

---

[99] *Cf.* H. Schlier, *Christus und die Kirche im Epheserbrief* (Tübingen, 1930); E. Käsemann, *Leib und Leib Christi* (Tübingen, 1933); R. Bultmann, *Theology of the NT,* i (Eng. tr., London, 1951), pp. 178 f.

[100] *Cf.* W. D. Davies, *op. cit.,* pp. 53 ff.

[101] *Cf.* A. Schweitzer, *The Mysticism of Paul the Apostle* (Eng. tr., London, 1931), *passim* (but the particular aspect of corporate personality on which Schweitzer bases his argument is the predestined solidarity of Messiah with the messianic or elect people, a conception which he derives from apocalyptic literature); E. Best, *One Body in Christ* (London, 1955), pp. 93 ff., 203 ff.

[102] *Cf.* E. Percy, *Der Leib Christi* (Lund, 1942), pp. 18 ff. Among other attempts to account for the origin of Paul's use of the term "body of Christ" for the church we may note those of A. E. J. Rawlinson ("Corpus Christi" in *Mysterium Christi,* ed. G. K. A. Bell and A. Deissmann [London, 1930], pp. 225 ff.), who finds in it the eucharistic presentation of the body of Christ, and of C. Chavasse (*The Bride of Christ* [London, 1940], pp. 70 ff.), who finds it in the nuptial union of bridegroom and bride in "one flesh." But both the eucharistic (1 Cor. 10:16b–17) and the nuptial (Eph. 5:28 ff.) applications of Paul's thought on this subject are derived from his conception of the church as the body of Christ rather than *vice versa.* J. A. T. Robinson points out that the germ of the conception in Paul's mind may well go back to the words of Christ which he heard at his conversion: "why persecutest thou me?" (*The Body* [London, 1952], p. 58). At this early stage the implication would simply have been that of the Christian community as Christ corporate. It is true enough to say, as Augustine did (*Sermons* 279, 1) that "while the members were still upon earth the head cried out in heaven," but this distinction does not seem to have formed itself in Paul's mind until later.

Christar,[103] or as the building of which He is at one time the foundation[104] and at another time the chief corner-stone,[105] and so on. There is a marked tendency to regard the presentation of the church as the body of Christ differently from these other presentations—to admit that they are metaphors while maintaining that the term "body of Christ" is to be taken "ontologically and realistically."[106] But if that were so, we could go on to make assertions about the church's relation to Christ, on the analogy of the functions of the human body and its parts in relation to the head, beyond what Paul has to say. It is better to recognize that Paul speaks of the church as the body of Christ for certain well-defined purposes, and to follow his example in using it for these same purposes. We can appreciate that those presentations which bring out the vital relationship between Christ and the church are more adequate than others (there is no organic relationship between a building and its foundation or coping-stone); for this reason the head/body and husband/wife analogies have a specially firm grasp on reality.[107]

Thus, when we speak of the church as the body of Christ, we think of it as being vitalized by His abiding presence with it and His risen life in it; we think of it as being energized by His power; we may even (without transgressing legitimate bounds) think of it as the instrument through which He carries on His work on earth.[108] But to think of it as the extension of our Lord's incarnation, as is widely done today, is to exceed the limits which the

---

[103] Cf. Eph. 5:22 ff.
[104] Cf. 1 Cor. 3:11.
[105] Cf. Eph. 2:20.
[106] The phrase is E. L. Mascall's *Christ, the Christian and the Church* [London, 1946], p. 112. See the critique of this tendency in E. Best, *op. cit.*, pp. 98 ff.
[107] T. F. Torrance, while acknowledging that all the terms with which the NT speaks of the church "must be used to correct and modify each other in our understanding and in any full discussion," gives reasons for regarding the body as "the central and all-important conception" (*Royal Priesthood* [Edinburgh, 1955], p. 29).
[108] Cf. E. Schweizer, *Das Leben des Herrn in der Gemeinde und ihren Diensten* (Zürich, 1946); T. W. Manson, *The Church's Ministry* (London, 1948); T. F. Torrance, *op. cit.*, pp. 23 ff. E. Best, however, demurs to this on the ground that the body-metaphor in the NT "looks inward and not outward" (*op. cit.*, pp. 113, 137, 157 f., 188); D. Cairns, reviewing Best's book in SJTh viii (1955), pp. 419 ff., goes farther and says "that probably it would be wrong even to claim that the Church continues Christ's mission." But the claim is surely unexceptionable if it means, as it should, that Christ continues His mission by His Spirit in His people.

Pauline exposition of the body permits. (The same might have to be said of the fashion of describing the church as Christ's "mystical body", if one could be sure what those who use this phrase mean by it.) Our Lord's incarnation cannot be dissociated from His atoning sacrifice, and that was offered once for all and can have no "extension" in the life of the church. And the view of the church as the extension of His incarnation takes insufficient account of the contrast between His sinlessness and the church's sinfulness.[109]

It is probably from this conception of the church as the body of Christ that we can best understand how Paul can speak of believers as being "in Christ" and at the same time of Christ as being in them. For they are "in Christ" as members of His body, "baptized into Christ" (Gal. 3:27); He is in them because it is His life that animates them.[110] We may compare the use made of another organic analogy in John 15:1 ff.; there the branches are in the vine and the vine at the same time is in the branches.[111]

It is the *risen* Christ who is head of His body the church; He receives the titles "the beginning"[112] and "the firstborn"[113] in resurrection as well as in creation. His resurrection marked His triumph over all the forces which held men in bondage.[114] That first Easter morning saw the dawn of a new hope for mankind. Now Christ is the firstborn among many brethren;[115] He is "the firstfruits of those who have fallen asleep";[116] His resurrection is the harbinger of the great resurrection-harvest of His people. But the resurrection day is anticipated here and now by those who know Him as the resurrection and the life and enjoy eternal life through their participation in Him.[117] By His primacy in creation and resurrection alike the divine purpose is fulfilled "that in all

---

109   Cf. A. M. Hunter, *Interpreting Paul's Gospel* (London, 1954), p. 43.
110   Cf. v. 27 (pp. 218 f.).
111   Cf. L. S. Thornton, *The Common Life in the Body of Christ* (London, 1944), p. 144; also his essay "The Body of Christ in the NT" in *The Apostolic Ministry*, ed. K. E. Kirk (London, 1946), pp. 53 ff.
112   Gk. ἀρχή as in Prov. 8:22 (cf. p. 195).
113   Gk. πρωτότοκος (cf. v. 15). With the expression used here (πρωτότοκος ἐκ τῶν νεκρῶν) cf. πρωτότοκος τῶν νεκρῶν in Rev. 1:5 (see n. 64 above).
114   Cf. Heb. 2:14 f.; 1 John 3:8b.
115   Rom. 8:29 (πρωτότοκος ἐν πολλοῖς ἀδελφοῖς); cf. Rom. 8:11.
116   1 Cor. 15:20, 23.
117   Cf. John 3:15 f., 36; 6:51; 10:27 f.; 11:25 f.

things—new creation as well as old[118]—He might be preeminent."[119]

(d) Christ as Reconciler of all things

Ch. 1:19–20

> 19 For it was the good pleasure *of the Father* that in him should all the fulness dwell;
> 20 and through him to reconcile all things unto himself, having made peace through the blood of his cross; through him, *I say,* whether things upon the earth, or things in the heavens.

19 The statement that God decreed the preeminence of Christ over every order of being is now repeated in different terms—terms which were probably calculated to appeal with peculiar force to the Colossian Christians in their present situation. It was the divine will,[120] says Paul, that in Christ all the "fulness" should take up its abode.[121] The Greek word translated "fulness" (*pleroma*) is one that Paul and other NT writers use in a variety of senses.[122] But the peculiar force of its use here lies in the probability that it was employed in a technical sense by the heretical teachers at Colossae (as it was in a number of gnostic systems) to denote the totality of divine emanations or agencies, those supernatural powers under whose control men were supposed

---

[118] In καὶ αὐτός ἐστιν ἡ κεφαλὴ τοῦ σώματος, τῆς ἐκκλησίας, M. Dibelius (HNT, *ad loc.*) considers that the addition of τῆς ἐκκλησίας is intended to indicate that Christ is head of the body, the church, as well as being head of the body, the κόσμος, which has been dealt with in vv. 15–17. But in that case we should have expected καὶ before τοῦ σώματος. H. A. Wagenführer (*Die Bedeutung Christi für Welt und Kirche* [Leipzig, 1941], p. 62) would expunge τῆς ἐκκλησίας as a gloss, taking σῶμα here (and in Ch. 2:19) to refer to the κόσμος. This is a completely unwarranted proceeding.

[119] Gk. πρωτεύων. Strack–Billerbeck, *op. cit.*, i, p. 65, Anm. C (on Matt. 1:21), compare the use of *rishon* ("first") as a title of Messiah.

[120] Gk. ὅτι ἐν αὐτῷ εὐδόκησεν πᾶν τὸ πλήρωμα κατοικῆσαι. It is best to understand ὁ θεός as subject of εὐδόκησεν ("God saw fit that all the 'fulness' should take up its abode in him"), rather than to take πλήρωμα as subject ("the 'fulness' saw fit to take up its abode in him").

[121] The verb is aorist infinitive, κατοικῆσαι.

[122] In the Synoptic Gospels πλήρωμα is used of the patch put in to "fill up" the rent in an old garment (Matt. 9:16 // Mark 2:21) and of the left-over fragments which "filled" several baskets after the miraculous feedings (Mark 6:43; 8:20). In Rom. 11:12, 25, it is used of the final sum-total of believing Jews and Gentiles respectively. In Rom. 13:10 it is used of love as the "fulfilling" of the law; in Rom. 15:29 of the "fulness" of Christ's blessing with which Paul hopes

to live.[123] These powers were considered to be intermediaries between God and the world; any communication between God and the world, in either direction, must pass through the spheres in which they exercised rule. It was therefore necessary to treat them with becoming respect. Paul undermines the whole of this theosophical apparatus in one simple, direct affirmation: the fulness or totality of divine essence and power has taken up its residence in Christ. In other words, He is the one mediator between God and the world of mankind, and all the attributes and activities of God—His spirit, word, wisdom and glory[124]—are displayed in Him.

20 It was God's good pleasure, moreover, to reconcile[125] all

---

to visit Rome. In 1 Cor. 10:26 it appears in a quotation from Ps. 24:1 (LXX 23:1) of that which fills the earth. In Gal. 4:4 and Eph. 1:10 it denotes the completion of an appointed period of time (and consequently the arrival of an epoch; *cf.* συμπληροῦσθαι in Acts 2:1). There remain those occurrences which have theological or Christological significance. In John 1:16 it is used of the "fulness" of Christ out of which (as the Evangelist says) "we have all received." There the thought is of the inexhaustible resources of grace ("grace upon grace") which the people of Christ find in Him, and on which they may freely draw. In Eph. 3:19 we read of the "fulness of God"; in Eph. 4:13 of the "fulness of Christ" (in the sense of the Christian maturity to which believers attain as members of His body); and in the much disputed occurrence of the word in Eph. 1:23 *(τὸ πλήρωμα τοῦ τὰ πάντα ἐν πᾶσιν πληρουμένου)* attention should be paid to C. F. D. Moule's argument that here too, as in Col. 1:19 and 2:9, it is Christ who is referred to as the fulness of God (ExT lx [1948–9], pp. 53, 224; he recalls the earlier statement of this interpretation by A. E. N. Hitchcock in ExT xxii [1910–11], p. 91). If this interpretation were sound, it would remove the basis of the argument that Colossians and Ephesians cannot be by the same hand because in the former Christ is the πλήρωμα and in the latter the church is the πλήρωμα. But in any case, the wide variety of senses in which πλήρωμα is used even in the Pauline Epistles would make this argument precarious. See p. 42, with n. 41 (on Eph. 1:23).

[123] *Cf.* Irenaeus' account of Valentinianism (*Heresies* i. l. 1, etc.). See Lightfoot, *Colossians*, pp. 257 ff.; J. A. Robinson, *Ephesians*, pp. 255 ff.; C. A. A. Scott, *Christianity according to St. Paul* (Cambridge, 1927), pp. 266 f. E. Percy, however, doubts if πλήρωμα was such a technical term in the Colossian heresy as is usually supposed. He suggests that Paul may have chosen the word independently, so as to emphasize the supremacy of Christ over against the false teaching (*Probleme der Kolosser- und Epheserbriefe* [Lund, 1946], pp. 76 f.).

[124] *Cf.* Ps. 72:19; Isa. 6:3; Jer. 23:24.

[125] Here and in v. 21 the verb for "reconcile" is ἀποκαταλλάσσω, found also in Eph. 2:16 and nowhere else in NT. The simpler verb καταλλάσσω appears in Rom. 5:10 (twice); 2 Cor. 5:18, 19, 20 (also in 1 Cor. 7:11, but not there in a theological sense); its cognate noun καταλλαγή is used in Rom. 5:11; 11:15; 2 Cor. 5:18, 19. The longer verb ἀποκαταλλάσσω "is not found before the New Testament where it occurs in Ephesians and Colossians, Epistles in which

things to Himself[126] through Christ. The fulness of the divine energy is manifested in Christ not only in His creative work but in reconciliation also. And while this reconciling activity has particular reference to redeemed humanity, it has a universal reference too.[127] In reconciliation as in creation the work of Christ has a cosmic significance; as we are told in Eph. 1:10, it is God's eternal purpose to sum all things up in Christ.[128]

Christ has accomplished this peace-making work through the shedding of His blood on the cross.[129] This is an aspect of the gospel which Paul emphasizes in other places; in Rom. 5:1 ff., for example, he speaks of the "peace with God" which belongs[130] to those who have been justified by faith; when they were His enemies, in rebellion against Him, they were "reconciled to God through the death of his Son." Here, as against the line of teaching which had been introduced into the Colossian church, Paul "declares that the universal reconciliation has been effected through something done in history, in a human body of flesh, and on a cross of shame; and it was done through physical dying. So 'the blood of His cross' can mean no other than the pouring out in death of His earthly human life by crucifixion on a common gibbet. That is the deed that avails to put men right with God."[131] The term "blood" speaks of the voluntary yielding up of His life in death—a death which thus was not only violent but sacrificial and

---

καταλλάσσω is not found. The meaning is much the same as that of the last-mentioned verb, but probably with an intensification" (L. Morris, *op. cit.*, p. 187). F. Büchsel (TWNT i [Stuttgart, 1933], p. 259, s.v ἀλλάσσω) thinks it probable that Paul coined ἀποκαταλλάσσω. See p. 61, n. 28 (on Eph. 2:16).

[126] It is strange that editors have regularly spelt εἰς αὐτόν here with a smooth breathing instead of εἰς αὑτόν (=ἑαυτόν) with a rough breathing (*cf.* C. F. D. Moule, IBNTG, p. 119).

[127] *Cf.* Rom. 8:19 ff.; 2 Cor. 5:19 *(κόσμον καταλλάσσων ἑαυτῷ)*; Rev. 5:13 *(πᾶν κτίσμα)*.

[128] Eph. 1:10 is thus a commentary on εἰς αὐτόν, Col. 1:16; everything was created with a view to Christ.

[129] The same thought, of reconciliation effected by our Lord's death on the cross, appears in Eph. 2:11 ff.; there, however, the special application of the thought is to the bringing together of Jew and Gentile to form "one new man" in Christ, since both have been reconciled in one body to God (v. 16).

[130] Reading ἔχομεν in Rom. 5:1 rather than ἔχωμεν.

[131] A. M. Stibbs, *op. cit.*, p. 24. This view seems preferable to that expressed, *e.g.*, by B. F. Westcott, that the shedding of a victim's blood means not only its death but also "the liberation, so to speak, of the principle of life by which it had been animated, so that this life became available for another end" (*The Epistles of St. John* [London, 1902], p. 35).

redemptive, procuring the justification and reconciliation of the sinner.[132]

Paul has been criticized at times for analysing the divine forgiveness into justification and reconciliation, especially by those who deprecate the expression of this forgiveness in judicial categories at all.[133] Paul had little choice in the matter; he had inherited the conception of God as the Judge of all the earth. Nor is this conception absent from the teaching of Jesus; He speaks of the day of judgment and tells His hearers what will secure their acquittal on that day and what will procure their condemnation. In fact the distinction between justification and reconciliation, in which logical priority is given to justification, is rooted in the insight that peace, to be worthy of the name, must be founded on righteousness. If we are to be reconciled to God, to enjoy peace with Him, we must have the assurance that He who will by no means clear the guilty has nevertheless accepted us, sinful as we are. It is as those who have been justified by faith that we have peace with God through our Lord Jesus Christ. Formerly offenders, we have been brought into a right relationship with Him through the merit of another; formerly hostile to Him, we have become His friends; His love, revealed in Christ, is poured forth and wells up in our hearts.

Paul's statement that Christ's reconciling work, in accordance with the divine purpose, is to embrace in its scope "all things... whether things upon the earth, or things in the heavens," has been taken to mean that he looked for the ultimate reconciliation to God not only of all men but of hostile spiritual powers as well—that, in fact, he anticipated Origen[134] in the view that fallen angels benefit by the redemption accomplished by Christ. The present passage, however, has to be understood in relation to Paul's general teaching on this subject; and it is very difficult to press his language to yield anything like universal reconciliation in the sense in which the phrase is commonly used nowadays. It is contrary to the whole analogy of Scripture (the Pauline writings included) to apply the idea of reconciliation in the ordinary sense to the fallen angels.[135]

---

132   *Cf.* also Rom. 3:25; 5:8 ff.; Eph. 1:7; 2:13.
133   *Cf.* J. Knox, *Chapters in a Life of Paul* (London, 1954), pp. 146 ff.
134   *Commentary on John,* i. 35.
135   *Cf.* J. Denney, *The Death of Christ* (London, 1951), pp. 113 ff. (and on the general interpretation of this passage, pp. 85 ff.). E. Percy (*op. cit.,* p. 95) holds that Ch. 1:21 must be understood in the light of Ch. 2:15. Both passages

And even with regard to mankind, to deduce from such a passage as this the conclusion that every human being, irrespective of his record or his attitude to God, will at last enjoy celestial bliss, is to deduce something which is contrary to recorded sayings of our Lord, not to mention the teaching of the NT in general.[136]

The peace effected by the death of Christ may be freely accepted, or it may be compulsorily imposed. When Paul speaks here of reconciliation on the widest scale, he includes in it what we should distinguish as pacification.[137] The principalities and powers whose conquest by Christ is described in Ch. 2:15 are certainly not depicted there as gladly surrendering to His grace, but as submitting against their wills to a power which they cannot resist. Everything in the universe has been subjected to Christ even as everything was created for Him. By His reconciling work, "the host of the high ones on high"[138] and sinful men on earth have been decisively subdued to the will of God, and can but subserve His purpose, whether they please or not. So in Phil. 2:11 "things in heaven and things on earth and things under the earth" ultimately unite to bow in the name of Jesus and to acknowledge Him as Lord.

(e) Christ as Reconciler of His People to God

Ch. 1:21-23

21 And you, being in time past alienated and enemies in your mind in your evil works,

22 yet now hath he reconciled[139] in the body of his flesh

---

presume a certain hostility on the part of these powers towards God and Christ; they are reconciled through subjugation (cf. 1 Cor. 15:28), and Christ's victory has reduced them to the status of πτωχὰ καὶ ἀσθενῆ στοιχεῖα (cf. Gal. 4:9). Cf. also J. Michl, "Die Versöhnung Kol. 1:21", Theologische Quartalschrift cxxviii (1948), pp. 442 ff.; B. N. Wambacq, "Per eum reconciliare...", RB lv (1948), pp. 35 ff.

[136] Cf. A. M. Hunter, op. cit., p. 54; for the contrary view see W. Michaelis, Versöhnung des Alls (Bern, 1950).

[137] In 1 Cor. 15:24 ff. Christ is to "abolish (Gk. καταργέω) all rule and all authority and power"; but there it is mainly the destructive powers, of which death is the chief, that are in view.

[138] Isa. 24:21.

[139] The chief "ancient authorities" which, according to ARV margin, read "ye have been reconciled" are P[46], B and Hilary. This reading (ἀποκατηλλάγητε) involves an anacoluthon after the accusative pronoun ὑμᾶς ("you") but for that reason may be regarded as original; the reading represented in ARV text (ἀποκατήλλαξεν) will then be the most successful of several attempts to mend the breach of concord.

210

> through death, to present you holy and without
> blemish and unreprovable before him:
>
> 23 if so be that ye continue in the faith, grounded and
> stedfast, and not moved away from the hope of the
> gospel which ye heard, which was preached in all
> creation under heaven, whereof I Paul was made a
> minister.

21 The central purpose of Christ's peace-making work, however, is seen most clearly in its bearing upon those who have heard
the message of reconciliation and willingly rendered their submission, gratefully accepting the amnesty which the message holds
out. Such were the people to whom Paul was writing.[140] Once
they had been estranged[141] from God, in revolt against His
authority. For sin is not only disobedience to the will of God;
it effectually severs our fellowship with Him, and forces us to
live "without God in the world" (Eph. 2:12). Hence men, estranged
from the One in whom alone true peace is to be found, are estranged
also from one another, and lead lonely lives in a universe which is
felt to be unfriendly. The barrier which sin sets up between men
and God is also a barrier set up between men and their fellows.
That is why Paul, dealing with this matter of alienation and
reconciliation in Ephesians, thinks of the most impenetrable barrier
which the ancient world knew—the barrier between Jews and
Gentiles—and describes how it has been abolished in Christ. When
Jews and Gentiles are both reconciled to God in Christ, they are
by that very fact reconciled to one another—a spectacle for
unending wonder and praise in Paul's eyes.[142]

22 But now the great change has been effected; those who were
once far away from God have been brought close to Him; those
who used to be at war with Him are at peace with Him. For Christ

---

[140] With the passage beginning "and you..." (Gk. καὶ ὑμᾶς ...) cf. Eph.
2:1 ff.

[141] But not in the sense that they, as individuals, had ever been in any other
relation to God than one of estrangement. Here, as in Eph. 2:12 and 4:18, the
perfect participle passive ἀπηλλοτριωμένοι is equivalent to the adjective ἀλλότριοι.
Cf. Eph. 2:13, "ye that once were far off." As for their being hostile in their
"mind" (Gk. διάνοια), it is noteworthy that in NT Greek, as in the LXX, this
word corresponds to the OT "heart" (Heb. leb, lebab). See C. Masson, L'Épître
aux Éphésiens, p. 159, n. 3.

[142] Cf. C. H. Dodd, New Testament Studies, p. 72. This reconciliation of
Jews and Gentiles may be viewed as a microcosm of the larger and "macro-
cosmic" reconciliation one day to be revealed.

has reconciled us to God "in the body of his flesh, through his[143] death." The historic act accomplished on our behalf once for all by the death of Christ is brought into close relation with what takes place in our own experience when we enter into peace with God, when the work done *for* us is made effective *in* us. If in v. 20 we were told that the reconciliation was won for us by the blood of Christ, here we are told that it was procured for us "in the body of his flesh."[144] Both expressions denote His self-oblation in death (as they also do in the Eucharist); but here the emphasis is on the fact that He endured that death in His physical body.[145] It is highly probable that some such insistence on the true incarnation of our Lord was a necessary corrective to the tendency of the Colossian heresy; more particularly, we should observe here the necessary bond between His incarnation and His atoning death. So, in Rom. 8:3, we read how God achieved "what the law could not achieve because it was weak by reason of the flesh" when, "having sent His own Son *in the likeness of sinful flesh* and as an offering for sin, He condemned sin *in the flesh*." The incarnation of the Son of God was real and necessary for the vindication of God's righteousness in the bestowal of His peace on sinful men. And now that we have received His peace, we have direct access to Him already[146] and shall have it in all its fulness when at length we are introduced[147] into His presence "holy, blameless, and free

---

143 Thus the force of the article may be brought out, διὰ τοῦ θανάτου.

144 Gk. ἐν τῷ σώματι τῆς σαρκὸς αὐτοῦ. The preposition ἐν probably has instrumental force; His body of flesh was the instrument or organ of the reconciliation which He established in His death. Yet the apostle's thought can move without difficulty from our Lord's incarnate body by means of which He accomplished His reconciling work to His body the church in which the reconciliation becomes effectively apparent—the "one body" in which He has reconciled both Jew and Gentile "unto God through the cross" (Eph. 2:16). "The thought which finds clear expression in Eph. 2:16, that the human beings to be reconciled are included in the body of Christ, and that at the very time when Christ died for them on the cross, also lies plainly behind ἐν τῷ σώματι τῆς σαρκὸς αὐτοῦ in Col. 1:22" (E. Percy, *op. cit.*, p. 382).

145 *Cf.* Ch. 2:11, ἐν τῇ ἀπεκδύσει τοῦ σώματος τῆς σαρκός. The expression "body of flesh" in the sense of "physical body" is evidently a Hebraism; *cf.* the Qumrân Habakkuk commentary on Hab. 2:7, *bi-gewiyyath besaro* (the exact verbal equivalent of ἐν τῷ σώματι τῆς σαρκὸς αὐτοῦ here).

146 Compare the sequence of blessings which flow from justification by faith in Rom. 5:1 ff.

147 Gk. παραστῆσαι. The time referred to is the *parousia* of Christ; the same verb appears in this eschatological sense in v. 28; *cf.* Rom. 14:10; 2 Cor. 4:14; 11:2; Eph. 5:27.

from every charge against us." "In Christ this accused person becomes unaccused; he is awarded not condemnation but liberty."[148] The sentence of justification passed upon the believer here and now anticipates the pronouncement of the judgment day; the holiness which is progressively wrought in his life by the Spirit of God here and now is to issue in perfection of glory on the day of Christ's *parousia*.

23 This, then, is the prospect which lies before them, provided that they remain firmly founded and established in their faith. If the Bible teaches the final perseverance of the saints, it also teaches that the saints are those who finally persevere—in Christ. Continuance is the test of reality. The apostle's language may suggest that his readers' first enthusiasm was being dimmed, that they were in danger of shifting from the fixed ground of the Christian hope. And indeed, to hold fast to hope is throughout the NT an indispensable condition of attaining the goal of full salvation to be revealed at the *parousia* of Christ.[149] Hope forms an essential part of the gospel—that gospel which (as Paul has already emphasized) is spreading and bearing fruit in all the world, having been proclaimed (as he puts it here, perhaps indulging in a prophetic prolepsis) "in the whole creation under heaven."[150] The catholicity of the gospel is a token of its divine origin and power.[151] And of this gospel—wonder of wonders!—"I Paul have become a minister." He sees his personal ministry as closely bound up with God's gracious plan for the world.[152]

---

148 A. Deissmann, *Paul* (Eng. tr., London, 1926), p. 168.
149 *Cf.* Eph. 1:18; Heb. 3:6; 6:11; 10:23; 1 Pet. 1:13; 1 John 3:3.
150 *Cf.* v. 6 above (p. 181), with exposition and note *ad loc.*
151 *Cf.* A. S. Peake *ad loc.* in EGT iii (London, 1903), p. 513.
152 *Cf.* Rom. 11:13; Eph. 3:2 ff., and see J. Munck, *op. cit.*, p. 33.

3. PAUL'S STEWARDSHIP OF THE REVELATION OF GOD

Ch. 1:24-29

24 Now I rejoice in my sufferings for your sake, and fill up on my part that which is lacking of the afflictions of Christ in my flesh for his body's sake, which is the church;

25 whereof I was made a minister, according to the dispensation of God which was given me to you-ward, to fulfil the word of God,

26 *even* the mystery which hath been hid for ages and generations: but now hath it been manifested to his saints,

27 to whom God was pleased to make known what is the riches of the glory of this mystery among the Gentiles, which is Christ in you, the hope of glory:

28 whom we proclaim, admonishing every man and teaching every man in all wisdom, that we may present every man perfect in Christ;

29 whereunto I labor also, striving according to his working, which worketh in me mightily.

24 Paul's introductory expression of thanks now passes into an account of his own spiritual exercise in relation to the people whom he is addressing.[153]

The hardships which he endures in the course of his apostolic service are endured for their sakes.[154] And he could even rejoice in these hardships,[155] because of the advantage that accrued through them to his converts (whether their conversion was due to his direct witness or, like that of the Colossians, to the witness of one of his colleagues). For he realized that by bearing hardship on behalf of the people of Christ, he was entering into the fellowship of Christ's sufferings—a fellowship which, as he told his

---

[153] *Cf.* a similar transition in Rom. 1:8 ff.

[154] *Cf.* 2 Tim. 2:10.

[155] *Cf.* Rom. 5:3; 2 Cor. 12:10, where other reasons are mentioned for rejoicing in such tribulations. For θλίψεις ("tribulations") see p. 77, n. 21 (on Eph. 3:13).

214

friends at Philippi, he desired to know more fully.[156] "In my own person",[157] he says, "I am filling up[158] those afflictions of Christ which have yet to be endured on behalf of His body, the church."

This remarkable statement can best be understood if we remember the oscillation in Hebrew thought between individual and corporate personality. In the present instance, the Biblical portrayal of the Suffering Servant is most helpful and relevant. The Servant is, in one place at least, a corporate entity, the Israel of God (Isa. 49:3):

> "Thou art my servant,
> Israel, in whom I will be glorified."

But Israel as a whole proved to be a disobedient servant, and the prophecy of the Servant's triumph through suffering found its fulfilment in one person, in whom the ideally obedient Israel was realized. Jesus Christ, by His obedience and passion and victory over death, fulfilled the prophecy, and therefore He is henceforth proclaimed as a light to the nations, as the agent of God's delivering grace throughout the world. But the identity of the Servant, which narrowed in scope until it was concentrated in our Lord alone, has since His exaltation broadened out again and become corporate in His people. So, to take the most notable example from the NT, Paul and Barnabas at Pisidian Antioch announce to the members of the Jewish synagogue there that, in view of their opposition to the gospel, they will henceforth turn to the Gentiles. And they find their authority for this course of action in one of the Isaianic Servant Songs: "For so hath the Lord commanded us, saying,

I have set thee for a light of the Gentiles,

---

156 *Cf.* Phil. 3:10. "What Paul refers to as being still 'lacking', or 'imperfect', was not the sacrifice and suffering of Christ, but it was his own fellowship with that sacrifice and suffering" (J. S. Stewart, *A Man in Christ* [London, 1935], p. 190).

157 Gk. ἐν τῇ σαρκί μου, "in my flesh."

158 Gk. ἀνταναπληρῶ. The force of ἀντι- in this compound is disputed; J. B. Lightfoot (*ad loc.*) renders it "I fill up on my part", "I supplement," and argues, on the basis of classical and Hellenistic occurrences of the verb, that "it signifies that the supply comes *from an opposite quarter* to the deficiency." But T. K. Abbott (in ICC [Edinburgh, 1897], *ad. loc.*) points out that in the two places in the NT where ἀναπληρόω is used with ὑστέρημα, the supply equally comes from a different quarter to the deficiency (1 Cor. 16:17; Phil. 2:30); it does not require the ἀντι- in ἀνταναπληρῶ to indicate this. It is simplest to regard the prefix as suggesting correspondence: to the deficiency corresponds the supply. See also n. 164 below.

That thou shouldest be for salvation unto the uttermost
part of the earth" (Acts 13:47, quoting Isa. 49:6).
That is to say, the Servant's mission of enlightenment among the
nations is to be carried on by the disciples of Christ.[159] But here
Paul goes farther: the Servant's sufferings are also to be carried
on by the disciples of Christ—at least, by one of them, Paul
himself.

We must distinguish, of course. The sense in which the suffering
and death of Christ have won justification and reconciliation for
men is unique, unrepeatable. When Paul is so concerned as he
is here to assert the sole sufficiency of Christ as Saviour and
Mediator, it would be absurd to suppose that he means that he
himself, by the hardships he endures, is in some way supplementing
the saving work of Christ.[160] Paul is as sure as the writer to the
Hebrews was that Christ's saving work was accomplished "once
for all" by His obedience unto death.[161]

But in the sense which Paul intends here, Christ continues to
suffer in His members, and not least in Paul himself. This truth
was impressed on Paul's mind in the very moment of his conversion, when he heard the voice of Christ say: "Why persecutest
thou *me?*"[162] Up to that moment, Paul had been actively engaged
in making Christ suffer in the person of His followers in Judaea;
from that time forth, he experienced in his own flesh the fulfilment
of the words of Christ to Ananias: "I will show him how many
things he must suffer for my name's sake" (Acts 9:16). To suffer
for the sake of the name of Christ and to suffer on behalf of His
body which is the church are two expressions that mean the same
thing. And as Christ Himself suffers in His members, this suffering
of theirs may be regarded as a filling up of Christ's personal
suffering.[163]

There may be the further thought here that Paul's own endur-

---

[159] See *Acts* in NICNT, pp. 282 f.; *cf.* C. K. Barrett, SJTh vi (1953), p. 242.

[160] *Cf.* E. Best, *op. cit.*, pp. 130 ff., 134 ff. He takes these "sufferings of the
Messiah" to be the messianic birth-pangs which had to be completed before the
parousia; Paul is anxious to fill up as full a measure as possible of these in his
own person.

[161] There is, indeed, a Pauline sense in which the believer shares in this
"once for all" act, but in that sense the believer's death with Christ is an event
in the past, expressed in the aorist or perfect tense. See below on Chs. 2:20;
3:3 (pp. 253, 260).

[162] See p. 203, n. 102. *Cf.* Matt. 25:40, 45.

[163] *Cf.* also 1 Cor. 15:31, and especially 2 Cor. 1:5–7; 4:10–12.

ance of hardship in the cause of Christ may relieve his converts and other members of the body of Christ of part of the suffering that would otherwise fall to their lot.[164] So conscious was Paul of the special significance of his vocation to service and suffering.[165]

25 For he knew very well that he had been called to be a servant of the church for the discharge of a unique stewardship.[166] This stewardship, entrusted to him by Christ, was (as he puts it) the "fulfilment" of the word or message of God. The word of God is fulfilled in this sense when it is proclaimed in the world and accepted by men in faith; thus it achieves its purpose.[167] It was Paul's responsibility to discharge this stewardship by the exercise of his special apostleship to the Gentiles, among whom the Colossians were included. "Unto me," as he says in the parallel passage in Ephesians, "...was this grace given, to preach unto the Gentiles the unsearchable riches of Christ" (Eph. 3:8); and the Colossians were among the beneficiaries of this apostolic commission of his, even if he had never visited them in person.

---

[164] *Cf.* J. A. T. Robinson, *op. cit.*, p. 70, for this view: the apostle "is glad to absorb in his flesh what should be the share of his Colossian brethren and to fill up in *their* stead ... the tax of suffering still outstanding to them." This ("in *their* stead") is his interpretation of the prefix ἀντι- in ἀνταναπληρῶ. C. F. D. Moule (IBNTG, p. 71) allows his interpretation (ἀντι-"may anticipate the force of the ὑπέρ which follows"), but he admits the view preferred in n. 158 above, that ἀντι- "may merely imply that fulness *replaces* lack."

[165] Ignatius (*Ad Eph.* 8:1; *Ad Trall.* 13:3) speaks of his imminent martyrdom as an offering on behalf of his Christian friends, but does not describe it as part of the suffering of Christ. On the other hand, the *Letter from the Churches of Vienne and Lyons* (Eusebius, *Hist. Eccl.* v. 1) expressly speaks of Christ as suffering in the martyrs.

[166] Gk. οἰκονομία, rendered "dispensation" in AV and ARV ("divine office" in RSV). Other examples of Paul's use of this word for his special service are found in 1 Cor. 9:17 and (more particularly) Eph. 3:2, 9. There, as here, he speaks of himself as a steward of the divine mystery, *i.e.* the divine purpose formerly concealed but now at length revealed and put into effect through his ministry—the bringing of Gentile believers into a common life with Jewish believers, as fellow-heirs of the promises of God and fellow-members of the body of Christ. See p. 33, n. 19 (on Eph. 1:10).

[167] *Cf.* Rom. 15:19, where Paul, early in A.D. 57, claims that he has "fulfilled (ARV margin, Gk. πεπληρωκέναι) the gospel of Christ" in the area between Jerusalem and Illyricum. Here the aorist infinitive πληρῶσαι may indicate the fulfilment of the purpose for which the word was sent forth. J. Munck (*op. cit.*, pp. 39 f.) connects our present passage and Rom. 15:19 (as also 2 Tim. 4:17, "that through me the message might be fully proclaimed [Gk. πληροφορέω], and that all the Gentiles might hear") with the bringing in of the πλήρωμα τῶν ἐθνῶν in Rom. 11:25.

THE EPISTLE TO THE COLOSSIANS

26-27 He now enlarges upon the message with which he has been entrusted. It is a "mystery"—that is to say, something formerly concealed and now unveiled.[168] It is "the mystery which was kept secret from[169] ages and generations (of the past), but which has now been revealed to God's holy people,[170] those to whom he has been pleased to make known the glorious wealth of this mystery[171] among the Gentiles—the mystery which may be summed up in these words 'Christ in you, the hope of glory'."

The saving purpose of God was, of course, a major theme of the OT prophets, and that Gentiles as well as Israelites were embraced within its scope was also foreseen.[172] But the manner in which that purpose would come to fruition—by the incorporation of Gentile and Jewish believers alike in the common life of the body of Christ—was not made known. That had remained a mystery, a secret, until the time of fulfilment, and now Paul, as first steward of this mystery, unfolds its wonder to his readers, that they may admire and worship the glory of God's rich grace thus lavishly dispensed. Had this grace been shown to believing Jews alone, it might not have excited such wonder; they, after all, were

---

[168] Cf. Rom. 16:25. "In the ordinary sense a mystery implies knowledge withheld; its Scriptural significance is truth revealed" (W. E. Vine, *Expository Dictionary of NT Words*, iii [London, 1940], p. 97). (In Dan. 2:18 f., 27 ff., etc., and in the Qumrân texts the term "mystery" [Heb. *raz*] refers to the way in which God will fulfil His prophetic word.) In Colossians and Ephesians two distinct, but related, aspects of the mystery entrusted to Paul are respectively emphasized: in Colossians, the fact that the indwelling Christ is, for Gentiles as well as Jews, the hope of glory; in Ephesians, the fact that in Christ Gentiles are fellow-heirs with Jewish believers.

[169] Gk. ἀπὸ τῶν αἰώνων καὶ ἀπὸ τῶν γενεῶν, where ἀπό has the temporal sense of "since" and does not mean that the "ages" and "generations" were the beings to which the mystery remained unrevealed, as it did to the spirit-rulers of 1 Cor. 2:8. Cf. Eph. 3:9 (p. 74, n. 14).

[170] In Eph. 3:5 the mystery has "now been revealed to his holy apostles and prophets by inspiration." (See p. 72 with n. 8.) It was then communicated by these to the saints in general. (With the reference to prophets cf. Rom. 16:26.)

[171] Gk. τὸ πλοῦτος τῆς δόξης τοῦ μυστηρίου τούτου. Paul is particularly given to the use of πλοῦτος with a following genitive; cf. Ch. 2:2; Rom. 2:4; 9:23; 2 Cor. 8:2; Eph. 1:7; 2:7; 3:8.

[172] See Paul's catena of OT quotations to this effect in Rom. 15:9 ff.; cf. also Isa. 49:6, quoted in Luke 2:32 and Acts 13:47 (see pp. 215 f. above). The prophets spoke of Christ and His salvation (Eph. 2:17; 4:8; 1 Pet. 1:10) and the gospel was proclaimed to Abraham (Gal. 3:8); yet before faith came (Gal. 3:23)—*i.e.* with the appearance of Christ—a veil overhung the true understanding of the OT (2 Cor. 3:14). "The apostles are the first to *know* what the prophets *said*" (H. J. Holtzmann, *Kritik der Epheser- und Kolosserbriefe* [Leipzig, 1872], p. 212).

recognized as the messianic people. But non-Jews are included
as well, and included on an equal footing with Jews, and it is
Paul's supreme joy, as it is his divinely-imposed obligation, to
make known "the riches of the glory of this mystery among the
Gentiles."[173] "Christ is in *you*," he assures his Colossian readers;
"Christ is in you (even in you Gentiles) as the hope of glory"; the
fact that here and now, as members of His body, you have His life
within you, affords you a firm hope that you will share in that
fulness of glory which is yet to be displayed, on the day of "the
revealing of the sons of God."[174] Christ Himself is the centre and
circumference of this mystery; by His death and exaltation He has
brought it to accomplishment, and those who are united to Him
are inevitably involved in its accomplishment—in measure now,
and in perfection hereafter.

28 This Christ, whose life flows in all His people, is the One
whom we proclaim, Paul continues. He is the sum and substance
of our message, whether in the saving news which we announce
in the world to bring men to repentance and faith, or in the
teaching which we impart to those who have believed. For they
have not learned all there is to know when once they have
come to Christ; that is only the beginning. Therefore we go on
"admonishing every man and teaching every man in all wisdom."
The repetition of "every man" carries a certain emphasis. There
is no part of Christian teaching that is to be reserved for a spiritual
élite. All the truth of God is for all the people of God. This verse
has been described as "one of the great slogans of what might be
called Christian democracy."[175] A later NT writer, taking issue

---

[173] *Cf.* the expansion of this thought in Eph. 3:2–12. The difference between
the use of μυστήριον in the two epistles is not so great as is suggested by M.
Dibelius (HNT xii, p. 84) and C. L. Mitton, *The Epistle to the Ephesians*
(Oxford, 1951), pp. 86 ff. According to Dibelius, the "mystery" in Col. 1:26 f. is
"das eschatologisch-mystische Christusgeheimnis"; according to Mitton, it is the
indwelling of Christ in His people. The "mystery" of Ephesians, on the other
hand, is God's acceptance of the Gentiles which, says Dibelius, "is no μυστήριον
for Paul." But the μυστήριον is not simply their acceptance; it includes their
incorporation, along with Jewish believers, in the community of the Messiah.
And in the present passage the emphasis is not just Christ's indwelling in His
people, but more particularly His indwelling in *Gentile* believers. *Cf.* E. Percy,
op. cit., pp. 379 ff.; C. F. D. Moule, ExT lx (1948–9), p. 224.

[174] Rom. 8:19; *cf:* also Rom. 5:2; 1 Cor. 2:7; 2 Cor. 4:17; Col. 3:4 (see
pp. 261 ff.); 1 Thess. 2:12; 2 Thess. 1:10; 2:14.

[175] S. C. Carpenter, in a sermon on "The Spiritual Capacity of the Plain
Man", ExT l (1938–9), pp. 394 ff.

with an incipient gnosticism which professed a special brand of knowledge for a favoured few, by contrast with the rank and file for whom elementary half-truths were good enough, assures even the "little children" among his Christian readers that, because they have been anointed by the Holy One, they all have access to the true knowledge.[176] And it may well be that at this earlier date Paul was confronted with a similar situation, where certain teachers professed a form of "wisdom" higher than anything taught by Paul and his colleagues, a form of wisdom which not everyone could appreciate, and which therefore marked off those who accepted it and affected its jargon as an intellectually superior group. No, says Paul, in the proclamation of Christ we bring all wisdom within the reach of all,[177] and our purpose is that we may present each believer before the face of God in a condition of complete spiritual maturity. There should be no exceptions; there are no heights in Christian attainment which are not within the reach of all, by the power of divine grace.

When Paul speaks of presenting every man "perfect" or fully grown in Christ, he probably has the *parousia* in mind.[178] We may compare his assurance to the Christians of Thessalonica that they are his hope and joy and crown of glorying "before our Lord Jesus at His *parousia*" (1 Thess. 2:19 f.); and his prayer that they may be completely sanctified, and that their spirit and soul and body may be kept sound and blameless "at the *parousia* of our Lord Jesus Christ" (1 Thess. 5:23).[179] It is then that the gracious work in the believer's life is completed; it is then that perfect conformity to the likeness of Christ is attained.[180] When "that which is perfect" comes, we shall see "face to face" instead of obscurely, as in a mirror; we shall know fully, as we ourselves are

---

176   1 John 2:20, ARV margin ("and ye all know"), reading πάντες (with ℵ B P 398 and the Sahidic version) instead of πάντα.

177   The accumulation of various parts and compounds of πᾶς ("all") is an effective rhetorical device appearing several times in the Pauline and other NT writings. Cf. Ch. 3:11; Eph. 1:23, etc.

178   The tense is aorist (παραστήσωμεν) as in v. 22 (cf. p. 212, n. 147).

179   In 1 Thess 5:23 the verbs ἁγιάσαι and τηρηθείη are aorist, and the explicit mention of the *parousia* indicates the epoch referred to. Sanctification begins with the new birth, it progresses throughout the Christian life, and is consummated at the *parousia*.

180   Cf. 1 John 3:2. Here and now it is the work of the Holy Spirit to transform the people of God increasingly into the image of our Lord (2 Cor. 3:18).

known, instead of knowing in part as we do at present.[181] But this prospect of glory, which is the perfection of holiness, is held out to *all* Christians.

29 For this blessed consummation, so devoutly to be wished, Paul himself expended all his strength.[182] His apostolic work was not finished with the conversion of his hearers. That was a beginning; the end would not be reached until the day of Christ, and the quality of his ministry would then be tested by the quality and maturity of those whom he could present as his children in the faith. What joy would be his if they were genuine and worthy believers; what shame, if they were not! No wonder that he toiled and strove for their spiritual health with this day of review and reward before him. But here he gladly acknowledges that the strength requisite for such unremitting labour is not his own; it is the strength powerfully wrought within him by his enabling Lord.[183]

---

[181] 1 Cor. 13:10, 12. *Cf.* Eph. 4:13, "a fullgrown man" (ἄνδρα τέλειον), where the completion of the body of Christ is in view.

[182] Gk. κοπιῶ, a strong word, implying toil to the point of weariness or exhaustion (*cf.* 1 Cor. 4:12; 15:10; Gal. 4:11; Phil. 2:16, and the similar use of the substantive κόπος in 1 Cor. 15:58; 2 Cor. 6:5; 11:23, 27; 1 Thess. 2:9; 3:5; 2 Thess. 3:8). See Munck, *op. cit.*, p. 100.

[183] Gk. κατὰ τὴν ἐνέργειαν αὐτοῦ τὴν ἐνεργουμένην ἐν ἐμοὶ ἐν δυνάμει. The present participle ἐνεργουμένην is probably passive and not middle here. *Cf.* Eph. 3:20 (p. 84, n. 31). For the general sense *cf.* Eph. 3:7, κατὰ τὴν ἐνέργειαν τῆς δυνάμεως αὐτοῦ (where a distinction is drawn between God's power which was active in Paul, as in his fellow-apostles, and his own weakness) and Phil. 2:13. θεὸς ... ὁ ἐνεργῶν. Paul uses ἐνέργεια of supernatural power.

CHAPTER II

4. PAUL'S CONCERN FOR THE CHRISTIANS OF THE LYCUS VALLEY

Ch. 2:1–5

(a) Reassurance of his prayers for them

Ch. 2:1–3

1 For I would have you know how greatly I strive for you, and for them at Laodicea, and for as many as have not seen my face in the flesh;

2 that their hearts may be comforted, they being knit together in love, and unto all riches of the full assurance of understanding, that they may know the mystery of God, *even* Christ,[1]

3 in whom are all the treasures of wisdom and knowledge hidden.

1 The toil and spiritual conflict[2] in which Paul was engaged on his converts' behalf embraced not only those whom he had met

---

[1] Gk. εἰς ἐπίγνωσιν τοῦ μυστηρίου τοῦ θεοῦ, χριστοῦ. This reading appears in P46 and B, and is attested by Hilary, Pelagius and Pseudo-Jerome. Cod. D and some other Western authorities give the same sense in the expanded form "the mystery of God which is Christ" *(τοῦ μυστηρίου τοῦ θεοῦ ὅ ἐστιν χριστός).* Other authorities omit χριστοῦ or θεοῦ, or insert καί so as to yield the reading "the mystery of God and Christ" (variously amplified to "the mystery of God the Father and Christ" or even, as in TR, followed by AV, "the mystery of God, and of the Father, and of Christ"), or change χριστοῦ to [τοῦ] ἐν χριστῷ ("the mystery of God in Christ"). The reading of P46 and B, which underlies ARV and RSV, is the point of departure for all these variants. ARV and RSV take χριστοῦ in apposition with μυστηρίου—Christ Himself is the mystery of God. This seems to be the true sense. Some, however, regard the genitive χριστοῦ as dependent on θεοῦ, as if the meaning were "the God of Christ" (*cf.* J. Moffatt, "the open secret of God, the Father of Christ"). J. N. Darby, *The New Testament: A New Translation* (London, 1871), *ad loc.*, W. Kelly, *Lectures on Colossians* (London, n.d.), p. 40, and E. Lohmeyer (MK, *ad loc.*) take χριστοῦ as an early gloss (very early, since it is present in P46), and follow those texts which read simply "the mystery of God" (*e.g.*, Db H P 31 424**); the following ἐν ᾧ (v. 3) then means "in which."

[2] F. Field (*Notes on the Translation of the NT* [Cambridge, 1899], p. 195) argues that AV "what great conflict I have" is more expressive than the wording of ARV; he suggests (unconvincingly) that the phrase may be based on a reminiscence of Isa. 7:13, LXX: "Is it a small thing for you to cause conflict (ἀγῶνα παρέχειν) to men? How then do you cause conflict to the Lord?"

face to face, and who had accepted the gospel as they heard it from his lips; but those also who, like the Colossian Christians,[3] had been converted through the ministry of Paul's colleagues and assistants. Into this category came also the Christians of the neighbouring city of Laodicea[4] and of other places in the Lycus valley,[5] who appear to have owed their souls to Epaphras.

2 The purpose of his constant concern for these young Christians was that they might be strengthened[6] in heart and firmly bound together[7] in Christian love. For (no matter what some teachers might pretend) only thus could they attain that wealth of spiritual experience which lay in a full discerning[8] of the divine revelation. Others might lead them astray with specious talk of mysteries; but there was one mystery above all others—the mystery of God, unfolded in Christ alone—and Paul's concern was that they should come to know this all-surpassing mystery, and know it as an indwelling presence.

As against all those who tried to intellectualize the Christian faith, speaking of knowledge (*gnosis*) as if it were an end in itself, Paul emphasizes that the revelation of God cannot be properly known apart from the cultivation of brotherly love within the Christian community. So, in Eph. 3:17 f., it is only as Christians are "rooted and grounded in *love*" that they can acquire the power to "apprehend *with all the saints*" the fulness of God's revelation.[9]

---

[3] A few of them may have met Paul elsewhere (*e.g.*, in Ephesus); thus it appears from the Epistle to Philemon that Philemon and his household were personally known to him (see further on Archippus, Ch. 4:17).

[4] *Cf.* Ch. 4:16; Rev. 3:14 ff. Laodicea, founded by the Seleucid king Antiochus II about the middle of the 3rd century B.C., lay farther down the Lycus valley than Colossae. See W. M. Ramsay, *Cities and Bishoprics of Phrygia* I (Oxford, 1895), pp. 32 ff.; *Letters to the Seven Churches of Asia* (London, 1909), pp. 413 ff.

[5] Including, no doubt, Hierapolis (see further on Ch. 4:14).

[6] Gk. παρακαλέω, which implies more than comfort (ARV). RSV renders "that their hearts may be encouraged".

[7] Gk. συμβιβάζω (ARV, "knit together"). M. Dibelius's view (HNT, *ad loc.*) that the word means "instructed" here ("durch Belehrung in Liebe") finds some support from usage elsewhere (especially in LXX; *cf.* the quotation from Isa. 40:13 in 1 Cor. 2:16); but the analogy of Ch. 2:19 (with Eph. 4:16) is decisive here. See p. 99, n. 34 (on Eph. 4:16).

[8] Gk. σύνεσις (as in Ch. 1:9), implying the capacity to distinguish true from false.

[9] Eph. 3:17 f. is not documentarily dependent on Col. 2:2 (or 2:19); it is a fuller expression of the same thought from the same mind. For "in love" (ἐν ἀγάπῃ) *cf.* Eph. 4:15.

And this revelation is personal; Christ Himself is the mystery of God revealed—Christ, with whom they have now become one. There can be no appreciation of divine wisdom without a personal knowledge of Christ.

3 For it is in Christ that all the treasures of divine wisdom and knowledge[10] have been stored up—stored up in hiding formerly, but now displayed to those who have come to know Christ. As once to the Corinthians, so now to the Colossians Paul insists that Christ alone is the Wisdom of God.[11] In Him we have the true knowledge, as contrasted with the counterfeit *gnosis* of the false teachers.

(b) *His anxiety lest they be misled*

Ch. 2:4–5

> 4 This I say, that no one may delude you with persuasiveness of speech.
> 5 For though I am absent in the flesh, yet am I with you in the spirit, joying and beholding your order, and the stedfastness of your faith in Christ.

4–5 "What I mean is this," says Paul; "don't let anyone talk you round with plausible arguments.[12] Although I am physically absent from you, I am with you in spirit, rejoicing as I watch your orderly Christian behaviour and your firm Christian faith."[13] Paul's sense of being spiritually present with his absent friends could be quite extraordinarily strong and vivid. Perhaps the most remarkable example is found in 1 Cor. 5:3–5, where he speaks of himself as being present in spirit at a church meeting in Corinth

---

10 The phrase "treasures of wisdom" (Gk. θησαυροὶ τῆς σοφίας) appears in Ecclesiasticus 1:25; here Paul adds "and knowledge" (καὶ γνώσεως), "with a side-glance at the shibboleths of Gnosticism" (W. D. Davies, *Paul and Rabbinic Judaism* [London, 1948], p. 173).

11 See p. 195 above (on Ch. 1:15).

12 Gk. τοῦτο λέγω ἵνα μηδεὶς ὑμᾶς παραλογίζηται κτλ. C. F. D. Moule (IBNTG, p. 145) points out that this is the imperative use of ἵνα, not its final use (in which case Paul would mean "I am saying this *in order that* no one may mislead you").

13 Gk. τὸ στερέωμα τῆς εἰς χριστὸν πίστεως ὑμῶν, "the solidity of your faith in Christ." H. Chadwick suggests that this use of στερέωμα, though possibly a military metaphor, may echo the important part played in Gnostic thought by the στερέωμα, the barrier between the upper realm and the lower (NTS i [1954–5], pp. 272 f.).

(at a time when he was resident in Ephesus), in order to take a
decisive part in a solemn act of discipline. Here he speaks of
himself as spiritually present with a distant church for a much
happier purpose. Whereas in the case of Corinth his spiritual
presence was promised to a church with which he was well
acquainted, here he gives the same assurance to a church in whose
midst he had never been present in body; so vivid, we may infer,
was the description which Epaphras had given him of the believing
community at Colossae.

5. GO ON AS YOU HAVE BEGUN!

Ch. 2:6-7

> 6 As therefore ye received Christ Jesus the Lord, *so* walk in him,
> 7 rooted and builded up in him, and established in your faith, even as ye were taught, abounding[14] in thanksgiving.

6-7 This short sentence introduces us to the whole concept of tradition in apostolic Christianity. The idea of tradition, together with the terminology used to express it, is common in Judaism, where it specially designates the handing down of the oral law and its interpretation from one generation to another. The best known Jewish exposition of the idea is found at the beginning of the Mishnaic tractate *Pirqe Aboth* ("The Sayings of the Fathers"): "Moses received the Torah from Sinai, and he delivered it to Joshua, and Joshua to the elders,[15] and the elders to the prophets, and the prophets delivered it to the men of the Great Synagogue." Then we are told how from the time of Simon the Just,[16] one of the last survivors of the "Great Synagogue", the Torah was handed down to successive pairs of scholars, generation by generation, until Hillel and Shammai (*c.* 10 B.C.). This was "the tradition of the elders" (Mark 7:3) which Jesus denounced because it nullified the basic principles of the divine law which it was intended to safeguard and interpret.[17]

When Paul says that his readers have "received" Christ Jesus as their Lord, he uses the verb which was specifically employed to denote the receiving of something which was delivered by tradition.[18] In other words, the Colossians have received Christ Himself

---

14 Cod. B and a few other authorities insert ἐν αὐτῇ ("in it"); ℵᶜ D* and some other authorities insert ἐν αὐτῷ ("in him").

15 *I.e.*, the elders of Josh. 24:31; Judg. 2:7.

16 Probably the high priest Simon II (*c.* 200 B.C.).

17 *Cf.* R. A. Stewart, *The Earlier Rabbinic Tradition* (London, 1949).

18 Gk. παραλαμβάνω (equivalent to Heb. *qibbel*, used in the first clause of the quotation from *Pirqe Aboth* above). It appears in this sense in Ch. 4:17; 1 Cor. 11:23; 15:1, 3; Gal. 1:9, 12; Phil. 4:9; 1 Thess. 2:13; 4:1; 2 Thess. 3:6. In 1 Cor. 11:23 and 15:3 it is accompanied by its correlative verb παραδίδωμι, "deliver" (the equivalent of Heb. *masar*, so used in the quotation from *Pirqe Aboth*); *cf.* Luke 1:2; Acts 6:14; 16:4; Rom. 6:17; 1 Cor. 11:2; 2 Pet. 2:21; Jude 3.

as their "tradition",[19] and this should prove a sufficient safeguard against following "the tradition of men" (v. 8). Emphasis is laid on the continuity of the transmission of Christian truth; the teaching which has been delivered to them is identical with the apostolic witness, depending on the supreme authority of Christ, and maintained in purity by the indwelling Spirit of God. Let them therefore see to it that their way of thought and life conforms continually to this teaching. Let them send their roots deep down into the truth as it is in Jesus, and their faith would not be easily uprooted. Or (to change the figure) let them make sure that this truth was the foundation on which they were built up, and they would not be quickly overturned. Faith in Christ would give them a stability which nothing could subvert. Thus firmly based on the indubitable facts of divine revelation, they would not be exposed to uncertainty and doubt, but would have ample occasion to over-flow with gratitude to God. This gratitude is the spontaneous manifestation of the Holy Spirit within, as they enjoy daily fellowship with Christ; it is a sign that they are indeed living in the new age.

It is well to note that in the New Testament "tradition" has this better sense as well as a worse one; it is good to recognize and hold fast the true tradition, while rejecting those that are false.[20]

---

[19] *Cf.* O. Cullmann, "The Tradition," in *The Early Church* (London, 1956), pp. 55 ff.; D. F. Mitchell, "The New Approach to Paradosis", RThR xii (1953), pp. 43 ff. For ἐρριζωμένοι, "rooted" (v. 7), see p. 78, n. 27 (on Eph. 3:18).

[20] Cf. 1 Cor. 11:2; 2 Thess. 2:15; 3:6, for the noun παράδοσις in a Christian sense.

III. FALSE TEACHING AND ITS ANTIDOTE

Chs. 2:8–3:4

1. CHRIST IS ALL—AND ALL YOU NEED

Ch. 2:8–15

What was this *gnosis* which was being pressed upon the Colossian Christians with such specious arguments? The answer to this question, in so far as it is available, must be gathered from this new section of Paul's letter to them. For it is here that he deals most fully and expressly with the erroneous teaching which his readers were being invited to accept, and here, too, that he prescribes the proper antidote. But we cannot be sure that we have grasped all the features of the controverted teaching. This is because Paul could assume an acquaintance with it on the part of his friends at Colossae which his twentieth-century readers lack. It appears, however, to have included elements of both Jewish and pagan origin. Its Jewish elements were not identical with those principles which at an earlier date Judaizing Christians had endeavoured to graft on to the faith of the young churches of Galatia, although there was an area of common ground between them. The teaching which Paul had to counter in Galatia was such as might have proceeded from "certain of the sect of the Pharisees who believed" (Acts 15:5). At Colossae, while the legal element is prominent, it is associated with an asceticism which was not characteristic of the main stream of Jewish life. The pagan elements were of the type which was later to be designated by the epithet "gnostic" (more especially of the Valentinian tradition);[21] in particular, a complete antithesis was maintained between spirit and matter, and therefore between the supreme God and the created universe. The existence of a specifically Jewish *gnosis* of this kind in the first century is becoming clearer as the result of recent discovery and research.[22]

---

[21] See W. L. Knox, *St. Paul and the Church of the Gentiles* (Cambridge, 1939), p. 155; H. Chadwick in NTS i (1954–5), p. 271.

[22] *E.g.*, in the beliefs of the Qumrân sect; *cf.* B. Reicke, "Traces of Gnosticism in the Dead Sea Scrolls?", NTS i (1954–5), pp. 137 ff.; O. Cullmann, "The Significance of the Qumrân Texts for Research into the Beginnings of Christianity", JBL lxxiv (1955), pp. 213 ff.

The effect of such a system of thought was the undermining of the basic Christian doctrines of creation and of the incarnation and mediation of Christ. For if God and the material world cannot come into direct relation, the world cannot be God's immediate handiwork, the Divine Word could not really have become flesh, and communication between God and man, in both directions, must be carried on through an indefinite series of intermediaries. These intermediaries, frequently viewed as the *archons* or lords of the seven planetary spheres,[23] appear to be further identified in this section of the epistle with the "rudiments" or elemental powers[24] served by those who have not yet exchanged legal bondage for the freedom that is found in Christ. (This is a point of contact between Colossians and Galatians.)

Against the implied attack on the Biblical doctrine of creation, Paul has already insisted that the universe was brought into being through the solitary agency of Christ. Against the enticing claim that a higher wisdom was offered by the new teaching, he has emphasized that all the treasures of wisdom and knowledge are stored up in Christ. Against the doctrine of an indefinite series of intermediary powers through which the divine essence was distributed until it reached man in a diluted form, he sets Christ as the personal embodiment of the fulness of deity. Against the idea that these intermediary or elemental powers should receive some meed of homage from men who must approach God through them, he affirms that these powers have all been conquered by Christ and can no longer claim the allegiance of men. The whole body of teaching which the Colossians were being urged to accept was a refurbishing, in its Jewish and pagan features alike, of old patterns of thought and life which Christ had rendered obsolete; it should receive no countenance from those who had died with Christ and risen with Him to newness of life.

(a) *The Fulness of Christ*

Ch. 2:8-10

8 Take heed lest there shall be any one that maketh

---

[23] The planetary spheres were those in which the planets (Sun, Moon, Mercury, Venus, Mars, Jupiter and Saturn) moved; each was believed to be governed by an ἄρχων. *Cf.* H. Bietenhard, *Die himmlische Welt im Urchristentum* (Tübingen, 1955), pp. 15, 44, 96, 109.

[24] Gk. στοιχεῖα. See p. 231 with nn. 30-33 (on v. 8).

> spoil of you through his philosophy and vain deceit, after the tradition of men, after the rudiments of the world, and not after Christ:
>
> 9 for in him dwelleth all the fulness of the Godhead bodily,
> 10 and in him ye are made full, who is the head of all principality and power:

8 Having encouraged his readers to continue firmly anchored to Christ and to His teaching, Paul now warns them not to be shifted from this impregnable position by any plausible form of persuasion. Possibly he has one particular teacher in view when he says: "Take heed lest there shall be any one..."[25]; at any rate, he warns them against any attempt to lead them astray by persuasive arguments. The verb which ARV renders "maketh spoil" —a rare one—has been variously translated "rob" or "kidnap"[26]; does the apostle mean "Don't let anyone plunder you" or "Don't let anyone carry you off as plunder"? On the whole, the latter alternative seems preferable; they are in danger of being carried off into captivity, and must be put on the alert, lest they become the prey of those who wish to take away their freedom. The spiritual confidence-tricksters against whom they are put on their guard did not inculcate a godless or immoral way of life; the error of such teaching would have been immediately obvious. Their teaching was rather a blend of the highest elements of natural religion known to Judaism and paganism; it was, in fact, a philosophy. It is not philosophy in general, but a philosophy of this kind—one which seduces believers from the simplicity of their faith in Christ—that Paul condemns. "Everything that had to do with theories about God and the world and the meaning of human life was called 'philosophy' at that time, not only in the pagan schools but also in the Jewish schools of the Greek cities."[27] But, for all its attractiveness, this particular philosophy was but

---

25 So C. Masson, CNT, *ad loc.*

26 Gk. συλαγωγέω. The only other occurrence quoted by W. Bauer, *Griechisch-Deutsches Wörterbuch z. NT* (Berlin, 1952), col. 1412, comes from Heliodorus (3rd cent. A.D.) with the meaning "kidnap." LS[9] adds a further occurrence from Aristaenetus (uncertain date) with the meaning "despoil." See J. B. Lightfoot, *ad loc.* Cf. the similar sense of αἰχμαλωτίζω in 2 Tim. 3:6.

27 A. Schlatter, *Erläuterungen zum NT*, Part 7 (Stuttgart, 1949), p. 273. Compare the way in which Josephus describes the various Jewish parties (even the Zealots) as φιλοσοφίαι (*War* ii. 8. 2 ff.; *Antiquities* xviii. 1. 1 ff.).

empty illusion.[28] If the Colossians embraced it, they would be the losers and not the gainers thereby. For those who had "received Christ Jesus the Lord" it must be unacceptable; it was a human tradition[29] which ran counter to the essential truths of their Christian faith and life. It sounded well, it appealed to natural religious instincts, but there was nothing in it for Christians. It was not a teaching "according to Christ"— in accordance with the tradition handed down from Him—but one which accorded with the elemental spirits of the *kosmos*.

There are two epistles in which Paul uses this term *stoicheia*, which AV and ARV render here by "rudiments" and RSV by "elemental spirits."[30] This Epistle to the Colossians is one; the Epistle to the Galatians is the other. In Gal. 4:3, 9, the "elemental spirits" of the world (*kosmos*) are associated, if not identified, with the angelic powers through whom the law was mediated (Gal. 3:19)[31]; the Galatians were properly under the tutelage of these powers until their coming of age, which coincided with the advent and redemptive work of Christ. But to remain under their control after that was to continue in a state of spiritual immaturity. One way of remaining under their control was to regulate religious life by the movements of the heavenly bodies—to "observe days and months and seasons and years"[32]—and this supports the identification of the powers in question with the rulers of the planetary spheres.[33]

---

[28] In the Greek text κενῆς ἀπάτης comes under the same regimen as φιλοσοφίας, and so the "philosophy" and the "vain deceit" are one and the same thing.

[29] "The tradition of men" might be Jewish or Gentile or both; *cf.* Mark 7:5 ff., where it is Jewish, and 1 Peter 1:18 (Gk. πατροπαράδοτος), where it is probably Gentile. In both these places the vanity or emptiness of such traditions is stressed.

[30] In Heb. 5:12 στοιχεῖα is used in its primary sense, of the "rudiments" or ABC of the gospel; in 2 Peter 3:10, 12, it is used of the "elements" of the material universe.

[31] Possibly the Colossian heresy contained features in common with the teaching of Cerinthus, according to whom—if we may believe Epiphanius (*Heresies*, xxviii)—the law and the prophets were inspired by angelic beings, the angelic giver of the law being one of the angels who made the world (κόσμος).

[32] Gal. 4:10; *cf.* Col. 2:16.

[33] *Cf.* E. Percy, *Probleme der Kolosser- und Epheserbriefe*, pp. 156 ff.; W. Bauer, *op. cit.*, cols. 1398 f. (with bibliographical notes in both works). Against the identification see H. N. Ridderbos, "Vrijheid en Wet volgens Paulus' Brief aan de Galaten," in *Arcana Revelata* (Grosheide FS, Kampen, 1951), pp. 89 ff. (especially pp. 92 ff.); *Galatians* (NICNT, Grand Rapids, 1953), p. 153, n. 5.

So, too, the form of teaching which was gaining currency at Colossae was something which belonged to a pre-Christian stage of experience; therefore, whatever its precise nature might be, to accept it would be a sign of spiritual retrogression. As Paul goes on to emphasize later,[34] they bade a long farewell to all such powers when they died with Christ to begin a new life in Him. Formerly, while they were "in the flesh," they were unable to throw off the domination of the powers which controlled the present world-order in opposition to God.[35] But now, One has appeared to conquer these powers and liberate men from their sway[36]; how foolish, then, it is for those who have enjoyed this liberation to go back and put themselves under the yoke of these discredited tyrants all over again! They have transferred their allegiance to the Ruler of a new order, to the Master and Conqueror of all such hostile powers; let the will and teaching of Christ therefore be the rule of their lives henceforth.

9–10ᵃ The teachers of error might talk as they would of the fulness of divine being which was filtered down to this world through a hierarchical succession of spirit-powers; Christians had something better. They had Christ, the personal revelation of the Father, the one Mediator between God and man, the One in whom the plenitude of deity was embodied.[37] Far from there being any inherent impossibility in the nature of things for God to communicate directly with this world, One who shared fully in the

---

[34] In v. 20 (p. 253).

[35] These powers, which dominate the present αἰὼν πονηρός (Gal. 1:4), are probably the same as the ἄρχοντες of 1 Cor. 2:6, 8, and the κοσμοκράτορες of Eph. 6:12.

[36] Cf. Mark 3:27; Luke 11:20.

[37] Gk. ὅτι ἐν αὐτῷ κατοικεῖ πᾶν τὸ πλήρωμα τῆς θεότητος σωματικῶς. The terms ἐν αὐτῷ, κατοικέω and πᾶν τὸ πλήρωμα are repeated from Ch. 1:19 (see p. 206 with n. 122). This is the only NT occurrence of θεότης. J. B. Lightfoot (ad loc.) aptly quotes two passages from Plutarch's Moralia to illustrate the difference between it and θειότης (also found once in NT, in Rom. 1:20). Paul "tells us in Romans (1:20) how God's eternal power and divinity (θειότης) reveal themselves by the light of nature to the heathen mind, but of Immanuel, that in Him dwelleth all the fulness of the Godhead (θεότης) embodied (Col. 2:9). The hand of omnipotence may be traced in the countless orbs that bespangle the heavens, and in the marvellous coadjustments of our comparatively tiny globe; but in the Son we behold the face of God unveiled, the express image and transcript of His very Being" (E. K. Simpson, Words Worth Weighing in the Greek NT [London, 1946], pp. 12 f.). The adverb σωματικῶς does not refer to the incarnation as such, but to Christ's complete embodiment of the πλήρωμα, as contrasted with its supposed distribution through other intermediaries.

divine nature had become flesh and tabernacled among men. Not only so, but Christians by their union with Him shared His very life. If the fulness of deity resided in Him, His fulness was imparted to them. Without Him we must remain forever *disiecta membra*—uncompleted, unable to attain the true end of our existence. But united with Him, incorporated in Him, we find ourselves joined in a living bond with Him in which He and we complement each other as the body does the head and the head the body.[38]

10ᵇ No need then to pay our respects to principalities and powers! He in whom we are made complete is the One who has shown Himself Lord and Master over all such beings. When Christ is described as "the head of every principality and power," are we to understand this headship in the same sense as His headship over the church in Ch. 1:18? Some commentators have held this view.[39] But it is unlikely that Paul wished to suggest that the principalities and powers, or the world to which they belong, form in any sense the body of which Christ is the head. What he emphasizes here, as in Ch. 1:15-18, is Christ's primacy over all things, including the principalities and powers. His primacy over all things springs from the fact that "He is before all things, and in him all things hold together" (Ch. 1:17, RSV); but He has established a further basis for His primacy over the principalities and powers, by His victory over them. Why should those who are united to Christ be in bondage to forces over which He has vindicated His preeminence by the twofold right of creation and conquest?

(b) The New Circumcision

Ch. 2:11-12

> 11 in whom ye were also circumcised with a circumcision not made with hands, in the putting off of the body of the flesh,[40] in the circumcision of Christ;

---

[38] *Cf.* Eph. 1:23.

[39] *E.g.* Dibelius (HNT, *ad loc.*); *cf.* H. Lietzmann, *The Beginnings of the Christian Church* (Eng. tr., London, 1949), p. 215. See also p. 206, n. 118 (on Ch. 1:18), and p. 251 (on Ch. 2:19).

[40] AV "the body of the sins of the flesh" represents the reading of later authorities which insert τῶν ἁμαρτιῶν between τοῦ σώματος and τῆς σαρκός.

12   having been buried with him in baptism,[41] wherein[42]
ye were also raised with him through faith in the
working of God, who raised him from the dead.

11 If only they called to mind their baptism, and all that was
involved and implied in it, they would be delivered from all such
inconsistent syncretism. What was their baptism?

It was, in the first place, a participation in "the circumcision of
Christ." This "circumcision of Christ" is not primarily His
circumcision as a Jewish infant of eight days old (Luke 2:21); it is
rather His crucifixion, "the putting off[43] of the body of the flesh,"
of which His literal circumcision was at best a token-anticipation.
That is to say, their baptism was a symbolical sharing in Christ's
death; as an initiatory ceremony it was "a circumcision not made
with hands." Even in the OT the symbolical character of circumcision was emphasized; what God really desired was not the external
sign for its own sake, but the "circumcision of the heart"[44]—an
inward purification, which to Paul was the true circumcision.[45]
For the Israelite of earlier days, however, the circumcision of the
the heart could not be regarded as a substitute for literal circumcision;[46] but now the work of Christ has so thoroughly exhausted the
significance of the physical ordinance (as of the whole ceremonial
law) that it is henceforth superseded.[47] Paul's choice of language

---

[41]   The rarer βαπτίσμῳ (P46 B D* G) is probably the original form, rather
than the commoner βαπτίσματι of the majority of authorities.

[42]   Gk. ἐν ᾧ, possibly to be rendered "in whom" (as at the beginning of v. 11).

[43]   Gk. ἀπέκδυσις. No independent instance of this noun is attested; it may be
a Pauline coinage. Cf. the verb ἀπεκδύομαι in v. 15 and Ch. 3:9. The double
prefix gives the word special emphasis—"stripping right off."

[44]   Cf. Deut. 10:16; 30:6; Jer. 4:4. See p. 58, n. 18 (on Eph. 2:11).

[45]   Cf. Rom. 2:28 f.; Phil. 3:3.

[46]   Cf. Philo, Migration of Abraham, 92.

[47]   Justin Martyr allegorizes the narrative of the Israelites' second circumcision at Joshua's hands with knives of stone (Josh. 5:2 f.) as the spiritual circumcision which Christians receive at the hands of the true Joshua (Jesus)
"from idolatry and all manner of wickedness, by sharp stones, that is, by the
words of the apostles of Him who is the corner-stone cut out without hands"
(Dialogue with Trypho, 114). Early Christian apologetic against the Jews
grouped together circumcision, sacrifice and sabbath as having been abolished
by Christ. (Cf. V. Burch, "Circumcision of the Heart", ExT xxix [1917–18],
pp. 330 f.; J. R. Harris, Testimonies ii [Cambridge, 1920], pp. 105 f.) But, as
O. Cullmann points out, the understanding of Christian baptism as a repeal of
Jewish circumcision "is not just a theological foundling, appearing only at a late
date after the Apologist Justin"; it is explicit in our present passage, and
implicit elsewhere in NT (Baptism in the NT [Eng. tr., London, 1950], pp. 56 f.).

here would be specially apt if circumcision was one feature of the
syncretism which was being inculcated in the Colossian church.
No longer is there any place for a circumcision performed by hands;
the death of Christ has effected the inward cleansing which the
prophets associated with the new covenant,[48] and of this our
baptism is the visible sign.

In so far as "the putting off of the body of the flesh" refers to
the death of Christ, the expression is readily intelligible, especially
in the light of the earlier mention of "the body of his flesh" in
connection with His death in Ch. 1:22a. But the expression in our
present passage includes also the Christian's baptismal experience.
What is involved is much more than the removal of a small piece
of flesh, as in the old circumcision; it is the removal of the whole
"body of flesh"—what Paul elsewhere describes as "putting off
the old man," reckoning one's former self with its desires and
propensities to be dead, as a necessary prelude to "putting on the
new man," putting on Christ Himself in His resurrection life.[49]
What the believer puts off is "the whole personality organized for,
and geared into rebellion against God."[50]

12 Their baptism might, secondly, be viewed as their participation in Christ's burial.[51] The "putting off of the body of the
flesh" and its burial out of sight alike emphasized that the old life
was a thing of the past. They had shared in the death of Christ;
they had also shared in His burial. Similarly, in Rom. 6:3 ff. Paul
argues that those who have been buried with Christ "through
baptism into death" can no longer go on living as slaves to sin.

But baptism not only proclaims that the old order is over and
done with; it proclaims that a new order has been inaugurated.
The convert did not remain in the baptismal water; he emerged

---

[48] E.g., Jer. 31:31 ff.; Ezek. 36:25 ff.
[49] Cf. Ch. 3:9 f.; Eph. 4:22 ff.; Rom. 13:14; see also Rom. 6:6; Gal. 2:20;
5:24, where Paul speaks of "crucifying" instead of "putting off."
[50] J. A. T. Robinson, The Body, p. 31.
[51] The burial of Christ might be viewed as setting the seal upon His death,
and symbolizing His descent to the realm of the dead (cf. Eph. 4:9 f.). His own
baptism in Jordan was a symbolical anticipation of this descent into death and
Sheol; we may recall His references to His approaching passion in baptismal
terms (Mark 10:38 f.; Luke 12:50). On the imagery involved cf. A. R. Johnson,
"Jonah 2:3-10," in Studies in OT Prophecy (T. H. Robinson FS, Edinburgh,
1950), pp. 82 ff., especially 102. This whole passage (vv. 9-15) has been sugges-
tively described as "a baptismal homily on the anti-gnostic kerygmatic hymn in
Col. 1:15-20" (J. M. Robinson in Interpretation x [1956], p. 349).

from it to begin a new life. Baptism, therefore, implies a sharing in Christ's resurrection as well as in His death and burial.[52]

The resurrection of Christ is presented by Paul as the supreme manifestation of the power of God. Those who have been raised with Christ have been raised through faith in the divine power[53] which brought Christ back from the dead, and henceforth that power energizes them and maintains the new life within them— the new life which is nothing less than Christ's resurrection life imparted to all the members of His body.[54] In Him they already enjoy eternal life—the life of the age to come.

This whole conception is thoroughly and characteristically Pauline. It may well be that the idea of the believer's participation in the risen life of Christ finds clearer expression here (together with Ch. 3:1 and Eph. 2:6) than it does elsewhere in the Pauline Epistles; but to imagine that someone other than Paul is responsible for this phraseology is to imagine that this other person gave clearer expression to Paul's central thought than Paul himself could give.[55]

And be it noted: it is through faith that the believer bids farewell to the old life and embarks upon the new; the sacrament of baptism derives its efficacy not from the water or from the convert's token burial in it but from the saving act of Christ and the regenerating work of the Holy Spirit, producing that faith-union with the risen Lord of which the sacrament is the outward sign.[56]

(c) *The Triumph of Christ*

Ch. 2:13-15

> 13 And you, being dead through[57] your trespasses and the uncircumcision of your flesh, you, *I say,* did he make alive together with him, having forgiven us all our trespasses;

---

[52] *Cf.* Ch. 3:1; Eph. 2:6; Rom. 6:4 f.

[53] Gk. ἐνέργεια, which is here the object of faith. See Eph. 1:19 ff. for the elaboration of this thought of the divine ἐνέργεια.

[54] Rom. 6:4-11; Gal. 2:20; Eph. 2:5.

[55] *Cf.* E. Percy, *op. cit.,* p. 113.

[56] *Cf.* J. S. Stewart, *A Man in Christ* (London, 1935), pp. 171, 192. On the subject-matter and interpretation of vv. 11 f. see also, in addition to the standard commentators and other authors mentioned in the foregoing footnotes, G. W. H. Lampe, *The Seal of the Spirit* (London, 1951), pp. 5, 56, 83, 85, *et passim.*

[57] Gk. τοῖς παραπτώμασι, the instrumental dative. A number of authorities (including P46 ℵ * A C D G) read ἐν before the dative ("being dead *in* your trespasses . . .").

14 having blotted out the bond written in ordinances
that was against us,[58] which was contrary to us: and
he hath taken it out of the way, nailing it to the cross;

15 having despoiled[59] the principalities and the powers,
he made a show of them openly, triumphing over
them in it.

13-14 Yes, the apostle insists, this is what has happened to
you.[60] You were really dead in those earlier days of your
paganism.[61] But now you have come to life again—come to life
in Christ, who was Himself dead and came alive again. Your
new life, indeed, is a sharing in the new life which Christ received
when He rose from the dead. And in giving you this new life with

---

[58] Gk. τὸ καθ' ἡμῶν χειρόγραφον τοῖς δόγμασιν, of which ARV margin,
"the bond that was against us by its ordinances", is an alternative translation.
The dative τοῖς δόγμασιν (cf. Eph. 2:15, ἐν δόγμασιν, discussed on p. 61, n. 26)
is taken by E. Percy (op. cit., pp. 88 ff.) with the following clause ὃ ἦν
ὑπεναντίον ἡμῖν, so that the meaning is "the handwriting that was against us,
which by virtue of the ordinances testified against us." The ordinances are, in
his view, the law of Moses. It is rather awkward to construe τοῖς δόγμασιν
with the following adjective clause, in spite of the parallels which he adduces.
He maintains that, on any other construction, the clause ὃ ἦν ὑπεναντίον ἡμῖν
is a superfluous repetition of καθ' ἡμῶν. J. A. T. Robinson, however, takes
καθ' ἡμῶν to mean "in our name" (op. cit., p. 43 n.), an attractive suggestion
which one could accept with greater alacrity if such a sense could be substan-
tiated for κατά with the genitive (the use of this construction with verbs of
swearing and asseveration is not a sufficient parallel). The same writer construes
τὸ ... χειρόγραφον τοῖς δόγμασιν as "our subscription to the ordinances" (ibid.).
C. F. D. Moule (IBNTG, p. 45) pays tribute to the plausible and ingenious
character of this interpretation, and appears to regard it as preferable to
Percy's, which involves "too much violence to word-order"; but he himself
renders the phrase "the document with its decrees (meaning, apparently, a
document containing, or consisting of, decrees)". It seems simplest to recognize
a dative of accompaniment here—"the bond, decrees and all"—but the difficulties of construction and interpretation make it advisable to treat every
reasonable suggestion with respect. See p. 238.

[59] Gk. ἀπεκδυσάμενος, the verb corresponding to ἀπέκδυσις in v. 11, possibly
a Pauline coinage, as has been suggested of ἀπέκδυσις (p. 234, n. 43). In Ch. 3:9
the verb means "put off" (as clothes); if that is the sense here, then the marginal
rendering of ARV, "having put off from himself the principalities...", is to be
preferred. But see p. 239, n. 68.

[60] Note the successive aorists: περιετμήθητε (v. 11), συνταφέντες (v. 12),
συνηγέρθητε (v. 12, Ch. 3:1), συνεζωοποίησεν (v. 13), ἐδειγμάτισεν (v. 15), ἀπεθάνετε
(v. 20, Ch. 3:3). Note, too, how many of them are συν- compounds, indicating
that what was accomplished for us has also been accomplished in us, so that we
are reckoned as having participated with Christ in His death, burial and
resurrection.

[61] With "the uncircumcision of your flesh" (v. 13) cf. the rather fuller
phraseology of Eph. 2:11.

Christ, God has broken you clean away from your past. He has freely forgiven[62] your sins. Those sins represented, so to speak, a mountain of bankruptcy which you were bound to acknowledge but could never have any hope of discharging. You had violated the ordinances of the law, and nothing that you might do could afford redress. But Christ has wiped the slate clean and given you a fresh start. He took that signed confession of indebtedness[63] which stood as a perpetual witness against you, and cancelled it in His death;[64] you might actually say that He took the document, ordinances and all,[65] and nailed it to His cross as an act of triumphant defiance in the face of those blackmailing powers who were holding it over you as a threat.

---

[62] Gk. χαρίζομαι, used also, as here, in Eph. 4:32, of God's forgiving men. Cf. χάρισμα in Rom. 6:23. For the similar use of ἀφίημι and ἄφεσις see p. 191, n. 54 (on Ch. 1:14). For χαρίζομαι used of men's forgiving one another cf. Ch. 3:13 (and also Eph. 4:32). Its use here may be due to the fact that it is so suitable a verb for the cancellation of a debt (cf. Luke 7:41, 43).

[63] Gk. χειρόγραφον, a term (found also in Plutarch and Artemidorus) very common in the papyri, among which many original χειρόγραφα have been preserved (cf. G. A. Deissmann, Bible Studies [Edinburgh, 1909], p. 247). Cf. also Moulton–Milligan, VGT, p. 687. J. A. T. Robinson (op. cit., p. 43 n.) describes this χειρόγραφον as "our written agreement to keep the law, our certificate of debt to it" (he compares the undertakings of Ex. 24:3; Deut. 27:14–26). But our failure to keep the law has turned this certificate into a bond held against us to prove our guilt. It is this bond, representing the power which the law has over us, rather than the law itself, which Paul views as cancelled by Christ. This is decidedly preferable to E. Lohmeyer's view that the χειρόγραφον represents an I.O.U. (a Schuldschein) which Adam gave to the devil in Paradise at the time of the fall of man (MK, pp. 116 f.).

[64] He removed it (Gk. ἦρκεν ἐκ τοῦ μέσου); this removal is elaborated in two figures: He blotted it out (Gk. ἐξαλείψας), He nailed it to His cross (Gk. προσηλώσας αὐτὸ τῷ σταυρῷ). According to Deissmann, papyrus debt-records illustrate the popular appeal of this double metaphor; the bond is first blotted out and then cancelled (Paul [Eng. tr., London, 1926], p. 172). We may compare two successive petitions in the Jewish prayer Abinu Malkenu: "Our Father, our King! blot out our transgressions, and make them pass away from before thine eyes. Our Father, our King! erase in thine abundant mercies all the records of our debts" (cf. S. Singer, The Authorised Daily Prayer Book [London, 1939], p. 56). As for the bold conception of the cancelled bond being nailed to the cross of Christ, Deissmann thinks of the cancellation of a bond or similar document by crossing it out with the Greek cross-letter X (chi) (Light from the Ancient East [London, 1927], p. 333). But would σταυρός suggest the X shape? (The Greek word for such "crossing out" is χιάζω.) On the "supposed 'ancient custom' of cancelling a bond by driving a nail through it" see F. Field, op. cit., pp. 195 f.; he can find no real authority for it, and thinks rather of the custom of hanging up spoils of war in temples (but it is unlikely that any such analogy was in Paul's mind).

[65] See p. 237, n. 58.

There is perhaps an allusion here to the fact that our Lord's own accusation was fixed to His cross. Jesus nails the accusation against us to His cross, just as His own accusation had been nailed there.[66] Thus His victorious passion liberates us from our bankruptcy and bondage.

> Jesus for thee a body takes,
> Thy guilt assumes, thy fetters breaks,
> Discharging all thy dreadful debt—
> And canst thou then such love forget?[67]

15 Christ by His cross releases His people not only from the guilt of sin but from its dominion over them. Not only has He cancelled our indebtedness but He has subjugated those powers whose possession of the damning indictment kept us in their grip. The very instrument of disgrace and death by which the hostile forces thought they had Him in their grasp and had conquered Him for ever was turned by Him into the instrument of their defeat and captivity. As He was suspended there, bound hand and foot to the wood in apparent weakness, they imagined they had Him at their mercy, and flung themselves upon Him with hostile intent. But, far from suffering their assault without resistance, He grappled with them and mastered them, stripping them of all the armour in which they trusted,[68] and held them aloft in His mighty, out-stretched hands, displaying to the universe their helplessness and

---

[66] There is the scarcely veiled implication that the real crimes for which He suffered were crimes that we had done. *Cf.* 2 Cor. 5:21; Gal. 3:13.

[67] Krishna Pal.

[68] The interpretation of this passage depends on two main considerations: (*a*) the subject of the sentence and (*b*) the force of the middle voice in the aorist participle ἀπεκδυσάμενος.

(*a*) Grammatically there is no indication of a change of subject in vv. 13, 14 and 15. In vv. 13 and 14 God is the subject. But is is commonly held that a change of subject from God to Christ must be understood somewhere in v. 14 (at ἦρκεν ἐκ τοῦ μέσου, J. B. Lightfoot suggests *ad loc.*), since vv. 14b, 15, seem to require Christ as subject. For the view that God is the subject throughout see E. Percy, *op. cit.*, pp. 96 f. The question is not of primary moment, for the action throughout is that of God in Christ; Paul himself may not have been conscious of any change of subject. "Perhaps the very ambiguity teaches us not to dissociate the work of the Father and of the Son" (T. W. Crafer *ad loc.*, in *A New Commentary on Holy Scripture*, ed. C. Gore [London, 1928], N.T., p. 562).

(*b*) More important is the interpretation of ἀπεκδυσάμενος (*cf.* p. 237, n. 59). The middle voice of this verb in Ch. 3:9 denotes putting off, as of clothes. So here some have thought of Christ as stripping off the hostile powers from Himself as they clung to Him on the cross like a shirt of Nessus. This was

His own unvanquished strength. Had they but realized the truth, those "archons of this age"—had they (as Paul puts it in another epistle) known the hidden wisdom of God which decreed the glory of Christ and His people—"they would not have crucified the Lord of glory" (1 Cor. 2:8). But now they are disabled and dethroned, and the shameful tree[69] has become the victor's triumphal chariot,[70] before which His captives are driven in humiliating procession, the involuntary and impotent confessors of their over-comer's superiority.[71]

The cross of Christ is the answer to the theosophy which was beguiling the minds of the Lycus churches. How foolish it now appeared to pay tribute to those principalities and powers through whom they believed the law to have been given, as though they controlled the way from God to man and back from man to God! That way is controlled by One Person only—the One who vindicated His sovereignty over those principalities and powers. Their envious enmity to men can no longer be indulged; they have been

the general view of the Greek fathers, and is approved by Lightfoot (cf. ARV margin). The Latin fathers in general prefer the view that what Christ stripped off was His body (cf. v. 11, ἐν τῇ ἀπεκδύσει τοῦ σώματος τῆς σαρκός); cf. the alternative rendering of ERV margin ("having put off from himself his body"). This view has been maintained more recently by C. A. A. Scott, Christianity according to St. Paul. pp. 34 ff.; E. Käsemann, Leib und Leib Christi, p. 139 (he adduces irrelevant Manichaean texts in its support); W. L. Knox, St. Paul and the Church of the Gentiles, p. 169 n.; G. H. C. Macgregor, NTS i (1954–5), p. 23; J. A. T. Robinson, The Body, pp. 41 f. ("By His death, Christ, as it were, 'died out on' the forces of evil without their being able to defeat or kill Him, thereby exhibiting their impotence and gaining victory over them".) It may well be, however, that the middle voice here simply indicates the personal interest of the subject in the action of the verb; in fact, there are not lacking in Hellenistic Greek examples of the middle voice of such verbs in an active sense (cf. A. Oepke in TWNT ii [Stuttgart, 1953], p. 319 ; W. Bauer, op. cit., col. 151). In that case the sense will be "having completely disarmed." So E. Percy, op. cit., p. 98: "These angel-powers have been deprived of all their previous power through the removal of the charges which the law brought against men and therewith also of the demands of the law itself."

[69] Taking ἐν αὐτῷ (v. 15) to mean "by means of the cross"; if God were the subject of this verse the phrase might mean "in Christ."

[70] The masculine αὐτούς after θριαμβεύσας is a sense-construction, referring to the ἀρχαί and ἐξουσίαι, but treating them as personal beings, not as abstractions. For the figure of a triumphal procession cf. 2 Cor. 2:14, τῷ . . . θριαμβεύοντι ἡμᾶς (where, however, it is Paul and his fellow-Christians who are the willing captives of Christ and witnesses to His victory).

[71] In Eph. 3:10 the principalities and powers are spectators of the many-hued wisdom of God displayed in the church; but there perhaps good as well as hostile beings are intended.

pacified[72] by a stronger than themselves.[73] Whatever power they once exercised, they are now the "weak and beggarly elemental spirits" which Paul declares them to be in Gal. 4:9.

The lords of the planetary spheres may play no part in the world-outlook of most of our contemporaries—although the number of those who accept the invitation to "plan with the planets" in the astrological columns of the popular press should warn us not to frame such a statement in absolute terms. The elemental spirits through whom the law was held to have been mediated may mean nothing to modern man. Angels and demons may be unknown to him by name. But is not modern man unprecedentedly aware of powerful and malignant "demonic" forces operating against him, which he is quite unable to master, whether by his individual strength or by united action? These forces may be Frankenstein monsters of his own creation; they may be subliminal horrors over which he has no conscious control. "We are still conscious that, apart from the victory of Christ, man is a helpless victim in a hostile cosmos. It is little comfort to us that the inexorable fate which was once expressed in terms of the influence of the stars, conceived as personal demons, is now expressed in terms of psychological, or physical or economic determinism. We still ask how a man is to triumph over an evil heredity, or how he can be free and victorious in a world of rigid law and scientific necessity. We still suffer from 'astronomical intimidation'—terror at the insignificance of man and the vastness of the material universe encompassing him."[74] Moreover, we are acutely conscious of our inevitable involvement in situations from which our moral sense revolts—but what can be done about it?[75]

---

[72] Cf. p. 209, n. 135 (on Ch. 1:21).

[73] Cf. the overpowering of the "strong man armed" in Matt. 12:29; Luke 11:21 f.; of the devil in John 12:31 (with 14:30 and 16:11); Heb. 2:14 (where the partaking of "blood and flesh" and the words "through death" are specially significant); and of death itself in 1 Cor. 15:26. We might regard the conquest of Col. 2:15 as the first stage in that victorious progress which ends with the destruction of the "last enemy."

[74] G. H. C. Macgregor, NTS i (1954–5), p. 27, in an article "Principalities and Powers" (pp. 17 ff.). He quotes to much the same effect from A. Galloway, The Cosmic Christ (London, 1951), p. 28. We need not demythologize Paul's language in order to appreciate how directly he speaks to the condition of modern man as described by these writers.

[75] Cf. J. S. Stewart, SJTh iv (1951), pp. 296 f., in an article "On a Neglected Emphasis in NT Theology" (pp. 292 ff.) which is a penetrating treatment of this same subject.

But for the gospel, we might well think of ourselves as puppets in the hand of a blind and unfriendly fate. And what does it matter whether we resist and be crushed sooner, or acquiesce and be crushed a little later?

There is only one message of hope to modern man in his frustration and despair, and it is the message which Paul proclaimed to the Colossians. Christ crucified and risen is Lord of all; all the forces of the universe are subject to Him, not only the benign ones but the hostile ones as well. They are all subject to Him as their Creator; the latter are subject to Him also as their Conqueror. And therefore to be united to Him is to be liberated from their thraldom, to enjoy perfect freedom, to overcome all the power of evil because Christ's victory is ours. The redemption that is in Christ Jesus is a cosmic redemption; its healing virtue streams out to the farthest bounds of creation; but it is a personal redemption too. The Conqueror who is enthroned at God's right hand, supreme above the universe and filling it with His presence, is the One who reigns as King in each believer's heart. Though "now we see not yet all things subjected to him" (Heb. 2:8), yet we are assured that because of His redemptive act, all creation will yet be "delivered from the bondage of corruption into the liberty of the glory of the children of God" (Rom. 8:21). And even here and now those who have already entered into that liberty may well be persuaded, with Paul himself, "that neither death, nor life, nor angels, nor principalities, nor things present, nor things to come, nor powers, nor height, nor depth, nor any other creature, shall be able to separate us from the love of God, which is in Christ Jesus our Lord" (Rom. 8:38 f.).

2. GUARD YOUR FREEDOM!

Ch. 2:16–19

Since the new teaching was an ascetic discipline which combined food-restrictions and calendar regulations with a form of angel-worship, Paul goes on to warn the Colossians of the necessity of guarding on those particular fronts the freedom which Christ had won for them.

(a) Freedom in respect of Food and Festivals

Ch. 2:16–17

> 16 Let no man therefore judge you in meat, or in drink, or in respect of a feast day or a new moon or a sabbath day:
> 17 which are a shadow of the things to come; but the body is Christ's.

16 Don't let anyone sit in judgment on you, he tells them, in respect of food or drink. He may not simply be referring to the Jewish food-laws (which did not extend to beverages), or to such abstentions as are enjoined in the apostolic letter of Acts 15:23–29,[76] but to more stringent regulations of an ascetic nature, probably involving the renunciation of animal flesh and of wine and strong drink, after the Nazirite fashion. In any case, he lays down the principle of Christian liberty in all such matters, in the spirit of his Master who, by one comprehensive pronouncement, made all meats clean.[77]

Elsewhere, in dealing with these subjects, the apostle introduces a further principle which might impose a voluntary limitation on one's Christian liberty—the principle of respect for the tender conscience of a "weaker brother" (cf. Rom. 14:1 ff.; 1 Cor. 8:1 ff.; 10:23 ff.). But this latter principle is invoked when Christians are asserting their liberty at all costs (even at the expense of Christian charity); at Colossae it is precisely Christian liberty that requires to be asserted in the face of specious attempts to undermine it.

And don't let anyone sit in judgment on you, he continues, in

---

76 Cf. Acts in NICNT, pp. 311 ff.
77 "This he said, making all meats clean" (Mark 7:19).

respect of holy days. Under the levitical economy the observance of such days, like the food-laws, was obligatory upon the Jews. But now the Christian has been freed from obligations of this kind. If a Christian wishes to restrict himself in matters of food and drink, or to set aside certain days for special observance or commemoration, good and well; these are questions to be settled between his conscience and God. Concerning such questions Paul writes in another epistle: "Let each man be fully assured in his own mind. He that regardeth the day, regardeth it unto the Lord: and he that eateth, eateth unto the Lord, for he giveth God thanks; and he that eateth not, unto the Lord he eateth not, and giveth God thanks" (Rom. 14:5 f.). But to regard them as matters of religious obligation is a retrograde step for Christians to take. When the churches of Galatia were minded to adopt the observance of special days and months and seasons and years, Paul told them that this was nothing less than placing themselves afresh under the yoke of the "weak and beggarly" elemental ordinances which regulated these time-divisions (Gal. 4:9 f.). He now uses a similar argument for the benefit of the Colossian church which was being criticized by the innovators for not observing festivals and new moons and sabbaths.[78] To accept the observance of these occasions as obligatory now would be an acknowledgment of the continuing authority of the powers through whom such regulations were mediated—the powers that were decisively subjugated by Christ. How absurd for those who had reaped the benefit of Christ's victory to put themselves voluntarily back under the control of those powers which Christ had conquered!

Had this lesson been kept in mind in the post-apostolic generations, there might have been less friction than there was in the early Church over the divergent calculations of the date of Easter. No doubt it was awkward (as it still is) for Christians to have

---

[78] We have no means of knowing whether the religious calendar followed by those innovators was that observed in the temple at Jerusalem, or one which deviated from it. The Qumrân sect attached great importance to calendrical questions, but apparently differed from the national authorities in their calculation of sacred seasons (perhaps following the calendar enjoined in the Book of Jubilees). Even the Pharisees and Sadducees, who accepted the common lunar calendar of 354 days to a year (with intercalations to correct the rapidly accumulating discrepancy with the solar calendar), disagreed on several details of the sacred year. Cf. L. Finkelstein, *The Pharisees* (Philadelphia, 1946), pp. 115 ff., 601 ff.; A. Jaubert, "Le calendrier des Jubilés," VT iii (1953), pp 250 ff.; vii (1957), pp. 35 ff.; J. Morgenstern, "The Calendar of the Book of Jubilees," VT v (1955), pp. 34 ff.

differing procedures for fixing the anniversary of their Lord's death and resurrection when they wished to commemorate these saving events in a special manner year by year; but the adjustment of such discrepancies is a matter of expediency, not of principle. And something similar might be said about the charge that Christians who do not observe the seventh day as a sabbath have accepted the mark of the beast. "Let no man judge you in respect of a sabbath day" is all the answer that such a charge requires.

17 Why must they refuse to be judged in these matters? Because all these matters belonged to a transitory order. The legal prescriptions of days gone by were but a shadow, of which the substance is Christ,[79] together with the new régime of liberty which He has introduced. This antithesis of the shadow and the substance is specially elaborated in the Epistle to the Hebrews,[80] but Paul also uses it here and there. Thus, in 1 Cor. 5:7 f., the sacrifice of Christ is the reality which was foreshadowed by the passover in Egypt; and the festival of unleavened bread which followed the passover is used as a picture of the Christian life which the sacrifice of Christ makes possible.[81]

In developing this argument, Paul was not necessarily contradicting the principles which he had learned in the course of his rabbinical education. For many Jews looked upon their festivals and sacred seasons as adumbrations of Messiah's age. There are rabbinical texts which treat even the sabbath as a foretaste of that coming time[82]—the time which, for Paul and other Christians, has come already in Christ.

---

[79] Gk. τὸ δὲ σῶμα τοῦ χριστοῦ, "the substance belongs to Christ" (so J. B. Lightfoot, *ad loc.*). This is not a sense in which σῶμα is used elsewhere in this Epistle. But attempts to understand σῶμα τοῦ χριστοῦ here as the "body of Christ" are unsatisfactory; such are the suggested translation "but (let) the body of Christ (judge such matters)," and the punctuation mentioned by H. Grotius which takes τὸ ... σῶμα τοῦ χριστοῦ in apposition with ὑμᾶς in the following verse: "But let no man rob you, (you who are) the body of Christ..." (see G. Farmer in ExT vi [1894-5], p. 137; xvii [1905-6], p. 430).

[80] *Cf.* Heb. 8:5; 10:1.

[81] *Cf.* F. W. Grosheide, *First Corinthians*, NICNT, *ad loc.*

[82] E. Lohmeyer (MK, *ad loc.*) quotes from *Aboth de-Rabbi Nathan* 2 a comment on the title of Ps. 92 ("A Psalm, a Song for the sabbath day") which interprets it of "that day which is all sabbath, on which there is no eating or drinking, ... but the righteous sit with crowns on their heads and refresh themselves with the vision of the Shekhinah." *Cf.* Heb. 4:9. Other references in the same sense are provided by Strack–Billerbeck, IV, pp. 839 f. See also H. J. Schoeps, *Aus frühchristlicher Zeit* (Tübingen, 1950), p. 163.

(b) Freedom in respect of Asceticism and Angel-Worship
Ch. 2:18-19

18 Let no man rob you of your prize[83] by a voluntary
humility and worshipping of the angels, dwelling in
the things which he hath seen,[84] vainly puffed up by
his fleshly mind,
19 and not holding fast the Head, from whom all the
body, being supplied and knit together through the
joints and bands, increaseth with the increase of God.

18 Don't let anyone condemn you, Paul goes on, by a show
of superior humility. There are some people who love to make a
parade of exceptional piety, and there are others who are over-
prone to be taken in by them. They pretend to have found the
way to a higher plane of spiritual experience, as though they had
been initiated into sacred mysteries which give them an infinite
advantage over the uninitiated. Naturally this kind of claim
impresses those who always fall for the idea of an "inner ring."[85]
But (says the apostle) don't be misled by such people. For all their
lofty pretension, for all the delight which they take in self-

[83] Gk. μηδεὶς ὑμᾶς καταβραβευέτω. The verb καταβραβεύω is very rare (cf.
Ch. 3:15 for the simple verb βραβεύω) and literally means "give an unfavourable
ruling" upon a competitor in some athletic contest, the ruling being given by the
umpire. Hence the rendering of ARV (so also J. B. Lightfoot, W. M. Ramsay,
etc.). RSV renders: "Let no one disqualify you." In all the passages quoted for
the use of the compound verb, it conveys the idea of depriving someone of
something which he would otherwise have possessed. Here, however, F. Field
(op. cit., p. 196) is probably right in regarding the thought of a "prize" as otiose;
the verb, then, will mean "give an adverse decision against" and so "condemn";
it is simply a stronger synonym for κρίνω in v. 16. Cf. T. K. Abbott, *Ephesians
and Colossians* (ICC, Edinburgh, 1897), pp. 265 f.; H. N. Bate, *Guide to the
Epistles of St. Paul* (London, 1926), p. 140 n.
[84] Gk. ἃ ἑώρακεν ἐμβατεύων. A large number of authorities for the text
insert μή before ἑώρακεν (so that the clause means "the things which he has *not*
seen"); these include אᶜ C Dᵇᶜ G H, the bulk of the later Greek manuscripts, the
Latin Vulgate, the Syriac Peshitta, the Armenian and Gothic versions, and
several of the Fathers (*e.g.*, Chrysostom, Ambrose, Augustine and Pelagius). But
the weight of the evidence confirms the omission of the negative; it is absent in
P⁴⁶א* A B D* and several other Greek manuscripts (including some known to
Jerome and Augustine), in the Coptic and Ethiopic versions, and in such earlier
patristic authorities as Marcion, Tertullian, Origen, Lucifer and Ambrosiaster.
The addition of μή was due to failure to understand the idiom here used by
Paul; see further p. 248, n. 93.
[85] Cf. C. S. Lewis, *Transposition and Other Addresses* (London, 1949),
pp. 55 ff.

humiliation and angel-worship, for all their boasting of the special insight which they have received into divine reality, they are simply inflated by the pride of their own unspiritual minds, having lost contact with Him who is the true head and fount of life.

The phrase translated "by a voluntary humility" probably reflects a Semitic idiom and might be rendered "delighting in humility."[86] We may recall Uriah Heep and others of that tribe which makes a parade of humility, although the humility referred to here took the form of asceticism (as v. 23 makes plain). But a self-conscious humility, not to speak of an advertised humility, is no humility. One only could say "I am meek and lowly in heart" without thereby denying the truth of His words.

> Humility! the sweetest, loveliest flower
> That bloomed in Eden, and the first that died,
> Has rarely blossomed since on mortal soil.
> It is so frail, so delicate a thing,
> 'Tis gone if it but look upon itself;
> And he who ventures to esteem it his
> Proves by that single thought he has it not.

As for the angel-worship, this seems to go beyond such speculation about angels as was common in many of the Jewish schools (not only among the Essenes and apocalyptists), and to denote an actual cult[87] of angels. While Paul may have the "elemental spirits" chiefly in mind—those principalities and powers to which he has made earlier allusion—he refers here more generally to angels as a class.[88] There is, however, extremely little evidence for the worship of angels among Jews. Some have therefore

---

86 Gk. θέλων ἐν ταπεινοφροσύνῃ, where ἐν is probably to be taken with θέλων, as a Septuagintalism (following the Hebrew use of the preposition *be* after the verb *haphetz*, "to delight in"). C. F. D. Moule (IBNTG, p. 183) compares Ps. 112:1 (LXX 111:1), where ἐν ταῖς ἐντολαῖς αὐτοῦ θελήσει σφόδρα renders Heb. *be-mitzwothaw haphetz me'od* ("he will greatly rejoice in his commandments"). E. Percy (*op. cit.*, p. 145) also quotes the *Testament of Asher* 1:6, ἐὰν οὖν ἡ ψυχὴ θέλει ἐν καλῷ ("if therefore the soul delight in good"). There is no need to emend the text as Hort suggested to ἐν ἐθελοταπεινοφροσύνῃ ("with voluntary humility")—this noun being a conjectural coinage of similar stamp to Paul's ἐθελοθρησκεία in v. 23 (see p. 255, n. 116). For ταπεινοφροσύνη, "humility" (*cf.* v. 23; Ch. 3:12) see p. 88, n. 5 (on Eph. 4:2).

87 Gk. θρησκεία, which denotes more particularly the external practice of religion. *Cf.* K. L. Schmidt, TWNT iii (Stuttgart, 1938), pp. 155 ff., *s.v.* θρησκεία.

88 This seems to be the natural inference from the definite article in θρησκεία τῶν ἀγγέλων.

suggested that this feature of the Colossian heresy was due to a local tendency which persisted for some centuries. Thus Sir William Ramsay[89] quotes from Canon XXXV of the Synod of Laodicea (A.D. 363) and from the commentary of Theodoretus (c. 420–450) on this Epistle (*ad loc.*) statements which indicate that the practice of praying to angels was maintained in Phrygia and Pisidia despite official ecclesiastical prohibition. (In later centuries the practice which had once been condemned as idolatrous came to be reckoned as piety in the form of the veneration of Michael the archangel, who was credited from the ninth century onward with being the author of the natural phenomenon in the vicinity of Colossae—the "miracle of Khonai," as Ramsay calls it.[90]) It is very unlikely, however, that the practices attested by the Canons of Laodicea and by Theodoretus have any direct connection with the situation to which Paul is here addressing himself. Percy suggests that the angel-cult is simply subjection to law and legalism, since that involved subjection to the angels through whom the law was mediated. "By their legalism and asceticism the heretics are worshipping the angels instead of God."[91] But something more than this is required to satisfy Paul's strong language about an angel-cult "figuring centrally in the plan of salvation."[92] We must probably think of this cult as an ingredient of non-Jewish provenience in the amalgam of Jewish legalism and Gnostic asceticism which we call the Colossian heresy.

The expression which ARV renders "dwelling in the things which he hath seen" has puzzled interpreters and expositors, many of whom have had recourse to the art of conjectural emendation in order to reduce it to intelligible terms.[93] But Sir William

---

[89]   *The Church in the Roman Empire* (London, 1897), p. 477.

[90]   *Op. cit.*, pp. 465 ff. Such legends, involving a Christian saint or angel, often go back to pagan times, the saint or angel having displaced an earlier god or *genius loci*.

[91]   E. Percy, *op. cit.*, p. 168.

[92]   E. Percy, *op. cit.*, p. 155. The whole question of this angel-cult, with all the light that can be thrown on it from Jewish and other sources, is treated exhaustively in Percy's work, pp. 149–169. It is noteworthy that Colossians concerns itself with the angels' relation to Christ more than any other Pauline letter does. *Cf.* Heb. 1:4 ff., and T. W. Manson's suggestion that Hebrews deals with a rather later development of the same situation as is treated in Colossians ("The Problem of the Epistle to the Hebrews", BJRL xxxii [1949], pp. 3 ff.).

[93]   One of the earliest attempts to make sense of this expression was to insert a negative (*cf.* p. 246, n. 84); hence AV "intruding into those things which he hath not seen." The intrusive negative denies the reality of the experience claimed.

Ramsay solved the problem for many in a communication to the *Athenaeum* for January 25, 1913,[94] where he drew attention to a recently published inscription from the temple of Apollo of Klaros, dating from the second century A.D. This inscription contains the Greek verb *embateuo,* which had baffled so many readers of Col. 2:18, and uses it as a technical term for some act in a mystery ritual.[95] The effect of the verb as used here by Paul, says Ramsay,

---

F. Field, who approves the retention of μή, would render ἃ μὴ ἑώρακεν ἐμβατεύων as "searching into [the more familiar use of the verb ἐμβατεύω] the things which he has not seen" (*op. cit.*, pp. 197 f.). But it is generally recognized that the textual evidence forbids the retention of the negative. Many have been attracted by the simple device (first propounded by Alexander More and Curcellaeus) of detaching -κεν from ἑώρακεν and making it a prefix to ἐμβατεύων, so that the phrase reads ἃ ἑώρα (imperfect instead of perfect) κενεμβατεύων ("talking emptily of what he saw"). Lightfoot carried the process of emendation a little farther, suggesting as the original text ἑώρᾳ (or αἰώρᾳ) κενεμβατεύων, "treading the void while suspended in air" (*i.e.*, "indulging airily in vain speculations"). Percy (*op. cit.*, pp. 173 f.) is inclined to follow Lightfoot; he is unconvinced by Ramsay's interpretation. A similar emendation to Lightfoot's, ἀέρα κενεμβατεύων, "emptily treading on air" (*i.e.*, "treading on empty air") was suggested by C. Taylor in the *Journal of Philology* xiii (1877), pp. 130 ff. "Taylor's brilliant conjecture," as H. N. Bate calls it (*op. cit.*, p. 142, n. 1), was approved by Hort (*Notes on Select Readings* [Cambridge, 1882], p. 127); while J. W. Burgon (who naturally preferred the Received Text) satirized it as something "which (if it means anything at all) may as well mean 'proceeding on an airy foundation to offer an empty conjecture' " (*The Revision Revised* [London, 1883], p. 356). "That was witty, but not very wise," says J. R. Harris (*Sidelights on NT Research* [London, 1908], p. 200). Harris himself, for whom there was nothing more certain in life than a good conjectural emendation, found Taylor's "charming simplification" a "very simple and convincing solution"; he went on in later years to suggest ("St. Paul and Aristophanes", ExT xxxiv [1922–3], pp. 151 ff.) that Paul had *The Clouds* of Aristophanes in his mind at the time, more particularly line 225, where Socrates (pictured by the poet as an ascetic) says ἀεροβατῶ καὶ περιφρονῶ τὸν ἥλιον, "I tread on air and overlook the sun"! This led him on to imagine that περιφροσύνη might have been the original reading in this verse and v. 23 rather than ταπεινοφροσύνη of all our texts! See p. 255, n. 116. All these emendations based on the conjecture κενεμβατεύων have to surmount the obstacle that this word is unknown, although κενεμβατέω is quite classical in the sense "indulge in empty speculation." (W. Bauer in his *Wörterbuch*, col. 775, wrongly quotes Plutarch, Galen, Lucian, etc., as authorities for κενεμβατεύω. The word for which they should have been quoted is κενεμβατέω.) While Lightfoot defends κενεμβατεύω as an "unobjectionable" formation, Field (*loc cit.*) dismisses it as a ghost-word, a *vox nulla*, "the inviolable laws regulating this class of compound verbs stamping κενεμβατεῖν as the only legitimate, as it is the only existing, form."

⁹⁴ Expanded in the *Contemporary Review* for August 1913; further expanded in the chapter, "The Relation of St. Paul to the Greek Mysteries" in *The Teaching of Paul in Terms of the Present Day* (London, 1913), pp. 283 ff.

⁹⁵ The inscription contained the words παραλαβὼν τὰ μυστήρια ἐνεβάτευσεν

"depends on the fact that it was a religious term familiar to his Phrygian readers."[96] They would catch the suggestion that the person alluded to had formally "entered upon" his higher experience like someone being admitted to a higher grade in one of the mystery religions, and was now appealing to that superior enlightenment in support of his teaching. The use of quotation-marks may convey something of the force of the apostle's words, as when Ramsay himself translates:[97] "Let no one cozen you of the prize of your life-race, finding satisfaction in self-humiliation and worshipping of angels, 'taking his stand on' what he has seen (in the Mysteries), vainly puffed up by his unspiritual mind,[98] and not keeping firm hold on [Christ] the Head."

Whatever may have been the precise nature of the spiritual experience which this teacher had undergone, his exploitation of it forms a remarkable contrast to Paul's apologetic account of the strange thing that happened to him once when he was "caught up into Paradise, and heard unspeakable words, which it is not lawful for a man to utter" (2 Cor. 12:4).

The phrase "the mind of his flesh"[99]—"his unspiritual mind," as Ramsay puts it—is a striking locution, quite out of keeping with the Greek concept of the relation between body and mind. Here it means the attitude and outlook which are characteristic of the old nature, before the regenerating power of the Holy Spirit has taken effect. Even afterwards this antiquated way of thinking may linger on; so to the Christians of Corinth Paul could write that, despite their conversion to faith in Christ, they were still

---

("having had the mysteries delivered to him he trod the sacred area"). Another inscription from the same shrine contains the words μυηθέντες ἐνεβάτευσαν ("having been initiated they trod the sacred area"). Both inscriptions refer to θεοπρόποι, delegations who came to secure an oracular response from the god. (For a non-mystery usage of ἐμβατεύειν cf. 2 Macc. 2:30, where ERV translates "to occupy the ground.")

96 Op. cit., p. 300. Cf. A. D. Nock, JBL lii (1933), p. 132.

97 Op. cit., p. 298.

98 Or might we take ἃ ἑώρακεν as accusative after εἰκῇ φυσιούμενος ("who is vainly puffed up in his unspiritual mind over the things which he has seen at his initiation")?

99 Gk. τοῦ νοὸς τῆς σαρκὸς αὐτοῦ. The νοῦς is that part of a man's mentality which can distinguish good from evil, can recognize and respond to the claims of God (cf. Rom. 7:21 ff.; 12:2), but may remain subservient to the old nature so long as one goes on living κατὰ σάρκα. See J. Behm, TWNT iv (1942), pp. 950 ff. (s.v. νοῦς, etc.); W. Bauer, op. cit., cols. 987 ff.; Ch. Masson, Éphésiens (CNT, 1953), p. 200, n. 3; J. A. T. Robinson, op. cit., p. 25, n. 2.

"carnal" or "fleshly" in their outlook and conduct, "babes in Christ", "walking after the manner of men", unfit as yet to be treated as "spiritual" men (1 Cor. 3:1 ff.).

19 This self-inflation and pride in private religious experiences comes of not maintaining contact with the head. Every part of the body will function properly so long as it is under the control of the head; if it escapes from this control and begins to act independently, the consequences can be very distressing. So it is under the direction of Christ that the various parts of His body function harmoniously together, since they all share one common divine life and grow to maturity under the fostering care of God,[100] supplied with nutriment and fitted to each other by means of the "joints and ligaments."[101]

In spite of Dibelius' argument, developed in agreement with his exposition of Chs. 1:18 and 2:10, that the "body" here is the cosmos, since the head is the head of every principality and power,[102] it seems quite certain that the present passage is to be taken in the same sense as Eph. 4:16, and that the body is accordingly the Church.[103] Dibelius' interpretation, according to which the false teachers hold to the members of the cosmos-body (*i.e.*, to the principalities and powers) instead of to Christ as the head of that body, introduces an un-Pauline element into the argument. What is really meant here is that the false teachers, by failing to maintain contact with Him who is head of His body the Church, have no true part in that body, since it is from Christ as their head that all the members of the body acquire their capacity to function aright in harmony with one another.

---

[100]   Gk. αὔξει τὴν αὔξησιν τοῦ θεοῦ. *Cf.* Eph. 4:15 f., "that we may grow up in love altogether into Him who is the head, even Christ, from whom the whole body, adjusted and fitted together by every joint with which it is supplied, according to the harmonious functioning of each separate part, acquires the power to grow up as a complete organism, so that it is built up in love." See exposition and notes *ad loc.*, p. 100.

[101]   Gk. διὰ τῶν ἁφῶν καὶ συνδέσμων. *Cf.* διὰ πάσης ἁφῆς in Eph. 4:16 (quoted in previous note). Paul may be developing in both these places a conception (the interlinking of bodily joints and ligaments) which had already taken shape in his mind as a figure of the mutual dependence and harmonious cooperation of believers as members of the body of Christ (*cf.* 1 Cor. 12:27). For σύνδεσμος (*cf.* Ch. 3:14), see p. 88, n. 7 (on Eph. 4:3).

[102]   HNT, *ad loc.*, and on Ch. 2:10. The same view is maintained by C. L. Mitton, *The Epistle to the Ephesians* (Oxford, 1951), p. 84.

[103]   *Cf.* Ch. 3:15, "in one body." See C. F. D. Moule, ExT lx (1948-9), p. 224: "I very much doubt whether there is any essential difference between the two uses" (i.e. of σῶμα in Eph. 4:16 and Col. 2:19 respectively).

3. YOU DIED WITH CHRIST; THEREFORE...

Ch. 2:20–23

20   If ye died with Christ from the rudiments of the
     world, why, as though living in the world, do ye
     subject yourselves to ordinances,
21   Handle not, nor taste, nor touch
22   (all which things are to perish with the using), after
     the precepts and doctrines of men?
23   Which things have indeed a show of wisdom in will-
     worship, and humility, and severity to the body;
     but are not of any value against the indulgence of
     the flesh.

Paul has already told his readers that they were participators
in the death of Christ (v. 11). Now he takes up this crucial fact
again and applies it to them in a practical way. You died with
Christ (he says); and therefore your former relation of bondage
to the elemental powers of the world has been terminated. That
old life, which they dominated, has come to an end. From their
point of view, you are dead. Why, then, do you go on serving
them as though that old life was still in being?[104] You submit to
their restrictive regulations: "Hands off this! Don't eat that! Don't
touch that other thing!"[105] And you imagine that asceticism of
this kind is true holiness! But how wrong you are! Only consider:
the things which these prohibitions deal with are all material
things, belonging to this transitory order of time and sense. They
are things which come to an end through the very use that is made
of them. Handling them, eating them, or the like, involves their
destruction. Food, once eaten, ceases to be food. These are not
the things that matter most; these are not the ultimate realities.
Yet these are the things that are the burning concern of those

---

104   The style of the argument in v. 20 is quite reminiscent of that used
against Peter in Gal. 2:14.
105   It is amazing that some commentators, both in antiquity and more
recently, have taken the prohibitions of v. 21 to be those imposed by the apostle
himself! So Hilary, Ambrose and Pelagius; Jerome and Augustine, on the other
hand, grasped the true sense. Paul is thinking here not of the negative commandments of the Decalogue, nor even perhaps primarily of their amplification in the
tradition of the elders, but rather of the special restrictions laid down in the
ascetic philosophy which he is concerned to refute .

"commandments and teachings of men." The commandments and teachings of Christ give you more important matters than these to engage your attention. O, I agree that the acceptance of these prohibitions looks very well; it makes a favourable impression on many people and suggests that you have attained a high plane of wisdom from which you can despise the material world. There is something very specious about all this voluntary piety, this self-humiliation, this severity to the body. But does it really get you anywhere? Let me assure you that it does not. The acceptance of all these ascetic restrictions is of no account when it comes to a real struggle against the indulgence of the "flesh". In fact, the sternest asceticism can exist along with an insufferable spiritual pride, one of the subtlest and most intractable of the "works of the flesh." You are following the wrong road, one which can never lead you to your true goal, and one, moreover, which is barred to all believers in Christ, to all who have shared in His death.

20 The idea of the believer's "dying with Christ" appears in earlier Pauline letters. The outstanding instance of its use is in Rom. 6:1 ff.,[106] where the proposal that believers should continue in sin, to give God's grace further opportunity of being displayed in its superabundance, is refuted by the argument that those who have died to sin can no longer live in sin. Baptism proclaims the believer's death with Christ: "all of us who were baptized into Christ Jesus were baptized into His death." The finality of that death-with-Christ has been confirmed by their burial-with-Christ —a burial from which they are risen-with-Christ to begin a new life-in-Christ. As death severs the bond which binds a slave to his master, so their death-with-Christ has severed the bond which bound them to sin.[107] As death severs the bond which binds a wife to her husband, so their death-with-Christ has severed the bond which bound them to the ordinances of the Jewish law.[108] Here the argument which is presented to the Colossian Christians is that, as death severs the bond which binds a subject to his ruler, so their death-with-Christ has severed the bond which bound them to the service of the principalities and powers.[109] Why should

---

[106] *Cf.* 2 Cor. 4:10 ff.; Gal. 2:20; 2 Tim. 2:11.
[107] Rom. 6:16 ff.
[108] Rom. 7:1 ff.; *cf.* Gal. 2:19.
[109] Gk. ἀπεθάνετε σὺν Χριστῷ ἀπὸ τῶν στοιχείων τοῦ κόσμου, "ye died with Christ out from under the elements of the world" (J. A. T. Robinson, *op. cit.*, p. 43).

they then go on submitting to the rules[110] imposed by these powers? All these rules and regulations belong to the sphere of the "flesh" —the old life[111]—and only in that sphere have they binding validity. Those who live "not after the flesh, but after the spirit" are under no obligation to obey them.

21 What sort of regulations are these which the elemental powers impose? Completely negative ones: "Don't, don't, don't." There may be a stage in a child's development when he must be told not to do this and not to touch that, before he can understand the reason for such prohibitions. But when he comes to years of discretion he can appreciate his parents' point of view, he can look at life from a responsible angle, and do what is proper without having to conform to a list of prohibitions such as are suitable and necessary for the years of infancy. These would-be teachers were trying to keep the Colossian Christians in leading-strings; Paul insists on the liberty with which Christ has set them free.[112] The imposition of prohibitions from without can do nothing to create a new nature within. "Merely negative rules do not avail for the maintenance and the growth of Christian life, for life is not offered merely to our acceptance, it is offered to our acquisition. Not abstinence, not indulgence, not mystic immersion into an external symbolism, as in the mysteries of Eastern Greece—not in these, but in the appropriation of Christ in His person and His work does the Christian life consist. The Christian must live over again the experience of the Christ; he must die with Him, rise with Him, live with Him in an endless, ever-growing life."[113]

22 Besides, all the things covered by these tabus are perishable objects of the material world, doomed to pass away by the very use that is made of them.[114] Paul may be thinking especially,

---

110 Gk. τί ... δογματίζεσθε; similarly the calendrical rules to which the Galatian Christians were disposed to submit were part of the domain of the στοιχεῖα according to Gal. 4:8–10, where these powers are described as φύσει μὴ οὖσιν θεοῖς (so-called gods that are really no gods at all).

111 For this use of σάρξ see Rom. 7:5; Gal. 3:3; Eph. 2:11.

112 *Cf.* Paul's argument in Gal. 3:23 ff.

113 J. Iverach, ExT xxv (1913–4), p. 208 (in an article on "The Epistle to the Colossians and its Christology", pp. 150 ff., 205 ff.).

114 Gk. ἀπόχρησις ("using", ARV); used in this sense by Plutarch and Dionysius of Halicarnassus. The sense "abuse" which this word sometimes has is impossible in the present context. The transitory character of the things referred to is emphasized by the consideration that they pass away merely by

but not exclusively, of food (which bulks so largely in ascetic regimens); food ceases to exist as such by the very act of being digested. So Paul puts it elsewhere: "Food for the stomach and the stomach for food; but God will do away with food and stomach alike" (1 Cor. 6:13).

Moreover, these tabus are of purely human invention; they are imposed "according to the commandments and teachings of men." Behind this phrase lies the wording of Isa. 29:13, where God says of His people: "their hearts are far from me, and their fear of me is a commandment of men learned by rote" (RSV). These words are quoted by Christ in the Gospels (Matt. 15:9 // Mark 7:7) in reference to the "tradition of the elders" by which, He averred, the scribes of His day had nullified the word of God. From His use of the text it passed into general Christian usage as one of several OT "testimonies" by which the Jews' refusal to accept the gospel was explained.[115] When Paul echoes the passage here, therefore, it is with the implication that these tabus, by very reason of their human origin, frustrate the pure teaching of God with its emancipating emphasis.

23 These prohibitions carry with them a reputation for wisdom, it is true. They are associated in people's minds with the ascetic philosophical schools, such as that of the Pythagoreans, and win for those who inculcate and practise them a veneration which is, after all, cheaply acquired. But there is no necessary connection between such impressive asceticism and the true spirit of the gospel. By contrast with the spiritual service which true Christianity inculcates in harmony with the "good and acceptable and perfect will of God," this "will-worship"[116] is a "self-made cult", as

---

being used in the proper and ordinary manner. Therefore it shows a gross lack of any sense of proportion to make such transient and perishable matters so central in religious teaching. J. B. Lightfoot compares Seneca (*On the Blessed Life*, 7), *in ipso usu sui periturum* ("doomed to perish by the very use that is made of it"), which is exactly Paul's point. *Cf.* W. Bauer, *op. cit.*, *s.v.* ἀπόχρησις (and Moulton and Milligan, VGT, p. 72, for the parallel usage of the verb ἀποχράομαι).

[115] *Cf.* Justin, *Dialogue with Trypho* 48, 140.

[116] Gk. ἐθελοθρησκεία, a *hapax legomenon*. RSV renders "rigor of devotion." But Moulton and Milligan (VGT, p. 181) are on the right lines in regarding it as probably a Pauline coinage on the analogy of ἐθελοδουλεία (used by Plato and others in the sense of "voluntary subjection"). J. R. Harris, pursuing his comparison of the language of this passage with that of Aristophanes (see p. 249, n. 93), conjectured νεφελοθρησκεία ("cloud-worship") as the original reading here. He points out that the clouds are acclaimed as deities worthy of worship

Deissmann puts it[117]—a "faked-religion," as Bate has it.[118] The term which Paul uses suggests that these people thought they were offering God a voluntary addition to His basic requirements—a supererogatory devotion by which they hoped to acquire superior merit in His sight. Far from being of any avail against the indulgence of the flesh,[119] as its proponents claimed, it could and often did coexist with overweening self-conceit, making it extremely difficult for those who accepted it to admit the truth that in God's sight they were sinners in desperate need of His salvation. When they commended harsh usage of the body as a specific against fleshly indulgence, they thought in terms of the Greek antithesis between body and soul. But this is not Paul's thought. When he speaks of "unsparing treatment of the *body*" he means the body in its ordinary sense; but when he speaks of "indulgence of the *flesh*" he means the old Adam-nature in its rebellion against God.[120] A chief ingredient in that rebellion is the proud spirit of self-sufficiency which has nothing to do with the body in the ordinary sense, but springs from the will. And the asceticism attacked by Paul feeds this particular indulgence of the flesh instead of starving it.[121]

---

in line 316 of *The Clouds* (ExT xxxiv [1922–3], pp. 151 ff.). But the conjecture νεφελοθρησκεία really belongs to the Aristophanic region of Νεφελοκοκκυγία ("Cloud-cuckoo-land").

[117] *Paul*, p. 118 (he contrasts it with the λογικὴ λατρεία of Rom. 12:1).
[118] *Op. cit.*, p. 143.
[119] Gk. πρὸς πλησμονὴν τῆς σαρκός.
[120] *Cf.* E. Percy, *op. cit.*, p. 262; J. A. T. Robinson, *op. cit.*, p. 27.
[121] *Cf.* E. Percy, *op. cit.*, p. 139.

CHAPTER III

4. YOU ROSE WITH CHRIST; THEREFORE...

Ch. 3:1–4

1 If then ye were raised together with Christ, seek the
things that are above, where Christ is, seated on the
right hand of God.

2 Set your mind on the things that are above, not on the
things that are upon the earth.

3 For ye died, and your life is hid with Christ in God.

4 When Christ, *who is* our[1] life, shall be manifested,
then shall ye also with him be manifested in glory.

Paul reminds the Colossians now that they did not only die with
Christ; they were raised from the dead with Him too (as he had
already told them in Ch. 2:12). When Christ left the tomb (he
says), He was raised on high, and is now enthroned at God's right
hand. What does this mean for you? It means that since you have
shared in His resurrection, your interests are now centred in Him,
in that place of highest honour to which God has exalted Him.
You must therefore pursue those things which belong to the
heavenly realm where He reigns; your mind, your attitude, your
ambitions, your whole outlook must be characterized by your living
bond with the ascended Christ. Is this not a reasonable conclusion?
You died with Christ; now you live with Him and in Him. Your
life is bound up with His; that is to say, it is laid up in safe keeping
with Him, securely hidden in God. The world cannot see your real
life at present, just as it cannot see Christ. A day is coming,
however, when Christ will be revealed in glory; and since Christ
Himself is our true life, it follows that you too—you whose life is
at present hidden with Him—will then be revealed with Him and
share His glory.

1 The Colossians knew that, like their fellow-Christians
throughout the world, they had been "raised with Christ through
faith in the power of God, who raised him from the dead"; that

---

[1] The weight of the manuscript evidence is slightly in favour of the marginal
variant "your" (Gk. ὑμῶν) as against "our" (Gk. ἡμῶν); ὑμῶν is the reading of
P⁴⁶ℵ C D* etc., ἡμῶν of B Dᵇᶜ etc.

they had been "quickened with Christ when they were spiritually dead" (Ch. 2:12 f.). Every time that they recalled their baptism and its meaning, they ought to be impressed afresh with the reality of their participation in Christ's death and resurrection, and draw the logical and practical conclusions. If their death with Christ severed the links that bound them to the old world order, which was trying to impose its dominion on them again, their resurrection with Christ established new links—links with a new and heavenly order, with that spiritual kingdom in which Christ their Lord was sovereign, ruling from the place of supremacy to which He had been raised at God's right hand.

Christ's ascension to the right hand of God was an essential and constant element in the earliest apostolic preaching; it finds echoes throughout the NT.[2] It goes back, of course, to the messianic interpretation of Ps. 110:1[3]—

> "Jehovah saith unto my Lord,
> Sit thou at my right hand,
> Until I make thine enemies thy footstool"—

words which Jesus claimed for Himself when He was arraigned before the Sanhedrin in Jerusalem.[4] With His resurrection and ascension, the apostles proclaimed, this enthronement had actually taken place; from the right hand of the Almighty Christ was now reigning as King, and would continue so to reign until all opposing forces in the universe had submitted to Him.[5]

The apostles knew very well that they were using figurative language when they spoke of Christ's exaltation thus; they no more thought of a location on a literal throne at a literal right hand of God than we do. The static impression made by conventional artistic representations of such a literal enthronement of Christ is quite different from the dynamic New Testament conception. It was the conventional representation that occasioned Luther's outburst: "Oh, that heaven of the charlatans, with its golden chair and Christ seated at the Father's side vested in a choir cope and a golden robe, as the painters love to portray Him!"[6] For he realized

---

2 *Cf.* Acts 2:33 ff.; 5:31; 7:55 f.; Rom. 8:34; Eph. 1:20; Heb. 1:3, 13; 8:1; 10:12; 12:2; 1 Pet. 3:22; Rev. 3:21.
3 *Cf.* Matt. 22:43 ff. // Mark 12:35 ff. // Luke 20:41 ff.
4 *Cf.* Matt. 26:64 // Mark 14:62 // Luke 22:69.
5 *Cf.* 1 Cor. 15:24 ff. for Paul's elaboration of this.
6 *Weimarer Ausgabe* XXIII, p. 131.

that such a representation quite obscured the apostolic picture of
the exalted Christ going forth by His Spirit conquering and to
conquer throughout the world. What the apostles understood by
the enthronement at God's right hand is plain from other terms
which they used to convey the same idea: Christ has been given
"the name which is above every name, that in the name of Jesus
every knee should bow..., and that every tongue should confess
that Jesus Christ is Lord" (Phil. 2:10 f.); Christ has "ascended far
above all the heavens, that he might fill all things" (Eph. 4:10).
Because He has been elevated to the position of highest sovereignty
over the universe, He pervades the universe with His presence.

This extract from the apostolic preaching or *kerygma* is not
introduced here for an ornamental purpose; Paul is about to
commence the parenetic section of his letter, and his parenetic
sections regularly presuppose the *kerygma,* by implication if not
expressly.[7] What God has done for us in Christ is the grand
argument and incentive for Christian living. The apostolic
teaching or *didache* may be distinguished from *kerygma,* but it is
founded upon *kerygma.* Whatever affinities may be traced between
Paul's ethical exhortations and those of contemporary moralists,
their whole emphasis in Paul's writings depends upon the fact
that they arise directly out of the work of Christ.[8] It is because
believers have died with Christ and risen with Him that their life
henceforth is to be different.

But what are the practical implications of being raised with
Christ? This, that believers have now no life of their own. Their
life is the life of Christ, maintained in being by Him at God's right
hand and shared by Him with all His people.[9] Their interests
must therefore be His interests. Instead of waiting until the last
day to receive the resurrection-life, those who have been raised
with Christ possess it here and now. The new creation[10]—the
"regeneration"[11]—has already begun in them. Spiritually—that
is to say, "in Christ"—they belong already to the age to come and
enjoy its life.

---

[7] *Cf.* Rom. 6:1-11; 1 Cor. 5:7 f.; 6:11, etc.
[8] *Cf.* W. D. Davies, *Paul and Rabbinic Judaism* (London, 1948), pp. 88.
112, 136.
[9] *Cf.* Rom. 8:10; Gal. 5:25.
[10] *Cf.* 2 Cor. 5:17; Gal. 6:15.
[11] *Cf.* Matt. 19:28.

2 "Aim then at what is above,"[12] says Paul. The Gnostics would have said this too. They were intensely interested in living on a higher plane. But Paul has in mind a higher plane than theirs. Go in for the higher things (he says)—higher things than the principalities and powers which dominate the planetary spheres, for Christ has ascended far above these.[13] Don't let your ambitions be earth-bound, set on transitory and inferior objects. Don't look at life and the universe from the standpoint of these lower planes; look at them from Christ's exalted standpoint. Judge everything by the standards of that new creation to which you now belong, not by those of the old order to which you have said a final farewell.

3 For, you see, you *died* to that old order. The idea is so strange that it must be repeated and emphasized. You *died*, I say, and as for the new life upon which you have entered, its true abode is where Christ Himself is. "When our Forerunner triumphed, 'He bore up with Him into safety the spiritual life of all His people.' "[14]

There is a widespread belief among "primitive" peoples that a person's life is bound up with some external object, some "life-token."[15] This object, sometimes actually referred to as his "life," is safely hidden away, in the belief that, so long as it is preserved intact, no harm can befall him. There is no such idea in Paul's mind here, and yet the belief may serve as a parable of the truth that he is expressing. The believer's life is safely "hidden away" with Christ. Its well-being depends on His. So long as He lives, His people live also.[16] Their true life is an extension of that indissoluble life which is His at the Father's right hand.

Bishop Handley Moule tells how Sir Arthur Blackwood always referred to these words as the means of his conversion. They were brought home by the Spirit of God to his seeking heart "in a final crisis of glad assurance" in the church at Barnet, near London, when William Pennefather gave out John Newton's hymn in which Col. 3:3 is quoted.

---

12 Gk. τὰ ἄνω ζητεῖτε.
13 *Cf.* Eph. 1:20 f.
14 E. K. Simpson, *The Pastoral Epistles* (London, 1954), p. 63.
15 *Cf.* E. S. Hartland in ERE viii (Edinburgh, 1915), pp. 44 ff. (*s.v.* "Life-Token"); C. M. Draper in ExT xxvii (1915–16), p. 427.
16 *Cf.* John 14:19.

Rejoice, believer, in the Lord,
  Who makes your cause His own;
The hope that's founded on His word
  Can ne'er be overthrown.

Though many foes beset your road,
  And feeble is your arm,
Your life is hid with Christ in God,
  Beyond the reach of harm.

"Who does not know," the Bishop goes on, "that fear often lies near great joy, and that a treasure may seem far too precious to be safe? But here, he felt, was a safety equal to the treasure; 'with Christ in God', a double rampart, all divine."[17]

"With Christ—in God." With Christ, because we died with Him and have been raised to new life with Him. In God, because Christ Himself has His being in God,[18] and therefore those who belong to Christ have their being there too.[19]

4 You know your life to be safely hidden with Christ, although in the eyes of the world you are, spiritually speaking, without visible means of support. But when Christ, the true life of all His people, is manifested in His *parousia,* then you who share His life will share His glorious epiphany.[20]

"Christ our life." The apostle who could say, "For to me to live is Christ" (Phil. 1:21),[21] does not think of this as something which is true of himself alone. Christ is the life of all those who are united to Him by faith, members of His body.

Bishop Moule tells of a friend of his to whom, "early in his course, those five words, *'Christ, who is our life'*, were made a new world. ... As he walked back to his home over the dark fields from a mission-service he had been conducting, these simple, these familiar words passed through his soul in one of those moments of insight which God alone can explain. 'Within ten paces, as I walked, life was transformed to me,' he said; so wonderful was

---

[17] H. C. G. Moule, *Colossian Studies* (London, 1898), p. 190.
[18] *Cf.* John 1:18 *(ὁ ὢν εἰς τὸν κόλπον τοῦ πατρός);* 10:27–30.
[19] *Cf.* J. S. Stewart, *A Man in Christ* (London, 1935), pp. 171 f. Deissmann says: "The faith of Paul is then the union with God which is established in fellowship with Christ" and describes Christians as ἔνθεοι ἐν Χριστῷ Ἰησοῦ (*Paul* [London, 1926], pp. 164 f.). But we are not impressed by his endeavour to illustrate this spiritual relationship by means of a geometrical diagram (p. 298)!
[20] *Cf.* Ch. 1:27 (p. 219).
[21] *Cf.* Rom. 8:2, 10; 2 Cor. 4:10; Gal. 6:8.

the discovery that the Lord Christ is not merely Rescuer, Friend, King, but Life itself, Life central, inexhaustible, 'springing up within my heart, rising to eternity.' "[22]

Nor is Christ our life only; because He is our life, He is also our hope.[23] The inward revelation of His saving glory which has come home to us already is the earnest of a fuller revelation yet to come, the grand consummation of the union between Christ and His people. "The same man whose daily thanksgiving was that 'it pleased God to reveal His Son' in him could also hope for a day 'when Christ, who is our life, shall appear.' "[24] That is the day for which, as Paul tells us in another place,[25] the whole creation looks with eager expectation. Hitherto it is fast held in the bondage of frustration; as old Qoheleth saw, "Vanity" is written large over it.[26] But what Qoheleth did not see was that a day would dawn when creation would be liberated from the frustrating cycle of change and decay, and share the glorious liberty of the children of God.[27] That glorious liberty will be manifested on the day of their revelation, for the day of the revelation of the *Son* of God is also the day of the revelation of the *sons* of God[28]—His by victorious right; theirs by His grace which unites them with Him.

Another New Testament writer voices the same thought in his own characteristic phraseology: "Beloved, now are we children of God, and it is not yet made manifest what we shall be. We know that, if he shall be manifested, we shall be like him; for we shall see him even as he is" (1 John 3:2). To participate in the revealed glory of Christ is to attain His likeness, as indeed Paul indicates again, when he tells the church in Philippi that its constitution is laid up in heaven, "whence also we wait for a Saviour, the Lord Jesus Christ, who shall fashion anew the body of our humiliation, that it may be conformed to the body of his glory" (Phil. 3:20 f.). And what is this but the fulness of Christian sanctification? Here and now it is the province of the Holy Spirit

---

[22] H. C. G. Moule, *op. cit.*, pp. 190 f.
[23] *Cf.* Ch. 1:5 (p. 180).
[24] J. S. Stewart, *op. cit.*, p. 202.
[25] Rom. 8:19.
[26] Eccl. 1:2, etc. Paul may have had Ecclesiastes in mind when he describes the creation as subjected to ματαιότης (Rom. 8:20).
[27] Rom. 8:21.
[28] Rom. 8:19.

within the people of God to reproduce increasing likeness to Christ in their lives;[29] but the consummation of this sanctifying work awaits the day of Christ.[30] Indeed, the presence and activity of the Spirit here and now is an "earnest"[31] of the heritage which is reserved for believers against that day.[32] But the day of resurrection and glory will only bring to complete and public fruition something that is already true—that Christians have died with Christ and been raised with Him, and in Him are partakers of the age to come.[33]

When that day will dawn Paul does not suggest. Its date is unknown; its advent is certain. The consummating act in the series of saving events is assured by those which have already been accomplished. Those whom God foreknew, "he also foreordained to be conformed to the image of his Son, that he might be the firstborn among many brethren; and whom he foreordained, them he also called; and whom he called, them he also justified; and whom he justified, them he also glorified"[34] (Rom. 8:29 f.). The day of glory may be future, but its arrival is as sure as if it had already come. The hope of glory will then give place to glory realized; but as it is Christ Himself who is now in us the hope of glory (Ch. 1:27), so it is Christ Himself who will eternally be to us glory realized.

With this reaffirmation of the Christian hope, the apostle concludes the more strictly "doctrinal" section of his letter.

---

[29]   2 Cor. 3:18.
[30]   1 Thess. 5:23.
[31]   Eph. 1:14.
[32]   *Cf.* 1 Pet. 1:4.
[33]   *Cf.* C. H. Dodd, *The Apostolic Preaching and its Developments* (London, 1936), pp. 147 f.; W. D. Davies, *op. cit.,* pp. 318 f.; O. Cullmann, *Christ and Time* (Eng. trans., London, 1951), pp. 139 ff.
[34]   The aorist ἐδόξασεν in Rom. 8:30 may be in imitation of the Hebrew "prophetic perfect."

IV. THE CHRISTIAN LIFE

Chs. 3:5–4:6

We come now to the practical application of the teaching contained in the preceding sections of this letter. As in other Pauline letters, the transition from the "doctrinal" to the "practical" sections is marked by the conjunction "therefore."[35]

It may be that the ethical teaching of Paul is cast in forms which were in widespread use among early Christians. These forms may be traced back to the ethical teaching of Jesus Himself. But Paul emphasizes the logical connection between Christian doctrine and Christian practice. He does not inculcate theological doctrine simply in order that his readers may have a firm intellectual grasp of it; he insists that it must find expression in Christian living. On the other hand, his ethical teaching is never left suspended in air; it is firmly founded upon the saving revelation of God in Christ. If his theology is a theology of grace, the practical response to that grace is one of gratitude.

Samuel Chadwick, a renowned preacher among English Methodists in the earlier years of this century, used to tell of a converted burglar who was a member of his congregation. One day in conversation the ex-burglar mentioned that he was going through the Epistle to the Romans in his private Bible study. Chadwick suggested that he must find some parts of the apostolic argument rather difficult. "Yes," said the other, "it *is* difficult; but I stumble on till I come to a 'therefore', and then I get a blessing!" He had grasped the logic of Pauline ethics![36]

Here, then, Paul enunciates general Christian maxims: there are old practices to be abandoned; there is a new way of life to be adopted. The old must be "put off"; the new must be "put on" (a figure of speech which may be associated with the wearing of new garments at one's baptism).

There is much to be said for the view that the Church at a rather early date began to classify its ethical teaching in categories

---

[35] *Cf.* Rom. 12:1 ("I beseech you therefore..."); Eph. 4:1 ("I therefore... beseech you...").

[36] The principle finds simple expression in John 13:17, "if ye know these things, blessed are ye if ye do them."

which would be easily taught and remembered, each being introduced by a sort of catchword. The steady increase in the number of believing Gentiles made it desirable that they should receive the elements of Christian ethics in forms which they could readily assimilate.[37] These catechetical "forms" are recognizable in several NT epistles,[38] and their recurrence is not to be accounted for by the dependence of one epistle on another but by the dependence of all on a common *paradosis* of practical teaching. Of these "forms" with their distinctive catchwords four are present here; they consist of the paragraphs which expand the injunctions "Put off" (Ch. 3:5–11); "Put on" (Ch. 3:12–17); "Be subject" (Ch. 3:18–4:1); "Watch and pray" (Ch. 4:2–6).

---

[37] *Cf.* A. Seeberg, *Der Katechismus der Urchristenheit* (Leipzig, 1903); G. Klein, *Der älteste christliche Katechismus* (Berlin, 1909); A. M. Hunter, *Paul and his Predecessors* (London, 1940); P. Carrington, *The Primitive Christian Catechism* (Cambridge, 1940); E. G. Selwyn, *The First Epistle of Peter* (London, 1946), Essay II (pp. 363 ff.); C. H. Dodd, *Gospel and Law* (Cambridge, 1951); G. B. Caird, *The Apostolic Age* (London, 1955), pp. 109 ff. The inclusion of Archbishop Carrington's book in this list does not imply approval of his view of the Church as a neo-levitical community!

[38] *Cf.* Rom. 12:1–13:14; Gal. 5:13–26; Eph. 4:17–6:18; 1 Thess. 4:1–12; Heb. 13:1–17; Jas. 1:2–4:12; 1 Pet. 1:13–4:11.

1. "PUT OFF"

Ch. 3:5–11

5 Put to death therefore your members which are upon the earth: fornication, uncleanness, passion, evil desire, and covetousness, which is idolatry;

6 for which things' sake cometh the wrath of God upon the sons of disobedience:[39]

7 wherein[40] ye also once walked, when ye lived in these things;

8 but now do ye also put them all away: anger, wrath, malice, railing, shameful speaking out of your mouth:

9 lie not one to another; seeing that ye have put off the old man with his doings,

10 and have put on the new man, that is being renewed unto knowledge after the image of him that created him:

11 where there cannot be Greek and Jew, circumcision and uncircumcision, barbarian, Scythian, bondman, freeman; but Christ is all, and in all.

Now that you are new men in Christ, says the apostle, live like new men. You have said good-bye to your old life; therefore have done with all those things that were characteristic of it. You have died with Christ; act and speak and think therefore so as to make it plain that this "death" is no mere figure of speech, but a real event which has severed all the links which bound you to the dominion of sin. In short, be (in actual practice) what you now are (by a divine act).

There is a true Christian *askesis,* but it is quite different from the *askesis* which the innovators were trying to impose upon the Colossians. The Christian *askesis* consists in renouncing all sinful propensities and pursuits, and allowing the new nature, divinely implanted within, to find outward expression in the fair fruit of a holy life.

---

[39] The words "upon the sons of disobedience" (Gk. ἐπὶ τοὺς υἱοὺς τῆς ἀπειθείας) probably represent an intrusion into the text from Eph 5:6; they are omitted by P^{46} B C (D*?), by the Sahidic Coptic version, and by Clement of Alexandria, Cyprian, Macrobius, Ambrosiaster and Jerome.

[40] Gk. ἐν οἷς. If "upon the sons of disobedience" were retained, this might be rendered "among whom."

5 While the first of the four ethical paragraphs contains the catchword "Put off" (v. 8), the paragraph is introduced by the synonymous injunction "Put to death," or, as we might put it, "reckon as dead."[41] "Reckon as dead things those 'members' of yours which partake of the nature of the old earthly life." Paul is not talking here of the actual members of the human body, nor is he expressing himself in quite the same sense as Jesus intends where He says that the offending hand or foot should be cut off, or the offending eye plucked out, if entrance into life cannot otherwise be gained (Matt. 5:29 f.; 18:8 f.; Mark 9:43 ff.). This seems plain from the apposition of the word "members" with the following catalogue of vices. Yet this apposition is so abrupt that attempts have been made to ease the difficulty of the construction by expedients which nevertheless are unconvincing. Thus Lightfoot makes a heavy stop after "your members which are upon the earth" and regards the following nouns ("fornication, uncleanness...") as "prospective accusatives" governed by some such verb as "put off" or "put away" in v. 8.[42] On this showing, Paul intended to make the accusatives directly dependent on the verb "put off", but before he reached that verb he introduced intervening clauses which led to a change in the construction of the sentence. To be sure, such breaches of construction (anacolutha) are by no means uncommon in Paul's epistolary style; but in this place, if he had meant to make the accusatives directly dependent on the verb "put off", he would almost certainly have put that verb in front of them.[43] Even less convincing is Charles Masson's expedient; he takes "members" as vocative, and interprets the verse thus: "You members [of the body of Christ] are therefore to reckon as

---

41 Gk. νεκρώσατε. This is the only place in NT where νεκρόω is used in this sense. It occurs in two other places (Rom. 4:19; Heb. 11:12) in the perfect participle passive νενεκρωμένος to describe Abraham's body in old age, "as good as dead." In Rom. 6:11 λογίζεσθε... νεκρούς ("reckon as dead") is synonymous with νεκρώσατε here, except that the tense is aorist here and present there. There must be a decisive initial act (aorist), introducing a settled attitude (present). In Rom. 8:13 the verb rendered "put to death" is θανατόω (translated "made dead" in Rom. 7:4); elsewhere in NT it means "put to death" in the literal sense.

42 J. B. Lightfoot, *St Paul's Epistles to the Colossians and to Philemon* (London, 1879), p. 211. On this A. S. Peake justly says: "It is true that the apposition of μέλη and the list of sins that follows is strange, but not so strange as to make this very forced construction preferable" (EGT, *ad loc.*).

43 As in Rom. 13:12; Eph. 4:22, 25; *cf.* Jas. 1:21; 1 Pet. 2:1.

dead the things which are on the earth—fornication, uncleanness, etc."[44]

What we have here is rather an extension of the ordinary sense of "members". Since these people's bodily members had been used as instruments of sin in the old life (cf. Rom. 6:19), they are viewed here as comprehending the various kinds of sin which were committed by their means and in which the "flesh" (the old nature) expressed itself actively.[45] In Rom. 7:23 Paul speaks of "the law of sin which is in my members"; here he goes farther and practically identifies his readers' members with the sins of which they were formerly the instruments. But what he is really thinking of is the practices and attitudes to which his readers' bodily activity and strength had been devoted in the old life. Of these he mentions first of all fornication, impurity, lust, evil desires, and covetousness in general, proceeding from the more overt to the less overt. These things had to be regarded as dead. Since believers have died with Christ, the domination of the old habits and instincts has been broken. But this severance of the old relation by reason of death can equally well be expressed the other way round: if, from one point of view, believers have died to these things, then, from another point of view, these things are dead so far as believers are concerned; they are no longer able to enforce their claims as they once did. So, in Rom. 6:11, Paul exhorts his readers to reckon *themselves* as dead to sin but alive to righteousness, while in Rom. 8:13 he says: "if by the Spirit[46] ye put to death the deeds of the body, ye shall live" (the "deeds of the body" being such things as are listed in the present passage of Colossians).

It has been held that, in his oscillation between the idea of the Christian's having died with Christ and the idea of his still having to "put to death" the old bad habits, or to reckon himself as dead,

---

[44] CNT, *ad loc.* Such an absolute use of μέλη in this sense would be tolerable only if their membership of the body of Christ were explicitly stressed in the immediate context.

[45] This transition of thought "is easily explained on psychological grounds by the inrush of various associations when a picture-word is being used" (M. Dibelius, HNT, *ad loc.*). With this extended use of the word "members" we may compare the use of the word "body" in Rom. 6:6 ("the body of sin"); 7:24 ("this body of death", ARV margin); 8:10 ("the body is dead because of sin"). In these places it is not the physical body pure and simple that is intended. *Cf.* the exposition of Ch. 2:11 (p. 235).

[46] Cf. Gal. 5:16. In the present passage in Colossians the πνεῦμα is not actually mentioned, but is certainly implied.

Paul is guilty of an unmistakable inconsistency. "He is working with an abstract theological idea which does not fit in with the facts of life, and in his effort to assert it he is involved in constant trouble."[47]. This criticism does less than justice to the reality of the believer's union with Christ and reception of new life from Him, which is much more than an "abstract theological idea." The difficulty arises rather from the circumstance that the believer, in fact and in his conscious experience, is living on two planes so long as he remains in this mortal body: spiritually he already belongs to the age to come, while temporally he is involved in this present age; spiritually he is united to Christ at God's right hand, while temporally he lives on earth. The new nature imparted by Christ does not effect the immediate annihilation of the old nature inherited from his ancestors; so long as he lives in "this age," the "flesh" persists like a dormant force which may spring into activity at any time. Hence the tension, which does not arise from any inconsistency between Paul's premises and his recognition of the facts of Christian life, but from well-known conditions of Christian experience.

The believer is dead to the world with Christ (Chs. 2:20; 3:3), having put off the "flesh" in Him (Chs. 2:11; 3:9) and been liberated from sin (Rom. 6:6 f., 11, 18, 22); on the other hand he is still in the world, with his old "flesh", exposed to the temptations of sin. Hence this antinomy in the apostle's thought-world; hence his transition back and forth between the indicative and imperative:[48] "Be what you are!"[49]

In moving from the outward manifestations of sin to the cravings of the heart—from acts of immorality and uncleanness to their inner springs—Paul proceeds in the manner of our Lord, who in the Sermon on the Mount traces murder back to the angry thought, and adultery to the lustful glance (Matt. 5:21 ff., 27 ff.). Catalogues of vices were common form among the pagan moralists and in the anti-pagan polemic of Jewish propagandists. In the Pauline letters such lists appear in Rom. 1:29 ff.; 1 Cor. 5:11; 6:9 f.; Gal. 5:19 ff.;

---

47 E. F. Scott, MNTC (London, 1930). *ad loc.*, pp. 65 f. In a later work, *Paul's Epistle to the Romans* (London, 1947), Scott shows a truer appreciation of Paul's thought.

48 In the Johannine literature the indicative predominates.

49 *E.g.*, in 1 Cor. 5:7 f., Christians are exhorted to be "unleavened" because they *are* "unleavened."

Eph. 5:3 ff., etc.; but they receive their special significance from the Christian context within which they are set. The climax of the present list is covetousness, which is equated with idolatry,[50] as in Eph. 5:5.[51] Covetousness is idolatry because it involves the setting of our affections on earthly things and not on things above, and therefore the putting of some other object of desire in the central place which Christ should occupy in our hearts.[52] So, in Phil. 3:19 f., the contrast is pointed between those who "mind earthly things" and those whose "citizenship is in heaven." The part that the commandment against covetousness played in Paul's own moral and religious experience [53] no doubt revealed to him the special deadliness of this subtle sin. The sins which precede covetousness in the catalogue appear regularly in such lists, and certainly they were sins against which Gentile converts needed to be put on their guard; but covetousness is the more dangerous because it may assume so many respectable forms.[54]

6 As Paul emphasizes elsewhere, and above all in his great arraignment of the pagan world in Rom. 1:18 ff., these are the things that incur divine retribution.[55] God has written His decree against such sins not only in the law as Israel received it, but in the conscience and in the very constitution of man, so that it cannot be violated with impunity. The phrase "upon the sons of disobedience"[56] denotes those whose lives are characterized by

[50] In Gal. 5:20 idolatry is one of "the works of the flesh" and is listed along with other sins of the kind mentioned here; *cf.* 1 Cor. 5:10 f.; 6:9 f.

[51] With $\pi\lambda\varepsilon o\nu\varepsilon\xi i\alpha\nu$ $\eta\tau\iota\varsigma$ $\dot{\varepsilon}\sigma\tau\dot{\iota}\nu$ $\varepsilon i\delta\omega\lambda o\lambda\alpha\tau\varrho\varepsilon i\alpha$ here *cf.* $\pi\lambda\varepsilon o\nu\dot{\varepsilon}\varkappa\tau\eta\varsigma$, $\ddot{o}$ $\dot{\varepsilon}\sigma\tau\iota\nu$ $\varepsilon i\delta\omega\lambda o\lambda\dot{\alpha}\tau\varrho\eta\varsigma$ in Eph. 5:5 (p. 118, n. 10). The parenetic sections of the two epistles have several parallel passages which exhibit close similarity in subject-matter but divergence of construction.

[52] The Greek word is $\pi\lambda\varepsilon o\nu\varepsilon\xi i\alpha$, which denotes not merely the desire to possess more than one has, but more than one ought to have, particularly that which belongs to someone else. *Cf.* W. Barclay, *A New Testament Wordbook* (London, 1955), pp. 97 ff.

[53] *Cf.* Rom. 7:7 ff.

[54] Sometimes, indeed, $\pi\lambda\varepsilon o\nu\varepsilon\xi i\alpha$ is used with a distinctly sexual reference, *e.g.* in 1 Thess. 4:6, where the injunction "that no man ... wrong ($\pi\lambda\varepsilon o\nu\varepsilon\varkappa\tau\varepsilon\tilde{\iota}\nu$) his brother in the matter" forbids a trespass of this kind against another man's family circle, by illicit relations with one of his womenfolk (*cf.* W. Hendriksen, *NT Commentary: I and II Thessalonians* [Grand Rapids, 1955], pp. 100 ff.).

[55] *Cf.* Eph. 5:6. A similar emphasis appears in the *Zadokite Fragments*, ii. 14–iii. 12. On the general subject *cf.* R. V. G. Tasker, *The Biblical Doctrine of the Wrath of God* (London, 1951).

[56] On the text see p. 266, n. 39. The locution $o\dot{\iota}$ $\upsilon i o\dot{\iota}$ $\tau\tilde{\eta}\varsigma$ $\dot{\alpha}\pi\varepsilon\iota\theta\varepsilon i\alpha\varsigma$ (*cf.* Eph. 2:2; 5:6) is probably a Hebraism, meaning "disobedient people." Deissmann

defiance of the law of God and consequent liability to His wrath; the opposite idea is conveyed by the phrase "obedient children" (literally "children of obedience"[57]) in 1 Pet. 1:14.

7 You yourselves used to practise these vices, he says; your lives were marked by them. This is not the only place in the NT epistles where a catalogue of pagan vices is immediately followed by a reminder to the readers that not so long ago these things characterized their own lives.[58] It was largely for this reason that many of Paul's critics thought him so foolishly unpractical in stressing gospel liberty where such people were concerned. Gospel liberty, they thought, might be all very well for Jews and God-fearers who had learned to acknowledge the law of God in their lives, but people so lately weaned from pagan immorality ought to be subjected first to a period of probation before they could properly be recognized as members of the Christian Church in the full sense. Paul's policy was different: pagans though these people had been, they had now received a new nature; they were in Christ and Christ lived in them; if they accepted the logic of this situation, looked upon themselves as dead to their former desires and alive to God in Christ, the Christ-life maintained within them by the Holy Spirit would manifest itself in a new pattern of behaviour.

8-9ᵃ So, he tells them, put off all those old habits, just as you would discard an outworn suit of clothes which no longer fitted you.[59] And a repulsive collection of habits they are, to be sure— anger, quick temper, malice, and the language which accompanies these things, slander and foul talk. Get rid of them all; don't let your mouths be polluted with the scurrilous and filthy language that used to flow readily from them, or with lying either. You used to tell lies to one another as though it were the natural thing

---

(*Bible Studies*, pp. 163 ff.) is unwilling to call such expressions Hebraisms pure and simple, preferring to regard them as "analogical formations" to similar Hebrew phrases which are reproduced literally in the Greek of the LXX (the distinction does not amount to much).

57 Gk. τέκνα ὑπακοῆς.

58 *Cf.* 1 Cor. 6:9 ff.; also Rom. 6:19 ff.; Tit. 3:3; 1 Pet. 4:1 ff.

59 Gk. ἀπόθεσθε (*cf.* Rom. 13:12; Eph. 4:22, 25; Heb. 12:1; Jas. 1:21; 1 Pet. 2:1 for this ethical use; the literal use in reference to clothes is found in Acts 7:58). For the representation of behaviour or character as a garment *cf.* Job. 29:14; Ps. 35:26; 109:29; 132:9; Isa. 11:5; 59:17; 61:10; Rom. 13:12, 14; 1 Thess. 5:8, in addition to passages quoted on p. 265, n. 38. The idea is extended to the putting off of the old (terrestrial) body and the putting on of the new (celestial) one in 1 Cor. 15:53 f.; 2 Cor. 5:2 ff.

to do; don't do it any more.[60] Your tongues were given you to speak the truth with.

9ᵇ–10 You see, you have stripped off[61] the "old man" that you used to be, together with the practices which he loved to indulge in.[62] This was emphasized in Ch. 2:11 f., where their baptism was said to be in effect the stripping off, not of an insignificant scrap of bodily tissue, as the old circumcision was, but of the whole "body of flesh"—the old nature in its entirety. They had done that already, and by the same token they had put on a new nature.[63] But what was that new nature? It was the "new man" who was being continually renewed[64] with a view to their progressive increase in the true knowledge—renewed in accordance with his Creator's image.

When Paul speaks of the renewal of the new man, his intention is much the same as when he says in 2 Cor. 4:16, "though our outward man is decaying, yet our inward man is renewed day by day." It is the life and power of Christ within that is thus being constantly renewed, as the Spirit of God reproduces more and more of the Christ-likeness in the believer's life.[65]

In the phrase "after the image of him that created him," we cannot miss the allusion to Gen. 1:27, where the first Adam is said to have been created by God "in his own image."[66] But the first

---

[60] The present imperative (Gk. μὴ ψεύδεσθε) implies: "Don't go on telling lies." (But see C. F. D. Moule, IBNTG, pp. 20 f.)

[61] Gk. ἀπεκδυσάμενοι, the verb used in Ch. 2:15 (cf. p. 237, n. 59; p. 239, n. 68 (b); cf. also the corresponding noun ἀπέκδυσις in Ch. 2:11). This verb is more forceful than ἀποτίθεμαι (v. 8; cf. n. 59 above); its use in the present passage gives much the same effect as συνσταυρόω in Rom. 6:6 ("our old man was crucified with him"); cf. Rom. 8:12 f. for a repetition of the same idea in yet another form of words.

[62] It was this passage that in part at least suggested to John Bunyan his picture of the sinister character of "Adam the First", who "dwelt in the town of Deceit", whose invitation to go with him and be his servant and son-in-law Faithful was "somewhat inclinable" to accept, until he noticed the words inscribed in his forehead: "Put off the old man with his deeds" (*The Pilgrim's Progress*, Part I).

[63] Perhaps the Colossian heresy made some play with the concept of the "new man." For the use of ἐνδύομαι here W. L. Knox compares *Bereshith Rabba* xlix. 2, where the *men* of Gen. 18:16 "put on" *angels* in Ch. 19:1 (*St. Paul and the Church of the Gentiles* [Cambridge, 1939], p. 173 n.).

[64] The participle (ἀνακαινούμενον) is in the present tense. Cf. Rom. 12:2, "be ye transformed by the renewing (ἀνακαίνωσις) of your mind."

[65] Cf. 2 Cor. 3:18.

[66] Lightfoot (*ad loc.*) quotes from Philo, *On the Making of the World*, 6, where the word (λόγος) of God is said to be "the archetypal exemplar, the

Adam is now seen as the "old man" who must be discarded, in order that the believer may put on the new man, the second Adam. Nor is there any doubt about the identity of the second Adam; as Paul had already told the Corinthian Christians, "the first man Adam became a living soul; the last Adam a life-giving spirit... the first man was from earth, earthy; the second man is from heaven... and as we have worn the image of the man of earth, we shall also wear the image of the heavenly Man"[67] (1 Cor. 15:45 ff.). The second Adam, that is to say, is Christ. This appears quite explicitly in Gal. 3:27 where, instead of telling his readers (as here) that they have put on "the new man", Paul says directly: "as many of you as were baptized into Christ did put on Christ."[68] To "put on" Christ is the necessary corollary of being "in Christ."

The conception of Christ as the second Adam, head of a new creation[69] as the first Adam was of the old creation, is thoroughly Biblical, and there is no need to look for possible Iranian sources of it, as has sometimes been done. The age to come is pictured as a new creation in the OT[70] and in post-Biblical Judaism,[71] and in that new creation (as in the old) dominion is bestowed by God upon "one like unto a son of man."[72] The consentient testimony

---

'form' of 'forms' " (ἰδέα τῶν ἰδεῶν), and where the first man is described as the "image of the Image" (εἰκὼν εἰκόνος). The words "him that created him" do not, of course, imply that Christ personally is a created being, although He is the "new man" whom believers have "put on"; the new man who is created is the new personality that each believer becomes when he is reborn as a member of the new creation whose source of life is Christ. Cf. Eph. 4:23 f.: "be renewed in the spirit of your mind, and put on the new man (καινός, not νέος as here), that after God hath been created in righteousness and holiness of truth." See p. 105, n. 53. Cf. also Ignatius, To the Ephesians, 20:1.

[67] According to C. H. Dodd, Paul's "doctrine of the heavenly Man, or Second Adam, has behind it the primitive 'Son of Man' Christology. The heavenly Man is the 'new man' which the believer assumes in becoming a member of the Church, and the 'perfect man' into which the entire Church grows up (Col. 3:10–11; Eph. 4:13)" (According to the Scriptures [London, 1953], p. 121).

[68] With this indicative compare the imperative of Rom. 13:14, "put ye on the Lord Jesus Christ."

[69] Cf. the καινὴ κτίσις of 2 Cor. 5:17; Gal. 6:15.

[70] E.g., in Isa. 65:17.

[71] See the exhaustive discussion by W. D. Davies in Paul and Rabbinic Judaism, pp. 36 ff.

[72] Dan. 7:13. There are possible contacts, too, with Ezek. 1:26 ("upon the likeness of the throne was a likeness as the appearance of a man upon it above"); Ps. 84:17 ("... the man of thy right hand, ... the son of man whom thou madest strong for thyself"). See J. Bowman, "The Background of the Term 'Son of Man' ", ExT lix (1947–8), pp. 283 ff.

of the NT is that this "one like unto a son of man" is He who became incarnate in Jesus of Nazareth.[73] While the presentation of Christ as the second Adam is predominantly Pauline in the NT, it is not exclusively so; it may be traced in the Gospels,[74], in Hebrews,[75] and in Revelation.[76] As the first Adam's posterity, by virtue of their solidarity with him in the old creation, are involved in his transgression, so the people of Christ, by virtue of their solidarity with Him in the new creation, share the redemption and eternal life which He has procured.[77] Thus, as the Puritan Thomas Goodwin put it, "there are but two men who are seen standing before God, Adam and Jesus Christ; and these two men have all other men hanging at their girdles."

One result of the putting on of the new man is a new and true knowledge. The "knowledge" that was held out to the Colossians by their would-be teachers was a distorted and imperfect thing in comparison with the full knowledge available to those who, through their union with Christ, had been transformed by the renewing of their minds. This full knowledge was, in short, nothing less than the knowledge of God in Christ, the highest knowledge that is accessible to men.

11 It is not only the old habits and attitudes that are abolished in this new creation. The barriers that divided men from one another are abolished as well. There were racial barriers, like that between Gentile[78] and Jew (that was a religious barrier too, as the reference to circumcision and uncircumcision indicates). There were cultural barriers, which divided Scythians and other barbarians from those who shared in the Graeco-Roman civilization of the Mediterranean world. There were social barriers, such as that between slaves and freemen. Outside the Christian fellow-

---

[73] *Cf. Acts* in NICNT, pp. 165 ff., 362.

[74] *E.g.*, in the Synoptic temptation narratives, where a comparison and contrast are implied between the first Adam's failure in the garden and the second Adam's victory in the wilderness. (Note the reference to the beasts in Mark 1:13.)

[75] Especially in Heb. 2:6 ff., where Ps. 8:4 ff., which echoes the creation narrative of Gen. 1:26 ff., is applied to Christ.

[76] *E.g.*, Rev. 1:13 ff.

[77] *Cf.* Rom. 5:12 ff.

[78] Here, as elsewhere (*e.g.*, Rom. 1:16; 2:9 f.; 3:9; 1 Cor. 1:24; 10:32; 12:13; Gal. 3:28). Ἕλλην is used in the wider sense of Gentile as opposed to Jew.

ship these barriers stood as high as ever, and there were Christians on the one side and on the other. From the viewpoint of the old order these Christians were classified in terms of their position on this side or that of the barriers. But within the community of the new creation—"in Christ"—these barriers were irrelevant; indeed, they did not exist.

There are other places in the Pauline letters where similar subdivisions of the human family are listed; e.g. in Rom. 1:14, where the apostle speaks of himself as "debtor both to Greeks and to Barbarians, both to the wise and to the foolish" (in other words, to all sorts and conditions of men); and in Gal. 3:28, where he says that for those who have been baptized into Christ and have put on Christ "there can be neither Jew nor Greek, there can be neither slave nor freeman, there can be no male and female." This latter passage is closely similar to the one we are considering at present, but in Gal. 3:28 the choice of antitheses is apparently made with a view to overthrowing the threefold privilege which a pious Jew recalls morning by morning when he thanks God that He did not make him a Gentile, a slave or a woman.[79]

The obliteration in Christ of the old distinction between Jew and Gentile, between circumcised and uncircumcised, was one of the most remarkable achievements of the gospel within a few decades. The wonder of it is specially elaborated in the second and third chapters of Ephesians. No iron curtain of the present day presents a more forbidding barrier than did the middle wall of partition which separated Jew from Gentile. As to the Galatians, so to the Colossians it was no doubt necessary for Paul to emphasize the abolition of the distinction between Jew and Gentile in view of the Jewish stamp of the teaching which he was countering in the one case as in the other. "There is no distinction between Jew and Greek"[80] either in respect of their need of salvation or in respect of the grace of God, bestowed impartially on both; "for God hath shut up all unto disobedience, that he might have mercy upon all."[81] Natural and racial idiosyncrasies may survive, but in such a way as to contribute to the living variety of the people of Christ, not so as to perpetuate any difference in spiritual status.

---

[79] Cf. S. Singer, *Authorised Daily Prayer Book* (London, 1939), pp. 5 f.
[80] Rom. 10:12; cf. Rom. 3:22 f.
[81] Rom. 11:32.

The two terms "barbarian" and "Scythian" are not set in contrast with each other like "Greek" and "Jew", or "bondman" and "freeman." Rather both "barbarian" and "Scythian" are set in implied contrast to such a term as "Greek" used in its cultural sense. Greeks divided mankind into two main categories, Greeks and barbarians. As the area of Greek civilization spread—especially after the Roman conquest, when "captured Greece led her savage captor captive"—so people like the Romans, who were not Greeks by nationality, came to be included in the wider Graeco-Roman civilization of the Empire, outside which were the barbarians. Among these barbarians the Scythians had for long been looked upon as particularly outlandish. Since the Scythian invasion of the "Fertile Crescent" towards the end of the seventh century B.C.,[82] these people's name had become a by-word for uncultured barbarians. In the fifth and fourth centuries B.C. Scythian slaves did police duty in Athens, and Scythian policemen are figures of fun in Attic comedy because of their uncouth ways and speech.[83] But the gospel overrides cultural frontiers; they have no place in a Christian church.

The same is true of the distinction between slave and freeman. For Greeks and Romans alike, a slave, legally speaking, was not a person but a piece of property. Aristotle could define a slave as "a living tool, as a tool is an inanimate slave."[84] But within the Christian community the slave, as much as the freeman, was a brother, for whom Christ died. Paul did something revolutionary when he sent Onesimus back to his former owner Philemon, "no longer as a slave, but as something more than a slave, a dear brother"—very dear to the apostle himself, but even more so now to Philemon, since to the previous temporal bond between them there was now added the bond which united them "in the Lord" (Philem. 16). Philemon might still receive obedience from Onesimus, but now it would be obedience gladly and willingly rendered by one Christian brother to another. The old relationship is transformed by the new. "We might say that the distinction of social function remains but the distinction of class is destroyed—because all are brothers in Christ. It is only when the latter is

---

[82] *Cf.* Zeph. 1:2 ff.; 2:4 ff.; Jer. 1:14 ff.; 4:5 ff.; Herodotus, *History*, i. 103 ff.
[83] *Cf.* Aristophanes, *Lysistrata* 451 ff.; *Thesmophoriazusae* 1017 ff.
[84] *Nicomachean Ethics* viii. 11. 6. See p. 139.

added to the former that snobbery is produced and ill-feeling is
bred between those of different social function."[85]

Perhaps this was the way in which the gospel made its deepest
impression on the pagan world. A slave might be a leader in a
Christian church by virtue of his spiritual stature, and freeborn
members of the church might humbly and gratefully accept his
direction.[86] In times of persecution slaves showed that they could
face the trial and suffer for their faith as courageously as freeborn
Romans. The slave-girl Blandina and her mistress both suffered
in the persecution which broke out against the churches of the
Rhone valley in A.D. 177, but it was the slave-girl who was the
hero of the persecution, impressing friend and foe alike as a
"noble athlete" in the contest of martyrdom.[87] And in the arena
of Carthage in A.D. 202 a profound impression was made on the
spectators when the Roman matron Perpetua stood hand-in-hand
with her slave Felicitas, as both women faced a common death for
a common faith.[88] What real difference could there be for a
Christian between bond and free?[89]

Nor has the time gone by when this note required to be sounded.
Our world is crossed and re-crossed by barriers of one kind and
another, and our life is scarred by the animosities cherished by
one side against the other. But in Christ these barriers must come
down—iron curtains, colour bars, class distinctions, national and
cultural divisions, political and sectarian partisanship. It is not
difficult to re-phrase, in terms of the divisions of modern life,
Paul's affirmation that "we were all baptized in one Spirit into
one body, whether Jews or Gentiles, whether slaves or freemen"
(1 Cor. 12:13). In the unity of that body there is no room for the
old cleavages: Christ is all, and in all. The Christ who lives in

---

[85] E. Best, *One Body in Christ*, p. 27. Similarly when Paul says in Gal.
3:28 that in Christ "there is no male and female," he does not mean that the
distinctive rôles and capacities of man and woman are abolished, but that in
Christ there is no inferiority of the one sex to the other, no difference in
spiritual status between them.

[86] The Roman bishops Pius (*c.* A.D. 150) and Callistus (217–222) were
apparently of servile origin.

[87] *Letter of the Churches of Vienne and Lyons*, quoted by Eusebius,
Ecclesiastical History v. 1.

[88] *The Passion of S. Perpetua* (ed. J. A. Robinson, Cambridge, 1891).

[89] Stoic humanitarianism held up the ideal of universal brotherhood in
which even slaves had equal rights. And we remember Epictetus. But did even
Stoicism produce a Blandina or a Felicitas?

each of His people is the Christ who binds them together in one. This "restoration of the original image of creation"[90] will be universally displayed on the day when the sons of God are revealed; but how good and pleasant it is when, as far as in us lies, we can display it in our Christian brotherhood here and now as an example to this divided world far more eloquent than all our preaching, so that men are constrained to confess, as they did in earlier days: "See how these Christians love one another!"[91]

---

[90] J. A. T. Robinson, *The Body*, p. 83.
[91] Tertullian, *Apology* 39.

2. "PUT ON"

Ch. 3:12–17

12 Put on therefore, as God's elect, holy and beloved,
   a heart of compassion, kindness, lowliness, meekness,
   longsuffering;
13 forbearing one another, and forgiving each other, if
   any man have a complaint against any; even as the
   Lord[92] forgave you, so also do ye:
14 and above all these things *put on* love, which is the
   bond of perfectness.[93]
15 And let the peace of Christ rule in your hearts, to
   the which also ye were called in one body; and be
   ye thankful.
16 Let the word of Christ[94] dwell in you richly;[95] in all
   wisdom teaching and admonishing one another with
   psalms *and* hymns *and* spiritual songs, singing with
   grace in your hearts unto God.
17 And whatsoever ye do, in word or in deed, *do* all
   in the name of the Lord Jesus, giving thanks to God
   the Father through him.

As those who have put on the new man, the apostle continues,
put on those qualities which are characteristic of him. Those
qualities, as we consider them, are seen to be the qualities which
were preeminently displayed in the life of Christ; no wonder, then,
that when Paul in another place wishes to commend to his readers
the whole body of Christian graces, he sums them up by saying:
"put on the Lord Jesus Christ."[96]

---

[92] P⁴⁶ A B D G and the Latin Bible exhibit "the Lord" (ὁ κύριος); ℵ * has
"God" (ὁ θεός); Cod. 33 with the Armenian version and one citation in
Augustine have "God in Christ" (ὁ θεὸς ἐν χριστῷ, under the influence of Eph.
4:32); the other witnesses to the text have "Christ" (ὁ χριστός), as in ARV
margin.

[93] The Western manuscripts D* F G read "the bond of unity (ἑνότητος) ,
a reading which had the support of Richard Bentley.

[94] The ancient authorities which, according to ARV margin, read "the word
of the Lord" are ℵ *, the Coptic (Bohairic) version and Clement of Alexandria;
those which read "the word of God" are A C* 33 and the Ethiopic version.

[95] On the punctuation of this verse see pp. 283 f. (with n. 114).

[96] Rom. 13:14.

279

12 Men and women who are God's chosen people—His choice souls, whom He has set apart for Himself and on whom He has placed His love—should inevitably exhibit something of His nature.[97] Jesus made this point in the Sermon on the Mount, when He said that the peacemakers would be known as the sons of God and that the sons of God ought to be merciful because their heavenly Father is merciful.[98] So here, and probably by way of echoing the teaching of Jesus, Paul tells his readers to "put on" a compassionate heart, kindness, humility, gentleness and patience —graces that were perfectly blended in the character and conduct of Christ.

13 Mutual forbearance, mutual tolerance, mutual forgiving-ness, should mark all their relations with one another.[99] Did not Jesus Himself inculcate the principle of unwearying and unceasing forgiveness, "until seventy times seven"?[100] More than that, had they themselves not received His forgiveness, in far greater measure than they were ever likely to have to emulate in forgiving others? The Teacher of unlimited forgiveness had taught His lesson by example and not only by precept. In His teaching, too, He had made it clear that those who seek the forgiveness of God must be ready to forgive others[101]—not that their forgiveness of others could be the basis of God's forgiveness of them (for God's forgiveness is ever prior to ours); but that an unforgiving spirit is a barrier to the reception of God's forgiveness. So, in a parallel passage in Eph. 4:32, Paul bids his readers to be kind and tender-hearted one to another, "forgiving each other, even as God also in Christ forgave you." In fact, he reproduces Jesus' insistence on the close connection between God's forgiveness of us and our

---

[97] *Cf.* Eph. 4:32; 5:1.

[98] Matt. 5:9; Luke 6:36. For χρηστότης ("kindness") see p. 52, n. 14 (on Eph. 2:7); for ταπεινοφροσύνη ("lowliness") see p. 88, n. 5 (on Eph. 4:2); for μακροθυμία ("longsuffering") see p. 88, n. 6 (on Eph. 4:2).

[99] The succession of present participles *(ἀνεχόμενοι ἀλλήλων, καὶ χαριζόμενοι ἑαυτοῖς...)* is characteristic of extended ethical injunctions in NT. The use of the participle in an imperative sense was a Hellenistic development; *cf.* J. H. Moulton, *Grammar of NT Greek* i (Edinburgh, 1906), pp. 180 ff.; D. Daube, "Appended Note: Participle and Imperative in I Peter," in E. G. Selwyn, *The First Epistle of St. Peter* (London, 1946), pp. 467 ff.; H. G. Meecham, "The Use of the Participle for the Imperative in the NT", ExT lviii (1946–7), pp. 207 f. *Cf.* Rom. 12:9 ff.; 13:11; Eph. 4:2 f.; 1 Peter 2:18; 3:1, 7 ff.

[100] Matt. 18:22.

[101] *Cf.* Matt. 6:14 f.; 18:23 ff.; Mark 11:25.

forgiveness of others in a way that suggests that he knew the Lord's Prayer.[102]

The verb here used for forgiving (on God's part and on men's alike) is not the common word for "remission" or "letting off",[103] but a word of richer content,[104] the word which AV translates "frankly forgave" in our Lord's parable of the two debtors (Luke 7:32).

14 And above all, Paul adds, put on the grace which binds all these other graces together, the crowning grace of love.[105] In Gal. 5:6 love (*agape*) is the motive power of faith; in 1 Cor. 13:13 it is the supreme Christian grace; in Rom. 13:9 f. all the commandments are summed up in the single commandment: "Thou shalt love thy neighbour as thyself." Love is the fulfilment of the law of God because love does a neighbour nothing but good. In all these places Paul's ethic is directly dependent on the teaching of Jesus, according to which the whole Old Testament ethic hung upon the twin commandments of love to God and love to one's neighbour. God's love in Christ to men and men's answering love to Him are presupposed here as the basis of that mutual Christian love which the readers of the epistle are called upon to practise. And it is by such love that the body of Christ is built up.[106]

15 From love the apostle moves to peace. It is noteworthy that in Eph. 4:3 peace itself is the bond in which the unity of the Spirit is to be maintained (the same word being used as is applied

---

[102] *Cf.* Matt. 6:12; Luke 11:4. For the argument that Paul was acquainted with the Lord's Prayer see E. F. Scott, *The Epistles to the Colossians etc.* (MNTC, London, 1930), pp. 72 f.; A. M. Hunter, *Paul and his Predecessors* (London, 1940), p. 59; W. D. Davies, *Paul and Rabbinic Judaism* (London, 1948), p. 139.

[103] Gk. ἀφίημι (*cf.* p. 191, n. 54).

[104] Gk. χαρίζομαι (*cf.* p. 238, n. 62).

[105] Simplicius (*Epictetus* 208a) says that the Pythagoreans regarded friendship (Gk. φιλία) as the σύνδεσμος πασῶν τῶν ἀρετῶν, "the bond of all virtues." See p. 88, n. 7 (on Eph. 4:3).

[106] *Cf.* 1 Cor. 8:1, Eph. 4:15 f. "*Love is ... the link of the perfect life*, as it holds Christians together in fellowship under the strain of all common life. Love checks the selfish, hard tempers which keep people apart and thus militate against the maturing of good fellowship. Here τελειότης is the full expression of the divine life in the Community, devoid of bitter words and angry feelings, and freed from the ugly defects of immorality and dishonesty. The argument is a parallel to that of Matthew 5:43–48" (J. Moffatt, *Love in the NT* [London, 1929], p. 191). See also G. Quell and E. Stauffer, *Love* (Bible Key Words, London, 1949).

here in v. 14 to love as the bond of perfection).[107] This is the sort of thing which suggests that the relation between Colossians and Ephesians is not so much one of direct dependence by the latter on the former; it is rather the relation between two works which are the product of one mind around the same time. If Paul had the general idea of love and peace linked in his mind at this time with the idea of a unifying bond binding all the graces of Christian life together, that would sufficiently account for the similar, if divergent, modes of expression.

"Let the peace of Christ arbitrate[108] in your hearts," he says. When hostile forces have to be kept at bay, the peace of God garrisons the believer's heart, as in Phil. 4:7. But here the mutual relations of fellow-members of the body of Christ are in view; where differences threaten to spring up among them, the peace of Christ[109] must be accepted as arbitrator. For if the members are subject to Him, the peace which He imparts must regulate their relations with one another. It was not to strife but to peace that God called them in the unity of the body of Christ.[110] In a healthy body harmony prevails between the various parts. Christians who have been reconciled to God, who have peace with Him through Christ, should naturally manifest peace with one another. Strife is the inevitable result when men are out of touch with Him who is the one Source of true peace; but there is no reason why those who have accepted the peace which Christ established by His death on the cross should have any other than peaceful relations among themselves.

"And be thankful," he adds, for Christian behaviour (if we may say so again) can be viewed as the response of gratitude to the grace of God. One of the counts in Paul's indictment of the pagan world in the first chapter of Romans is that "knowing God, they

---

[107] Gk. σύνδεσμος. In Eph. 4:3 (ἐν τῷ συνδέσμῳ τῆς εἰρήνης), τῆς εἰρήνης is a genitive of definition.

[108] Gk. βραβεύω (occurring here only in the NT) is the simple verb from which the compound καταβραβεύω (rendered "rob ... of your prize" in Ch. 2:18, ARV) is formed.

[109] Deissmann describes ἡ εἰρήνη τοῦ χριστοῦ as the "mystical genitive"— the sense of the phrase being "the peace which is yours in union with Christ" (*Paul* [Eng. tr., London, 1926], p. 163).

[110] With the words "ye were called in one body" *cf.* the fuller expression in Eph. 4:4, "one body, and one Spirit, even as also ye were called in one hope of your calling." In both places the Church is the community of those whom God has called.

glorified him not as God, neither gave thanks" (Rom. 1:21). If then thanksgiving is God's undoubted due from all men for His gifts of creation and providence, how much more is it His due from those who have received the surpassing gift of His grace?

16 What does Paul mean by saying: "Let the word of Christ dwell in you richly"? Does "in you" mean "within you" (as individual Christians) or "among you" (as a Christian community)? Perhaps he would not have cared to be pinned down too firmly to either alternative, although if one of the two had to be accepted, the collective sense might be preferred in view of the context. Let there be ample scope for the proclamation of the Christian message and the impartation of Christian teaching in their meetings. Christian teaching must be based on the teaching of Jesus Himself; it must be unmistakably "the word of Christ."[111] And it would "dwell richly" in their midst when they came together and in their hearts as individuals if they paid heed to what they heard, bowed to its authority, assimilated its lessons and translated them into daily living.

In ARV the phrase "in all wisdom" is attached to the words which follow (as also in RSV), and not to those which precede (as in AV and ERV). ARV and RSV are probably right in this. The Colossian Christians, like those at Rome,[112] should be able to admonish one another; but such admonition and other forms of teaching should be given wisely. Admonition, however well-intentioned it may be, can provoke the opposite result to that which is desired if it be given in an unwise or tactless manner.

But were they, as the punctuation of ARV (with AV and ERV) suggests, to teach and admonish one another[113] in "psalms and hymns and spiritual songs"? Or should we take the verse as RSV does: "Let the word of Christ dwell in you richly, as you teach and admonish one another in all wisdom, and as you sing psalms and hymns and spiritual songs with thankfulness in your hearts to

---

111 This takes the genitive in ὁ λόγος τοῦ χριστοῦ to be subjective (the word proceeding from Christ); less probably it might be the objective genitive (the word concerning Christ).

112 *Cf.* Rom. 15:14.

113 ARV margin suggests the alternative rendering: "teaching and admonishing *yourselves.*" But Gk. ἑαυτούς may in the Hellenistic period have the sense of ἀλλήλους (as in v. 13, χαριζόμενοι ἑαυτοῖς). A papyrus occurrence of this usage (*P. Oxy.* 115) is quoted by Deissmann, *Light from the Ancient East* (London, 1927), p. 176.

God"?[114] There is some plausibility in RSV's punctuation, but it involves an overweighting of the participial clause at the end of the verse.[115] In the parallel passage in Eph. 5:19 even RSV renders: "addressing one another in psalms and hymns and spiritual songs, singing and making melody to the Lord with all your heart" —which gives the same general sense as the commoner punctuation does in the present Colossians passage. But how could they teach and admonish one another in psalms and hymns and spiritual songs? We may find an explanation in Tertullian's description of the Christian love-feast at which, "after water for the hands and lights have been brought in, each is invited to sing to God in the presence of the others from what he knows of the holy scriptures or from his own heart."[116] Antiphonal praise or solo singing for mutual edification in their church meetings is probably what the apostle recommends.[117]

It is sometimes asked whether a strict threefold classification of praise is signified in the collocation of "psalms and hymns and spiritual songs." It is unlikely that any sharply demarcated division is intended, although the "psalms" might be drawn from the OT Psalter (which has supplied a chief vehicle for Christian praise from primitive times),[118] the "hymns" might be Christian canticles,[119] and the "spiritual songs" might be unpre-

---

[114] This is the punctuation given in Nestle's Greek text.

[115] Here, as in v. 13, it might be argued that the participles have imperatival force (see p. 280, n. 99).

[116] Tertullian, *Apology* 39. *Cf.* Pliny the Younger's account to the Emperor Trajan of the way in which the Christians of Bithynia met on a fixed day before dawn and "recited an antiphonal hymn to Christ as God" (*Epistles* x. 96).

[117] In 1 Cor. 14:26 Paul emphasizes that, when Christians come to their meetings prepared with a psalm or any other spiritual exercise, they must have regard to the essential conditions of edification and good order.

[118] It is unlikely that the $\psi\alpha\lambda\mu\omicron\iota$ and $\H{\upsilon}\mu\nu\omicron\iota$ and $\H{\omega}\delta\alpha\iota$ $\pi\nu\epsilon\upsilon\mu\alpha\tau\iota\varkappa\alpha\iota$ should be confined to three types of composition found in the OT Psalter—*mizmorim*, *tehillim* and *shirim* respectively. Nor should the etymological force of the terms be pressed, as though $\psi\alpha\lambda\mu\acute{o}\varsigma$ inevitably meant a song sung to the accompaniment of a stringed instrument (psaltery or lute), the strings of which were plucked by the hand. While such plucking of the strings is the original sense of $\psi\acute{\alpha}\lambda\lambda\omega$ (found in the parallel passage in Eph. 5:19), it is used in NT with the meaning "to sing psalms" (1 Cor. 14:15; Jas. 5:13; so too, probably, in the LXX quotation in Rom. 15:9). *Cf.* p. 125, n. 25 (on Eph. 5:19).

[119] Such as the *Magnificat* (Luke 1:46 ff.) and *Benedictus* (Luke 1:68 ff.), which have also been used in Christian praise from early times. Other canticles or fragments of canticles have been detected here and there throughout NT, *e.g.* in Eph. 5:14; Phil. 2:6 ff.; 1 Tim. 3:16, in several places in Revelation, and even in the Prologue to St. John's Gospel.

meditated words sung "in the Spirit," voicing holy aspirations.[120]

It is plain, at any rate, that when early Christians came together for worship, they not only realized the presence of Christ in the breaking of the bread but also addressed their prayers and praises to Him in a manner which tacitly, and at times expressly, acknowledged Him as no less than God. If here Paul encourages the Colossians to "sing with grace in their hearts to *God*," he speaks in the parallel Ephesians passage of "singing and making melody with your heart to *the Lord*" (presumably meaning Christ).[121] The voice must express the praise of the heart if the singing is to be really addressed to God. RSV may well be right in taking "grace"[122] here in the sense of "thankfulness"—which is, as has already been said, our proper response to God's grace.[123]

17 Finally, these general injunctions are summed up in an exhortation of universal scope, covering every aspect of life. The NT does not contain a detailed code of rules for the Christian, like those which were elaborated with ever-increasing particularity in rabbinical casuistry. Codes of rules, as Paul explains elsewhere,[124] are suited to the period of immaturity when he and his readers were still under guardians; the son who has come to years of responsibility knows his father's will without having to be provided with a long list of "Do's" and "Don't's." What the NT does provide is those basic principles of Christian living which may be applied to all the situations of life as they arise.[125] Such a principle is enunciated here: "And whatever you do, in word or deed, do[126]

---

[120]   *Cf.* 1 Cor. 14:15, ψαλῶ τῷ πνεύματι. A good example of such "spiritual songs" is the collection of early Christian hymns curiously known as the *Odes of Solomon*; another composition of the same character is the *Song of the Star* preserved in Ignatius, *To the Ephesians*, 19.

[121]   *Cf.* the quotation from Pliny on p. 284, n. 116. Whereas here Colossians has "God" and Ephesians has "the Lord", in Col. 3:13 we find "the Lord" as against "God" in Eph. 4:32.

[122]   Westcott and Hort's Greek text punctuates (less satisfactorily) *after* "with grace" *(ἐν χάριτι)*, as though the meaning were "teaching and admonishing one another in psalms and hymns and spiritual songs with grace."

[123]   *Cf.* Heb. 12:28, where χάρις is necessary for the acceptable worship of God, "with reverence and awe."

[124]   *E.g.*, in Gal. 3:23–4:7 (*cf.* pp. 243 ff., on Col. 2:16 ff.).

[125]   *Cf.* 1 Cor. 10:21, "Whether therefore ye eat, or drink, or whatsoever ye do, do all to the glory of God."

[126]   The imperative is not expressed in the Greek; on its omission see H. G. Meecham in ExT lviii (1946–7), p. 208, n. 5.

everything in the name of the Lord Jesus, giving thanks to God the Father through him" (RSV).

When the twentieth-century Christian is confronted by a moral issue, he may not find in the Bible any explicit word of Christ relating to its particular details. But he can ask himself: What is the Christian thing to do here? Can I do this without compromising my Christian confession? Can I do it (that is to say) "in the name of the Lord Jesus"? (For His reputation is at stake in the lives and conduct of His known followers.) And can I thank God the Father through Him[127] that He has given me the opportunity of doing this thing? (The repeated emphasis on thanksgiving is note-worthy.) Questions like these, honestly faced, will commonly provide surer ethical guidance than special regulations may do. One can often get round special regulations; it is not so easy to get round so comprehensive a statement of Christian duty as this verse supplies. In NT and OT alike it is insisted that our relation to God embraces and controls the whole of life, and not only those occasions which are sometimes described as "religious" in a narrower sense of the term.

---

[127] For giving thanks to God through Christ *cf.* Rom. 1:8; 7:25; 16:27, and especially the parallel passage in Eph. 5:20, where the duty of thankfulness is emphasized (as here): "giving thanks always for all things in the name of our Lord Jesus Christ to God, even the Father."

3. "BE SUBJECT"

Chs. 3:18–4:1

The duty of mutual deference is inculcated in several of the ethical sections of the New Testament epistles. Thus, in the section of Ephesians which corresponds to Col. 3:18 ff., the Christian wife's deference to her husband is enjoined as a particular expression of the general duty of submissiveness which all Christians are encouraged to show to one another: "submitting yourselves one to another in the fear of Christ," says Paul, "and you wives [in particular] to your own husbands, as to the Lord" (Eph. 5:21 f.).[128]

Here in Colossians, however, there is a more definite paragraph division between the preceding general instructions and the more specific injunctions regarding the Christian household. Even so, in Chs. 3:18–4:1 we are shown how the general principles of Christian behaviour laid down in the foregoing paragraph (vv. 12–17) are to be applied in the special relationships of the Christian home.

Codes of domestic behaviour were not unknown in pagan antiquity, setting forth the mutual duties of husbands and wives, parents and children, masters and slaves, and so on. The Byzantine anthologist Stobaeus has some very interesting collections of quotations from ancient authors on these mutual duties.[129] Similar summaries of domestic duties are found in the New Testament,[130] and one of these summaries is given here. Its relation to the summaries given elsewhere in the epistles suggests that such instruction formed part of a fairly well defined body of catechesis imparted to Christian converts from early times.[131]

It is no doubt true that many of the ethical emphases in these

---

[128] There is, strictly speaking, no sentence division between verses 21 and 22 of Eph. 5 in the Greek text, although in printed texts the punctuation between the two usually indicates not merely a sentence division but a paragraph division. See p. 126, n. 28; p. 128, n. 29.

[129] Stobaeus, *Anthologies* IV, 19, 23–26.

[130] *Cf.* Eph. 5:22 ff.; 1 Pet. 2:13–3:7; 1 Tim. *passim*; Tit. 2:1–10. See K. Weidinger, *Die Haustafeln* (Leipzig, 1928), with review by W. K. L. Clarke, *New Testament Problems* (London, 1929), pp. 157 ff.; E. G. Selwyn, *The First Epistle of Peter*, pp. 419–439.

[131] *Cf.* pp. 264 f., with n. 37 (on Ch. 3:5 ff.).

early Christian summaries can be paralleled from Jewish and Stoic sources.[132] But to say that the mere addition of such phrases as "in the Lord" (vv. 18, 20) to the formularies already existing "Christianizes them in the simplest possible way"[133] is really to say everything, for a new and powerful dynamic is now introduced. If the Stoic disciple asked why he should behave in this particular way, his master would no doubt tell him that this was the way which accorded with the nature of things; when a Christian convert asks the same question, he is told that this is the behaviour which "is fitting in the Lord": he must live thus for Christ's sake. The added words may be exceedingly simple, but they transform the whole approach to ethics.

> Teach me, my God and King,
> In all things thee to see,
> And what I do in anything
> To do it as for thee.
>
> A man that looks on glass
> On it may stay his eye;
> Or if he pleaseth, through it pass,
> And then the heaven espy.
>
> All may of thee partake;
> Nothing can be so mean,
> Which with this tincture, 'for thy sake,'
> Will not grow bright and clean.
>
> A servant with this clause
> Makes drudgery divine;
> Who sweeps a room, as for thy laws,
> Makes that and the action fine.
>
> This is the famous stone
> That turneth all to gold;
> For that which God doth touch and own
> Cannot for less be told.[134]

Paul's inclusion of such summaries of domestic duties here and

---

[132] Cf. C. H. Dodd's comparison of Paul's exposition of duties with the social ethics of Hierocles the Stoic (New Testament Studies [Manchester, 1953], pp. 116 f.).

[133] W. K. L. Clarke, op. cit., p. 159.

[134] George Herbert, The Elixir.

in Eph. 5:22 ff.[135] shows "a sense of the values of ordinary family life."[136] It is in the closest and most familiar relationships of daily living that the reality of Christianity will be manifest, if at all.

(a) *Wives and Husbands*

Ch. 3:18–19

> 18 Wives, be in subjection to your husbands, as is fitting in the Lord.
> 19 Husbands, love your wives, and be not bitter against them.

The household duties are here divided into three correlative pairs. First come the mutual duties of wives and husbands.

18 The wife is to take a place of subordination to her husband, for that is fitting not only (as others taught) in the natural order, but also within the new fellowship of those who own Christ as Lord. Paul does not suggest here or anywhere else that the woman is naturally or spiritually inferior to the man, or the wife to the husband. But he does hold that there is a divinely instituted hierarchy in the order of creation, and in this order the place of the wife comes next after that of her husband.[137] The Christian wife should therefore recognize and accept her subordinate place in this hierarchy, "as is fitting."[138] This phrase has a thoroughly Stoic ring about it; but the injunction ceases to be Stoic when Paul

---

[135] There is no need to see a dependence of Ephesians on Colossians here. Both reproduce a common Christian catechesis——Colossians in a more skeletal form, Ephesians with considerable expansion.

[136] C. H. Dodd, *New Testament Studies*, p. 81. But we do not see so great a contrast between the attitude of these two passages and that of 1 Cor. 7:32–34 as Dodd suggests—or any necessity to account for the change by Paul's "second conversion" or by an eschatological reorientation. The emphasis of 1 Cor. 7 may be partly due to the actual situation at Corinth.

[137] *Cf.* 1 Cor. 11:3, 7–9. This hierarchical argument for the submission of wives is made more explicit in Eph. 5:23 f.: "for man is the head of the woman just as Christ is the head of the church, He Himself being the Saviour of the body. Indeed, just as the church is subordinate to Christ, so also let wives be to their husbands in everything." The expansion of marital duties in Eph. 5:22–33 in terms of the relation between Christ and the Church emerges naturally from the subject-matter of Ephesians. See p. 129 with n. 31.

[138] Gk. ὡς ἀνῆκεν. The Stoics regularly referred to the ethical duties as τὰ καθήκοντα, "the things that are fitting" (*cf.* Rom. 1:28). See C. H. Dodd, *op. cit.*, p. 116.

baptizes it into Christ by adding the words, "in the Lord."[139] By treating the relation between the sexes in this context, Paul (contrary to much popular opinion) places the essential dignity of women in general and of wives in particular on an unshakable foundation.[140]

19 The wife's subordination to her husband has as its counterpart the husband's duty of love[141] to his wife. This is not only a matter of affectionate feeling or sexual attraction; it involves his active and unceasing care for her well-being. The addition "and be not bitter against them"[142]—don't treat them harshly—indicates the meaning of the positive injunction more precisely by prohibiting the opposite attitude and behaviour. The parallel passage in Eph. 5:25–33 is amplified to form an ecclesiological excursus, where Christ's love for the church is viewed as the archetype of the husband's love for the wife, and the words of Gen. 2:24, already quoted by Jesus as setting forth the basic principle of the marital bond,[143] are glossed with the comment: "This mystery is a great one, but I quote it in reference to Christ and to the church."

(b) Children and Parents

Ch. 3:20–21

20 Children, obey your parents in all things, for this is well-pleasing in the Lord.

---

[139] Eph. 5:22 omits "as is fitting" and the preposition "in," thus suggesting that the wife's obedience to her husband should go side by side with her obedience to the Lord. The phrase ἐν κυρίῳ occurs four times in Colossians (Chs. 3:18, 20; 4:7, 17); it appears some forty times in the Pauline corpus. Examples of its application to domestic relationships are found in 1 Cor. 7:22, 39; Eph. 6:1; Philem. 16. It sums up the relationship existing between fellow-members of Christ—a relationship which does not supersede earthly relationships but subsumes them and lifts them on to a higher plane.

[140] Cf. J. Foster, "St. Paul and Women," ExT lxii (1950–51), pp. 376 ff.

[141] Gk. ἀγαπάω, the characteristic verb for Christian love, more than φιλέω (to "feel affection" or "show affection") or ἐράω (to "love with sexual desire").

[142] Gk. καὶ μὴ πικραίνεσθε πρὸς αὐτάς. Plutarch similarly uses a compound of this verb in his essay On the Control of Anger (457a), where he condemns those who "behave harshly towards (or rage bitterly against) women" (πρὸς γύναια διαπικραίνονται). For the general thought cf. TB Baba Metzia 59a: "Rab said: 'One should always be on his guard against wronging his wife, for since her tears are frequent she is quickly hurt'."

[143] Mark 10:7 f.

21 Fathers, provoke not[144] your children, that they be not discouraged.

20 Then come the mutual duties of children and parents. Children are enjoined to render complete obedience to their parents, as something which is acceptable or delightful "in the Lord." RSV, "for this pleases the Lord," is based on a slightly different reading.[145] The parallel injunction in Ephesians has a somewhat different wording—"Children, obey your parents in the Lord, for this is right" (Eph. 6:1)—but this need not be thought to modify the completeness of the obedience ("in all things"[146]) which is enjoined in Colossians. It is assumed that such obedience is pleasing to the Lord; Paul has a Christian family in view ("in the Lord"), and does not contemplate the situation where parental orders might be contrary to the law of Christ. In that situation the law of Christ must inevitably take precedence. In Ephesians the exhortation to children is reinforced by the quotation of the Fifth Commandment—"the first of the commandments which has a promise attached to it."

21 If children are exhorted to render obedience, fathers—or more generally parents[147]—are enjoined not to irritate their children lest they lose heart and come to think that it is useless trying to please their parents. Sir Robert Anderson has some wise remarks to make on this in a little-known book:

"The late Mr. Justice Wills, who combined the heart of a philanthropist with the brain of a lawyer, used to deplore the ill-advised legislation which so multiplies petty offences that high-spirited lads, without any criminal intention, are caught in the meshes of the criminal law. But the traps laid by modern bye-law legislation are few as compared with the 'don'ts' which confront the children of many a home during all their waking hours. And against this it is that the Apostle's 'Don't' is aimed: 'You fathers, don't irritate your children.'

---

144 Gk. μὴ ἐρεθίζετε. The parallel passage in Eph. 6:4 has the synonymous clause μὴ παροργίζετε, whence παροργίζετε has found its way into our present text in many authorities (ℵ A C D* and others) and extruded ἐρεθίζετε.

145 In v. 20 a few authorities (notably Cod. 81 and Clement of Alexandria) have τῷ κυρίῳ for ἐν κυρίῳ.

146 Gk. κατὰ πάντα, as in v. 22.

147 Gk. πατέρες ("fathers") may have the sense of parents, as in Heb. 11:23, where Moses "was hid three months by his parents" (ὑπὸ τῶν πατέρων αὐτοῦ).

"For the children his only precept is 'Obey your parents'; let parents see to it that they deserve obedience: and more than this, that they make obedience easy. The law, which for the Christian is summed up in the word 'love,' is formulated in 'thou shalt not' for the lawless and disobedient. And the 'thou-shalt-not's' of Sinai have their counterpart in the 'don't's' of the nursery. Grace teaches us to keep His commandments, law warns us not to break them. And it is on this latter principle that children are generally trained. 'Don't be naughty' is the nursery version of it. . . .

"William Carey . . . wrote to his son: 'Remember, a gentleman is the next best character to a Christian, and the Christian includes the gentleman.' And if a little of the effort used to teach the children not to be naughty were devoted to training them to be gentlemen and ladies, parents would come nearer to fulfilling the Apostolic precept!"[148]

Stobaeus follows up a consideration of the duty of children with a collection of passages from ancient authors under the general heading: "How fathers ought to behave to their children."[149] He quotes many sayings to much the same effect as Paul's injunction, including these two from Menander: "A father who is always threatening does not receive much reverence," and "One should correct a child not by hurting him but by persuading him." In the setting of this epistle, however, these ethical observations, good as they were in their pagan expression, are given a Christian significance and emphasis, which are made still more explicit in Eph. 6:4, where the positive injunction is added: "but bring them up in the discipline and instruction of the Lord" (RSV).

(c) Servants and Masters

Chs. 3:22–4:1

22   Servants, obey in all things them that are your masters according to the flesh; not with eye-service, as men-pleasers, but in singleness of heart, fearing the Lord:

23   whatsoever ye do, work heartily, as unto the Lord, and[150] not unto men;

---

[148] R. Anderson, *The Entail of the Covenant* (London, 1914), pp. 20 ff.

[149] *Anthologies* IV, 26.

[150] We should probably follow those texts (P^{46} B 177 1739 and the Sahidic Coptic) which omit "and" (*καί*). Among the authorities which exhibit "and," Cod. A and Clement of Alexandria add "doing service" (*δουλεύοντες*) after "unto men" (*ἀνθρώποις*).

24   knowing that from the Lord ye shall receive the recompense of the inheritance: ye serve the Lord Christ.[151]

25   For he that doeth wrong shall receive again for the wrong that he hath done: and there is no respect of persons.

1   Masters, render unto your servants that which is just and equal; knowing that ye also have a Master in heaven.

22-24   Christian slaves are next addressed. Both here and in Ephesians the injunctions to slaves are more extended than those to masters, and are accompanied by special encouragements. This, it has been suggested, is "a reflection of the social structure of these churches."[152] That may well be so. The companion Epistle to Philemon affords an illuminating commentary on the mutual duties of slaves and masters within the Christian fellowship, and the transforming effect of this fellowship upon their relationship.[153] The relationship belongs to this present temporary world-order; it is a relationship "according to the flesh."[154] In the higher and abiding relationship which is theirs in Christ, believing slaves and masters are brothers. The slave-and-master relationship might persist in the home and business life; within the church it was swallowed up in the new relationship. Thus, a Christian slave might be recognized as an elder in the church by reason of his spiritual stature, and receive due deference from his Christian master. But the Christian slave would not presume on this new relationship or make it an excuse for serving his master less assiduously; on the contrary, he would serve him the more faithfully because of this new relationship. And if a Christian slave had an unbelieving master, he would serve him the more faithfully now because the reputation of Christ and Christianity was bound

---

151   For the dative "the Lord Christ", dependent upon "ye serve" *(τῷ κυρίῳ χριστῷ δουλεύετε)*, a few Western authorities (*e.g.* D F Ambrosiaster) have the genitive "of the (our) Lord (Jesus) Christ," dependent upon "the inheritance," with a following relative pronoun *ᾧ*, yielding the reading *τῆς κληρονομίας τοῦ κυρίου (ἡμῶν Ἰησοῦ) Χριστοῦ, ᾧ δουλεύετε* ("the inheritance of the [our] Lord [Jesus] Christ, whom ye serve").

152   Deissmann, *Paul*, p. 243. *Cf.* G. B. Caird, *The Apostolic Age* (London, 1955), p. 103. In the "house-tables" of 1 Peter (2:18–3:8) the instructions to slaves (2:18–25) have no correlative instructions to masters.

153   But there is no ground for thinking that Paul had Onesimus specially in his mind in the present passage.

154   Gk. *κατὰ σάρκα* (v. 22); so in Eph. 6:5.

up with the quality of his service.[155] Slaves in general might work hard when the master's eye or the foreman's eye was on them;[156] they would slack off as soon as they could get away with it. And why not? They owed their masters nothing. Far more culpable is the attitude of the modern "clock-watcher," who has contracted to serve his employer and receives an agreed remuneration for his labour. But the Christian slave—or the Christian employee today —has the highest of all motives for faithful and conscientious performance of duty; he is above all things else a servant of Christ, and he will work first and foremost so as to please Him.[157] Not fear of an earthly master, but reverence[158] for "the Lord Christ," should be the primary motive. This would encourage Christian servants to work eagerly and zestfully even for a master who was harsh, unconscionable and ungrateful; for they would not expect their thanks from him, but from Christ.[159] A rich recompense is the assured heritage[160] of all who work for Christ; and the Christian servant can work for Christ by serving his earthly employer in such a manner as to "adorn the doctrine of God our Saviour in all things" (Tit. 2:10).

25 The promise of reward is expanded in Eph. 6:8 in these words: "knowing that whatsoever good thing each one doeth, the same shall he receive again from the Lord, whether he be bond or free." Here, however, we find, expressed in similar terms, the warning which corresponds to the promise of Ephesians: "he that doeth wrong shall receive again[161] the wrong that he hath done."

---

[155] Cf. 1 Tim. 6:1 f.; Tit. 2:9 f.; 1 Pet. 2:18 ff.

[156] This is the usual interpretation of ὀφθαλμοδουλεία ("eye-service"), here and in Eph. 6:6. C. F. D. Moule, however, suggests that the meaning is not "while the master's eye is on you" but "with reference to what the eye can see" —i.e. what is external. Eye-service will thus (as lip-service) refer to the eye (as to the lip) of the servant. Cf. "A Note on ὀφθαλμοδουλία," ExT lix (1947–8), p. 250. For ἀνθρωπάρεσκοι ("men-pleasers") see p. 138, n. 6 (on Eph. 6:6).

[157] Cf. A. Richardson, The Biblical Doctrine of Work (London, 1952), passim.

[158] Gk. φοβούμενοι τὸν κύριον (v. 22); cf. Eph. 6:5, μετὰ φόβου καὶ τρόμου.

[159] "Knowing" (Gk. εἰδότες) in v. 24 (as in the following injunction to masters in Ch. 4:1) suggests that Paul is invoking a pattern of teaching well known to Christians (cf. J. Munck, Paulus und die Heilsgeschichte [Copenhagen, 1954], p. 119, n. 103).

[160] For the thought of the "inheritance" (κληρονομία) cf. Gal. 3:18; 4:1 ff.; Eph. 1:14; 5:5, etc. Here it is brought into close association with the most practical issues of daily life.

[161] So ARV margin, rightly, omitting "for" of ARV text. (Gk. κομίσεται ὃ ἠδίκησεν.)

The judgment on disobedience is as certain as the reward for faithfulness. While salvation in the Bible is according to grace, judgment is always according to works, whether good or bad, for unbeliever and believer alike. It is to believers that Paul writes elsewhere: "we must all be made manifest before the judgment-seat of Christ; that each one may receive the things done in the body, according to what he hath done, whether it be good or bad."[162] What is clearly stated there is probably implied here too—that, while the sowing is here, the reaping is hereafter. It may seem difficult to understand how one who by grace is blessed with God's salvation in Christ may yet before the divine tribunal "receive again the wrong that he has done." But it is in accordance with the teaching of Scripture throughout that judgment should "begin at the house of God";[163] and even if the tribunal be a domestic one, for members of the family of God, it is none the less a solemn reality.

It is noteworthy that here the statement "there is no respect of persons"[164] is attached to the injunction to slaves, whereas in Eph. 6:9 it is attached to the injunction to masters. As between masters and servants God arbitrates with impartial fairness. So in the OT legislation similar impartiality was prescribed in lawsuits between rich and poor: "thou shalt not respect the person of the poor, nor honour the person of the mighty" (Lev. 19:15).

---

[162] 2 Cor. 5:10; *cf.* Rom. 14:10–12; 1 Cor. 3:12 ff.; 4:4 f.

[163] 1 Pet. 4:17; *cf.* 1 Cor. 11:29–32; Heb. 10:30 f.

[164] Gk. προσωπολημψία. *Cf.* p. 138, n. 7 (on Eph. 6:9); also *Acts* in NICNT, p. 224, n. 38 (on Acts 10:34).

CHAPTER IV

1 If slaves like Onesimus have their duties, so have masters like Philemon; they must treat their slaves fairly and justly. They are masters on earth, but they themselves have a Master in heaven; let them treat their servants with the same consideration as they themselves hope to receive at the hands of their heavenly Master. Such consideration is the opposite of the threatening or browbeating attitude which is forbidden in Eph. 6:9. No command is given for the manumission of slaves. Onesimus' master, to be sure, receives a broad hint of what is expected of him in this respect (Philem. 12–14); but at the same time it is made clear that the whole virtue of such an act lies in its not being done "as of necessity, but of free will."

Paul does not give detailed advice for the complexities of modern industrialism, nor could he be expected to do so. For that matter, he does not even give detailed advice for the critical situations which might arise in the first century between master and slave, when one or both belonged to the Christian fellowship. Had he given such advice, in place of the exhortations which he does give, we in our day should have derived less help from these ethical sections than in fact we do. His teaching embodies basic and abiding Christian principles, which can be applied in the changing social structures of every time and place.[1]

---

[1] *Cf.* A. Richardson, *The Biblical Doctrine of Work*, p. 50.

296

4. "WATCH AND PRAY"

2 Continue steadfastly in prayer, watching therein with thanksgiving;

3 withal praying for us also, that God may open unto us a door for the word, to speak the mystery of Christ, for which I am also in bonds;

4 that I may make it manifest, as I ought to speak.

5 Walk in wisdom toward them that are without, redeeming the time.

6 Let your speech be always with grace, seasoned with salt, that ye may know how ye ought to answer each one.

2 Prayer and thanksgiving can never be dissociated from each other in Christian life. The remembrance of former mercies not only produces spontaneous praise and worship; it is also a powerful incentive to renewed believing prayer. And believing prayer will be persevering prayer. "Persevere in prayer," says Paul, "maintaining your watchfulness therein." Our Lord's words to His disciples, "Watch and pray that you may not enter into temptation,"[2] have their message for His people at all times. He taught "that men ought always to pray and never lose heart";[3] and the man of persistent prayer is the man who is constantly awake[4] and alive to the will of God and the need of the world, and constantly prepared to give account of himself and his stewardship to his Master. The parallel passage in Eph. 6:18 enjoins "with all prayer and supplication praying at all seasons in the Spirit, and watching[5] thereunto in all perseverance and supplication for all the saints." And there as here the exhortation to general prayer is immediately followed by a request for prayer on the apostle's own behalf.

---

[2] Matt. 26:41 // Mark 14:38 // Luke 22:40, 46.

[3] Luke 18:1. For the use of προσκαρτερέω in relation to prayer cf. Acts 1:14; 2:42; 6:4; Rom. 12:12. In Eph. 6:18 the noun προσκαρτέρησις is used in a similar context (cf. p. 153, n. 34).

[4] For this catechetical use of γρηγορέω cf. Acts 20:31; 1 Cor. 16:13; 1 Thess. 5:6; 1 Pet. 5:8; Rev. 3:2 f. Cf. E. G. Selwyn, *The First Epistle of St. Peter*, pp. 439 ff.

[5] Here the verb is not γρηγορέω but the synonymous ἀγρυπνέω (cf. Mark 13:33 // Luke 21:36). See p. 153, n. 33.

3-4 "Pray for us also,"[6] says Paul. The plural pronoun no doubt includes his friends and companions who are mentioned later in this chapter; but he is thinking primarily of his own spiritual need, as is evident from the later clauses of the present sentence, in which he slips into the first person singular. "Pray for us also," he says; "pray God to open a door for the message, for the utterance of His purpose once kept secret and now revealed.[7] It is for the sake of this divine purpose that I am a prisoner; pray that I may publish it openly in the words which I ought to speak."[8]

The idea of a door being opened for the gospel message (and for the messenger) to enter is found elsewhere in the NT; we may compare 1 Cor. 16:9 ("a great door and effectual is opened unto me") and 2 Cor. 2:12 ("a door was opened unto me in the Lord").[9] Deissmann thinks that Paul may have found the expression current in general speech;[10] this may very well be so, as we are familiar with similar phrases in contemporary idiom. That an open door was indeed set before Paul in Rome is evident from the closing words of Acts.[11] The opportunities were great, but the circumstances called for special wisdom, whether Paul was proclaiming the kingdom of God and telling the story of Jesus day by day to those who frequented his lodging, or looking forward to his appearance before the imperial tribunal to give an account of his missionary activity. So much might hang on the way in which he made his defence there that he was consciously in need of special prayer, and for this he asks.

5 Reverting from his personal situation to the general principles of Christian conduct, he bids his readers behave themselves

---

[6] For such requests for personal remembrance in prayer *cf.* Rom. 15:30 ff.; Eph. 6:19 f.; 1 Thess 5:25; 2 Thess. 3:1 f.

[7] This is the force of "the mystery"; *cf.* Ch. 1:26 (p. 218 with n. 168).

[8] These two verses of Colossians are followed very closely by Eph. 6:19 f.: "(pray) too for me, that utterance may be granted me as I open my mouth with all freedom of speech to make known the 'mystery' of the gospel—for the sake of which I am a prisoner, and yet an ambassador at the same time—that I may speak freely therein, as I ought to speak." See p. 154, with nn. 36, 37.

[9] *Cf.* also Acts 14:27; Rev. 3:8. It has been suggested that in Col. 4:3 θύρα τοῦ λόγου does not mean (as in 1 Cor. 16:9; 2 Cor. 2:12) an opportunity to preach the gospel but access by Paul to the right thing to say (*cf.* E. Lohmeyer, MK, *ad loc.*; contrariwise, E. Percy, *Probleme der Kolosser- und Epheserbriefe*, pp. 393 f.). This is a less likely interpretation.

[10] *Light from the Ancient East*, p. 301, n. 2.

[11] A similar situation (whether the same one or not) is pictured in Phil. 1:12 ff.

wisely in the sight of non-Christians. Distorted accounts of Christian behaviour and belief were in circulation; it was important that Christians should give no colour to these calumnies, but should rather give the lie to them by their ordinary manner of life. Even today it is true that the reputation of the gospel is bound up with the conduct of those who claim to have experienced its saving power. Non-Christians may not read the Bible or listen to the preaching of the word of God; but they can see the lives of those who do, and form their judgment accordingly. Let Christians then make full use of this present season of opportunity. Here the exhortation to "redeem the time"[12] seems to have special application to their duty to unbelieving neighbours; in Eph. 5:15 f.[13] it seems to have a more general reference to the duty of Christian prudence. In either case, Paul wishes to emphasize that, while he has a special opportunity of witness at the heart of the empire, every Christian has his opportunity and should use it to the full while it lasts.

6 The grace and wisdom that Paul desires for his own utterance he enjoins upon his readers too. They never know when they may be called upon to give an answer in regard to their faith, whether in private conversation or more publicly. If they practise grace of speech, it will not desert them when they find themselves suddenly confronted by the necessity of defending their Christian belief. Nor will their speech be acceptable if it is insipid.[14] Those who are the salt of the earth[15] may reasonably be expected to have some savour about their language.[16] In pagan usage "salt" in such a context means "wit";[17] here perhaps it is rather the saving grace

---

[12] For τὸν καιρὸν ἐξαγοραζόμενοι (ARV margin, "buying up the opportunity") here and in Eph. 5:16, see R. M. Pope, "Studies in Pauline Vocabulary," ExT xxii (1910–11), pp. 552 ff. The common rendering is inadequate; καιρός implies a critical epoch, a special opportunity, which may soon pass; "grasp it," says the apostle; "buy it up while it lasts."

[13] "Be careful how you live; live like wise men, not like fools, making good use of this present opportunity, because the days are evil (and so the opportunity may soon be ended)." Cf. p. 124, n. 22.

[14] Cf. J. B. Phillips, "Speak pleasantly to them, but never sentimentally" (Letters to Young Churches [London, 1947], pp. 125 f.).

[15] Cf. Matt. 5:13; Mark 9:49 f.; Luke 14:34 f.

[16] Since salt prevents corruption, this injunction has a parallel in Eph. 4:29: "let no corrupt speech (λόγος σαπρός) proceed from your mouth, but language which is good for building up the hearers in accordance with their need, that it may give them grace (χάρις)."

[17] Cf. Lat. sales Attici, meaning "Attic wit."

of common sense. The replies of some of the early martyrs to their interrogators may illustrate what is meant; there is no lack of this kind of salt, for example, in the narrative of the trial of Justin Martyr and his companions. "No right-thinking person," said Justin, "turns away from true belief to false." "Do what you will," say his companions, "for we are Christians, and Christians do not offer sacrifice to idols."

Moreover, the conversation of Christians must not only be "opportune as regards the time; it must also be appropriate as regards the person."[18] The importance attached in primitive Christianity to giving right answers to questions about the faith is evidenced by various passages in the Gospels,[19] as also by the exhortation in 1 Pet. 3:15, "Always be ready to defend your faith to anyone who asks you to give account of the hope that resides within you, and do it in a gentle and respectful manner."

---

[18] J. B. Lightfoot, *Colossians*, p. 233, on ἐν ἑκάστῳ (*ad loc.*).
[19] *Cf.* Matt. 10:19; Mark 13:11; Luke 12:12; 21:14.

V. PERSONAL NOTES

Ch. 4:7–17

1. PAUL'S MESSENGERS

Ch. 4:7–9

7 All my affairs shall Tychicus make known unto you, the beloved brother and faithful minister and fellow-servant in the Lord:

8 whom I have sent[20] unto you for this very purpose, that ye may know our state,[21] and that he may comfort your hearts;

9 together with Onesimus, the faithful and beloved brother, who is one of you. They shall make known unto you all things that *are done* here.

7–8 The reference to Tychicus is almost word for word identical with Eph. 6:21 f.[22] Evidently he was the bearer of the Epistle to the Ephesians as well as of this one, and possibly of a letter to Laodicea as well (see v. 16). Tychicus was probably Paul's special envoy on this occasion to the churches of provincial Asia which had been founded in the course of the apostle's Ephesian ministry. He was himself a native of the province of Asia, as we learn from Acts 20:4, where he appears in the list of delegates from Gentile churches who accompanied Paul to Palestine in A.D. 57 with those churches' gifts for their brethren in Jerusalem. He is also mentioned on two occasions as a messenger of Paul in the

---

[20] In English idiom, "I am sending" (ἔπεμψα is an instance of the "epistolary aorist").

[21] Gk. ἵνα γνῶτε τὰ περὶ ἡμῶν. The variant reading of TR, "that he may know your state" (ἵνα γνῷ τὰ περὶ ὑμῶν), is less suitable to the context. While, however, it could be said in Lightfoot's time that "the preponderance of ancient authority" was decidedly against it, is now known to be the reading of P46, and this fact must give us pause before we dismiss it too readily.

[22] While the practical identity of the two parallel passages has been used (*e.g.* by E. J. Goodspeed and C. L. Mitton) as an argument for the secondary character of Ephesians, such a self-conscious effort on the part of a "deutero-Paulinist" seems much less likely than the view that Paul repeated in a second letter the same words about the messenger as he had recently used in another letter to be carried to the same province by the same man. See C. F. D. Moule, "E. J. Goodspeed's Theory regarding the Origin of Ephesians," ExT lx (1948–9), pp. 224 f.

301

Pastoral Epistles (2 Tim. 4:12; Tit. 3:12). Paul speaks of him as a faithful colleague and helper[23] in his service for the Lord, who will give the Colossians all his news and strengthen and cheer their hearts.

9 Onesimus, unlike Tychicus, is not mentioned in Ephesians; he was bound for Colossae under the circumstances which we may learn in detail from the Epistle to Philemon.[24] Onesimus was a slave of Philemon, who was a member of the Colossian church. He had run away from his master, and in Rome[25] he came somehow into touch with Paul and through his ministry became a Christian. He quickly proved himself a devoted attendant and friend to the apostle while he remained with him, but when Tychicus' journey to Asia provided a suitable opportunity, Paul sent Onesimus along with him, so that he might return to Philemon "no longer as a slave but more than a slave, as a beloved brother" (Philem. 16). It was necessary that the difference which had parted two men who were now fellow-Christians should be resolved in reconciliation.

Onesimus was now in good standing as a church member (probably he was attached to one of the "house-churches" of Rome), and he would naturally receive from the Colossian church the same welcome as would be given to any other visiting Christian, especially one armed with a letter of commendation from an apostle. Naturally, since Philemon had been wronged personally, it was necessary in addition that a personal letter should be sent to him, persuading him to forgive and welcome his former slave. But Onesimus' welcome by the whole church at Colossae, on Paul's commendation, would be a powerful lever for Philemon's accept-

---

[23] He applies to Tychicus the term σύνδουλος ("fellow-slave") applied to Epaphras in Ch. 1:7 (see p. 182, n. 17). This term is omitted from the description of Tychicus in Eph. 6:21, but the idea that the omission is due to a later writer's unwillingness to appear to bring Paul down to Tychicus' level is far-fetched.

[24] See J. J. Müller, *The Epistles of Paul to the Philippians and to Philemon* (NICNT, Grand Rapids, 1955), pp. 157 ff.

[25] The argument that Onesimus would have been more likely to seek refuge in Ephesus, a city "comparatively near at hand ... with which he was no doubt already familiar, and which was of sufficient size to afford him all the security that he was likely to require" (G. S. Duncan, *St. Paul's Ephesian Ministry* [London, 1929], p. 73) may be countered by the surmise that "it is as likely that the fugitive slave, his pockets lined at his master's expense, made for Rome *because* it was distant, as that he went to Ephesus because it was near" (C. H. Dodd, *New Testament Studies* [Manchester, 1953], p. 95).

ance of him too. And the fact that the Epistle to Philemon has been preserved is sufficient evidence for the success of Paul's plea.

Whether Onesimus in fact played such a part in bringing together the several units which made up the Pauline corpus of letters as has been ingeniously argued by a well-known scholar of our day,[26] need not concern us here. Nor need we stay to consider whether he could have been identical with the Onesimus whom Ignatius of Antioch names as bishop of Ephesus fifty years later.[27] Here Paul presents him to the Colossian Christians as one of themselves, one who, along with Tychicus, will be able to answer all their questions about the apostle and his affairs.

---

[26] J. Knox, *Philemon among the Letters of Paul* (Chicago, 1935); *The Interpreter's Bible* xi (New York, 1955), pp. 557 ff. *Cf.* C. L. Mitton, *The Formation of the Pauline Corpus of Letters* (London, 1955), pp. 50 ff.; E. J. Goodspeed, *The Key to Ephesians* (Chicago, 1956), pp. xiv ff.

[27] Ignatius, *To the Ephesians* 1:3. The name Onesimus ("useful") was a very common type of slave-name. In the *Apostolic Constitutions* (vii. 46) Philemon's Onesimus appears as subsequently bishop of Beroea, but nothing can be built on this insecure foundation.

2. GREETINGS FROM PAUL'S COMPANIONS

Ch. 4:10–14

10 Aristarchus, my fellow-prisoner saluteth you, and Mark, the cousin of Barnabas (touching whom ye received commandments; if he come unto you, receive him),

11 and Jesus that is called Justus, who are of the circumcision: these only *are my* fellow-workers unto the kingdom of God, men that have been a comfort unto me.

12 Epaphras, who is one of you, a servant of Christ Jesus, saluteth you, always striving for you in his prayers, that ye may stand perfect and fully assured in all the will of God.

13 For I bear him witness, that he hath much labor for you, and for them in Laodicea, and for them in Hierapolis.

14 Luke, the beloved physician, and Demas salute you.

Greetings are now sent to the Colossian church from six Christian men who are in Paul's company while he is writing—three of Jewish birth (Aristarchus, Mark and Jesus Justus) and three of Gentile birth (Epaphras, Luke and Demas).

10 Aristarchus appears in the narrative of Acts as a native of Thessalonica, who was with Paul at Ephesus and was exposed to personal danger in the riot in the Ephesian theatre (Acts 19:29). Later he went to Jerusalem with Paul as one of the two delegates from the Church of Thessalonica (Acts 20:4), and accompanied him along with Luke when they set sail from Caesarea for Rome (Acts 27:2). It is not said explicitly in the narrative of Acts that he went as far as Rome, and some have thought that he stayed in the company of Paul and Luke only as far as Myra, where they changed boats (Acts 27:5 f.), and then went home to Thessalonica;[28] but we are probably to understand that he went the whole way with them.[29] At any rate, he was with Paul at this time (in Rome,

---

[28] So J. B. Lightfoot, *St. Paul's Epistle to the Philippians* (London, 1913), pp. 11, 35.

[29] So C. H. Dodd, *New Testament Studies*, p. 92. See *Acts* in NICNT, p. 501.

as we judge), and is described by Paul as his "fellow-prisoner"—
literally, his fellow-prisoner-of-war.[30] Aristarchus may have
shared Paul's captivity voluntarily, perhaps passing as his
servant.[31] One who looked upon himself as a soldier of Jesus
Christ, as Paul did,[32] would not unnaturally think of himself
during his captivity as a prisoner-of-war.

Greetings are also sent from Mark, another of Paul's companions
at the time. It is from this passage alone that we learn that Mark
was Barnabas's kinsman[33]—a piece of information which throws
light on the special consideration which Barnabas gives to Mark
in the narrative of Acts.[34] Some twelve years before he had
disgraced himself in Paul's eyes by deserting him and Barnabas at
Perga instead of going on with them to evangelize South Galatia;
by this time, however (no doubt in great measure owing to the
kindly tutelage of Barnabas, that true "son of encouragement"),
he had completely redeemed his reputation. Under what circumstances he had come to Rome we are not told. It may be that he
had already begun to accompany Peter as that apostle's interpreter
or aide-de-camp on his more extended ministry,[35] but it is unlikely
that Peter himself was in Rome at this time, for in that case we
might have expected some reference to him here.

The fact that Paul identifies Mark here in terms of his relationship to Barnabas suggests that the Colossian Christians knew
Barnabas well by name, even if they had never met him personally.[36]

They had already received some communication with regard to
Mark. It is perhaps best, with Lightfoot, to suppose that the
"commandments" came from Paul himself, and that the words,
"if he come unto you, receive him," sum up the substance of these

---

[30]   Gk. συναιχμάλωτος. In Philem. 23 Epaphras receives this designation,
although Aristarchus is mentioned in the same sentence. In Rom. 16:7 Andronicus and Junia are so styled; they may have won the right to this description
during Paul's Ephesian ministry.

[31]   *Cf.* W. M. Ramsay, *St. Paul the Traveller and the Roman Citizen* (London, 1920), p. 316.

[32]   Compare his application of the term "fellow-soldier" (Gk. συνστρατιώτης)
to Archippus (Philem. 2) and Epaphroditus (Phil. 2:25).

[33]   Gk. ἀνεψιός, "cousin" (not "sister's son," as in AV).

[34]   *Cf.* Acts 15:36 ff. (and *Acts* in NICNT, p. 319).

[35]   For a tentative reconstruction of the movements of Peter and Mark around
this time *cf.* T. W. Manson, "The Foundation of the Synoptic Tradition," BJRL
xxviii (1944), pp. 132 f.

[36]   He was evidently well known to the Corinthian Christians too, to judge

commandments. Another interpretation is that they had received the communication about Mark from someone else who could speak with authority, such as Peter or Barnabas, and that Paul is endorsing the instructions given to them by that other party; in that case the words, "if he come unto you, receive him," will be Paul's personal confirmation of the "commandments" given by someone else. We have no further information about a visit by Mark to the province of Asia, and we have no means of knowing whether he actually made his way to Colossae or not.[37]

11 Jesus, surnamed Justus, also sends his greetings. All we know about him is that he was a Jewish Christian, who was with the apostle at the time when he wrote this letter. He is not mentioned elsewhere, not even in the Epistle to Philemon, where the five other companions of Paul mentioned here send their greetings again. Jesus is, of course, the Greek form of Joshua or Jeshua; Justus was a common Latin cognomen.[38]

These three men—Aristarchus, Mark and Jesus Justus—were the only Christians of Jewish birth who were actively cooperating with Paul in his gospel witness at this time.[39] "Fellow-workers for the kingdom of God," he calls them. When Paul speaks of the kingdom of God he usually thinks of its future manifestation, retaining such an expression as "the kingdom of Christ" for its present aspect.[40] But such a passage as Rom. 14:17 ("the kingdom of God is not eating and drinking, but righteousness and peace and joy in the Holy Spirit") shows that "the kingdom of God" may also have a present reference in Paul's writings, and so it may be here.

---

by the way in which Paul refers to him in 1 Cor. 9:6.

[37] A special interest on Peter's part in the Christians of Asia and the surrounding provinces may be inferred from 1 Pet. 1:1; and Mark's greetings are sent to them in 1 Pet. 5:13.

[38] Another Jewish Christian with the additional name of Justus is mentioned in Acts 1:23 (see *Acts* in NICNT, p. 50). *Cf.* J. Munck, *Paulus und die Heilsgeschichte* (Copenhagen, 1954), p. 108, n. 76.

[39] For the construction οἱ ὄντες ἐκ περιτομῆς οὗτοι μόνοι ... see C. F. D. Moule, IBNTG, p. 31. This is not necessarily to be taken as a "pessimistic remark," as Deissmann says (*Light from the Ancient East*, p. 438), "thrown off in a mood comparable with that of the peevish lines in Phil. 2:20 f., which also need not be weighed too nicely." Deissmann's judgment seems to be quite unwarranted (with regard to Phil. 2:20 f. as well as to the present passage). Nor is there much to be said in favour of his further note that "it is not certain whether Paul is describing all three men as Jews; Aristarchus might be a pagan convert to Christianity" (*ibid.*, n. 3). See n. 45 below.

[40] See p. 190, n. 47 (on Ch. 1:13).

We recall that in Acts 28:30 f. Paul is said to have spent these two years in Rome "proclaiming the kingdom of God and telling the story of the Lord Jesus Christ"; in this work he had these three Jewish Christians to assist him at this particular point in the course of the two years, and he found great comfort[41] in their presence and help.

12–13 But he had fellow-Christians of Gentile birth with him also, and they too sent their greetings to Colossae. First among these he mentions the Colossians' own evangelist and friend, Epaphras, whose name we have met earlier in this letter (Ch. 1:7). Epaphras was a true bondman of Christ, devoted to Him and to His people, and specially solicitous for the welfare of his own beloved converts and friends in the Lycus valley. Now that he was far distant from them, they were never out of his mind; he was continuously engaged in intense intercession to God on their behalf, praying for their perfect establishment in all God's will. Praying is working; and by such fervent prayer Epaphras toiled effectively on behalf of the churches of Colossae and Laodicea[42] and Hierapolis.[43]

14 The other two Gentile Christians who sent their greetings to Colossae were Luke and Demas. It is from Paul's reference to Luke here that we know what his profession was: "my dear physician," the apostle calls him. W. K. Hobart's arguments that the author of Luke and Acts must have been a physician have received severe criticism, but when all necessary discount has been made (and that is not a little), they retain considerable illustrative value.[44] That the author of Luke-Acts was in Rome with Paul is evident from the last two chapters of Acts; there is no evidence that he was with Paul in Ephesus. It is from this reference, too, that we may most surely conclude that Luke was a Gentile by

---

[41]   Gk. παρηγορία. "The idea of consolation, comfort, is on the whole predominant in the word," probably owing to its special medical usage (Lightfoot, *ad loc.*).

[42]   See p. 223, n. 4 (on Ch. 2:1).

[43]   Hierapolis, probably so called because it was the "sacred city" (Gk. ἱερὰ πόλις) of the tribe of the Hydrelitae, lay about 12 miles north-west of Colossae and some 6 miles due north of Laodicea. See W. M. Ramsay, *Cities and Bishoprics of Phrygia*, Vol. I (Oxford, 1895), pp. 84 ff.

[44]   *Cf.* F. F. Bruce, *The Acts of the Apostles* (London, 1951), pp. 4 f.

birth—as the author of Luke-Acts appears to have been, to judge by some internal evidence.[45]

Of Demas[46] we know very little. He is mentioned along with Luke in Philem. 24 and later in 2 Tim. 4:10 f.; but in the latter passage Paul says that Luke alone remains with him; Demas had left him, "having loved this present world."[47]

---

[45] Quite unconvincing is Deissmann's argument (*Light from the Ancient East*, p. 438) that we need not infer from this passage that Luke was a Gentile, as is also his suggestion that Luke might be Paul's kinsman (συγγενής) Lucius in Rom. 16:21. Luke (Gk. Λουκᾶς, Lat. *Lucas*) may well be a shortened or familiar form of Lucius, but Lucius was a very common praenomen throughout the Roman world.

[46] Demas is an abridged form of some such name as Demetrius, Democritus, Demosthenes, etc.

[47] What exactly is implied in this expression is uncertain, but the natural inference is that some temporal interest took him off to Thessalonica at a time when the imprisoned apostle would have valued his continued presence.

Ch. 4:15–17

15 Salute the brethren that are in Laodicea, and Nymphas,[48] and the church that is in their[49] house.

16 And when this epistle hath been read among you, cause that it be read also in the church of the Laodiceans; and that ye also read the epistle from Laodicea.

17 And say to Archippus, Take heed to the ministry which thou hast received in the Lord, that thou fulfil it.

15 Paul now asks the Colossian Christians to convey his greetings to their fellow-Christians in the neighbouring city of Laodicea, which lay about ten miles to the north-west. One member of the Laodicean church is mentioned specially—Nympha (for the name should probably be read as feminine)—perhaps because it was in her house that the local church, or part of it, met. House-churches are frequently referred to in the NT epistles. Sometimes the whole church in one city might be small enough to be accommodated in the home of one of its members; but in other places the local church was quite large, and there was no building in which all the members could conveniently congregate. This was certainly true of the early Jerusalem church; there we find one group meeting in the house of Mary, the mother of Mark (Acts 12:12); and although Luke does not specifically call that group the church in her house, it might very well have been described thus. Priscilla and Aquila were accustomed to extend the hospitality

---

48 Probably Νύμφαν, accusative from the feminine nominative Νύμφα (Nympha), rather than Νυμφᾶν, accusative from the masculine nominative Νυμφᾶς (Nymphas). Lightfoot's argument (*ad loc.*) that the feminine is "in the highest degree improbable" because of its Doric form is answered by J. H. Moulton, who sees here an Attic feminine form with short *alpha* (alongside the normal Attic Νύμφη) and not the Doric form with long *alpha* ("Nympha," ExT v [1893–4], pp. 66 f.).

49 The manuscripts and other authorities vary between "their" (αὐτῶν, א A C P 33 1908 and the Bohairic Coptic), "his" (αὐτοῦ, the Western codices D C and the bulk of the later MSS.), and "her" (αὐτῆς, B, the accurate corrector of 424, the Sahidic Coptic, Origen and Ambrosiaster), owing in the main to the uncertainty of the gender of the preceding proper name. Read "Nympha and the church that is in her house."

of their home to such groups in the successive cities where they lived—*e.g.* in Ephesus (1 Cor. 16:19) and Rome[50] (Rom. 16:5). At Colossae itself Philemon's house was used for this purpose (Philem. 2). We may compare Lydia's house in Philippi (Acts 16:15, 40) and Gaius' at Corinth (Rom. 16:23). Such house-churches appear to have been smaller circles of fellowship within the larger fellowship of the city *ekklesia*.[51]

16 The Colossians are then told to pass on this letter, after it has been read to them at a church meeting, to the Laodicean church, in order that they may read it too. At the same time they are told to procure a certain letter from Laodicea and have it read in the Colossian church. Much discussion has been devoted to this "epistle from Laodicea", but to very little purpose. It was presumably a letter sent by Paul to that church (possibly by the hand of Tychicus), but if so it was probably lost at an early date—too early for it to be salvaged and included in the Pauline corpus towards the end of the first century.[52]

One view identifies it with the Epistle to the Ephesians.[53] But Ephesians appears almost certainly to have been written after Colossians, and not to one church only in the province of Asia. If it was written after Colossians, it is unlikely that it would be mentioned in Colossians—unless indeed Ch. 4:16 is a later addition (and of that there is no evidence). We know that Marcion in his Apostolic Canon gave the Epistle to the Ephesians the title "To the Laodiceans"; but he probably knew the Epistle to the Ephesians

---

[50] If Rom. 16 was meant for Rome (as I think) and not for Ephesus.

[51] *Cf.* A. Deissmann, *Paul*, p. 214; O. Cullmann, *Early Christian Worship* (Eng. tr., London, 1953), pp. 9 f.

[52] On this Professor N. B. Stonehouse writes: "It seems to me ... that one might allow for other possibilities than that the letter was lost and so not included in the Canon. Its contents might have made it unsuitable for inclusion in the Canon, possibly because, to take one extreme, they virtually were identical with the contents of another letter, or, to take the other extreme, the contents were lacking in universal significance. On a matter as obscure as this one I would prefer to allow also for other possibilities than the one which you mention."

[53] The first scholar of comparatively modern times to make this identification was John Mill (1707) in his *Prolegomena* (see A. Fox, *John Mill and Richard Bentley* [Oxford, 1954], p. 85). *Cf.* also J. B. Lightfoot (*ad loc.*); A. Harnack, *Sitzungsberichte der preussischen Akademie der Wissenschaften, phil.-hist. Klasse* (Berlin, 1910), pp. 698 ff.; J. Knabenbauer, *Commentarius in S. Pauli Apostoli Epistolas*, iv (Paris, 1912), pp. 7 ff.; B. W. Bacon, *Expositor* VIII. xvii (1919), pp. 19 ff.

in a form which lacked the words "at Ephesus" in the first verse, and found what seemed to be a pointer to its destination in Col. 4:16.[54] This is more likely than the view that he deliberately suppressed the reference to Ephesus in Eph. 1:1 because the church of that city had refused his doctrine.

Yet another suggestion about the "epistle from Laodicea" is E. J. Goodspeed's; he would like to identify it with the Epistle to Philemon.[55] But if Onesimus is commended to the Christians of Colossae as "one of you" (v. 9), it is more natural to think of Philemon as a member of the Colossian church.

We must, in short, remain in doubt about this Laodicean letter. It may be that the Laodicean church required a letter more or less on the same lines as the Epistle to the Colossians; yet the two were sufficiently dissimilar for Paul to direct that either letter should be read in the other church.[56]

The reference to an epistle not included (or not obviously included) in the NT canon led at a later date to the fabrication of an apocryphal "Epistle of Paul to the Laodiceans"[57] (just as the OT references to the Book of Jashar and other "lost books" have stimulated the composition of books bearing their titles).

17 A special message is sent to one member of the church— Archippus. "Look to the ministry which you have received 'in the Lord'; see that you fulfil it." Archippus appears from Philem. 2, where Paul calls him his "fellow-soldier," to have been a member of Philemon's household, perhaps the son of Philemon and Apphia.[58] We cannot determine the precise nature of the ministry

---

[54]   See A. Souter, *The Text and Canon of the NT* (ed. C. S. C. Williams, London, 1954), p. 152.

[55]   *Introduction to the NT* (Chicago, 1937), p. 224.

[56]   A. Deissmann, *Light from the Ancient East*, p. 238.

[57]   See B. F. Westcott, *Canon of the NT* (London, 1870), pp. 542 ff.; J. B. Lightfoot, *Colossians*, pp. 287 ff. (at the end of a thorough discussion of the whole question posed by Col. 4:16); A. Souter, *op. cit.*, pp. 176 f.; A. Harnack, "Der apokryphe Brief des Apostels Paulus an die Laodicener, eine marcionitische Fälschung aus der zweiten Hälfte des zweiten Jahrhunderts," *Sitzungsberichte der preussischen Akademie der Wissenschaften, phil.-hist. Klasse* (Berlin, 1923). This fabrication, originally composed in Greek, is extant in a Latin version. It is an obvious and pointless cento from the Pauline corpus, mainly from Philippians, and was known to Jerome at the close of the 4th century A.D. (Whether the Muratorian Canon's reference to "an alleged epistle to the Laodiceans" implies that the compiler knew such an uncanonical document, or merely knew that this title appeared in Marcion's ᾽ἀποστολικόν, is uncertain.)

[58]   So J. J. Müller, *op. cit., ad loc.*

with which he had been entrusted, but it was one to be discharged in a spirit of Christian faithfulness. And the fact that Paul's charge to him was read out in a letter to the whole church would impress him the more with the solemnity of his responsibility to carry out his service. May it not have been an embarrassment to him to have this personal commission given such publicity? We may be sure that Paul took this into consideration, and knew very well how to make his charge most effective.[59]

---

[59] Lightfoot (*op. cit.*, pp. 42, 308 f.) suggests that, while Archippus's parents were Colossians, he himself lived at Laodicea and was apparently chief pastor of the church there. One would like firmer evidence for this than the bare fact that Paul's charge to Archippus follows immediately upon his reference to Laodicea.

VI. FINAL GREETING AND BLESSING

Ch. 4:18

> 18 The salutation of me Paul with mine own hand.
> Remember my bonds. Grace be with you.

18 Paul writes his final greeting with his own hand, as he did
in all his letters, to confirm their genuineness.[60] Normally the
amanuensis (when one was employed) was left to compose the final
salutation himself.[61] But Paul had reason to fear that forged
letters in his name might be sent to churches and individuals;[62]
therefore, while he commonly dictated his letters, he regularly
appended the last few words in his own hand.[63]

A last plea, "Don't forget that I am a prisoner" (essentially, no
doubt, a request for their continued prayers on his behalf), and
the brief benediction, "Grace be with you," bring the letter to an
end.[64]

---

60 *Cf.* 1 Cor. 16:21; Gal. 6:11; 2 Thess. 3:17; Philem. 19.

61 Hence O. Roller argues (quite unconvincingly) that the fact that Paul
composed the final greeting himself means that he wrote the whole letter himself; he contrasts Romans, where an amanuensis was admittedly employed and
Paul makes no allusion to his own writing (*Das Formular der paulinischen Briefe*
[Stuttgart, 1933], p. 9 ff., etc.). Roller's arguments are criticized by E. Percy,
op. cit., pp. 10 ff.

62 *Cf.* 2 Thess. 2:2.

63 Deissmann (*Light from the Ancient East*, pp. 171 f.) quotes as a parallel
BGU 37, where a different hand at the end of a letter adds ἔρρωσο ("Farewell")
and the date. See also Deissmann's remarks in *Paul*, p. 13, on some practical
implications of the fact that Paul's letters were mostly dictated and not written
by him.

64 The added note in AV, "Written from Rome to the Colossians by Tychicus
and Onesimus," is no part of the original text; it is a patent inference from
Ch. 4:7–9.

INDEX OF PERSONS AND PLACES

Abraham, 94, 137
Adam, 136, 203, 238, 272, 273, 274
Alexander the Great, 125, 148
Alexandria, 201
Ananias, 216
Andronicus, 305
Antioch (Pisidian), 215
Antiochus II, 223
Antiochus III (the Great), 163
Apphia, 311
Aquila, 15, 309
Archippus, 223, 305, 311, 312
Aristarchus, 182, 304, 305, 306
Augustine, 151

Barnabas, 94, 215, 305, 306
Benjamin, 28
Bithynia, 284
Blackwood, Sir Arthur, 260
Blandina, 277
Bliss, Philip, 131

Caesarea, 19, 164, 304
Callistus, 277
Capernaum, 154
Caracalla, 144
Carthage, 277
Chadwick, Samuel, 264
Colossae, 163, 164, 165, 167, 170,
    177, 178, 180, 181, 182, 189, 192,
    198, 206, 223, 225, 228, 232, 243,
    248, 302, 306, 307, 310
Constantinople, 15
Corinth, 224, 225, 310
Cyrus, the younger, 163

Dagon, 151
David, 92, 142
Demas, 304, 307, 308

Eli, 137
Elijah, 94
Epaphras, 164, 177, 182, 184, 223,
    225, 302, 304, 305, 307
Epaphroditus, 305
Ephesus, 15, 16, 17, 18, 19, 47, 118,
    163, 164, 177, 182, 223, 225, 302,
    304, 307, 310, 311

Eve, 133
Ezekiel, 51, 81

Felicitas, 277
Flavel, John, 84

Gaius, 310
Galatia, 166, 228, 244, 305

Hierapolis, 163, 164, 182, 223, 307
Hierocles, 288
Honas, Khonai, 163, 248
Hutchinson, Col., 123

Illyricum, 181, 217
Isaac, 52

Jacob, 28
Jeremiah, 94
Jerusalem, 69, 181, 217, 244, 258,
    301, 304
Jesus Justus, 304, 306
Job, 149
John, 17, 33, 45
Joseph, 75, 89
Joseph (of Nazareth), 137
Joshua, 226, 234
Judaea, 164, 166, 216
Julius Caesar, 148
Junia, 305

Laodicea, 18, 163, 164, 182, 223, 301,
    307, 309, 312
Lot, 94
Lucius, 308
Luke, 16, 100, 304, 307, 308
Lycus Valley, 163, 164, 182, 223
Lydia, 310
Mark, 304, 305, 306
Mary, 137
Mary (mother of Mark), 309
Moses, 28, 91, 108, 226
Nathan, 28
Nero, 70
Nympha, 309
Onesimus, 276, 293, 296, 302, 303,
    311, 313

Palestine, 196, 301

314

Pennefather, William, 260
Perga, 305
Pergamum, 163, 186
Perpetua, 277
Peter, 19, 91, 305. 306
Philemon, 223, 276, 296, 302, 310, 311
Philippi, 187, 215, 262, 310
Phrygia, 163, 248
Pisidia, 248
Pius (Roman bishop), 277
Polyclitus, 96
Pompeii, 103
Priscilla, 15, 309

Rome, 19, 69, 103, 142, 164, 165, 177, 181, 182, 201, 207, 283, 302, 304, 305, 307, 310, 313
Ruth, 65

Silas, 187
Silvanus, 177
Simon II (the Just), 226
Socrates, 187

Sodom, 154
Solomon, 28, 92, 120
Stephen, 96

Thelwall, J., 136
Thessalonica, 220, 304, 308
Timon, 52
Timothy, 17, 177
Titus, 139
Titus (the emperor), 52
Trajan, 284
Tychicus, 19, 156, 182, 301, 302, 303, 310, 313
Tyrannus, 16

Vanderkemp, F. A., 151
Venice, 15

Wesley, Susannah, 136
Wilson, Margaret, 132

Xerxes, 163

Zacchaeus, 93

INDEX OF CHIEF SUBJECTS

Access, 63
Adoption, 26 f, 52
Air, 48 f
Angels, Angel-worship, 75 f, 79, 168, 198 f, 209, 231, 240, 241, 243, 247 f, 272
Apologetic, 170
Apostles, Apostleship, 65, 70, 72, 73, 94, 177 f
Apostolic Preaching, 258, 259
Ark, 92, 147
Artemis, 15, 16, 19
Ascension of Christ, 41, 91, 258
Asceticism, 167, 243 ff, 248, 252 ff, 266
Atonement, 116
Authorship of Ephesians, 17, 73, 172 f, 301

Baptism, 89, 90, 131 f, 167, 234 ff, 253, 258, 273
Barriers removed in Christ, 274 ff
Blood of Christ, 29, 42, 60, 191, 208
Body of Christ, 42 ff, 73, 89, 93 f, 100 f, 128, 155, 165, 171, 201 ff, 212, 215, 235, 240, 245, 251

Calendar, 244 f
Canticles, 284, 285
Captivity, Captivity Epistles, 19, 70 f, 88, 155, 164 f, 302, 313
Catechesis, 264 f, 287, 294, 297
Christology, 74, 168, 184, 192 ff, 199 f, 201, 232 f
Church, Churches, 42 ff, 50, 79, 81, 88, 89 f, 93, 94 f, 101, 129 ff, 200 ff, 215, 251, 309 ff
Circumcision, 58, 233 ff
Colossian heresy, 164, 165 ff, 189, 198, 206, 212, 228 f, 231, 248
Confession of faith, 171, 184, 201
Cornerstone, 65, 68
Corporate personality, 203, 215
Cosmic Christ, 77, 169, 195 f, 199, 200, 208 ff, 242
Covenants, 58, 62
Creation, 76, 193 ff, 197, 200, 229
Critical questions, 17 ff, 170 ff

Descent of Christ, 91

Destination of Ephesians, 17 f, 37, 71, 172 f
Dualism, 188
Dying with Christ, 51, 234 f, 253, 260

Easter, date of, 244
Election, 26
Elemental powers, 229, 231, 241, 244, 252, 253, 254
Eschatology, 181, 189
Eternal life, 50 f
Ethics, 87 ff, 106, 264 ff
Eucharist, 203, 212

Faith, 54 f, 80, 89 f, 149
Fall of man, 76
Family life, 128 ff, 287 ff
Fatherhood of God, 79, 89, 90, 115, 116, 120, 188
Food laws, 243, 247, 252
Forgiveness, 112
Fulness (pleroma), 42 ff, 91, 93, 206 f, 232

Gnosis, Gnosticism, 48, 167, 170, 172, 181, 185 f, 192, 203, 206, 220, 223, 224, 248, 260
Grace, 54, 113

Head, Headship, 42 f, 50, 93 f, 100, 129, 201 ff, 204, 233, 251
Heavenly places, 24 f, 75, 145, 157
House-churches, 309 f
Humility, 88

Image of God, 193 f, 272 f
Incarnation, 204 f, 212, 229, 232
Inheritance, 34 f, 39

Jews and Gentiles, 15. 58 ff, 64, 73, 211. 218 f, 274 ff
Justification, 54, 112, 147, 209, 213, 216

Kingdom of God, 45, 190, 200, 306 f

Laodicea, Epistle from, 18, 310 f
Law, Legalism, 61, 62, 238, 248, 286 f

Life-token, 260
Light and darkness, 119 f, 188 f
Logos, 197, 200, 272
Love of Christ, Love of God, 80 ff, 129, 131, 132
Love-feast, 284

Mediation, Mediatorship, 43, 65, 92, 168, 190, 197, 200, 207, 229, 232
Mysteries, pagan, 249 f
Mystery (of God), 31 f, 69, 70, 72, 75, 133, 218 f, 223 f

New birth, 56, 80
New man, 93, 103, 106, 272 ff, 279

Old man, 103, 105, 112, 272 f

Paganism, 58 f
Panoply of God, 142 ff
Parousia, 180, 190, 213, 216, 220, 262 f
Partiality, 138
Pastors, 94 ff
Pelagianism, 46
Perfection, 95, 167, 168, 213, 221, 262 f
Philosophy, 230, 255
Phrygian Jews, 166
Plan of the ages, 31, 32 f, 72
Prayer, 37 f, 78 f, 80, 83, 153 ff, 297 f, 307
Pre-existence, 195 f, 200
Priesthood, 95
Principalities and powers, 75, 144, 167 ff, 189, 198 f, 210, 229, 232 f, 239 ff, 253, 260
Prophets, 65, 73, 94
Proselytes, 58, 72

Rabbinism, 203, 226
Reconciliation, 61 ff, 207 ff, 216
Redemption, 27, 29, 190 f, 209, 242
Remission of sins, 191

Resurrection of Christ, 39, 205, 236
Rising with Christ, 51, 236 f, 257ff

Sabbath, 245
Salvation, 54 f, 150
Sanctification, 96, 120, 147
Satan, 45, 48 f, 56, 97, 103, 108, 109, 143, 145, 189
Seal of the Spirit, 35
Second Adam, 50, 96, 273 f
Semipelagianism, 46
Servant of Jehovah, 215 f
Shekinah, 92, 100
Sin, 46 ff, 60, 190 f
Slavery, 138 ff, 274 ff, 293 ff
Spirit of God, 26, 34, 35 f, 51, 56, 64, 68, 69, 80, 88, 89, 90, 94, 100, 110, 111, 125, 126, 150, 151, 152, 153 f, 182 f, 185, 187, 227, 262
Stewardship (Paul's), 33, 75, 217
Stoicism, 187, 197, 200, 201, 202, 288, 289

Temple, at Jerusalem, 61, 92
Temple, Ezekiel's, 81
Temple, of Artemis, 15, 19
Temple, spiritual, 18 f, 66 ff, 92
Tradition, 226 f, 255, 265
Tribulations, 77, 214 ff
Trinity, 24, 30, 64, 81, 89, 132
Truth, 99, 104, 107, 120, 146

Vices, catalogue of, 108 ff, 117 f, 267 ff
Virtues, catalogue of, 279 ff

Wisdom of God, 192 ff, 195, 197, 224
Word of God, 150
World-rulers (*kosmokratores*), 143 ff, 192

Zoroastrianism, 188

Abbott, T. K., 215, 246
Aeschines, 37
Ambrose, 29, 246, 252
Ambrosiaster, 69, 72, 246, 266, 293, 309
Anderson, Sir Robert, 291, 292
Apollonius Rhodius, 46
Appian, 78, 119
Aqiba, Rabbi, 197
Argyle, A. W., 194
Aristaenetus, 230
Aristeas, 25, 28
Aristophanes, 249, 255, 276
Aristotle, 46, 73, 108, 114, 117, 118, 139, 154, 276
Arius, 200
Arndt, W. F., 161
Artemidorus, 238
Athanasius, 78
Augustine, 26, 27, 44, 203, 246, 252, 279

Babrius, 65, 76, 156
Bacon, B. W., 310
Bacon, F., 89
Barclay, W., 270
Barrett, C. K., 216
Basil, 18
Bate, H. N., 246, 249, 256
Bauer, W., 161, 230, 231, 240, 249, 250, 255
Beck, J. T., 48
Behm, J., 191, 250
Bengel, J. A., 15, 44, 81, 110, 149
Benoit, P., 171
Bentley, Richard, 279
Best, E., 80, 203, 204, 216, 277
Bettex, F., 11
Beza, T., 18
Bietenhard, H., 229
Blass, F., 37, 67, 91, 117
Bonnard, P., 178
Bowman, J., 273
Bruce, F. F., 11 ff, 307
Büchsel, F., 190, 208
Bultmann, R., 185, 203
Bunyan, John, 96, 118, 144, 272
Burch, V., 234
Burgon, J. W., 249
Burke, E., 56, 124

Burney, C. F., 195
Burritt, Elihu, 115
Byron, G. G., 143

Caird, G. B., 198, 265, 293
Cairns, D., 204
Calvin, J., 79, 95, 111, 161
Candlish, R. S., 48, 115
Carey, William, 292
Carlyle, T., 54, 103
Carpenter, S. C., 219
Carrington, P., 265
Cerinthus, 231
Cerny, E., 194
Chadwick, H., 170, 171, 224, 228
Chalmers, T., 32
Charnock, S., 132
Chavasse, C., 203
Chrysostom, 43, 70, 107, 110, 131, 135, 246
Cicero, 33
Citron, B., 178
Clarke, W. K. L., 287, 288
Clement of Alexandria, 266, 279, 291, 292
Clement of Rome, 19, 84, 102, 142
Cole, A., 68
Coleridge, S. T., 49, 136, 137
Cook, Joseph, 113
Cowley, A., 124
Crafer, T. W., 239
Cross, F. L., 170, 173
Cudworth, R., 80
Cullmann, O., 227, 228, 234, 263, 310
Cunningham, W., 147
Curcellaeus, S., 249
Cyprian, 266

Dale, R. W., 30, 33, 54, 64, 85
Dana, J., 134
Daniel, Samuel, 79
Darby, J. N., 222
Daube, D., 280
Davies, W. D., 190, 191, 195, 203, 224, 259, 263, 273, 281
Deissmann, A., 19, 37, 63, 153, 179, 184, 186, 191, 213, 238, 256, 261, 270, 271, 282, 283, 293, 298, 306, 308, 310, 311, 313
Denney, J., 66, 112, 209
De Wette, W. M. L., 73

318

Dibelius, M., 192, 206, 219, 223, 233, 251, 268
Dilschneider, O. A., 169
Diodorus, 26
Dionysius of Halicarnassus, 97, 254
Dodd, C. H., 165, 188, 211, 263, 265, 273, 288, 289, 302, 304
Draper, C. M., 260
Duncan, G. S., 164, 165, 302
Dupont, J., 186

Edwards, Jonathan, 27
Ellicott, C., 75
Emerson, R. W., 155
Epictetus, 77, 88, 93, 97, 110, 153, 187, 277
Epiphanius, 167, 231
Eratosthenes, 61
Euripides, 114
Eusebius, 217, 277

Farmer, G., 245
Field, F., 93, 222, 238, 246, 249
Filson, F. V., 195
Findlay, G. G., 18, 44, 48, 62, 90, 120
Finkelstein, L., 244
Fison, J. E. 180
Forsyth, P. T., 30, 76, 90, 106, 115
Foster, J., 290
Fox, A., 310

Galen, 249
Galloway, A. 241
Geldenhuys, J. N., 178
Gingrich, F. W., 161
Glover, T. R., 182
Goodspeed, E. J., 73, 172, 301, 303
Goodwin, Thomas, 28, 30, 40, 52, 274
Grellet, Stephen, 105
Grimm, C. L. W., 45
Grosheide, F. W., 245
Grotius, H., 245
Gurnall, W., 55, 154, 155

Harnack, A., 310, 311
Harris, J. R., 193, 234, 249, 255
Harrison, P. N., 165
Hartland, E. S., 260
Haupt, E., 197
Heliodorus, 230
Henderson, I., 197
Hendriksen, W., 270
Herbert, George, 288
Hermann, G., 71

Hermas, 19
Herodotus, 63, 78, 163, 276
Hilary, 222, 252
Hippolytus, 167, 170
Hitchcock, A. E. N., 44, 207
Hobart, W. K., 307
Hodge, Charles, 87, 147
Holtzmann, H. J. 172, 218
Homer, 37, 45, 150
Hooke, S. H., 65
Hort, F. J. A., 142, 149, 247, 249, 285
Horton, W. M. 169
Howe, J., 67
Hunter, A. M., 180, 192, 196, 205, 210, 265, 281

Ignatius, 17, 19, 138, 217, 273, 285, 303
Irenaeus, 19, 29, 170, 192, 207
Iverach, J., 254

Jastrow, M., 143
Jaubert, A., 244
Jeremias, J., 65
Jerome, 61, 246, 252, 266, 311
Johnson, A. R., 235
Johnson, L., 164
Johnson, Samuel, 123
Johnston, G., 202
Jonas, H., 166
Josephus, 52, 61, 76, 88, 99, 135, 150, 154, 230
Justin Martyr, 234, 255, 300

Käsemann, E., 192, 203, 240
Kelly, W., 222
Kennedy, H. A. A., 31
Klein, G., 265
Knabenbauer, J., 310
Knox, J., 209, 303
Knox, W. L., 181, 185, 201, 202, 228, 240, 272
Krishna Pal, 239

Lachmann, C., 72
Laertius, Diogenes, 26
Lampe, G. W. H., 35, 236
Lathe, Herbert, 28
Lavater, J. C., 106
Lewis, C. S., 246
Lietzmann, H., 233
Lightfoot, J. B., 42, 91, 99, 167, 185, 194, 207, 215, 232, 239, 240, 245, 246, 249, 255, 267, 272, 300, 305, 307, 309, 310, 311, 312

Livy, 32, 201
Locke, John, 104
Loeb, J., 149
Lohmeyer, E., 184, 222, 238, 245, 298
Longus, 56
Lowell, J. R., 48, 118
Lucian, 52, 71, 77, 93, 97, 118, 119, 131, 142, 149, 153, 154, 156, 249
Luficer of Cagliari, 246
Luther, M., 54, 56, 146, 153, 258

Macgregor, G. H. C., 240, 241
Machen, J. G., 192, 196
Macrobius, 266
Mahaffy, Sir John, 63
Malinine, M., 170
Manson, T. W., 178, 204, 248, 305
Manton, T., 56
Manzoni, A., 89
Marcion, 19, 130, 246, 310, 311
Marcus Aurelius, 52, 124, 142, 157, 199
Martial, 124
Mascall, E. L., 204
Masson, Charles, 172, 178, 211, 230, 250, 267
McCheyne, R. M., 100
Meecham, H. G., 280, 285
Menander, 135, 140, 292
Meyer, H. A. W., 71, 91
Meyer, F. B., 55
Michl, J., 210
Michl, I., 210
Mill, J., 23, 310
Milton, J., 36, 69, 81, 95, 104, 125, 194, 198
Mimnermus, 73
Mitchell, D. F., 227
Mitton, C. L., 172, 219, 251, 301, 303
Moffatt, J., 222, 281
Monod, Adolphe, 63
Montgomery, James, 98
Moody, D. L., 151
More, Alexander, 249
Morgenstern, J., 244
Morris, L., 191, 208
Moule, C. F. D. 44, 161, 180, 200, 207, 208, 217, 219, 224, 237, 247, 251, 272, 294, 301, 306
Moule, H. C. G., 30, 55, 71, 260, 261, 262
Moulton, J. H., 35, 37, 52, 280, 309
Moulton, J. H., and Milligan, G.,

78, 144, 185, 186, 238, 255
Müller, J. J., 302, 311
Murray, J., 58
Munck, J., 181, 213, 217, 221, 294, 306

Nestle, E., 185, 186, 284
Newton, John, 260
Nineham, D. E., 173
Nock, A. D., 166. 250
Norden, E., 184, 192

Oepke, A., 240
Origen, 18, 43, 209, 246, 309
Ovid, 98
Owen, John, 34, 95, 113, 143

Payson, E., 25, 87
Peake, A. S., 172, 213, 267
Pelagius, 222, 246, 252
Percy, E., 165, 172, 184, 191, 199, 203, 207, 209, 212, 219, 231, 236, 237, 239, 240, 247, 248, 249, 256, 298, 313
Petronius, 117
Phillips, J. B., 299
Philo, 42, 45, 76, 91, 102, 167, 186, 194, 195, 197, 234, 272
Philodemus, 45, 46, 65, 88, 97, 153
Pierson, A. T., 17, 136
Plato, 37, 65, 78, 88, 97, 102, 103, 114, 117, 123, 135, 255
Plautus, 117
Pliny the younger, 284, 285
Plutarch, 25, 28, 52, 78, 88, 97, 108, 114, 117, 118, 124, 129, 131, 135, 153, 154, 232, 238, 249, 254, 290
Polybius, 33, 38, 46, 77, 97, 102, 150, 154
Polycarp, 19, 107
Pope, Alexander, 201
Pope, R. M., 299
Procksch, O., 190
Pseudo–Jerome, 222

Quarles, F., 131
Quell, G., 281
Quintilian, 33

Ramsay, W. M., 15, 16, 163, 166, 223, 246, 248, 249, 305, 307
Rawlinson, A. E. J., 203
Reicke, B., 228
Rengstorf, K. H., 178
Richardson, A., 294, 296

Ridderbos, H. N., 231
Robertson, A. T., 50, 117
Robinson, D. W. B., 178
Robinson, J. A., 42, 43, 46, 99, 100, 132, 185, 186, 207
Robinson, J. A. T., 190, 203, 217, 235, 237, 238, 240, 250, 253, 256, 278
Robinson, J. M., 235
Robinson, T. H., 235
Robinson, Wade, 157
Rochefoucauld, F. de la, 55
Roller, O., 313
Rutherford, S., 92, 145

Sanders, J. N., 173
Scaliger, J., 76
Schaff, P., 91
Schlatter, A., 230
Schlier, H., 203
Schmidt, K. L., 247
Schmitt, T., 202
Schoeps, H. J., 245
Schweitzer, A., 203
Schweizer, E., 204
Scott, C. A. A., 188, 195, 207, 240
Scott, E. F., 269, 281
Seeberg, A., 265
Selden, J., 87
Selwyn, E. G., 265, 280, 287, 297
Seneca, 79, 133, 139, 141, 255
Sextus Empiricus, 68, 76
Shakespeare, W., 48, 69, 73, 82, 97
Shedd, W. G. T., 60, 112
Simplicius, 281
Simpson, E. K., 11 ff, 104, 131, 161, 186, 187, 190, 191, 232, 260
Singer, S., 238, 275
Smalley, S. S., 91
Socinus, F., 29
Sophocles, 111, 131
Souter, A., 93, 311
Spurgeon, C. H., 29, 50, 55, 85
Stalker, J., 55
Stauffer, E., 145, 281
Stewart, J. S., 215, 236, 241, 261, 262
Stewart, R. A., 226
Stibbs, A. M., 191, 208
Stobaeus, 287, 292

Stonehouse, N. B., 310
Strabo, 99, 163
Strack, H. L., and Billerbeck, P., 194, 206, 245
Suetonius, 52

Tacitus, 146
Tasker, R. V. G., 270
Taylor, C., 249
Tertullian, 19, 143, 246, 278, 284
Theodoretus, 248
Thornton, L. S., 205
Thornwell, J. H., 41
Thucydides, 38
Tischendorf, C., 114
Torrance, T. F., 204
Trapp, J., 99
Tregelles, S. P., 72
Trench, R. C., 52, 77, 88, 105, 108, 111, 125, 135
Turrettine, F., 132
Tyndale, W., 62

Ussher, J., 18

Vettius Valens, 78, 97, 118, 143
Vine, W. E., 218
Vinet, Alexander, 104
Virgil, 46, 71
Vos, G., 190

Wagenführer, H. A., 206
Wambacq, B. N., 210
Wardlaw, R., 116
Warfield, B. B., 29, 30, 50, 91, 190
Watts, I,, 112
Weidinger, K., 287
Wessel, John, 115
Westcott, B. F., 43, 208, 311
Westcott, B. F., and Hort, F. J. A., 142, 149, 285
Whittier, J. G., 76, 100
Williams, R. R., 89
Winer, G. B., 61, 91
Wordsworth, W., 79

Xenophon, 28, 46, 63, 97, 117, 133, 163

Yochanan, Rabbi, 199
Young, E., 109, 122

GENESIS
1 — 197
1:1 — 195
1:4 — 189
1:26 f — 193
1:26 ff — 274
1:27 — 272
2:23 — 133
2:24 — 130, 133, 290
18:16 — 272

EXODUS
4:22 — 27
24:3 — 238

LEVITICUS
19:15 — 295

DEUTERONOMY
10:16 — 234
27:14 - 26 — 238
30:6 — 58, 234
33:12 — 28

JOSHUA
5:2 f — 234
24:31 — 226

JUDGES
2:7 — 226
6:34 (LXX) — 142

I SAMUEL
4:9 — 142

II SAMUEL
13:25 — 28
19:27 (LXX) — 97

ESTHER
2:12 — 131

JOB
29:14 — 271
31:2 (LXX) — 188
33:24 — 29

PSALMS
3:8 — 54
4:3 — 35
4:5 (LXX) — 108

8:4 ff — 274
8:6 — 41
13:3 — 38
19:4 — 181
22 — 92
23:1 (LXX) — 207
24:1 — 207
29 — 92
29:3 — 38
32:1 — 191
33:6 — 197
35:26 — 271
40:16 (LXX) — 115
45 — 28
49 — 29
52:6 (LXX) — 138
68:18 — 91, 92
71:20 — 92
72:17 — 196
72:19 — 207
84:17 — 273
87:6 — 91
89:27 — 194
92 — 245
109:29 — 271
110:1 — 41, 258
111:1 (LXX) — 247
111:10 — 186
112:1 — 247
118:22 — 65
119 — 157
119:8 — 132
132:9 — 271
132:14 — 66
136:23 — 92
139:15 — 92

PROVERBS
1:7 — 186
3:9 — 31
8:22 — 205
8:22 ff — 192, 195
8:30 — 197
9:10 — 186
12:22 — 107

ECCLESIASTES
1:2 — 262

SONG OF SOLOMON
— 28, 133

ISAIAH
5:1 — 28
6:3 — 207
7:13 (LXX) — 222
8:22 — 77
11:5 — 271
24:21 — 210
28:16 (LXX) — 65
29:13 — 255
30:6 (LXX) — 77
40:13 — 223
43:3 — 29
44:23 — 92
49:3 — 215
49:6 — 216, 218
52:7 — 63
53:10 — 27
53:11 — 106
56:5 — 72
57:19 — 59, 63, 64
59:17 — 147, 150, 271
61:10 — 271
65:17 — 273

JEREMIAH
1:14 ff — 276
4:4 — 234
4:5 ff — 276
15:9 (LXX) — 77
23:24 — 207
31:31 ff — 235

EZEKIEL
1:26 — 273
36:25 ff — 131, 235

DANIEL
2:18 f — 218
2:27 ff — 218
4:27 (LXX) — 29
7:13 — 273

JONAH
2:3 - 10 — 235

HABAKKUK
2:7 — 212

ZEPHANIAH
1:2 ff — 276

ZECHARIAH
8:16 — 108
13:1 — 132

INDEX OF SCRIPTURE REFERENCES
NEW TESTAMENT

MATTHEW

1:21	206
4:21	93
5:9	280
5:13	299
5:21 ff, 27 ff	269
5:29 f	267
5:43 - 48	281
5:48	115
6:12	281
6:14 f	280
6:27	93
7:17 f	110
9:16	206
10:17	98
10:19	300
10:20	155
10:37	186
12:28	190
12:29	241
12:33	110
13:48	110
15:9	255
18:8 f	267
18:22, 23 ff	280
19:28	259
21:33	61
22:43 ff	258
25:40, 45	216
26:28	191
26:41	297
26:64	258
28:18	67

MARK

1:4	191
1:13	274
2:21	206
3:27	232
4:8	181
5:23	130
6:48	206
7:3	226
7:5 ff	231
7:7	255
7:19	243
8:20	206
9:43 ff	267
9:49 f	299
10:7 f	130, 290
10:38 f	235

11:25	280
12:1	61
12:35 ff	258
13:11	300
13:33	297
14:38	297
14:62	258

LUKE

1:2	226
1:28	28
1:46 ff	284
1:48	92
1:68 ff	284
1:77	191
1:80	78
2:21	234
2:32	218
2:40	78
3:3	191
6:36	280
6:43	110
7:32	281
7:41, 43	238
11:4	281
11:20	190, 232
11:21 f	241
12:12	300
12:50	235
13:7	61
14:9	108
14:23	61
14:34 f	299
15:17	139
18:1	77, 297
19:3	93
20:41 ff	258
21:14	300
21:36	297
22:40, 46	297
22:52 f	189
22:69	258
24:26	42
24:27	191

JOHN

1:1	200
1:1 f	196
1:1 ff	184, 284
1:1 - 4	192
1:3	197
1:15	194

1:16	207
1:18	193, 261
3:5	131
3:15 f	205
3:20	122
3:36	205
6:37	26
6:51	205
8:12	120
8:58	196
10:11	114
10:27 f	205
11:25 f	205
12:31	241
12:35	120
13:17	264
14:6	102
14:9	193
14:19	260
14:30	241
15:1 ff	205
15:3	132
15:13	114
16:11	241
17:17	131
17:22, 23	43
18:37	102

ACTS

1:14	297
1:23	306
2:1	207
2:33	91
2:33 ff	258
2:38	191
2:39	64
2:42	297
4:11	65
5:31	191, 258
6:4	297
6:14	226
7:55 f	258
7:58	271
9:16	216
10:34	295
10:43	191
12:12	309
13:10	108
13:38	191
13:47	216, 218
14:27	298

15:5	228	5:1 - 5	180	10:17	150
15:23 - 29	243	5:2	219	10:18	181
15:36 ff	305	5:3	214	11:12	206
16:4	226	5:8 ff	209	11:13	213
16:15	310	5:10	207	11:15	207
16:23	310	5:11	207	11:22	52
16:25	187	5:12 ff	274	11:25	206, 217
16:40	310	6:1 ff	253	11:32	275
17:28	79	6:1 - 11	259	11:36	199
19:2	35	6:3 ff	51, 235	12:1	256, 264
19:10	163	6:4	187	12:1 - 13:14	265
19:22	177	6:4 f	236	12:2	105, 185
19:29	304	6:4 - 11	236		186, 250, 272
20:4	301, 304	6:6	235, 268, 272	12:4 f	202
20:30	97	6:6 f	269	12:9 ff	280
20:31	297	6:11	268, 269	12:12	297
20:32	188	6:16 ff	253	13:1	180
21:29	61, 71	6:17	226	13:4	273
22:14	185	6:18	269	13:9 f	281
24:18	170	6:19	268	13:10	206
26:18	188, 191	6:19 ff	271	13:11	280
26:28 f	69, 70	6:21	120	13:12	143, 267, 271
27:2	304	6:22	269	13:14	235, 271, 279
27:5 f	304	6:23	238	14:1 ff	243
28:20	154	7:1 ff	253	14:5 f	244
28:30 f	307	7:4	267	14:10	212
		7:5	254	14:10 - 12	295
ROMANS		7:7 ff	270	14:17	190, 306
	147, 165	7:21 ff	250	15:9	284
	170, 171, 264, 313	7:22	78	15:9 ff	218
1:7	178	7:23	268	15:14	186, 283
1:8	179, 181, 286	7:24	268	15:15 : 32	69
1:8 ff	214	7:25	286	15:19	217
1:9	153	8:2	261	15:29	206
1:14	275	8:3	212	15:30 ff	298
1:16	274	8:10	259, 261, 268	16	310
1:18 ff	270	8:10 f	51	16:5	310
1:20	193, 232	8:11	205	16:7	305
1:21	283	8:12 f	272	16:21	308
1:28	289	8:13	267, 268	16:25	218
1:29 ff	269	8:15	27	16:26	218
2:4	218	8:19	180, 219, 262	16:27	286
2:9	77	8:19 ff	196, 208		
2:9 f	274	8:19 - 22	169	**I CORINTHIANS**	
2:28	185	8:21	242, 262		15, 100
2:28 f	234	8:23	36		165, 170, 171
3:9	274	8:29	205	1:3	178
3:22 f	275	8:29 f	263	1:4	179
3:24 f	191	8:30	52, 189, 263	1:6	186
3:25	32, 191, 209	8:34	258	1:24	60, 169, 195, 274
3:27	55	8:35	77	1:31	195
4:7	191	8:38 f	242	2:3	139
4:19	267	9:1	102	2:6	232
5:1	208	9:23	218	2:6 ff	186
5:1 ff	208, 212	10:12	275	2:6 - 10	169

2:7	219	14:5	284	8:2	218
2:8	218, 232	14:15	153, 285	8:7	186
2:16	223	14:23	125	11:2	212
2:18	240	14:26	284	11:6	186
3:1 ff	251	15:1, 3	226	11:23	221
3:2	186	15:10	221	11:27	221
3:11	204	15:20	205	12:4	250
3:12 ff	295	15:23	205	12:10	214
4:4 f	295	15:24	190		
4:12	221	15:24 ff	200, 210, 258	GALATIANS	
4:20	190	15:26	241		170, 171, 229, 231
5:3 - 5	224	15:27	41	1:3	178
5:7 f	259, 269	15:28	210	1:4	232
5:10 f	270	15:31	216	1:9, 12	226
5:11	269	15:45 ff	273	2:15	46
6:9 f	190, 269, 270	15:50	190	2:19	253
6:9 ff	271	15:53 f	271	2:20	235, 236, 253
6:11	259	15:58	221	3:3	254
6:13	255	16:9	298	3:8	218
6:15	202	16:10	130	3:13	239
7:11	207	16:13	78, 142, 297	3:18	294
7:22	290	16:17	215	3:19	231
7:29	142	16:19	310	3:23	218, 254
7:30, 31	123	16:21	313	3:23 - 4:7	285
7:39	290			3:26	180
8:1	281	II CORINTHIANS		3:27	205, 273
8:1 ff	243		170, 171	3:27 f	202
8:6	169, 196, 197, 199	1:1	177	3:28	274, 275, 277
8:12	202	1:2	178	4:1 ff	294
9:6	306	1:5 - 7	216	4:3	231
9:17	217	1:22	35	4:4	207
9:22 f	170	2:12	298	4:8 - 10	254
10:16 f	202	2:14	188, 240	4:9	210, 231, 241
10:16b - 17	203	3:5 f	188	4:9 f	244
10:21	285	3:14	218	4:10	231
10:23 ff	243	3:18	220, 263, 272	4:11	221
10:26	207	4:1	77	4:14	202
10:32	274	4:4	46, 193	4:16	99
11:2	226, 227	4:6	188, 193	4:25	91
11:3	129, 202, 289	4:10	261	5:2	187
11:7	193	4:10 ff	216, 253	5:5 f	180
11:7 - 9	289	4:14	212	5:6	180, 281
11:23	226	4:16	77, 78, 272	5:13 - 26	265
11:29	202	4:17	219	5:16	268
11:29 - 32	295	5:2 ff	271	5:19 ff	269
12:4 - 6	89	5:10	295	5:20	270
12:12	43	5:14	114, 202	5:21	190
12:12 f	107, 165	5:17	259, 273	5:22	119
12:12 - 27	202	5:18 - 20	207	5:24	235
12:13	183, 274, 277	5:19	208	5:25	259
12:21	202	5:21	239	6:8	261
12:27	251	6:4	77	6:9	77
12:28	15, 65, 93	6:5	221	6:10	65
13:10, 12	221	6:7	181	6:11	19, 313
13:13	180, 281	7:15	139	6:15	61, 259, 273

EPHESIANS
165, 171,
172, 177, 185,
187, 188, 202,
207, 218, 282,
289, 301, 310
1:1   18, 178, 311
1:2   178
1:3   38
1:4   28, 41, 197
1:5   25
1:6   52
1:7   185, 191, 209, 218
1:9   32
1:10   69, 200,
       207, 208, 217
1:12   180
1:13   110, 181
1:14   263, 294
1:15   180
1:16   179
1:17   78, 110
1:18   180, 213
1:19   187
1:19 ff   236
1:20   258
1:20 f   260
1:21   75
1:22   33
1:23   80, 187, 202,
       207, 220, 233
2   81, 275
2:1 ff   211
2:2   186, 270
2:3   118
2:5   46, 54, 236
2:6   236
2:7   218, 280
2:11   234, 237, 254
2:11 ff   208
2:12   102, 211
2:13   209, 211
2:15   93, 237
2:16   202, 207, 208, 212
2:17   59, 218
2:18   154
2:19   188
2:20   73, 93, 204
2:20 ff   93
2:21   99
3   275
3:1   69, 88
3:2   33, 217
3:2 ff   213
3:2 - 12   219

3:5   65, 93, 218
3:7   187, 221
3:8   217, 218
9:9   33, 217, 218
3:10   76, 198, 240
3:13   214
3:14   69
3:16   37. 110, 187
3:17   149
3:17 f   223
3:18   227
3:19   207
3:20   187, 221
4   157
4:1   264
4:2   280
4:2 f   280
4:2 - 4   180
4:3   251, 281, 282
4:3 ff   183
4:4   171, 180, 202, 282
4:6   199
4:8   121, 218
4:9 f   235
4:10   43, 259
4:11   65, 73
4:12   202
4:13   42, 61, 80,
       207, 221, 273
4:15   223
4:15 f   251, 281
4:16   68, 93, 202,
       223, 251
4:17 - 6:18   265
4:18   58, 211
4:19   102
4:22   267, 271
4:22 ff   235
4:23 f   57, 273
4:25   100, 267, 271
4:27   143
4:29   299
4:32   88, 238, 279,
       280, 285
5   157
5:1   280
5:3 ff   270
5:5   270, 294
5:6   47, 266, 270
5:11   119
5:14   91, 284
5:15 f   299
5:16,   146, 299
5:19   284
5:20   286

5:21   128
5:21 f   287
5:22   290
5:22 ff   204, 287, 289
5:22 - 33   289
5:23   202
5:23 f   289
5:25   114
5:25 - 33   290
5:26   131, 150
5:27   212
5:28 ff   202
5:30   202
5:31   133
6:1   290, 291
6:4   291, 292
6:5   293, 294
6:6   294
6:8   140, 294
6:9   295, 296
6:10   187, 189
6:11   108
6:12   75, 198, 232
6:17   131
6:18   297
6:19 f   298
6:20   69
6:21   302
6:21 f   23, 301

PHILIPPIANS
       42, 164
1:2   178
1:3 f   179
1:6   189
1:9 f   186
1:12 ff   298
1:19   99
1:21   261
2:6 ff   284
2:6 - 11   91
2:10   41
2:10 f   259
2:11   210
2:16   221
2:20 f   306
2:25   182, 305
2:30   215
3:3   234
3:10   186, 215
3:19 f   270
3:20 f   262
4:7   282
4:9   226
4:11 - 13   188

4:13	73	2:8	199, 227, 272	4:7	182, 290	
4:18	182	2:9	207	4:7 f	156	
		2:9 f	42, 80	4:7 - 9	313	
COLOSSIANS		2:10	43, 143, 198, 251	4:9	311	
	75, 128,	2:11	58, 212, 237, 240,	4:10	182	
	138, 156, 165,		252, 268, 269, 272	4:11	190	
	170, 171, 172,	2:11 f	272	4:12	182	
	202, 207, 218,	2:11 ff	51	4:12 f	164	
	229, 282, 289,	2:12	55, 187, 237, 257	4:16	18, 223, 301, 310	
	310	2:12 f	258	4:17	223, 226, 290	
1:4	37, 39	2:13	47			
1:5	262	2:14	61	**I THESSALONIANS**		
1:6	186, 213	2:15	94, 143, 198,	1:2	178, 179	
1:7	177, 302, 307		210, 234, 237, 272	1:3	180	
1:7 f	164	2:16	231, 246	1:8	181	
1:9	31, 182, 223	2:16 f	166	2:9	221	
1:9 - 23	171	2:16 ff	285	2:12	186, 190, 219	
1:10	88	2:18	88, 102, 183, 282	2:13	226	
1:12 f	119	2:19	88, 99, 100,	2:16	177	
1:12 - 17	171		206, 223, 233	2:19 f	220	
1:13	28, 45, 306	2:20	216, 232, 237, 269	3:5	221	
1:14	29, 238	2:20 ff	51	3:5, 6	37	
1:15	205, 224	2:23	88, 247, 249	4:1	226	
1:15 f	200	3:1	236, 237	4:1 - 12	265	
1:15 ff	195	3:3	216, 237, 260, 269	4:6	270	
1:15 - 17	206	3:4	219	5:6	297	
1:15 - 18	233	3:5 ff	105, 118, 287	5:8	143. 150, 180, 271	
1:15 - 20	235	3:6	47	5:23	220, 263	
1:16	32, 33, 34,	3:7	186	5:25	298	
	75, 143, 208	3:8	110	**II THESSALONIANS**		
1:17	64, 233	3:9	105, 107, 234,	1:2	178	
1:18	42, 194, 233, 251		237, 239, 269	1:3	179	
1:19	42, 80, 207, 232	3:9 f	235	1:5	190	
1:20	32, 34, 200	3:10	105, 185, 194	1:10	219	
1:20 ff	61, 62	3:10 f	273	2:2	313	
1:21	58, 207, 241	3:11	220	2:14	219	
1:21 f	61	3:12	88, 111	2:15	227	
1:22	220, 235	3:12 - 17	287	3:1 f	298	
1:23	78, 180, 181	3:13	111, 238,	3:6	226, 227	
1:24	77		283, 284, 285	3:8	221	
1:25	69	3:14	88, 251, 282	3:13	77	
1:26	69, 72, 74, 298	3:15	246, 251	3:17	313	
1:26 f	32, 219	3:16	125	**I TIMOTHY**		
1:27	180, 261, 263	3:18	129, 135		287	
1:28	38, 80, 185, 212	3:18 ff	128	1:14	180	
1:29	84, 187	3:20	290	1:15	73	
2	198	3:20 ff	137	3:13	180	
2:1	307	3:21	136	3:16	284	
2:1 ff	185	3:22	138, 291, 294	6:1 f	294	
2:2	70, 78, 99,	3:25	138, 140			
	218, 223	4:1	294	**II TIMOTHY**		
2:3	104	4:2	153	1:11	104	
2:5	180	4:3	155, 298	1:13	180	
2:6	186	4:5	124, 186	1:16	154	
2:7	78	4:6	110	2:10	214	

2:11	51, 253
3:6	230
3:15	180
4:1	190
4:10 f	308
4:12	23, 156, 302
4:17	217
4:18	190

TITUS

1:4	178
2:1 - 10	287
2:9 f	294
2:10	294
3:3	271
3:4	52
3:5	131
3:12	302

PHILEMON

	141, 165, 173, 177, 223, 293, 302, 303, 311
2	305, 310, 311
4	179
6	186
12 - 14	296
16	276, 290, 302
19	313
23	182, 305
24	308

HEBREWS

	245
1:1 - 4	184
1:2	194, 196, 197
1:2 f	200
1:2 - 4	192
1:3	193, 258
1:4 ff	248
1:13	258
1:14	198
2:6 ff	274
2:8	41, 242
2:14	133, 241
2:14 f	205
3:6	213

4:9	245
4:12	151
5:12	231
6:5	150
6:10 - 12	180
6:11	150, 213
8:1	258
8:5	245
10:1	245
10:5	93
10:5 ff	196
10:12	258
10:22 - 24	180
10:23	213
10:30 f	295
11	149
11:8 - 16	188
11:12	267
11:23	291
11:35	29
12:1	271
12:2	258
12:27	91
12:28	285
13:1 - 17	265

JAMES

1:2 - 4:12	265
1:21	106, 267, 271
5:12	200
5:13	284

I PETER

1:1	306
1:3 : 8	180
1:4	188, 263
1:10	218
1:13	213
1:13 - 4:11	265
1:14	271
1:18	231
1:21 f	180
2:1	106, 267, 271
2:6	65
2:13 - 3:7	287
2:18	280
2:18ff	294
2:18 - 25	293

2:18 - 3:8	293
2:22 - 24	184
3:1, 7 ff	280
3:15	300
3:22	184, 258
4:1 ff	271
4:8	200
4:17	295
5:8	297
5:13	306

II PETER

2:21	226
3:10, 12	231

I JOHN

1:5 - 7	188
1:6	120
1:6 f	120
2:2	66
2:8	122
2:20	220
3:2	220, 262
3:3	213
3:8b	205
5:4	149

III JOHN

6	186

JUDE

3	226
20	153

REVELATION

	284
1:5	132, 194, 205
1:13 ff	274
1:17	196
2:4	97
2:8	196
3:2 f	297
3:8	298
3:14	197
3:14 ff	223
3:21	258
4:4	198
5:13	208
18:13	72
22:13, 16	196